ALLE ZEIT WACH
SJ
1842

Multiple Criteria Decision Methods and Applications

Selected Readings of the
First International Summer School
Acireale, Sicily, September 1983

Edited by Günter Fandel and Jaap Spronk

In Collaboration with Benedetto Matarazzo

With 56 Figures and 35 Tables

Springer-Verlag
Berlin Heidelberg New York Tokyo

Prof. Dr. Günter Fandel
Lehrstuhl für Betriebswirtschaft, Fernuniversität Hagen
Roggenkamp 6, D-5800 Hagen 1, FRG

Prof. Dr. Jaap Spronk
Department of Business Finance and Portfolio Investment
Erasmus University, P. O. Box 1738, NL-3000 DR Rotterdam
The Netherlands

Sponsored by
CREST (EEC) ERO Università di Catania
Erasmus University Rotterdam AIRO Regione Siciliana
Banco di Sicilia

ISBN-13:978-3-642-70585-4 e-ISBN-13:978-3-642-70583-0
DOI: 10.1007/978-3-642-70583-0

Library of Congress Cataloging in Publication Data. Main entry under title: Multiple criteria decision methods and applications. Based on a selection of papers from the First International Summer School of Multiple Criteria Decision Making Methods, Applications and Software. Sponsored by CREST (EEC) ... and others. Includes bibliographies and index. 1. Decision-making - Congresses. I. Fandel, G. (Günter), 1943-. II. Spronk, Jaap. III. Matarazzo, Benedetto. IV. International Summer School on Multiple Criteria Decision Making Methods, Applications and Software (1st: 1983: Acireale, Sicily) V. CREST (EEC). HD30.23.M833 1985 658.4'033 85-9958

Softcover reprint of the hardcover 1st edition 1985

2142/3140-543210

Preface

Both the 'First International Summer School on Multiple Criteria Decision Making Methods, Applications and Software' and the present volume of readings could only be realised with assistance and support from many sides. We would like to express our gratitude to all those who have contributed to making a success of the first of a hopefully long series of summer schools in this field and to all those who have contributed to the present volume.

First of all we are grateful for the financial means supplied by a long list of sponsors, the most important of which are mentioned on the copyright page. Next, we are grateful to the members of the organising committee, Anna Ostanello and Giovanni Zambruno. Since this is the first of what will become a series of summer schools, the chairman of the organising committee, Benedetto Matarazzo, will start this volume with a brief account of the school held in Acireale. The programme committee consisted of Jean Fichefet, Anna Ostanello, Bernard Roy, Jaap Spronk (chairman) and Stanley Zionts. Their valuable contribution is gratefully acknowledged, as is the contribution of all the lecturers at the school. Of course, a school is not only made by its teachers, but just as much by its students. The primary aim of a school is to teach and to stimulate the students. It is a tribute to the quality of the students to notice that their presence and attitude was in its turn very stimulating and instructive to the lecturers. During the school, many contacts have been made, contacts of a long-lasting character, both at the professional and at the personal levels.

The present volume of readings is for the most part, a selection of what was presented at the school. A number of the papers was presented in pretty much the same form as they appear here. Others have been adapted and reworked in order to let them fit into the framework of this volume. In addition, one contribution (by Schaffers) has been especially prepared for this occasion.

A new venture like the summer school organised in Acireale and the publication of an associated volume of readings requires a lot of patient and skilful secretarial hands (and minds). It is in this context that we gratefully acknowledge the contribution of Miss Rossana Chiara and Mrs. Lia Matarazzo to the organisation of the school. Ms. Dianne Biederberg skilfully and efficiently typed this manuscript, but not only that. In addition, she corrected the English of the manuscript and contributed in many other ways to the present form of the book. We very much appreciate her careful work. We are very grateful to Marianne Leutscher for all her secretarial assistance during both the organising of the school and the editing of this book.

Finally, we thank our wives for their patience and their assistance.

Günter Fandel
Benedetto Matarazzo
Jaap Spronk

Table of Contents

The First International Summer School on MCDM

W. Matarazzo

1. The rapid development of the methods and techniques of Multiple Criteria Decision Making (MCDM) is reflected by a large number of applications in a wide variety of fields. The first studies on MCDM, carried out in the 1960s, ultimately led to a large number of research programmes being developed all over the world. Moreover, this was not merely a quantitative development, due to easily-aroused enthousiasm for a passing fashion. After a very short time, in fact, a number of results of primary importance were obtained, and new, extremely valuable paths of research were opened up.

As the most interesting of these studies were made public, the methods and problems of MCDM began to attract more and more attention from an ever-widening range of fields. Specialist groups of international experts were formed, (EURO working group on 'Aide à la Décision Multicritère', and Special Interest Group on MCDM. These groups have continued to meet regularly, developing their research on the subject and providing opportunities both for group discussions of the results presented and for a valuable exchange of ideas and experiences between the various participants.

Apart from these groups, especially since the approbation accorded by the authorities and the undeniable success obtained, there is also a growing number of people who, for scientific, technical or professional reasons, would like to discover, or to know more about, certain aspects of MCDM. Today we can confidently say that MCDM has outgrown its early phase of development and reached full maturity.

In the light of this fact, some years ago a number of scholars began to consider the possibility of organising, in the form of a summer school, an advanced course in MCDM, which would take into account, as far a possible, the basic requirements of all the different fields. This approach, in spite of the difficulties and limitations arising from the wide variety of subjects, and the ambitious nature of the objectives, seemed preferable to the organisation of a course at seminar level, dealing with specific aspects or a particular field of application of MCDM.

2. The idea was to deal with a variety of topics connected with MCDM, of both a general and a specific nature. Each topic was presented by one or more speakers, experts in that specific field, with the support of lecture notes and practical demonstrations with the computer. All the participants were continually encouraged to take an active part in the course, through critical group discussions, accounts of personal experiences and presentation of research data.

Owing to the large number of subjects to be discussed in a relatively short time (three periods of two hours daily for two weeks), many of the specialised topics and applications were discussed in parallel sessions. In view of this, once the specific problems of widest interest were established, the timetable of lectures and practical lessons on these subjects was programmed in such a way as to avoid clashes between two sessions on the same topic. In this way each participant was given the opportunity to organise his own course programme in the most suitable way, according to personal preferences and interests.

The main objectives of the Summer School were the following:

- To give a complete and up-to-date picture of MCDM problems, methods and software;
- To publicise results of the most recent theoretic and practical research;
- To encourage contacts between research workers of different countries and different education and background (universities, research centres, industries, government offices) and to promote a fruitful cooperation for the future, in the field of scientific research;
- To promote the application of MCDM methods, techniques and software in real-life operations, by informing and encouraging particularly active representatives of public and private concerns;
- To give each participant the opportunity to discuss real specific problems with experts, to the great advantage of the former (practical application of theoretic research, encouragement towards a deeper study of MCDM problems and methods, and towards the

organisation of special introductory courses to be held in their own companies); and of the latter (opportunities to check the practical possibilities of the MCDM methods proposed, and useful pointers for future research);

- To organise group discussions between research workers and practitioners in order to form a critical and comparative analysis of the methods and techniques suggested and to evaluate the available software.

3. In order to come as close as possible to the total achievement of these objectives, the Summer School was organised as a residential course, held in a quiet, comfortable hotel situated on a small bay of the Ionian coast near Catania. The aim was in fact, to render as easy as possible the contacts between teachers and participants, not only during the official 'lesson' periods, but also outside these. In this way, thanks to the utmost cooperation of the speakers, the fortnight's compulsory, but pleasant stay, was greatly instrumental in creating numerous opportunities for useful informal debates, and in giving rise to peaceful, but stimulating discussions, in a friendly atmosphere which was also partly responsible for the complete success of the Summer School.

Four personal computers and a terminal connected with a mainframe were established in one of the conference rooms of the hotel. These were used for practical demonstrations (software exhibitions) and were placed at the disposal of all the participants for the entire duration of the course. Moreover, to supplement the many papers and lecture notes distributed (about sixty), a small library was set up, where the participants could find some of the basic works published on the subject, together with bibliographical indications and information on further conferences and other initiatives connected with MCDM etc.

4. At a certain point, the organisers had some fear that the 'novelty' of the Summer School planned, the relatively long duration of the course and the distance of the site chosen from the main European capitals, would make the school less attractive. Fortunately, after a short time the large number of applicants for the course and requests for further information put an end to all fears. Evidently, the excellent qualifications of the lecturers, the outline of the programme, the suggested teaching methods, as well as the choice of Sicily, a land of enormous tourist and cultural attraction, had all contributed to arouse a widespread interest.

The participants, who came from sixteen different countries, were strongly motivated to maximise the 'take-home-value' of the course. For a variety of reasons, the group was extremely heterogeneous. First of all, the participants were not all in possession of the same university degree (Table 1): while 50 per cent of the participants had degrees in either mathematics or economics. In fact, a good 25 per cent had degrees in other subjects not directly concerned with careers generally associated with decision making. This fact can be considered

Table 1.

Division of Summer School Participants According to University Degree

Degree	%
Mathematics	25
Economics	25
Engineering	12.5
Computer Science	10
Architecture	10
Political Science	5
Others	12.5
	100.0

in direct relation to the real motivation of those who took part in the Summer School. Many of the participants, in fact, were already well acquainted with the basic outline and methods of MCDM; they were therefore interested in either acquiring further knowledge, especially

Table 2.

Division of Summer School Participants According to Profession

Profession	%
University professor	12.5
University research workers	37.5
Government employees	22.5
Industrial managers	7.5
Bank employees	7.5
Computer science consultants	7.5
Others	5.0
	100.0

with regard to specific formal-mathematical, technical or programming aspects - or in particular applications. Other participants, on the other hand, came into contact with MCDM for the first time at the Summer School; their aim was to get acquainted with the MCDM philosophy and methods; alternatively, they were interested in the practical aspects of real-life operational applications in one specific sector.

The division of the participants according to profession (Table 2) also underlines the interest that the Summer School aroused in different fields. While 50 per cent of the participants were university professors or research workers (not only in mathematics or economic subjects, however) 35 per cent of them were professionally involved in considerable responsibility in decision making, either in government (22.5%), in banking (7.5%) or in industrial management (7.5%). Finally, 10 per cent of the participants were consultants, 75 per cent of them working in the field of computer science. The large number of participants connected with the world of economics leaves room for hope in a wider and more valuable cooperation in this field in years to come. These economists, through the acquisition of an adequate 'forma mentis' will be able to face problems of decision making in the future with a new and more suitable approach, an approach which will not only be valuable in the practical application of the different techniques acquired, but will also give them the opportunity to recognise and understand the true essence of real problems, and therefore to face them in the best possible way. And this, in our opinion, is already a first advantage of notable entity to be gained from the Summer School.

Of course, it is still too early to draw definite, or even provisional, conclusions on the results of this first Summer School. Once more, however, we wish to extend our warmest thanks to all the speakers for their generous and greatly appreciated cooperation, and to all the participants for their active interest. Together, with their comprehension, they helped us to solve all the new problems and unforeseen difficulties which arose unavoidably during the course. The experience acquired will certainly be of great value for a better organisation of similar enterprises in the future.

We feel justified, nevertheless, in expressing a decidedly positive verdict on this first Summer School, even if our judgement is based on the limited number of elements already at our disposal. The most valuable of these, as we have already said, is the enormous interest shown during the course by the participants, who worked continually with the utmost diligence and enthousiasm. Apart from attending all the lectures and practical lessons, they also asked the organisers on several occasions to arrange for 'supplementary periods' in order to study and discuss further specific aspects of the subjects dealt with. The fact that the speakers placed themselves so willingly and so completely at their disposal, and the 'family' atmosphere which was immediately established at the Summer School, made it extremely easy to satisfy this, and other requests, greatly enriched the advantages to be drawn from the course.

Finally, we would like to underline that at the end of the course both speakers and participants expressed their desire for a periodic repetition of the initiative. We are particularly flattered by this choice, which clearly and eloquently expresses their approval and appreciation of the opportunities offered. We sincerely hope therefore that the First International Summer School of MCDM may really constitute the first link in a long chain of similar valuable initiatives, leading to better and better results, not only in the field of scientific research, but also in that of real-life applications. It is in this vein that we wish a lot of success to Jean Fichefet and Philippe Vincke, the organisers of the second school.

1 Introduction: MCDM on Its Way to Maturity

G. Fandel and J. Spronk

Since its early development a few decades ago, MCDM has reached maturity but not in all respects. Many conferences are being held in east and west, in north and south. Many proceedings and special issues of important journals have appeared. Scholars and teachers all over the world are involved in research and teaching programmes of different size. Monographs, textbooks and dissertations have appeared in respectable numbers. Undoubtedly many more will follow. Furthermore, MCDM has received a lot of attention from practitioners both in the private and the public sectors. MCDM is used in practice to support actual decision processes. Nevertheless, MCDM has not yet reached full maturity. A still too large part of research in this field concentrates on algorithms rather than problems and, if problems are discussed, it is quite often as an illustration of these algorithms. This does not mean that this type of research is not needed. It does mean, however, that more effort should be directed towards problem oriented approaches. Fortunately, more and more research work is problem oriented. More attention is being paid to problem characteristics and to the adaptation of tools to problems instead of the other way round. In this respect, MCDM is still on its way to maturity. It is even so far as to be mature enough to marry. In our opinion, it is rather likely that MCDM will be coupled more and more with Decision Support Systems. The concern for problems and decision makers in DSS constitutes a fruitful land-stage for the attention for preferences in MCDM which, by its very nature, is also directed towards problems and decision makers. Such a marriage between MCDM and DSS will certainly benefit the stimulating results of recent research in psychology, organisation theory and game theory as far as they are concerned with the study of decisions by individuals and groups.

Research in the field of multiple criteria decision making is concerned with a number of different activities:

1. identification of decision alternatives;
2. generation and selection of solutions for decision problems with multiple criteria, involving only one decision maker;
3. generation and selection of solutions for decision problems with multiple criteria and several decision makers;
4. evaluation of the use of instruments designed to support decision makers confronted with multiple objectives in real applications.

(1) Studies dealing with the identification of decision alternatives focus on the question how the 'complete solution' of a decision problem with multiple objectives can be described and characterised. This 'complete solution' consists of the set of functionally-efficient decision alternatives and/or the set of efficient vectors of objective values. For linear problem structures, efforts have been made to describe and identify functionally-efficient facets of the set of alternatives by assigned preference cones of weights given to objectives. Extensions are concerned with the question to what extent available computational techniques which have already been applied to linear problem formulations are useful and/or must be modified for the determination of the set of efficient points in nonlinear problems. A third category of research work seems to be of particular interest from the point of view of economics. Apart from dealing with degeneracies of the set of alternatives, this type of research is among others, concenred with the question how nonessential objective functions can be identified and eliminated ex ante in order to simplify the decision problem. Here the nonessential objective functions of a criteria system are defined in such a way that their deletion will not modify the 'complete solution' of the decision problem at hand.

(2) Contributions which are concerned with the generation and selection of solutions for decision problems with multiple criteria involving only one decision maker, frequently assume some decision rule which serves as the decision maker's guiding principle. One can distinguish between multiple objective programming problems and the so-called multiattribute decision problems. The former are usually characterised by the fact that several objective functions are to be optimised with respect to an infinite convex set (implicitly described by a set of contraints) of decision alternatives. Multiattribute decision problems are concerned with the task of ordering a finite number of decision alternatives, each of which is explicitly described in terms of different characteristics (attributes) which have to be

taken into account simultaneously. The crux of the problem is in obtaining information on the decision maker's preferences. This can be achieved in many different ways. The spectrum ranges from directly asking the decision maker for preference statements on the basis of strong orders over preference functions, to the attempt to decompose a cardinal utility function with respect to its arguments in order to be able to measure the effects of isolated changes of individual objectives.

In a relatively large number of procedures, a linear or locally linear approximisable utility function is assumed. An optimal solution is then detected gradually by asking the decision maker for certain values of the objectives, for weights given to the objectives or for marginal rates of substitution between pairs of objectives. Some of these approaches attempt to improve or extend the available set of decision alternatives. Presently, much effort is devoted to the acceleration of algorithms for larger problems. Obviously, most efforts try to maintain the formal elegance of the algorithms and the comprehensibility of the solution process while avoiding that the information requirements become too heavy a burden for the decision maker.

A large part of research is devoted to sensitivity analyses. How sensitive is a given problem solution to changes in the input data? This question is not only important because of uncertainty with respect to the instruments and their effectiveness, but also because of uncertainty about the 'rightness' of the statements on the decision makers' preferences.

(3) In recent years, researchers have taken a particularly great interest in the field of group decisions and organisational decision processes. This has led to a series of publications with different methodical starting points. One group of papers tries to apply the concepts which have proven to be successful in dealing with multiobjective problems with one decision maker to problems involving a multiplicity of decision makers using the same analytical instruments. Another group of contributions in this field has chosen a completely different methodical starting point which so far has been of relatively little importance for decision theory with multiple objectives. Partly availing themselves of game and bargaining theoretic approaches, the authors examine under what conditions the former can be applied to multiobjective decision problems in groups.

In the first group one can encounter similar considerations on preferences structures as within the framework of multiattribute utility theory. Examples of questions which are dealt with are: which axioms allow the aggregation of the individual utility functions into a group preference function? How to solve the conflict between pareto-optimal and fair utility distributions among the group members. What forms of group preference functions or social welfare functions may be contemplated from this standpoint? In comparison with the first group, the game and bargaining theoretic approaches generally possess a greater formal elegance, having its basis in utility theory as well as in other axiomatic points of view. But it is just this fact which is often also regarded as a disadvantage of these approaches. Critics point out that the axiomatic foundation has a large influence on the determination of the optimal solution, which consequently entails the loss of flexibility required for practical applications. However, this critique is counterbalanced by the presence of a great number of game and bargaining theoretic solution approaches which are able to deal adequately with real decision behaviour as observed in groups and organisations.

(4) A steadily increasing number of studies is devoted to multiple criteria decision problems in fields as business administration, economics and the military. Applications include production allocation, research and development planning and problems of manpower allocation. Other studies are concerned with quality control problems of multilevel multiproduct manufacturing or with questions of public power supply, wage bargaining, transportation and location problems. Another main field consists of those studies dealing with resource allocation problems in university planning or with general educational planning. More and more of these studies concentrate on problem characteristics and on the question of how these characteristics condition the way a problem at hand can be solved and how much a solution process can be supported by using formal procedures. This is very different from earlier studies in which 'applications' are treated as illustrations of the potential of formal procedures.

Results of research in this area enter into an increasing number of courses both within and outside the universities. In line with this recent development, it was the aim of the First International Summer School on MCDM to give interested students, beginning academic researchers in fields as computer science, operational research and management science and staff members in government and industry involved in planning and decision making, a state-of-the-art overview of multiple criteria decision methods, applications and software.

The first part of the summer school was devoted to the philosophy of multiple criteria decision making and to an overview of solution approaches for discrete problems. The second part was devoted to an evaluation of the usefulness of multiple criteria decision making in practice. This book contains selected readings of the summer school concerning methods and methodology (Part A) as well as applications (Part B).

The first paper in Part A by Jacquet-Lagrèze discusses 'Basic Concepts for Multicriteria Decision Support'. It describes concepts developed in very different research areas and their role in solving actual multiple criteria decision problems. The contribution 'Multiattribute Utility Theory as a Basic Approach' by Vincke starts with an overview of the three different directions in which multicriteria analysis has developed thus far: multiattribute utility theory, outranking relations or interactive methods respectively. Then basic concepts and principles of multiattribute utility theory are presented and methods of estimating utility functions will be discussed. The paper by Ostanello is especially devoted to 'Outranking Methods'. It is shown how outranking relations can be modelled and used within different problem formulations. After that, the outranking procedures of the ELECTRE type are characterised by their structures. In addition, flow charts of the ELECTRE procedures explain the course of selecting the best decision alternatives. Nijkamp/Voogd present 'An Informal Introduction to Multicriteria Evaluation'. A number of general evaluation issues in relation to public planning are dealt with regarding the feasibility and desirability of policy proposals. This paper is located at the cutting line between discrete and continuous multicriteria methods in so far as it gives an overview of methods of both categories. The contribution 'Multiple Criteria Mathematical Programming: an Overview and Several Approaches' by Zionts is designed as an introduction to continuous multiple criteria decision problems with a presentation of some of the methods that have been developed to solve the multiple objective mathematical programming problem. It defines and explores the relationship between objectives, constraints and related concepts and develops a typology of models. Naive methods of problem solving are analysed and it points out how the associated ideas have been transformed into effective methods. In his contribution 'Mathematics of the Multiple Objective Problem - a Tutorial', Isermann starts with a general description of the multiple objective decision problem. He discusses the efficiency concept and the linear multiple objective programming problem. A solution method for linear programmes is outlined and illustrated by different numerical examples. Furthermore, this author describes procedures to find compromise solutions in case only limited information about the decision maker's valuation system is available. In the paper 'Decision Concepts for Organisations', Fandel shows that decision processes in organisations can be described as decision problems with several decision makers and different utility functions. Game and bargaining approaches are taken into account as solution methods. They are characterised by the actual decision rule which describes, or rather determines, the decision behaviour of the organisation members. Colson criticises in his paper 'Theories of Risk and MCDM' the traditional approaches to the risk concept which can be found in the literature, because of their lack of generality. Therefore, he proposes enlarging the concept of uncertainty, taking account of three basic uncertainty factors, hazard, ambiguity amd complexity. The paper intends to show how MCDM literature can benefit from such a new analysis grid for uncertainty. Fichefet starts in his paper 'Data Structures and Complexity of Algorithms for Discrete MCDM Methods' from the viewpoint that microcomputers will play an increasingly important part in the use of multiple criteria decision aid methods. Thus the time complexity of algorithms becomes of special interest. This time complexity is rather dependent on the data structure used to represent and to manipulate the objects involved in the algorithms. The paper illustrates this message for discrete MCDM problems. The contribution by Jelassi/Jarke/Checroun focusses on data management aspects of computerised decision support systems which use interactive multiple criteria decision methods. In this context the technical requirements for such systems and the importance of the data management tool to multiple criteria decision support systems are pointed out. Schaffers' paper 'Design of Computer Support for Multicriteria and Multiperson Decisions in Regional Water Resources Planning', the last contribution in Part A, deals with technical, psychological, ergonomic and organisational conditions for effectiveness of design and use of decision support systems for regional water resource projects. These projects show a high complexity due to many interrelations between aspects, decision makers and planning procedures. A case study is used to discuss problems and opportunities in applying formal decision aids.

The applications in Part B begin with experiences in 'Financial Planning with Conflicting Objectives', reported by Spronk. He points out how financial planning problems become multiple criteria decision problems and gives an overview of different approaches to solve these planning problems. On the basis of a simplified case description, it is shown how these approaches may support the financial planning process. The second application oriented paper 'Interactive Multiple Goal Programming for Bank Portfolio Selection' by Spronk/Zambruno shows that goal programming approaches often proposed for bank portfolio selection possess some less desirable properties. An alternative approach is presented, circumventing these less desirable features while preserving the attractive properties of goal programming. This approach is illustrated by means of a simple example. In the paper 'MCDM Problems in Rabobank Nederland', Telgen describes two MCDM problems in a large organisation and also peculiar to the banking sector. The first problem concerns budgetting in which many different decision makers have conflicting objectives. The second problem is a bicriterion problem of bank balance sheet management. Both problems are tackled by non-standard methods; heuristic mathematical programming as well as graphic interaction are applied. The paper 'On the Applicability of Game-Theoretic and Bargaining Methods to a Wage Bargaining Problem' by Fandel reports on investigations concerning wage bargaining in the metal industry in the Federal Republic of Germany between 1961 and 1979. Formally, those processes may be treated as decision probles among two parties with different utility functions, so that solution methods of game and bargaining theory can be applied. In particular, the paper analyses the extent to which the methodical approaches of Nash, Zeuthen and Contini and Zionts can be used in practice in order to explain and reconstruct the course of and the agreements within wage bargaining processes. Fichefet starts in his contribution 'Computer Selection and Multicriteria Decision Aid' with the statement that computer selection is obviously a decision problem with multiple objectives. Scoring methods based on a value function are often used as a tool to tackle the computer selection problem. Given the complexity of the latter problem, the use of these scoring methods can be criticised from many points of view. The purpose of the paper is to show that decision aid models based on the ELECTRE approaches may be better suited to solving these decision problems in practice. In their contribution 'A Methodology for Multiple Criteria Environmental Plan Evaluation', Janssen/Nijkamp/Voogd address the question whether it is possible to identify a set of discriminating criteria for environmental management problems in order to be able to choose an appropriate evaluation method for a specific environmental management problem. The aim of the paper 'An Example of Comparison of Two Decision-Aid Models' by Roy/Bouyssou is to examine on a non-theoretical ground to what extent outranking and multiattribute utility theory as decision aid approaches differ. This question is answered by describing which decision would have resulted if the ELECTRE III model, instead of the Keeney-Nair approach would have been used. In his paper 'Multiple Criteria Analysis in Energy Planning and Policy Assessment', Grauer shows that in this problem field a wide range of quantifiable and not quantifiable objectives has to be considered. In order to combine 'hard' information about energy projects with 'soft' information concerning their social and political impacts, an interactive solution dialogue with a computerised decision support system is constructed and applied. The paper gives a survey of energy models using the reference-point optimisation method. These tools help policy makers to achieve the best compromise between conflicting strategic goals.

Part A: Multiple Criteria Decision Methods and Support

2 Basic Concepts for Multicriteria Decision Support

E. Jacquet-Lagrèze

1 MULTICRITERIA DECISION SUPPORT

By 'Multicriteria Decision Support', or more classically but more improperly by 'Multicriteria Decision Making', one refers usually to a set of methods enabling a user to aggregate several evaluative criteria in order to select one or several 'actions' (projects, solutions, elements of solutions to a problem, etc.). But these expressions refer also the activity of supporting decisions for a well-defined decision maker (individual, firm, public administration, ...).

1.1 A set of methods

Available methods come from very different horizons:

- Utility theory, born in the XVIIIth Century with the first works of Bernouilli was concerned at first with modelling preferences of an individual who must choose among alternatives with risky outcomes. Its recent development under the name of Multi-Attribute Utility Theory (MAUT) (cf. Keeney and Raiffa 1976, and Ph. Vincke thereafter).

- The theory of social welfare was also born in the XVIIIth Century with the works of the Marquis of Condorcet who was interested in the problem of aggregating individual preferences expressed under the form of ranking (orders or weak orders) into a collective unique order. This type of work led to axiomatic research on aggregation or voting procedures such as Arrow's (1974) well-known impossibility theorem. Some methods issued from this field of research use recent developments in linear programming such as the one by Marcotorchino and Michaud (1979). Some others such as ELECTRE I (Roy 1968) and Ostanello-Borreani thereafter) are at the origin of important concepts in multicriteria decision support such as 'incomparability' or 'outranking relation'.

- The theory of psychosensitive measurement has dealt with the development of mathematical concepts for modelling human appraisal and judgement. Luce introduced in 1956 the notion of semi-order which enables representation of situations when the indifference situation is not transitive, due to phenomena of underlying thresholds. These notions have been used in multicriteria decision analysis and generalised in order to include several thresholds, especially in the notion of pseudo-criterion (see Roy 1975, Vincke 1978).

- Operational research and mathematical programming always had to handle the difficult question of choosing a particular objective function leaving some aspects of the preference in the set of constraints. A pragmatic answer to this question has been given by Charnes and Cooper (1961) with the 'goal programming' approach. Other important concepts and methods have been developed in this field (efficient solution, methods to find the set of efficient solutions, interactive methods to find a compromise efficient solution, ...).

- Data analysis and multidimensional scaling have recently been conceived with the analysis of qualitative and often ordinal data (cf. Batteau, Jacquet-Lagrèze, Monjardet 1981). Regression methods were proposed in order to estimate the parameters of a model (additive value function) consistent with some hollistic ranking of alternatives. The UTA method (Jacquet-Lagrèze and Siskos 1982) and very recently the PREFCALC package were developed.

1.2 A decision support activity

Most of the authors have been interested in either axiomatic research or in the development of appropriate methods. Few are those such as B. Roy who have been interested in the question of how such a method could be or should be implemented in practical situations and more precisely in defining a conceptual framework to facilitate such an implementation.

The definition of Decision Support given by B. Roy (1980) is the following:

> "Decision Support is the activity of a person who relies on clearly explicit but more or less completely formalised models, in order to get answers to the questions posed to an actor (participant) in a decision making process. The answers should enable a prescription of the behaviour of the actor increasing the consistency

between the evolution of the decision process and the objectives of the actor'.

This definition refers to a very large conception of decision support, if compared with classical Operational Research whose aim is to find out the optimal solution; but it is also restrictive if compared with methodologies which do not use analytical approaches (or mathematical models). From a practical point of view, Decision Support leads to modelling activities at the three following levels:

- Level I - Nature of the decision and choice of a problem formulation

What are the alternatives or more generally the actions (alternatives are mutually exclusive, actions are not necessarily exclusive). In connection with a choice of a set A of actions, one has to choose a problem formulation which might be:

P.α : Choice of one and only one action - From a practical point of view, the decision support should enable the user to get a subset (eventually reduced to one) of incomparable and/or equivalent actions. Optimisation is a special case of P.α whenever incomparability is not introduced in the modelling of the preferences.

P.β : Choice of all the good actions - From a practical point of view, one has to use a predefined set of actions and/or norms in order to make a classification of the actions.

P.γ : Choice of some of the best actions - One has to rank-order in a total or partial way the actions in order to facilitate the selection of some among the best.

More recently, B. Roy introduced a fourth problem formulation (P.δ) which consists of giving a description of the actions and their consequences.

- Level II - Analysis of the consequences and construction of a set of criteria

If the choice of a single criterion is too difficult or arbitrary to make, one has to use several and often conflicting criteria. The concept of consistent family of criteria gives conditions to respect in the choice of a set of criteria:

(i) Exhaustivity

$$g_i(a) = g_i(a') \text{ for } i = i, n \Rightarrow a \; I \; a' \qquad \text{(indifference)} .$$

(ii) Non-decreasing preference according to each criterion

$$g_i(a) = g_i(a') \text{ for all } i \neq k \text{ and } g_k(a) > g_k(a') \Rightarrow a \; S \; a',$$

(a outranks a' : indifference, weak preference or strict preference)

(iii) Non-redundancy

Whenever a criterion is deleted in the family, it is possible to find situations which do not respect one of the two first situations.

- Level III - Choice of an approach in aggregating the criteria

In order to aggregate the criteria, one can choose one among the three following approaches:

- aggregation of the criteria into a single one called value/utility function

$$(g_1, \ldots, g_i, \ldots, g_n) \rightarrow u(g_1, \ldots, g_i, \ldots, g_n) \; ;$$

- partial aggregation of the criteria into one or several embedded outranking relations;
- interactive and local aggregation of the criteria in order to find a compromise solution.

2 PREFERENCE MODELLING

One can use either binary relations or functions to model preferences.

2.1 Modelling preferences using binary relations

- Using a single relation R defined on A x A it is possible to represent three basic situations:

1. Preference : a R b and not b R a : $a \longrightarrow b$

2. Indifference : a R b and b R a : 

3. Incomparability : not a R b and not b R a : a   b

Although relation R is sufficient, it is easier to introduce the two derived relations: P and I to represent the preference and the indifference:

$a \; P \; b \iff a \; R \; b$ and not $b \; R \; a$,

$a \; I \; b \iff a \; R \; b$ and $b \; R \; a$.

Classically, theories and methods which use a single relation R, use also the following equivalent notations:

$\geq \iff R, \; > \leftrightarrow P, \; \sim \leftrightarrow I$.

- Recently, Roy introduced a fourth basic situation which he called weak preference (a Q b). Since it is necessary to introduce this new relation, the four following binary relations are introduced by Roy:

P : Strict preference,	I : Indifference,
Q : Weak preference,	R : Incomparability.

He also introduced situations where one is not able to make the distinction between two or perhaps three of these relations:

The outranking relation (a S b) for instance is defined as a P b or a Q b or a I b without any possible distinction between the three situations.

2.2 Modelling preferences using functions

The second basic model is the real valued function defined on A called value or utility function depending on the fact that it enables comparison to be of certain risky outcomes (see for instance Fishburn 1970). Such a function is also called a criterion or an objective function (in mathematical programming).

- Threshold phenomena - the pseudo-criterion

g is a pseudo criterion if there exist two threshold functions q(g) and s(g) such that if $g(a) \geq g(b)$:

1. $g(a) > g(b) + s(g(b)) \Longleftrightarrow a \; P \; b$.
2. $g(b) + q(g(b)) < g(a) \leq g(b) + s(g(b)) \Longleftrightarrow a \; Q \; b$.
3. $g(b) \leq g(a) \leq g(b) + q(g(b)) \Rightarrow a \; I \; b$.

Furthermore, to avoid some inconsistency, the threshold functions must satisfy the following conditions:

$$g \geq g' \Rightarrow g + q(g) \geq g' + q(g') \text{ and}$$
$$g + s(g) \geq g' + s(g')$$

$$s(g) \geq q(g) \text{ for all } g \; .$$

A semi-criterion is a pseudo criterion such that $s(g) = q(g) = 0$.
A precriterion is a pseudo criterion such that $q(g) = 0$.
A true criterion is a pseudo criterion such that $s(g) = q(g) = 0$.

The true criterion is the classical model used in Decision Theory and Multicriteria Decision Making. The first two use the notion of thresholds and therefore enable modelling situations for which indifference is not transitive.

Example:

A	a	b	c
g	12	11	10

With $q(g) = 1$ and $s(g) = 0$, we get the following semi-order defined on A :

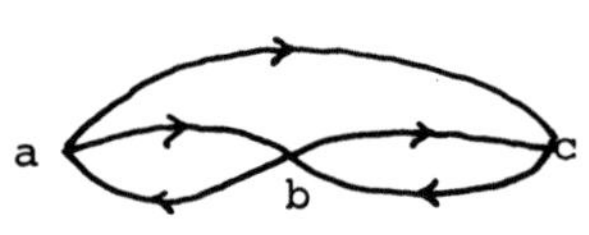

Intensity of preferences: cardinal versus ordinal criteria

- An ordinal criterion g is a criterion for which only the weak-order derived from g is meaningful. Therefore, if g is an ordinal criterion, any non-decreasing function $f(g)$ is also an ordinal criterion. Such a criterion does not enable the modelling of intensity of preference.

- A cardinal criterion is a criterion for which comparing the differences of values, or more generally intervals, is meaningful. This means we are able, or willing, to introduce an ordinal comparison of intervals.

let $\geq^*$ a relation defined on A x A. If $a \geq b$ and $c \geq d$, then $(a, b) \geq^* (c, d)$ means that the intensity of preference of a over b is greater than the one of c over d.

Krantz et al. (1971, pp. 147-151) give theorems which lead to the adoption of a criterion g defined up to a linear transformation.

g is a cardinal criterion iff $\alpha g + \beta$ is a cardinal criterion modelling the same preferences (with $\alpha > 0$).

3 NON-COMPENSATORY MODELS

We assume now that the consequences are multiple and modelled using n criteria $g_1, \ldots, g_n$, enabling us to evaluate any alternative or action a of A by a vector $\underline{g}(a)$.

Compensation is one of the main concepts in multicriteria decision making. To what extent can improving a value on one criterion compensate for a decrease on another criterion?

In some situations, compensation is not allowed. The corresponding models are non-compensatory.

3.1 Conjunctive model or aspiration levels model

Let g_i^* be an aspiration level (a goal) defined on criterion g_i.

Two judgements are possible for every alternative:

(i) $g_i(a) \geq g_i^*$ for all i, then a is accepted.

(ii) $\exists\ i \mid g_i(a) < g_{i*}$, then a is rejected.

This model is so simple that it has been shown that it is almost the only model used by individuals when they do not formalise explicitly their multicriteria decision problem (consumer behaviour, for instance).

3.2 Lexicographic model

This is the model used to put in order the words in a dictionary, the first letter playing the role of the first criterion, the second letter, the second criterion, and so on.

To use the model, the decision maker must give a total strict order on the criteria

$$1 > 2 \ldots > i \ldots > n$$

where g_1 would be the most important criterion and g_n the least important.

The output of the lexicographic model is a weak-order defined on A: $R = P \cup I$ such that:

$$a \; P \; b \Longleftrightarrow \exists \; i' \mid a \; I_i \; b \text{ for all } i = 1, \ldots, i' - 1 \text{ and } a \; P_{i'} \; b$$

$$a \; I \; b \Longleftrightarrow a \; I_i \; b \text{ for all } i.$$

4 AGGREGATION MODELS IN A VALUE (UTILITY) FUNCTION

4.1 Definitions

Multicriteria utility function

This model consists of aggregating the n criteria into a function $u(g_1, g_2, \ldots, g_n)$ such that u is an overall criterion:

$$u(g(a)) \geq u(g(b)) \Longleftrightarrow a \; R \; b \; .$$

R is a total weak order.

A utility function is the name often given to such a function. In utility theory, the distinction is made though between a value function when no risky outcomes are taken into account, and a utility function which allows the comparison of risky outcomes, through the computation of an expected utility.

When u can be derivated, the fact that g_i is a criterion implies that the partial derivate is non-negative:

$$\frac{\partial u(g)}{\partial g_i} \geq 0 \text{ for all } g_i \text{ and } g .$$

In some situations, it is preferable not to impose such a condition. The term <u>attribute</u> or <u>dimension</u> is then used instead of the term criterion.

Tradeoff ratio or marginal rate of substitution

This concept is the most important in the multicriteria utility theory. It formalises the notion of compensation and generalises therefore the notion of price.

Let g_r be a given criterion, a first and approximate definition of a tradeoff ratio is the necessary increase on criterion g_r to compensate the loss of one unit in criterion g_i

$$s_{ir}^{g} \text{ such that } (g_1, \ldots, g_{i-1}, \ldots, g_i + s_{ir}^{g}, \ldots, g_n) \; I \; (g_I, \ldots, g_n).$$

A more precise definition can be given whenever u(g) can be derivated:

$$s_{ir}^{g} = \frac{\partial u(g)}{\partial g_i} \Big/ \frac{\partial u(g)}{\partial g_r} .$$

4.2 Additive utility function

An additive utility function is such that:

$$u(g) = \sum_{i=1}^{n} u_i(g_i) .$$

$u_i(g_i)$ is called a <u>marginal utility function</u>.

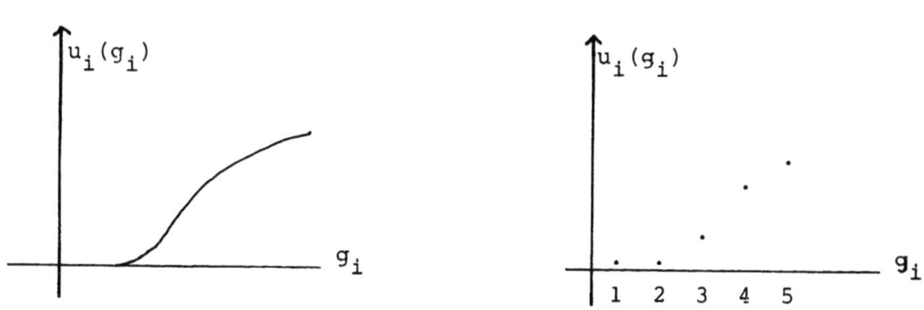

<u>Figure 1.</u> Continuous and discrete marginal utility functions

When the utility function is additive, the tradeoff ratio between two criteria are independent of the values on the n-2 other criteria.

Since $$\frac{\partial u(g)}{\partial g_i} = \frac{du_i}{dg_i}\ , \quad s^g_{ij} = \frac{du_i}{dg_i} \Big/ \frac{du_j}{dg_j}$$

The tradeoff ratio is in this case the ratio of the slopes of the two marginal utility functions.

This form of independence is called <u>preferential independence</u> (cf. Keeney and Raiffa 1976).

The <u>average sum</u> is a special and well-known case of an additive model:

$$u_i(g_i) = w_i g_i \text{ for all } i, \text{ so } U(g) = \sum_i w_i\, g_i\ .$$

In this model, the marginal utility functions are linear (slope w_i) and the indifference curves are linear (planes, hyperplanes). The tradeoff ratios are constant since $s^g_{ij} = w_i/w_j$.

5 AGGREGATION MODELS IN AN OUTRANKING RELATION

These models consist of aggregating the criteria into a partial binary relation (outranking relation) which is 'more complete' than, the dominance relation.

5.1 Dominance relation and efficient set

Let $R_1, \ldots, R_i, \ldots, R_n$ be the n weak-orders on A derived from the n criteria $(g_1, \ldots, g_i, \ldots, g_n)$.

Dominance relation

$a \geq b \Longleftrightarrow a\ R_i\ b$ for all $i = 1, n$: weak dominance.
$a > b \Longleftrightarrow a \geq b$ and not b a : strict dominance.

When the criteria are true-criteria (without thresholds):

$$a \geq b \Longleftrightarrow g_i(a) \geq g_i(b) \quad \text{for all } i\ .$$

Efficient set E

The efficient or non-dominated set is a subset of E and A whose alternatives are not dominated:

$$a \in E \text{ iff there is no } b \in A \text{ such that } b > A \ .$$

The dominance relation and the efficient set are interesting concepts when, but only when the problem formulation is P.α (select one and only one alternative). It is sometimes much easier to work on the set E than on the set A, since E can be much 'smaller' than A.

For other problem formulation, one has to work with the whole set A, to be sure not to eliminate the 'very bright second alternative', which is an excellent alternative but slightly dominated by the first one.

In multiobjective linear programming for instance, a lot of research has been done in order to describe or to explore the set E. A necessary and sufficient condition for an alternative $\tilde{a}$ to be efficient is that there exists a set of weights w with $w_i > 0$ for all i such that:

$$V(\tilde{a}) = \max_{a \in A} \sum_i w_i \, g_i(a) \ .$$

If A is not convex, this property is false as shown in the following example (Figure 2). Alternative b is efficient and cannot be an optimal solution for a weighted sum.

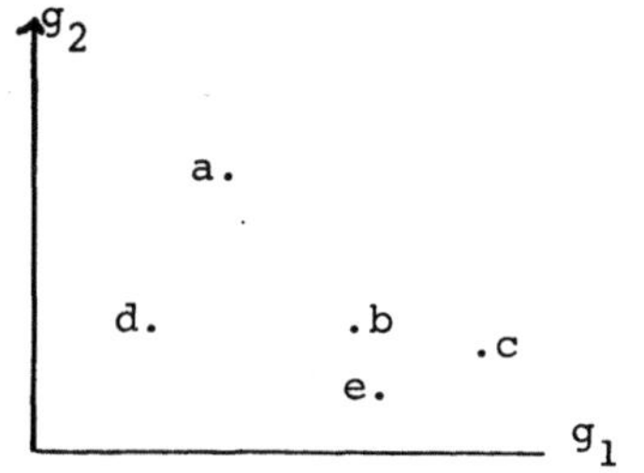

Figure 2. Efficient alternative (a, b, c) and dominated alternatives (d, e)

5.2 Some concepts for building outranking relations

Concordance

This is an ordinal concept which generalises the concept of majority rule in a voting procedure.

For each pair (a, b) of alternatives, let us consider the three following subsets of the criteria.

Criteria for which a is better than b :

$$I_{a>b} = \{i \mid a >_i b\}.$$

Criteria for which b is better than a :

$$I_{b>a} = \{i \mid a >_i b\}.$$

Criteria for which a and b are equivalent (indifference situation) :

$$I_{a\sim b} = \{i \mid a \sim_i b\}.$$

Let us assume we have a set of weights w_i such that $\sum_i w_i = 1$; then let us compute:

$$P_{a>b} = \sum_{i \in I_{a>b}} w_i,\ P_{b>a} = \sum_{i \in I_{b>a}} w_i,\ P_{a\sim b} = \sum_{i \in I_{a\sim b}} w_i .$$

The concordance test is satisfied if the following 'majority rules' are satisfied:

$$P_{a>b} + P_{a\sim b} \geq c \text{ and } P_{a>b} > P_{b>a} \text{ with } .5 \leq c \leq 1 .$$

Non-discordance

The concept is used to reject a situation of outranking of a over b whenever there exists a criterion for which b is 'much better' than a.

We can define for instance a 'big threshold' D_i and reject an outranking relation of a over b if there exists a criterion g_i such that $g_i(b) - g_i(a) > D_i$. This is a means to reintroduce some cardinal property in an ordinal aggregation rule, even if from a mathematical point of view, defining a constant threshold D_i is equivalent to define a semi-order structure on A.

Cardinal outranking relations

Roy and Bertier have proposed a cardinal method which uses the concept of tradeoff ratio (see de Montgolfier and Bertier 1978).

They chose one criterion g_r as a reference criterion and they assume that for each of the n-1 other criteria the decision maker (or a group of decision makers) agree on a lower bound and an upper bound of the tradeoff:

$$m_i \leq s^g_{ir} \leq M_i \ .$$

An outranking relation can be built, based on the following indicator:

$$\sigma(a, b, s) = \sum_i s^g_{ir}(g_i(a) - g_i(b)) \ .$$

An outranking relation S can be:

$$a \ S \ b \Longleftrightarrow \min_{S \in [m,M]} \sigma(a, b, s) \geq 0 \ .$$

Such a relation S has the following properties (see Jacquet-Lagrèze 1975):

- S is transitive;
- $m_i = 0$ and $M_i = +\infty$, S is the dominance relation (no information on the tradeoff;
- $m_i = M_i$ for all i : S is the weak-order derived from the average sum model $u(g) = \sum_i w_i \ g_i$ with $w_i = m_i = M_i$.

This principle can be generalised using a set μ of utility functions.

Let $\mu = (u(g))$ a set of utility functions considered as a model of the preferences of the decision maker. We may wish to consider such a set when the estimation of the parameters of a utility function remain imprecise. This is the case for instance when we use ordinal regression methods to estimate the weights of an average sum or more generally the parameters of an additive utility function as in the UTA method (see Jacquet-Lagrèze and Siskos 1982).

An outranking relation S can be built using the following sets:

$$a \ S \ b \Longleftrightarrow \min_{u \in \mu} (u(g(a)) - u(g(b)) \geq 0$$

$$\Longleftrightarrow u(g(a)) \geq u(g(b)) \text{ for all } u \in \mu \ .$$

6 INTERACTIVE AND LOCAL AGGREGATION OF THE CRITERIA IN ORDER TO FIND A COMPROMISE SOLUTION

This type of method was first proposed in the context of multi-objective linear programming.

Some of the methods use the notion of <u>ideal point</u> (cf. Roy 1968, Zeleny 1981).

This point is defined in the criteria space and is such that each coordinate equals the maximum value which can be obtained on the corresponding criterion without considering the other criteria.

$$g^* \text{ is such that } g_i^* = \max_{a \in A} g_i(a) \quad \text{for all } i \text{ .}$$

The interaction process can rely on the following types of phases (see Roy 1975):

<u>i) Search of a candidate for a compromise solution</u>
Considering the information we have on the preference of the decision maker (cf. phase (iii), the model searches for an alternative which could appear as a possible compromise solution.

<u>ii) Communication to the decision maker (DM)</u>
The solution found in phase (i) is shown to the DM, and also all the information which seems useful to him, for instance, the values of this solution on the different criteria.

<u>iii) Reaction of the DM</u>
The solution can be judged satisfactory and then the procedure stops. When it is not the case, information on the preferences of the DM is obtained from him. The type of the information differs from one method to the other. It can be the tradeoff ratio (Boyd 1973, Geoffrion et al.) hollistic judgement in the comparison of the compromise solution and adjacent solutions (Zionts 1981), aspiration levels (Winkels, forthcoming), new constraints which modify to the ideal point (Zeleny 1981).

7 CONCLUSION

We have given here most of the main concepts used in multicriteria decision making, and have also given some ideas on the different approaches.

As far as the concepts are concerned, we will probably see in the near future, some integrating work at an axiomatic level. Different concepts and mathematical models will then appear as special cases of a more general conceptual framework.

As far as the methods are concerned, we began to observe an increase of highly interactive (micro) computer programs. From a practical point of view, these new generation programs will make a major contribution to multicriteria decision support.

REFERENCES

Arrow, K.J., Social Choice and Individual Values, Wiley, New York, 1951, and 1983. Trad. française, Choix Collectif et Préférences Individuelles, Calman Lévy, Paris, 1974.

Batteau, P., Jacquet-Lagrèze, E. and Monjardet, B., Analyse et Agrégation des Préférences dans les Sciences Sociales, Economiques et de gestion, Economica, 1981.

Boyd, D.W., 'Interactive preference assessment for decisions with multi-attribute outcome', Paper presented at the fourth conference on subjective probability, Utility and Decision Making, Rome 1983.

Charnes, A. and Cooper, W.W., Management Models and Industrial Applications of Linear Programming, Vol. 1, Wiley, New York, 1961.

Fishburn, P.C., Utility Theory for Decision Making, Wiley, New York, 1970.

Geoffrion, A.M., Dyer, J.S. and Feinberg, A., 'An interactive approach for multicriterion optimization with an application to the operation of an academic department', Management Science, Vol. 19, no. 4, Part I, pp. 357-369.

Giordano, J.L. and Suquet, J.C., 'Une procédure multicritère interactive adaptée à la saisie de données non quantifiables', RAIRO, Vol. 12, no. 2, 1978, pp. 181-205.

Guilbaud, G.Th., 'Contenu physique et contenu expérimental', Mathématiques et Sciences Humaines, no. 62, 1978.

Jacquet-Lagrèze, E., 'How can we use the notion of semi-order to build outranking relations in multicriteria decision making', in: Wendt, D. and Vlek, C. (eds), Utility, Probability and Human Decision Making, Reidel Publ. Co., 1975.

Jacquet-Lagrèze, E., 'Quasi-ordres et relations probabilistes sous forme standard et méthodes d'approximation', Mathématiques et Sciences Humaines, no. 63, 1978.

Jacquet-Lagrèze, E., 'De la logique d'agrégation de critères à une logique dágrégation-désagrégation de préférences et de jugements', Cahiers de l'ISMEA, Série de Gestion no. 1, Tome XIII, no. 456, 1979, pp. 839-859.

Jacquet-Lagrèze, E., 'Binary preference indices, a new look at multi-aggregation procedures', European Journal of Operational Research, Vol. 10, no. 1, 1982, pp. 26-32.

Jacquet-Lagrèze, E., 'A behavioral model of the decision process and an application for designing a decision support system', Paper presented at the NATO-ARI on Understanding and Aiding Human Decision Making', Williamsburgh, USA, March 28-April 2, 1982.

Jaquet-Lagrèze, W. and Siskos, J., 'Assessing a set of additive utility functions for multicriteria decision making, the UTA method', European Journal of Operational Research, Vol. 10, no. 2, 1982, pp. 151-164.

Keeney, R. and Raiffa, H., Decision with Multiple Objectives: Preferences and Value Tradeoffs, Wiley & Sons, 1976.

Krantz, D.H., Luce, R.D., Suppes, P. and Tversky, A., Foundation of Measurement, Vol. 1: Additive and Polynomial Representations, Academic Press, London, 1971.

Marcotorchino, F. and Michaud, P., Optimisation en Analyse Ordinale des Données, Masson, Paris, 1979.

Montgolfier, J. de and Bertier, P., Approche Multicritère des Problèmes de Décision, Editions Hommes et Techniques, Paris, 1978.

Monjardet, B., 'Axiomatiques et propriétés des quasi-ordres', Mathématiques et Sciences Humaines, Vol. 63, 1978, pp. 51-82.

Roy, B., 'Classement et choix en présence de points de vue multiples (la méthode ELECTRE)', Revue Française d'Informatique et de Recherche Opérationnelle, no. 8, 1968, pp. 57-75.

Roy, B., 'Vers une méthodologie générale d'aide à la decision', METRA, Vol. XIV, no. 3, 1975, pp. 459-497.

Roy, B., 'ELECTRE III: Un algorithme de classements fondé sur une représentation floue des préférences en présence de critères multiples', Cahiers du CERO, Vol. 20, no. 1, 1978, pp. 3-24.

Roy, B., 'L'aide à la décision: Critères multiples et optimisation pour choisir, trier, ranger',

Roy, B. and Bertier, P., 'La méthode ELECTRE II: Une application au média-planning', in: Ross, M. (ed), O.R. 72, North-Holland Publ. Co., 1973, pp. 291-302.

Roy, B. and Vincke, Ph., 'Pseuso-critères et systèmes relationnels de préférences - Nouveaux concepts et nouveaux résultats en vue de l'aide à la décision', Université de Paris-Dauphine, Cahier du LAMSADE, no. 28, 1980.

Siskos, J., 'A way to deal with fuzzy preferences in multicriteria decision problems', European Journal of Operational Research, Vol. 10, no. 3, 1982, pp. 151-164.

Siskos, J., 'Evaluating a system of furniture retail outlets using an interactive ordinal regression method', Cahier du LAMSADE, no. 38, Université Paris-Dauphine, January 1982.

Vincke, Ph., 'Quasi-ordres généralisés et représentation numérique', Mathématiques et Sciences Humaines, Vol. 62, 1978, pp. 35-60.

Winkels, H.M., 'Efficiency projections', O.R. Spectrum, forthcoming.

Zeleny, M., Multiple Criteria Decision Making, McGraw Hill, New York, 1981.

Zionts, S., 'A multiple criteria method for choosing among discrete alternatives', European Journal of Operational Research, Vol. 7, 1981, pp. 143-147.

3 Multiattribute Utility Theory as a Basic Approach

Ph. Vincke

1 THREE BASIC APPROACHES

A Nature of a decision problem

A decision problem can often be formulated as a problem where a set A of potential actions (possible solutions, feasible decisions) is considered among which one must:

- either choose a single action considered as 'the best',
- or select a subset of actions considered as 'good',
- or order the actions from the best to the worst.

The set A may be defined in an enumerative way (i.e. by a list) or by means of mathematical constraints; it may be finite or infinite, fixed or evolutive (i.e. likely to be modified during the decision process).

Examples

1. A business concern must choose a site for a warehouse: seven locations are possible. Each site represents an action; the set A contains seven elements: it is finite and defined in an enumerative way. It is fixed if no new site can be considered.

2. In the travelling salesman problem in which a salesman must pass once and only once through each of N towns in a network, the set A is defined by constraints (the actions are the hamiltonian circuits of a graph with N vertices); it is finite (it contains $(N-1)!$ elements) and is fixed.

3. In a linear programme, the set of actions is defined by mathematical constraints (linear inequalities) and is infinite. It is evolutive if, during the decision process, modifications may be made to the constraints.

Before the advent of multicriteria analysis, the defintion of 'good' or 'best' actions is made according to a single point of view. This point of view in general is represented by a function g (objective function, value function, utility function) which associates with each action a number such that, $\forall$ a,b $\in$ A :

$$\text{a is better than b iff } g(a) > g(b) \ .$$

In this context, decision problems are well-defined mathematically: the set A and the function g being defined, it remains to study the existence and uniqueness of the solution and construct an algorithm which furnishes this solution: this is the objective of classical operational research.

It is rare however, to find concrete applications where a single point of view is sufficient to embrace all the necessary information to compare the elements of A. For example, the choice of a car rests simultaneously on its price, its looks, its comfort, its performance, its petrol consumption, ... The objective of multicriteria analysis is the study of decision problems in which several points of view must be taken into consideration.

The principal inconvenience of a multicriteria problem is that, mathematically, it is not well-defined. In general, there exist contradictions between the different points of view considered, in such a way that an action a might be 'better' than an action b on one criterion, and 'worse' on another. In these circumstances, the following two extreme attitudes are fruitless:

- leave the decision maker entire liberty for the decision,
- introduce consciouly or not restrictive hypotheses so that the problem can be solved by a 'classical' method.

The methods used in multicriteria analysis lie between these two extremes: they are based on models constructed partly from necessarily restrictive mathematical hypotheses, and from information gathered from the decision maker. In this sense, multicriteria analysis constitutes an example of the evolution of the scientist role in decision problems: the problems are no longer solved by replacing the decision maker by a mathematical model, but by helping the decision maker to construct his solution by enlightening him on his possibilities.

B Several definitions

Dominance: an action a dominates an action b if a is at least as good as b for all the considered points of view and strictly better than b for at least one point of view.

Efficient solution: an action a is efficient if there is no action b in A (the set of potential actions) which dominates a. It is clear that often only efficient solutions are of interest in a decision problem.

Criterion: in this introduction, a criterion is a real valued function g_i on A such that a is strictly better than b iff $g_i(a) > g_i(b)$.

Image of A in the criteria space: each element a of A may be represented in $\mathbb{R}^n$ by a point with coordinates $g_1(a), g_2(a), \ldots, g_n(a)$. The set of points thus obtained is the image of A in the criteria space.

Ideal point: the point which, in the criteria space, has coordinates

$$\max_{a \in A} g_1(a), \max_{a \in A} g_2(a), \ldots, \max_{a \in A} g_n(a)$$

is called the ideal point. It is clear that if an element of A has this point as its image, this element is the 'absolute best' because it maximises simultaneously all the criteria.

Tradeoff: the tradeoff between two criteria is the amount that the decision maker is ready to concede on one of the criteria to obtain one unit on the other. This concept is fundamental in some procedures as will be illustrated in the papers devoted to the applications.

Multiobjective linear programme: a multiobjective linear programme is a particular multicriteria problem in which the set A is defined by a set of linear constraints in $\mathbb{R}^p$ space, and the criteria are linear functions defined in this space. Mathematically, it may be formulated as follows:

$$\text{maximise } g_j = c_{j1} x_1 + c_{j2} x_2 + \ldots c_{jp} x_p , \quad j=1,2, \ldots, n$$

subject to the constraints

$$a_{i1} x_1 + a_{i2} x_2 + \ldots + a_{ip} x_p = b_i \quad , \quad i=1,2, \ldots, m$$

or, in the matrix form:

$$\begin{cases} (A) . (X) = B \\ \max (C) . (X) \end{cases}$$

where (A), (X), (B) and (C) are respectively m x p, p x 1, m x 1 and n x p matrices. Geometrically, the set A is a convex polyhedron in $\mathbb{R}^p$ space, and each criterion attains its maximum at a vertex (possibly an edge or a face) of this polyhedron.

C Efficient solutions

The set A and the criteria $g_1, g_2, \ldots, g_n$ being defined, the characterisation and determination of efficient solutions are obviously well-defined mathematical problems. In particular, the following result is entirely general.

Theorem: so that an action a of A is efficient, it is sufficient that there exist n real constants $\lambda_1, \lambda_2, \ldots, \lambda_n$, strictly positive, such that a maximises in A the function $\sum_{i=1}^{n} \lambda_i g_i$.

Proof: if a was not efficient, there would exist an action b in A such that $g_i(b) \geq g_i(a)$, $\forall$ i, at least one of the inequalities being strict. By multiplying each inequality by λ_i and summing, we obtain:

$$\sum_{i=1}^{n} \lambda_i g_i(b) > \sum_{i=1}^{n} \lambda_i g_i(a)$$

which contradicts the hypothesis.

In certain conditions, usually satisfied in real life cases (convexity of A), the converse of this theorem is true. The search for efficient solutions reduces to the study of a parametric unique criterion problem. Many authors have put forward methods to determine efficient solutions in the particular case of multiobjective linear programs (see for example Philip (1972) and Zeleny (1974).

More generally, the characterisations of efficient solutions in the form of the generalised KUHN and TUCKER conditions have been studied particularly by Geoffrion (1968).

Certain links may be established between efficient solutions and the points which, in the image of A in the criteria space, are the nearest to the ideal point for certain distances. More theoretical studies on the topological structure of the set of efficient solutions have been undertaken.

The determination of the efficient solutions of a multicriteria problem does not solve this problem. The set of efficient solutions may in fact be quite large; it often happens that all the actions of A are efficient.

D A first approach: multiattribute utility theory

This theory is based on the following hypothesis: in any decision problem there exists a real valued function U defined on A which the decision maker wishes, consciously or not, to examine. This function aggregates the criteria $g_1, g_2, \ldots, g_n$. The role of the scientist is to determine this function.

Essentially, three problems have been studied within the framework of this theory:

1. What must the properties of the decision maker's preferences be so that U is a certain function of $g_1, g_2, \ldots, g_n$ (for example so that $U = \sum_{i=1}^{n} g_i$)?
2. How to test these properties?
3. How to construct the function U?

The second part of this paper is devoted to this approach.

E A second approach: outranking methods

The dominance relation defined previously is in general too poor a relation to be used in a multicriteria problem. To construct an outranking relation consists of enriching the dominance in such a way as to advance in the solution of the decision problem. Nevertheless, contrary to multiattribute utility theory, the aim is not to make a pairwise comparison of the actions at all costs and the relation obtained is not necessarily transitive.

An outranking method comprises two distinct stages:
1. the construction of the outranking relation,
2. the exploitation of this relation.

Each of these stages may obviously be treated in a number of ways according to the problem formulation and the particular case considered.

In particular, the methods ELECTRE I, II and III, implemented by ROY and his collaborators, recommend different ways of envisaging each one of these stages. The methods are described in detail in the text of A. Ostanello. The paper by D. Bouyssou presents a comparison of the two previous approaches on a same concrete problem (see also Bouyssou 1984).

F A third approach: interactive methods

An interactive method is a procedure made up of an alternation of stages of calculation and discussion. The calculation stage allows the scientist to select an action and to put it to the decision maker during the discussion stage. This discussion stage allows the decision maker to consider the scientist's proposition, and provide supplementary information about his preferences. This additional information is then introduced into the model in the following calculation stage.

The majority of interactive methods up to date concern multiobjective linear programs. The papers by Zionts, Isermann, Spronk and Grauer are concerned with this third approach (see also Vincke 1982), so that we only give here some comments on the important question of the convergence of an interactive method. The problem of how to stop an interactive method has influenced the attitude of many scientists in the construction of their methods. Many inconveniences of these methods come from the fact that they are built in such a way that they converge independently of the decision maker. For example, many methods do not allow the decision maker to change his preferences during the procedure. Sometimes they only consider an arbitrary subset of A (for example the vertices of the polyhedron in multiobjective linear programming) or they reduce more or less arbitrarily the set of potential actions at each step. Some interactive methods assume the existence of an implicit utility function with which the answers of the decision maker are supposed to be coherent.

In fact, the purpose of an interactive method is to help the decision maker to obtain a satisfactory solution. A decision which is rejected by the decision maker at the beginning of the procedure may finally be chosen in the light of the information accumulated during the discussion. To impose a mathematical convergence of interactive methods is in opposition to their basic principle: it must be possible to come back to a decision which was rejected in a previous step.

It is, in fact, the decision maker who will stop the procedure when he is satisfied with a solution given the information he has obtained, the time devoted to the problem and its importance and other factors which are not included in the model.

2 THE MULTIATTRIBUTE UTILITY THEORY

A Introduction

Let A be the set of potential actions (feasible decisions), and let X_i be the set of possible states of the point of view (attribute) i. The tableau here below gives some illustrative examples.

Point of view i	X_i
Price	(1500 \$, 2000 \$)
Comfort	(bad, medium, good, very good)
Presence of a gadget	(yes, no)
Ranking by an expert	(1, 2, 3, ...,)

To each action a, in A, corresponds a state x_i for each point of view, so that a may be represented by the vector $(x_1, x_2, \ldots, x_n)$ element of $X = \Pi_{i=1}^{n} X_i$.

Multiattribute utility theory methods consist of two steps:

a) to build, for each point of view i, a criterion g_i (in the sense defined in the first part of the paper);

b) to combine the functions g_i in a global criterion U such that

$$U(g_1(x_1), \dots g_n(x_n)) > U(g_1(y_1), \dots g_n(y_n))$$

iff the action represented by $(x_1, x_2, \dots, x_n)$ is better than that represented by $(y_1, y_2, \dots y_n)$, when considering all the points of view simultaneously.

The multicrtieria decision problem is then reduced in a unicriterion decision problem.

The most usual combinations, in step b) are the sum of the g_i and the product of the g_i.

Now in many situations, the consequences of an actions a are not known with certainty. Given an action a and a point of view i, the consequence of a for i is x_i, y_i, z_i, ... respectively with a probability $p_a(x_i)$, $p_a(y_i)$, $p_a(z_i)$, ... these probabilities being calculated from technical aspects or being subjective. In this case, utility theory usually assumes that the value of a for the point of view i is given by the expected value of g_i:

$$u_i(a) = \sum_{x_i \in X_i} p_a(x_i)\, g_i(x_i)$$

The purpose of the next sections is to summarise some aspects concerning the two following questions:

a) Which assumptions are implicitly contained in this theory?

b) How to obtain the functions g_i, on a practical point of view?

We have to mention here that this presentation concerns only a small part of the lot of work which has been done in this field. The bibliography will help the reader to go into greater detail (see Keeney and Raiffa 1976, and von Neumann and Morgenstern 1947), and the papers by P.C. Fishburn.

B The assumptions

a) How must the preferences of the decision maker in the set X_i be in order to ensure the existence of criterion g_i? The answer to this question is well known: if X_i is finite, the necessary and sufficient condition is that the preference relation of the decision maker is a weak order, i.e.:

1. given two states x_i and y_i, one and only one of the following assertions must be true: x_i is preferred to y_i or y_i is preferred to x_i or x_i and y_i are indifferent; in other words, all the states are comparable;
2. if x_i is preferred to y_i and y_i is preferred to z_i, then x_i must be preferred to z_i (transitivity of the preference).
3. if x_i and y_i are indifferent and if y_i and z_i are indifferent, then x_i and z_i must be indifferent (transitivity of the indifference).

When X_i is infinite, a condition of topological nature, which is often satisfied in the applications, must be added.

Among the three assumptions, the third one has been the most criticised and can lead to a lack of realism in the model. This was illustrated by the famous example of the cup of coffee, by Luce (1956), showing that the third assumption is incompatible with the existence of an indifference threshold. The quasi and pseudo-criteria, introduced by B. Roy, try to bring more realism into preference modelling (see the text by E. Jacquet-Lagrèze).

b) How must the preferences of the decision maker be in the set X in order to be representable by an additive function

$$U(x_1, x_2, \ldots x_n) = \sum_{i=1}^{n} g_i(x_i) \ ?$$

It is easy to see that this assumption implies that if $(x_1, x_2, \ldots, x_k, x_{k+1}, \ldots, x_n)$ is preferred to $(y_1, y_2, \ldots, y_k, x_{k+1}, \ldots, x_n)$, then for every $y_{k+1}, \ldots, y_n$, $(x_1, x_2, \ldots, x_k, y_{k+1}, \ldots, y_n)$ must be preferred to $(y_1, y_2, \ldots, y_k, y_{k+1}, \ldots, y_n)$. This property is called the preferential independence of the set $(1, 2, \ldots, k)$ of points of view in the set of all points of view. The additive form implies that every subset of points of view must be preferentially independent in the set of all points of view. Nevertheless, this condition is not always sufficient. The reader will find in the references more details on the precise results concerning this problem but preferential independence is the essential property. The practitioners must know that this property implies, for example, that if you prefer spaghetti with red wine to mussels with red wine, then you must prefer spaghetti with white wine to mussels with white wine. Many applications present similar situations where preferential independence is too restrictive.

c) How must the preferences of the decision maker be in the set X_i in order to be representable by the function

$$u_i(a) = \sum_{x_i \in X_i} p_a(x_i)\, g_i(x_i)$$

in the probabilistic case. The answer is given by the well-known axioms of von Neumann and Morgenstern (1947). We will not recall and discuss these axioms here. Many papers have been devoted to this subject. The interpretation of the axioms depends upon the predictive or the prescriptive nature of the approach. In the predictive approach, the assumptions of utility theory are supposed to represent the preferences of the decision maker so that the model is able to predict the attitude of the decision maker (many experiments have shown that this seems rather optimistic). In the prescriptive approach, the assumptions of utility theory are supposed to define what is a rational attitude for the decision maker, so that the model is a guide for the decision maker. This point of view puts the interesting question of the concept of rationality. In any case, what is important is that the users of a model are conscious of the properties it implies.

d) We have seen that the additive model implies the property of preferential independence. In a probabilistic context, it also implies another property, illustrated by the following example.

Suppose that the actions a, b, c, and d give the following consequences:

$$\text{a gives}\begin{cases}(x_1 \ldots x_k, x_{k+1} \ldots x_n) \text{ with a probability } p,\\(y_1 \ldots y_k, x_{k+1} \ldots x_n) \text{ with a probability } 1-p;\end{cases}$$

$$\text{b gives}\begin{cases}(x_1' \ldots x_k', x_{k+1} \ldots x_n) \text{ with a probability } q,\\(y_1' \ldots y_k', x_{k+1} \ldots x_n) \text{ with a probability } 1-q;\end{cases}$$

$$\text{c gives}\begin{cases}(x_1 \ldots x_k, z_{k+1} \ldots z_n) \text{ with a probability } p,\\(y_1 \ldots y_k, z_{k+1} \ldots z_n) \text{ with a probability } 1-p?\end{cases}$$

$$\text{d gives}\begin{cases}(x_1' \ldots x_k', z_{k+1} \ldots z_n) \text{ with a probability } q,\\(y_1' \ldots y_k', z_{k+1} \ldots z_n) \text{ with a probability } 1-q.\end{cases}$$

It is easy to see that if a is preferred to b, then an additive model will impose that c is preferred to d.

This is called the utility independence of $(1, 2, \ldots, k)$ in the set of points of view and is fundamental in the additive and multiplicative models of utility theory.

c) Methods of estimating utility functions

We present in this section some methods which have been proposed in the literature to estimate the functions g_i. They are very simple and, in fact, everybody can imagine its own technique in function of the context of the application (see also Fishburn 1966).

i) Method 1

Let x_i be the least preferred and y_i the most preferred states in X_i. The decision maker is asked to determine the state z_i that is midway between x_i and y_i, so that

$$g_i(z_i) = \tfrac{1}{2}[g_i(x_i) + g_i(y_i)] .$$

After that, utility midpoints between x_i and z_i and between z_i and y_i are estimated, and so forth, until enough points are obtained to sketch a function.

ii) Method 2

The decision maker is asked to determine the state z_i which is indifferent to a (50, 50) gamble with x_i and y_i, so that $g_i(z_i)$ is calculated as in Method 1. The procedure begins again with x_i and z_i and with z_i and y_i, and so on.

iii) Method 3

The decision maker is asked to determine the states $z_{i,p}$ which are indifferent to (p, 1-p) gambles with x_i and y_i, for different values of p, so that

$$g_i(z_{i,p}) = p\, g_i(x_i) + (1-p)\, g_i(y_i)\ .$$

iv) Method 4

For some or all states z_i, the decision maker is asked to estimate the probability $p(z_i)$ such that z_i is indifferent to a $(p(z_i),\ 1-p(z_i))$ gamble with x_i and y_i, so that

$$g_i(z_i) = p(z_i) g_i(x_i) + (1-p(z_i))\, g_i(y_i)\ .$$

v) Method 5

The decision maker is asked to rank the elements of X_i and to rank the 'intervals' between these elements. Numerical values are given to the states according to the obtained rankings.

The first three methods may be applied when X_i is infinite and Method 5 when X_i is finite, while Method 4 is applicable in both situations. In the following method, a function g_j is obtained on X_j from the knowledge of the function g_i corresponding to another point of view, on the basis of an additive model.

vi) Method 6

Let x_j be the least preferred state in X_j and w_i an arbitrary state in X_i. For some states z_j in X_j, the decision maker is asked to determine the states t_i in X_i such that the couples (x_j, w_i) are indifferent to (z_j, t_i), so that

$$g_j(z_j) = g_j(x_j) + g_i(w_i) - g_i(t_i) ,$$

where $g_j(x_j)$ receives an arbitrary value and $g_i(w_i)$ and $g_i(t_i)$ are known.

d) Conclusions

Multiattribute utility theory has known important theoretical developments and has been useful in many applications. However, it is essential that the practitioners who want to use this approach, carefully study its theoretical grounds because of the strong character of the assumptions implied.

REFERENCES

Bouyssou, D., 'Approches descriptives et constructives d'aide à la décision: fondements et comparaison', thèse LAMSADE, Université Paris-Dauphine, 1984.

Fishburn, P.C., 'Methods of estimating additive utilities', Management Science, 13, 1966.

Fishburn, P.C., 'Utility theory', Management Science, vol. 14, 1968.

Fishburn, P.C., Utility Theory for Decision Making, John Wiley and Sons, New York, 1970.

Fishburn, P.C., 'A survey of multiattribute/multicriteria evaluation theories', in Zionts, S. (ed), Multicriteria Problem Solving, Springer-Verlag, Berlin, 1977.

Fishburn, P.C., The Foundations of Expected Utility, D. Reidel Publishing Company, 1982.

Geoffrion, A.M., 'Proper efficiency and the theory of vector maximization', Journal of Math. Anal. Appl., 22, 1968.

Keeney, R. and Raiffa, H., Decisions with Multiple Objectives, Preferences and Values Trade-offs, John Wiley and Sons, 1976.

Luce, R.D., 'Semiorders and a theory of utility discrimination', Econometrica, vol. 24, 1956.

Philip, J., 'Algorithms for the vector maximization problem', Mathematical Programming, 2, 1972.

Roy, B. and Vincke, Ph., 'Multicriteria analysis: survey and new tendencies', European Journal on Operations Research, vol. 8, no. 3, 1981.

Roy, B., L'aide à la décision: critères multiples et optimisation pour choisir, trier, ranger, (forthcoming).

Vincke, Ph., 'Preference modelling: a survey and an experiment', in Brans, J-P. (ed), Operational Research 81, North-Holland Publishing Company, Amsterdam, 1981.

Vincke, Ph., 'Présentation et analyse de neuf méthodes multicritères interactives', Cahier du LAMSADE no. 42, Université Paris-Dauphine, 1982.

Von Neumann, J. and Morgenstern, O., Theory of Games and Economic Behaviour, Princeton University Press, 1947.

Zeleny, M., 'Linear multiobjective programming', Lecture Notes in Economics and Mathematical Systems 95, Springer, 1974.

4 Outranking Methods

A. Ostanello

1 INTRODUCTION

1.1 Multicriteria problem formulation

In the perspective of decision aid, modelling activity (process) has substantially two roles: firstly in helping to comprehend, by mastering the various possible actions and by the reflections it gives to pre-existing preferences, and secondly in contributing to the formation and evolution of the preferences of the decision maker(s) (DM) on stage so as to make acceptable or discover possibilities which were previously refused or not considered.

Assuming the concept frame of the works of B. Roy (see for instance, Roy 1973, 1974, 1975), the formulation of a multicriteria problem can be summarised as follows:

A finite set of potential (feasible) actions, $A = (a_i/i = 1, \ldots, m)$ is considered; each of them is supposed perfectly identified but not necessarily exactly and completely known in all its quantitative and qualitative consequences. It is thus admitted that those consequences can be analysed by means of a 'consistent family' of criteria, $g = (g_j/j = 1, \ldots, n)$, see Roy (1975), where $g_j(a_i)$ will characterise the evaluation made - with more or less precision or subjectivism - of an action a_i on the j-th criterion. The technical problem consists of assessing, by an aggregation model, one of the three problems: to select one (or some) action (s) of A (the 'best' one(s)) - Problem α -; to accept actions which appear 'good' and reject those appearing 'bad', with a complementary analysis for the others - Problem β; to rank all the actions according to a complete weak order - Problem γ.

1.2 Outranking relation

An outranking relation is conceived so as to represent, in the aggregation model, the particular case where two actions are incomparable: in several decision situations indeed, the decision maker 'cannot', 'does not want', 'does not know how to' compare two actions (see Roy 1974). This situation is in practice frequently due to phenomena as unreliability linked with the personality of the DM, uncertainty of the actions or data imprecision. Thus, when accepting incomparability situations, willingness to clarify situations of preference and indifference, an outranking relation refers to preferences modelled only for those cases where the analyst is able to establish them with an objectivity and security that he/she judges satisfactory; that means, among other things, that he/she renounces the complete transitive comparability axiom (see Roy 1973).

According to the uncertainty level, deterministic or fuzzy outranking relations can be dealt with.

A deterministic outranking relation is a binary relation on the set A of actions defined as follows (see Roy 1974):

Given two potential actions, a and a' belonging to A, we say that

i) a outranks a' (a S_A a') if, taking into account the DM's known preferences, the quality of the evaluations of the criteria, the set A and the nature of the decision problem, we have enough reason to admit that 'a is at least as good as a' ' and no good reason to refuse it;

ii) a does not outrank a' (a $\not S_A$ a') if the arguments in favour of the proposition 'a is at least as good as a' ' are considered insufficient.

In terms of preferences, 'simple' outranking - a S_A a' - corresponds to the situation where a is preferred to a'; 'double' outranking - a S_A a' and a' S_a a - means that a is indifferent to a'; no outranking means that the two actions are incomparable (see Figure 1).

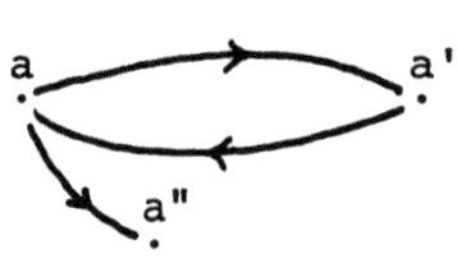

- a indifferent to a'
- a preferred to a"
- a' incomparable to a"

Figure 1. Graph of a deterministic outranking relation

When accepting to deal with the concept of outranking relation, the analyst may be more or less willing (may take more or fewer risks) to accept the outranking, whence the concept of 'fuzzy outranking'.

A fuzzy outranking relation is thus a relation finer than the deterministic one, since a 'credibility' of the outranking of one action on another is given. In other words, a fuzzy outranking relation is a fuzzy subset (see Zadeh 1975) of the set AXA of pairs of actions, characterised by a membership function δ(AXA), called by Roy (1977), the 'credibility degree' of the outranking (or 'outranking degree').

For instance, the fuzzy set

$$\left\{ \frac{(a,a')}{0.85}, \frac{(a',a)}{0.9}, \frac{(a,a")}{0.8}, \frac{(a",a)}{0.2}, \frac{(a',a")}{0.4}, \frac{(a",a')}{0.0} \right\},$$

defined for all pairs of actions of Figure 1, is a fuzzy outranking relation. It results that higher values of the credibility degree correspond to preference or indifference, whereas lower values in both comparisons of a couple imply incomparability.

In the following sections we shall present how an outranking relation could be modelled and used within different problem formulations.

2 MODELS OF OUTRANKING RELATIONS

We shall confine ourselves to describing the approaches applied in the ELECTRE methods, implemented by B. Roy and his collaborators (Roy 1968, Roy and Bertier 1973, Roy 1978, Roy and Hugonnard 1982). The 'ELECTRE approach' is founded on the concepts of 'concordance' and 'discordance'.

Other approaches can be found, for instance based on substitution rates (Roy and Bertier 1972) or on a family of utility functions (Siskos 1980).

2.1 Deterministic outranking relation

Let A = $(a_i/i\in I)$ be a finite set of potential actions, evaluated on a consistent family of true criteria (see Roy 1975), g = $(g_j/j\in J)$. Each criterion g_j is considered as a single point application from the set A to the criterion scale E_j, i.e. a completely ordered set (of quantitative or qualitative values) taken as the formal representation of the set of states associated with the j-th criterion:

$$g_j : a \in A \rightarrow e = g_j(a) \in E_j .$$

Thus the multicriteria evaluation of an action a A an be summarised by the vector $g(a) = [g_1(a), \ldots, g_n(a)] \in E = E_1 \times \ldots \times E_n$.

The model of the outranking relation consists of admitting that for any pair of actions (a,a') of A, 'a outranks a'' - a S_A a' - when both a 'concordance' test (c-test) and a 'non-discordance' test (nd-test) are satisfied (Figure 2). As it will be seen, the c-test corresponds to the acceptation of majority rule, introduced to enrich the unanimity rule, for admitting the outranking of a on a', without any veto expression (nd-test).

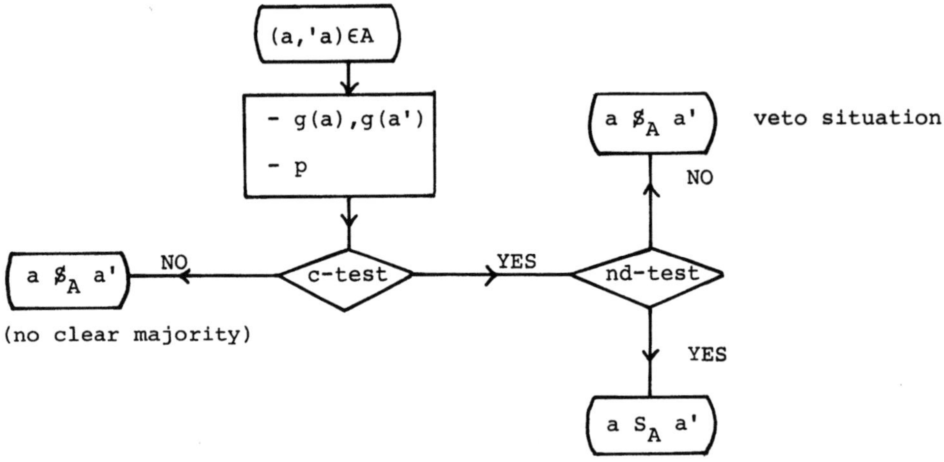

Figure 2. Structure of a model of outranking relation

2.1.1 Concordance test

For any pairs of actions a and a', let us consider the set of criteria for which a is strictly preferred to a', denoted as $J^+(a,a') \subseteq J$, the set of criteria where a and a' get equal evaluations, denoted as $J^=(a,a') \subseteq J$, and the set of criteria for which a' is strictly preferred to a, denoted as $J^-(a,a')$.

The c-test consists of verifying that the relative importance of the three sets is compatible with the hypothesis a S_A a' .

The main difficulty lies in judging the relative importance in a realistic and quick manner. It is - so to say - a question of assigning 'weights' to the criteria.

So let $p_j, j \in J$, be the weight (positive number) corresponding to the importance given to the j-th criterion within the family g, and denote by $p = (p_j / j \in J)$ the set of weights.

When the set of criteria deals with enough differentiated aspects of the consequences (see Roy 1974) used to compare the actions of A, one may simply define the importance of the above defined subsets respectively by:

$$P^+(a,a') = \sum_{j \in J^+} p_j \ , \ P^=(a,a') = \sum_{j \in J^=} p_j \ , \ P^-(a,a') = \sum_{j \in J^-} p_j \ .$$

Then a straight formulation of the c-test may be:

$$\text{i)} \quad c(a,a') = \frac{P^+(a,a') + P^=(a,a')}{P} \geq c, \text{ where } P = \sum_{j \in J} p_j$$

and (eventually equal to 1) (1)

$$\text{ii)} \quad \frac{P^+(a,a')}{P^-(a,a')} \geq 1$$

where c is a parameter, $0 \leq c \leq 1$, representing the minimum level of concordance or majority; it is supposed that this is discussed with the decision maker, otherwise it is assumed at the so-called 'natural' levels: $c_F = 3/4$, $c_f = 2/3$. $c(a,a')$ represents a 'concordance index'.

More sophisticated forms may be easily conceived.

2.1.2 Non-discordance test

The nd-test is introduced to represent veto situations so to inspect relative positions of two compared actions on the value scales, for those criteria which are 'in discordance' with the hypothesis a S_A a', i.e. the criteria of $J^-(a,a')$.

As the c-test, it can be formulated differently. Depending on the nature of the scale (continuous or not, quantitative or qualitative - case where the available evaluations can be transformed into numerical values or scores, without loss of generality) and on the decision maker's ability to identify possible veto situations, cardinal or ordinal forms may be adopted.

Cardinal forms

This kind of form has been adopted in the ELECTRE I method. The original formulation (Roy 1968) assumes a complete comparability between any pair of values of a scale with any other pair of all other scales. It is expressed as follows:

Considering the value scales of the criteria of $J^{-}(a,a')$, a 'discordance index' may be defined by

$$d(a,a') = \begin{cases} 0 \text{ if } J^{-}(a,a') = \emptyset \\ \frac{1}{d} \max\limits_{j \in J^{-}} [g_j(a') - g_j(a)] \quad \text{if } J^{-}(a,a') \neq \emptyset \\ \text{where } d = \max\limits_{j \in J^{-}} (\bar{e}_j - \underline{e}_j) \text{ , with } \bar{e}_j \text{ , } \underline{e}_j \text{ upper and lower state of } E_j \text{ respectively}, \forall\ j \in J. \end{cases} \tag{2}$$

Then the nd-test may be formulated as

$$d(a,a') \leq q \text{ , } 0 \leq q \leq 1 \text{ ,} \tag{3}$$

where q is a parameter, representing a maximum tolerance level of relative negative deviation, consistent with the hypothesis a S_A a'.

Remark: The analysis on data and preferences, required by the complete comparability assumption, does not always result in an easy or feasible task within real decision contexts. We experienced that the form (2) can be the source of misinterpretations and errors (mostly when introduced without any comment in a computer program). Whenever the nature of criteria or uncertainty of different kinds do not allow the maintaining of this assumption, a more 'technical' expression for d(a,a') is advisable.

A practical form we experienced (see Ostanello et al. 1976) is the following one: let us denote by

$$d_j(a,a') \triangleq \frac{g_j(a') - g_j(a)}{\bar{e}_j - \underline{e}_j} \quad j \in J^{-}(a,a') \text{ (marginal discordance index)} \tag{2'}$$

Then the nd-test is passed if

$$d_j(a,a') \leq k_j \qquad j \in J^-(a,a') \tag{3'}$$

where k_j, $0 \leq k_j \leq 1$, $\forall j$, is a parameter depending on the nature of the criterion and on the scale. It may be constant on E_j, but it may depend on the states of the two compared actions.

Ordinal forms

This kind of form is adopted in the ELECTRE II method (Roy 1971). Whatever $j \in J$, a set of pairs of values $D_j \subset E_j \times E_j$, called 'discordance set', is introduced so as to reflect possible veto situations.

By definition, a pair of values of E_j, (e,e'), $e < e'$, is an element of D_j, when the hypothesis a S_A a' is not admissible for a pair of actions such that $g_j(a) = a$, $g_j(a') = e'$.

In other words, a discordance pair corresponds to a negative deviation on the j-th criterion which cannot be surely compensated by the positive deviations on the criteria of $J^+(a,a')$ as soon as the concordance test is positive. It may be $D_j = \emptyset$.

Then, for the pair (a,a'), the nd-test is positive if

$$(g_j(a), g_j(a')) \notin D_j \quad \forall j \in J^-(a,a') . \tag{3"}$$

Remark: The pairs of values of a discordance set can be defined with more or less caution (severity); several inbricated sets can be identified. The set to be chosen may depend on the concordance level.

2.2 Fuzzy outranking relation

A fuzzy outranking relation S_A^δ, can be characterised by the definition of an outranking degree, associating each pair of actions (a,a') with a number $\delta(a,a')$, $0 \leq \delta(a,a') \leq 1$. δ is a criterion that fixes the more or less high credibility of the outranking of a' by a. (For the properties of δ see Roy 1977.)

When the set A of potential actions is evaluated on a family of pseudo-criteria, the model for the fuzzy outranking relation can be built by the notions of concordance and discordance.

The following formulation is adopted in the ELECTRE III Method (see Roy 1978).

2.2.1 Concordance index

For any pair (a,a'), a 'marginal credibility degree', $\delta_j(a,a')$, on the j-th criterion may be defined as a monotonous non-decreasing (with $g_j(a)$) function, such that:

$$\begin{cases} \delta_j(a,a') = 1 & \text{if } g_j(a) - g_j(a') \geq 0 \\ \delta_j(a,a') = 0 & \text{if } g_j(a') - g_j(a) \geq s_j(g_j(a)) \\ \delta_j(a,a') = 1 & \text{if } g_j(a') - g_j(a) \leq q_j(g_j(a)) \\ \delta_j(a,a') = \dfrac{s_j(g_j(a))-(g_j(a') - g_j(a))}{s_j(g_j(a)) - q_j(g_j(a))} & \text{(by linear interpolation)} \\ & \text{if } q_j(g_j(a)) \leq g_j(a') - g_j(a) \leq s_j(g_j(a)) \;. \end{cases} \tag{4}$$

Then a 'concordance index' can be defined by

$$c(a,a') = \sum_{j \in J} p_j \, \delta_j(a,a') \;. \tag{5}$$

It may be interesting to compare (5) with the corresponding definition of c(a,a') for the deterministic case.

2.2.2 Discordance index

On any criterion g_j, a veto threshold, $v_j(g_j(a))$, can be defined. It is a subjective parameter, representing the bound beyond which the opposition to the hypothesis 'a outranks a'' is sufficiently motivated.

When $g_j(a') - g_j(a) \geq s_j(g_j(a))$ ($\rightarrow \delta_j(a,a') = 0$) and a veto threshold is defined on g_j, $v_j \geq s_j$, then a 'discordance index', $D_j(a,a')$ can be defined as a monotonous non-increasing (with $g_j(a)$) function, such that:

$$D_j(a,a') \cdot \delta_j(a,a') = 0$$

$$D_j = 1 \quad \text{if } g_j(a') \geq g_j(a) + v_j(g_j(a)) \;.$$

See Figure 3 - case of linear interpolation.

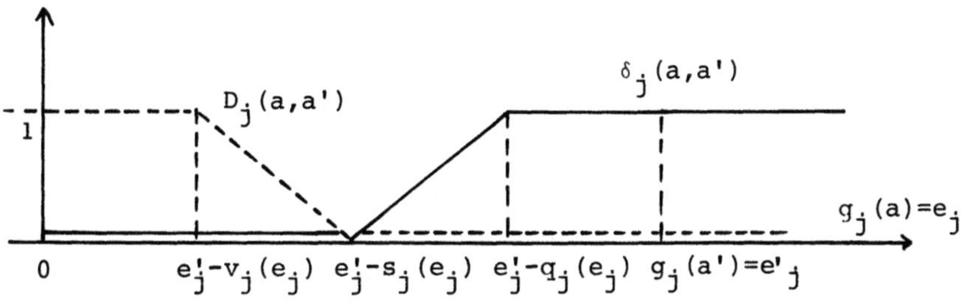

Figure 3. Marginal credibility degree $\delta_j(a,a')$ and discordance index on a pseudo-criterion g_j

2.2.3 Credibility degree

For the pair (a,a') under comparison, the outranking degree $\delta(a,a')$ can be defined as follows (see Roy 1978):

i) If $\forall\ j \in J : D_j(a,a') = 0$ then $\delta(a,a') \triangleq c(a,a')$;

ii) If $\exists\ j \in J$ such that $D_j(a,a') \neq 0$ and

a) if $D_j(a,a') \leq c(a,a')\ \forall\ j \in J$

then $\delta(a,a') \triangleq c(a,a')$;

b) if $D_j(a,a') > c(a,a')$ for at least one $j \in J^* \subseteq J$ then

$$\delta(a,a') = c(a,a') \prod_{j \in J^*} \frac{1 - D_j(a,a')}{1 - c(a,a')} . \qquad (6)$$

For other models of S_A see for instance Siskos (1982).

Remarks: Once a fuzzy outranking relation S_A^{δ} is defined, it may be interesting to introduce a non-fuzzy outranking relation, S_A^{λ}, defined by

$$a\ S_A^{\lambda}\ a' \leftrightarrow \delta(a,a') \geq \lambda .$$

For the analyst, to take into consideration a decreasing sequence of values λ, means to introduce a nested family of outranking relations that are richer and richer, but more and more risky (insufficiently justified). Conversely, the analyst may be led to build a sequence $S^1 \subset S^2 \subset S^3$ ... (strict inclusion in the set theoretical sense), referring to precise values of λ, except for the first index, generally corresponding to $\lambda = 1$. Such a sequence can be treated as a particular form of fuzzy outranking relation, S_A^δ, in which the criterion δ ranges upon a completely ordered discrete set of grades, but for which assigning a precise value is useless.

3 PROCEDURES TO EXPLOIT OUTRANKING RELATIONS (OUTRANKING PROCEDURES)

An outranking relation is a model, to aggregate the n criteria of a family g, built with fewer hypotheses than those required by a value function; however, it does not always allow a straight conclusion to be drawn. It is therefore particularly suitable to roughing out a problem. (On the basis of our rich experience with outranking procedures, we can assert that most of the expected information is produced by the outranking relation), but it may have to be completed by additional analysis of a more restricted problem.

How can the model be used to produce further information?

1. To choose one (or some) 'best' action(s): selection procedure (problem formulation α),
2. To sort out actions according to intrinsic value: segmentation procedure (problem formulation β),
3. To rank all the actions in decreasing order of preference: ordering procedure (problem formulation γ).

The ELECTRE methods have been conceived to work within these different problem formulations. They are particularly flexible, as it is shown by the fact that any solution to a γ-problem can be easily translated into a solution to a β or α-problem.

Other segmentation procedures, working with 'reference sets' cannot be reported in this paper. (See for instance, Moscarola and Roy 1977.)

The structure of all these methods is well characterised, as they are articulated into two distinct phases:
Phase I : construction of an outranking relation;
Phase II: exploitation of this relation, according to the problem formulation.

The main characteristics of the ELECTRE methods are summarised in Table 1.

Table 1.
Main characteristics of the ELECTRE methods

ELECTRE	I	II	III	IV
Kind of criteria	True criteria	True criteria	Pseudo criteria	Pseudo criteria
Additional preference information	- weights - concordance - discordance levels	- weights - conc. levels - discord-ance sets	- weights -	-
Problem formulation	α	γ	γ	γ
Outranking relation	determin.	determin.	fuzzy	deterministic, strong weak
Final information	kernel	partial ranking	partial ranking	partial ranking

3.1 Method ELECTRE I

Phase I: Model of the outranking relation.
Two decisional parameters p, q have to be defined.
Then for any pair of actions (a,a') we say that:

$$a\ S_A\ a' \text{ iff } \begin{cases} c(a,a') \geq p, \text{ defined as in (1i)} \\ d(a,a') \leq q, \text{ defined as in (2)} \end{cases} \tag{7}$$

Phase II: Exploitation of the relation (Problem formulation α).
Given S_A, we are required to determine a subset N of A such that
- each element of A - N is outranked by at least one element of N,
- the elements of N do not outrank each other. This may be expressed by:

  $\forall b \in A - N, \exists a \in N : a\ S\ b$ (external stability)

  $\forall a, a' \in N : a \not S a'$ and $a' \not S a$ (internal stability).

In mathematical terms, N is called a Kernel of the graph of S_A. Critical point: The kernel may not exist, may not be unique. A graph has a unique kernel if it has no circuits. A reduced graph, without circuits may be obtained by replacing the actions on a same circuit by a unique element and keeping external relations. This operation may however destroy a considerable amount of information contained in the outranking relation. In practice it is advisable to vary the parameters p, q and study the sensitivity of the results.

Another solution consists of using the concept of quasi-kernel (see Hansen 1976), whose definition includes outrankings up to second order. Whenever S_A, a quasi-kernel always exists.

3.2 Method ELECTRE II

Phase I : Model of the outranking relation.
Let the concordance test be modelled by (1) and the nd-test by (3"). The two non-fuzzy outranking relations, called 'strong' and 'weak' respectively, may be defined on the basis of two concordance levels c_F, c_f such that $c_F \geq c_f$ (for instance, the 'natural' levels) and, if needed, of two discordance sets $D_j^F \subseteq D_j^f$, $\forall j$.

Then, for any pair of actions (a, a') we say that

$$a\ S_A^F\ a' \text{ iff } \begin{cases} c(a, a') \geq c_F \text{ and (1ii) hold} \\ \text{and } \nexists\ j\ J : (g_j(a), g_J(a')) \in D_j^F . \end{cases} \tag{8}$$

Phase II: Exploitation of the strong and weak relations. (Problem formulation γ.) The actions of A must be regrouped into equivalence classes (as small as possible) and these classes must be put in a linear order, i.e. a weak order must be defined on A.

The method applies iteratively the following procedure (see Figure 4):

1. For a given subset A^κ of A, let $S^F_{A^\kappa}$ be the strong outranking relation. At the first iteration (κ=1), it is A^1 = A.
2. Select on A^κ the maximal subset B of elements not outranked by any element of A^κ. If the graph of the strong relation has no circuits, then $B^\kappa \neq \emptyset$. In order to meet this condition, the reduced graph has to be constructed, as in the method ELECTRE I.
   Then, if B^κ is not 'as small as needed', the weak outranking relation S^f is supplied on B^κ.
3. The κ-th class, $\bar{C}_\kappa$, of a weak order on A is then selected, as the maximal subset of elements of B^κ not weakly outranked by any element of B^κ.
4. Define $A^{\kappa+1} = A^\kappa - \bar{C}_\kappa$, set $\kappa := \kappa+1$, and go back to 1.

Stop condition : $|A^\kappa| = 1$ ($|B^\kappa| = 1$) or the outranking relation is an empty set.

A weak order on A is thus constructed, $\bar{P} : \bar{C}_1 > \bar{C}_2 > \ldots > \bar{C}_\kappa$ (downward ranking).

Before proposing this ranking to the decision maker, another weak order $\underline{P}$, must be constructed by the same procedure, working in the opposite direction, i.e. where B^{κ} is the maximal subset of elements which do not outrank any element of $A^{\kappa}, \forall \kappa$. Thus $\underline{P}$: $\underline{C}_1 < \underline{C}_2 < \ldots < \underline{C}_h$ (<u>upward ranking</u>) has to be confronted with $\bar{P}$. It may be $\bar{P} \neq \underline{P}$.

Evidently, there are no more reasons to opt for $\bar{P}$ than for $\underline{P}$. When the two rankings are too different, it may be wiser not to retain either of them but to reconsider the problem data and parameters. Vice versa, when they are closely related (the Kendall correlation index can be used to evaluate the proximity of the two rankings), an intermediary ranking P may be retained according to an 'acceptable' principle.

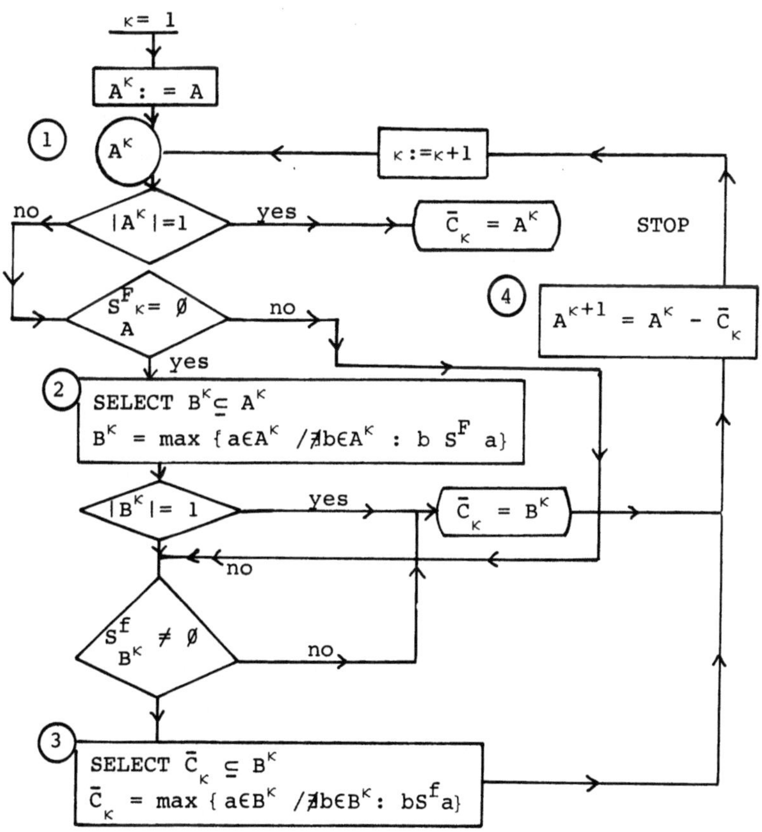

<u>Figure 4.</u> ELECTRE II: Flowchart of the downward ranking procedure

3.3 Method ELECTRE III

Phase I : Model of the outranking relation. For a finite set A of actions, evaluated on a family of pseudo-criteria, the model of a fuzzy outranking relation, S_A^{δ}, is constructed as in 2.2.

Phase II: Exploitation of the fuzzy relation. Taking into account the arbitrariness within the construction of S^{δ}, δ will be considered as a pre-criterion, i.e. a criterion endowed with a 'discrimination threshold', $s(\delta)$, such that if $\delta(a, a') = \lambda$ and $\delta(b, b') = \lambda-\sigma$, with $\sigma > s(\lambda)$, then a S^{λ}a' is strictly 'more credible' than b $S^{\lambda-\sigma}$b', $\forall(a, a'), (b, b') \in A$. The structure of the method is substantially the same as in the method ELECTRE II.

Two extreme rankings (downward and upward) are elaborated; but the classes are more sensible: they are established through the concept of 'λ-qualification' and controlled by 'separation levels', using so-called 'distillation procedures' respectively down the scale of qualifications and up the same scale.

The method applies iteratively the following main procedure on a sequence of sets B, deduced from A by successive suppressions of classes of the ranking.

A credibility level is associated to each set B.

At the first iteration ($\kappa=0$), it is : $B = A$, $\lambda_0 \hat{=} \max_{a,a' \in A} \delta(a,a')$.

Then, by defining $\lambda=\lambda_{\kappa}-s(\lambda_{\kappa})$, a 'separation level' in B,$\lambda_{\kappa+1}$, starting from λ, is defined as the maximum outranking degree attained by pairs of elements (a,a') in B such that $\delta(a,a') < \lambda$.

It may be: $\lambda_{\kappa+1} = 0$.

Given $\lambda_{\kappa+1}=0$, the $\lambda_{\kappa+1}$-qualification' of an action $a \in B$, $q_B^{\lambda\kappa+1}(a)$, is measured by the difference between the number of actions $a' \in B$ which are strictly outranked by a, 'strength of a' [i.e. $|\{a'/\delta(a,a' > \lambda_{\kappa+1}$ and $\delta(a',a) < \delta(a,a') - s(\delta(a,a'))\}|$] and the number of actions $a'' \in B$ which strictly outrank a, 'weakness of a" [i.e. $|\{a''/\delta(a'',a) > \lambda_{\kappa+1}$ and $\delta(a,a'') < \delta(a'',a) -s(\delta(a'',a))\}|$].

Within B, subsets of actions are successively separated and selected with so-called 'distillàtion procedures' producing finer and finer 'distillates' D_h (downward by choosing actions with max $q^\lambda(a)$ and upward by choosing actions with min $q^\lambda(a)$) and ending respectively to the classes $\bar{C}_{\kappa+1}$ and $\underline{C}_{\kappa+1}$ of the two rankings. (For more details on these procedures see Roy 1978.)

By defining $B = A - \bigcup_{\kappa\geq 0} C_{\kappa+1}$ (with $C_{\kappa+1} = \bar{C}_{\kappa+1}, \underline{C}_{\kappa+1}$ respectively) and setting $\kappa := \kappa+1$, the main procedure can be repeated.
Stop condition: $\lambda_\kappa = 0$ or $|B| = 1$.

The extreme rankings of the actions of A are thus produced as sequences of 'final distillates' of the distillation procedures.

It may be $\bar{P} \neq \underline{P}$. The same considerations as for ELECTRE II can be done. An intermediary ranking P can be proposed: obviously it will be more acceptable as the distance between $\bar{P}$ and $\underline{P}$ is reduced (the Kendall correlation index can be used to evaluate the proximity of the two rankings).

3.4 Method ELECTRE IV

The method has been designed to deal with two drawbacks frequently met in real cases: imprecision, uncertainty of action evaluation on the criteria and absence of weighting of the criteria.

A satisfactory answer to the first problem can be reached by the introduction of selected thresholds (of indifference, preference, veto) on each criterion, so to define a pseudo-criterion.

The second drawback requires an appropriate introduction of the concept of outranking. To get this concept to operate, rules have to be specified so to characterise proofs which will be considered sufficiently clear and positive to accept outranking.

The outranking may be established more or less plausibly.

The method ELECTRE IV (see Roy and Hugonnard 1982) distinguishes two plausibility levels: strong outranking, S_F, not subject to discussion, and weak outranking, S_f, a little more questionable.

Phase I : Modelling strong and weak outrankings.
For each pair of actions (a,a') let a Q_j a', a P_ja' denote respectively the weak and strict preference of a on a' on the j-th pseudo-criterion, j = 1, ..., n.

Then the conditions which have been specified (see Roy and Hugonnard 1982) to a conclusion in terms of 'a strongly outranks a'', a S_Fa', or 'a weakly outranks a'', a S_fa', are summarised in Figure 5. The specified rules can be easily interpreted as formal expressions of common sense principles, compatible with ignorance of the relative importance of the criteria.

With the same guiding ideas, somewhat different rules can be formulated.

Phase II: Exploitation of the outrankings.
As in ELECTRE III, two ranking procedures (downward and upward) are elaborated using distillation processes, through the concept of 'qualification' of an action a$\in$A.

Given a deterministic outranking relation S, for any subset B $\subseteq$ A, the 'qualification' of a$\in$B is given by the number of actions of B which are outranked by a ('strength' of a in B) less the number of actions of B which outrank a ('weakness' of a in B).

Given S_F, the actions of B having maximum qualification are qualified for first place. The weak outranking relation has been conceived (as in ELECTRE II) to handle ex aequo cases. Actions with maximum qualification, within S_f, are withdrawn before a new iteration is made.

One can proceed with the same rule to determine the next class in the ranking. That implies recomputing the qualifications, as withdrawing actions induces changes in some of them.

The procedure ends when all the actions have been ranked. The upward procedure is constructed on the same principle, but in reverse order, i.e. looking for actions have the minimum qualification within the sets B.

The two rankings $\bar{P}$, $\underline{P}$ may be different.

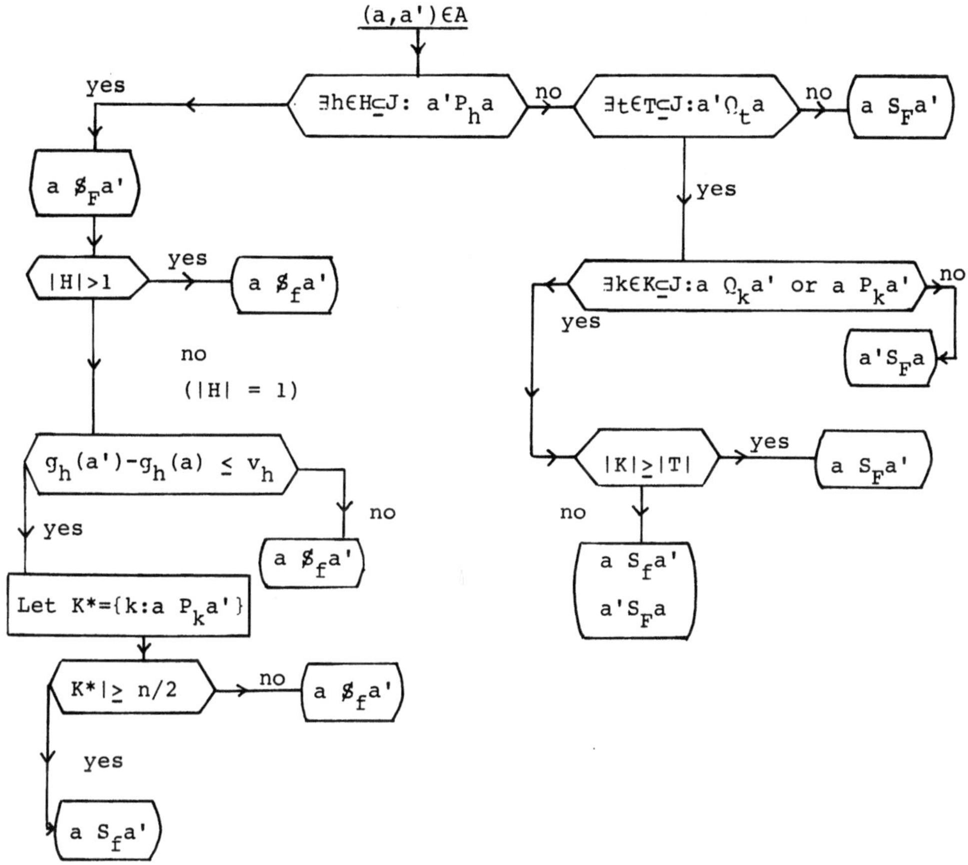

Figure 5. ELECTRE IV: Flowchart of the conditions to establish strong and weak outrankings

In order to obtain a partial weak order on A from them, when discrepancy results, a binary relation may be defined as follows:

- a and a' ex aequo iff they appear so in the two rankings,
- $a > a'$ iff they are not ex aequo in the two rankings and if a' does not come strictly ahead of a in either of them.

REFERENCES

Bona, B., Giorgi, N., Minini, U., Orlando, E. and Ostanello, A., 'An application of a multicriteria method to a diagnosis of public services in homogeneous areas of a town', (in Italian), Part I and Part II, Quaderni di Lavoro, no. 2,3, Politecnico di Torino, Gruppo R.O., 1976.

Hansen, P., Anciaux, M. and Vincke, P., 'Quasi-kernels of outranking relations', in: Thiriez, H. and Zionts, S. (eds), Multiple Criteria Decision Making, Lecture Notes in Economics and Mathematical Systems, No. 30, Springer-Verlag, Berlin, 1976, pp. 53-62.

Jacquet-Lagrèze, E., 'How we can use the notion of semi-orders to build outranking relations in multicriteria decision making', in: Wendt, D. and Vlek, C. (eds), Utility, Subjective Probability and Decision Making, Wiley, 1975.

Jacquet-Lagrèze, E. and Siskos, J., Méthode de Décision Multicritère, Editions Hommes et Techniques, Boulogne-Billancourt, 1983.

Montgolfier, P. de and Bertier, P., Approche Multicritère des Problèmes de Décision, Editions Hommes et Techniques, Suresnes, 1978.

Moscarola, J. and Roy, B., 'Procédure automatique d'examen de dossiers fondée sur un classement trichotomique en présence de critères multiples', RAIRO Recherche Opérationnelle, 22 (2), 1977.

Roy, B., 'Classement et choix en présence de points de vue multiples, (Le méthode ELECTRE)', RIRO, 2, no. 8, 1968, pp. 57-75.

Roy, B., 'La méthode ELECTRE II', METRA, Direction Scientifique, Note de Travail, No. 142, 1971.

Roy, B., 'How outranking relation helps multiple criteria decision making', in: Cochrane, J.L. and Zeleny, M. (eds), Multiple Criteria Decision Making, University of South Carolina Press, SC, 1973, pp. 179-201.

Roy, B., 'Critères multiples et modélisation des préférences: l'apport des relations de surclassement', Revue d'Economie Politique, 84, (1), 1974, pp. 1-44.

Roy, B., 'Vers une méthodologie générale d'aide à la décision', Revue METRA, XIV, (3), 1975.

Roy, B., 'Partial preference analysis and decision-aid: the fuzzy outranking concept', in: Bell, D., Keeney, R. and Raiffa, H. (eds), Conflicting Objectives in Decision, Wiley, New York, 1977, pp. 40-74.

Roy, B., 'ELECTRE III: un algorithme de classement fondé sur une représentation floue des préférences en présence de critères multiples', Cahiers Centre Etudes Recherche Opérationnelle, 20, (1), 1978, pp. 3-24.

Roy, B., 'Extension of the dominance concept: theoretical background and application', Communication to the 12th Meeting of the EURO Working Group 'Multicriteria Decision Aid', Bochum, October 1980.

Roy, B. and Bertier, P., 'La méthode ELECTRE II, une application au media-planning', in: Ross, M. (ed), OR'72, North-Holland Publ. Co., Amsterdam, 1973, pp. 291-302.

Roy, B. and Hugonnard, J.C., 'Ranking of suburban line extension projects on the Paris Metro System by a multicritèria method', Transport Research, 16A, (4), 1982, pp. 301-312.

Roy, B. and Vincke, Ph., 'Systèmes relationnels de préférences en présence de critères multiples avec seuils', Cahiers Centre Etude Recherche Opérationnelle, 22 (1), 1980a.

Roy, B. and Vincke, Ph., 'Pseudo-critères et systèmes relationnels de préférence: nouveaux concepts et nouveaux résultats en vue de l'aide à la décision', Cahiers du LAMSADE, Université de Paris Dauphine, No. 28, 1980b.

Roy, B. and Vincke, Ph., 'Multicriteria analysis: survey and new directions', European Journal of Operational Research, 8, 1981, pp. 207-218.

Siskos, J., 'Comment modéliser les préférences au moyen de fonctions d'utilité additives', RAIRO Recherche Opérationnelle, 14, 1980, pp. 53-82.

Siskos, J., 'A way to deal with fuzzy preferences in multi-criteria decision problems', European Journal of Operational Research, 10, 1982, pp. 314-324.

Vincke, Ph., 'Quasi-kernels to minimum weakness in a graph', Discrete Mathematics, 20, (2), 1977.

Zadeh, L.A., Fu, K.S., Tanaka, K. and Shimura, M., Fuzzy Sets and Their Applications to Cognitive and Decision Processes, Academic Press, New York, 1975.

5 An Informal Introduction to Multicriteria Evaluation

P. Nijkamp and H. Voogd

1 MULTICRITERIA EVALUATION AND PLANNING

1.1 Introduction

Evaluation is a crucial component of effective organisation behaviour. Organisations plan actions to cope with or exploit anticipated future conditions. However, they typically cannot predict all relevant conditions and they must therefore continuously adapt their planning to varying circumstances. Evidently, planning processes are usually very ubiquitous and quite uncertain. On the other hand, impact patterns of decisions and actions are often intricate, far-reaching and conflicting. In the past, this has evoked the need for many kinds of evaluation approaches to assist the decision making process.

Especially the field of public planning is often faced with difficult judgement problems regarding the feasibility and desirability of policy proposals, varying from a straightforward allocation of funds for a given project or policy measure to more general strategic plans or programs. Consequently, in public choice theory it has become more and more common to evaluate policy alternatives in an integrated and multidisciplinary welfare framework. This is a logical consequence of the interwoven structure of advanced societies, in which interest conflicts, external effects and - very often rather diffuse - social interactions at different levels exist. Current evaluation studies therefore, increasingly show a broad judgement framework, which includes among others private economic, socioeconomic, environmental, energy, equity and spatial-physical considerations.

In this paper, some recent integrated evaluation approaches will be introduced and discussed. In the first section a number of general evaluation issues in relation to public planning will be dealt with. Section 2 is devoted to a discussion of so-called discrete multicriteria methods, i.e. methods which are based on a given number of a priori known alternatives. In Section 3 an overview is given of so-called continuous multicriteria methods which are appropriate evaluation techniques in case alternatives are infinite in number.

1.2 Characteristics of systematic evaluation

The notion of evaluation can be described as an activity which includes two simultaneous steps: the attempt to achieve the objectivity of a certain (choice) situation and the appraisal of that situation. The word 'situation' refers to alternative choices in planning, for instance, alternative development plans or investment decisions.

Traditionally, income per capita has been used as the major criterion to judge economic developments, welfare increases, growth perspectives and the social value of plans. However, this unidimensional welfare approach is often criticised because it implicitly assumes a perfectly competitive system marked by full information and a fully operating price system; conditions which can hardly be met in practice. Even if they can be fulfilled, many essential elements of human life cannot be translated into a common denominator, whether money or not, e.g., residential living conditions, quality of working environment, risk, equity, and so forth (see Nijkamp 1977).

Therefore, the rise in average income is no longer being considered as the only indicator for the rise in welfare. During the last two decades the insight has grown that welfare is essentially a unidimensional variable which comprises _inter alia_ average income, growth, environmental quality, distributional equity, supply of public facilities, accessibility, etc. Consequently, not only monetary consequences but also unpriced impacts of policy decisions have to be taken into account. This implies that in public planning a broad evaluation framework is required of all relevant effects in order to assist in the selection of the most desirable project or to rank the successive alternative plans in a coherent and systematic way.

Any investment project, either in the private sphere (for example, a steel plant, an office building, a shop) or in the public sphere (for example, a motorway, a local community centre, a harbour) has a wide variety of impacts, not only in economic terms, but also in social and environmental terms. If through a systematic evaluation analysis a social appraisal has to be given to such a project, it should be kept in mind that 'the' decision maker does not exist, so that due to diverging preferences and lack of concensus within a public planning process the emergence of conflicting options cannot be avoided (see for a discussion: Voogd 1983). No evaluation framework whatsoever will solve such policy problems.

Consequently, the meaning of systematic evaluation for public decision making is not primarily the identification of 'the optimal and unambiguous solution'. This optimising paradigm is often criticised, for instance by Herbert Simon (1965) who advocated a more modest satisficing way of approach: not the 'best' alternative must be pursued but alternatives must be identified which meet or exceed a number of explicitly defined standards (for a discussion on the issue of optimising versus satisficing, see Chadwick 1971). More recently even another kind of approach emerged next to 'optimising' and 'satisficing' in which especially the accountability of the 'solution' is stressed. This may be denoted by the work 'justificing'. The rationale behind this point of view is that it is very important that decisions can be defined and justified. Both subjective information about the choices and facts must be made explicit, and can therefore be subject to (public) debate.

The three abovementioned points of view all imply some kind of a rationalisation of the decision problem at hand. The 'optimising' approach in public planning is often equated with a so-called 'rational comprehensiveness' paradigm (see for a discussion Lindblom 1968). The 'satisficing' approach acknowledges the limited capacity of the human mind to approximate full rationality. It is, in fact, based upon a recognition of what Simon (1965) calls the principle of 'bounded rationality'. The 'justificing' approach can be found back in some recent work in urban and regional planning, especially in Faludi (1981) who elaborated a so-called principle of 'critical rationalism'.

With respect to evaluation this means in all cases that an evaluation method should focus on the provision of all relevant information on the judgement criteria (e.g., costs, employment effects, energy use, pollution effects, balance of payments), on the generation of all relevant alternatives (e.g., various locations of a shopping center), on the existence of interest conflicts (e.g., environmentalists versus supporters of economic growth), on the existence of different priorities for various impacts (e.g., employment versus budget equilibrium) and on the development of procedures and techniques which guarantee the best use of the available information, given the institutional framework (e.g., process planning, multilevel planning, interactive policy making).

In general, an integrated appraisal of plans or projects requires the following activities to be undertaken:

1) Collection of information on criteria;
2) Identification of alternatives;
3) Identification of conflicts;
4) Estimation of priorities;
5) Use of suitable evaluation techniques.

Depending on the kind of evaluation which is pursued (e.g., discrete or continuous evaluation; see Sections 2 and 3), these activities will be undertaken simultaneously or (partial) sequentially. The results of this comprehensive evaluation procedure may be varying, dependent on the information required by the responsible authorities. Sometimes only an assessment of the impacts of an investment plan is sufficient, but in other cases much more emphasis may be placed on differences in priorities or on procedural questions. Thus an evaluation framework should be flexible enough to cover all these different demands. In addition, it should make the choice conflicts and the consequences of choices more transparent (cf. the 'justificing' approach). Finally, an evaluation has often a learning character, so that an evaluation framework must be adaptable to changing circumstances. This implies that - in general - an evaluation technique for public planning should be comprehensible for the users concerned (decision makers, civil servants, politicians and so forth), so that applicability and simplicity have to be strived for in any evaluation analysis. These conditions hold for both the provision of information on impacts or interest conflicts, and the ranking and selection of alternative plans or projects.

1.3 Multicriteria evaluation

As explained before, a systematic evaluation of public plans or projects has to be based on the distinction and measurement of a broad set of criteria. These criteria may be different in nature: private economic (investment costs, rate of return, scale economics, etc.), socioeconomic (employment, income distribution, access to facilities, etc., environmental (e.g., pollution, deterioration of natural areas, noise), energy (use of energy, technological innovation, risk, etc.), spatial physical planning (congestion, population density, accessibility, etc.), and so forth. In practice, the choice of criteria will also depend on the available data. However, it is better not to base the selection of criteria primarily on the availability of reliable data, but rather on the relevance of these criteria in the policy framework. It will be shown later that also 'soft' and qualitative information can be taken into account, so that there is no need to exclude a priori fuzzy information. This implies that various kinds of criteria can be distinguished, viz. monetary criteria and intangible criteria, quantitative and qualitative criteria, etc.

The ultimate selection of relevant judgement criteria is a political responsibility, supported by necessary information from the side of experts or analysts. It should be noted that the use of evaluation in a dynamic policy making environment often gives rise to the introduction of new (or adjusted) criteria which were neglected during the initial stages of the evaluation procedure. Therefore, the evaluation procedure should be flexible enough to include new criteria during a later stage.

Evaluation in public planning usually means that alternatives (plans, projects or proposals) have to be judged. The number of alternatives may vary between 1 (e.g., should a certain project be undertaken or not?), any discrete number (e.g., 10 alternative routes of a highway) and infinity (e.g., the quantity of oil to be imported).

The problem of only one alternative is essentially a 0-1 choice system in which a choice has to be made between the status quo and a new situation. Sometimes an intermediate stage has to be inserted, especially when the information is not sufficient to make a decision. In the latter case, one faces, in fact, a situation with three alternative choices: 'yes', 'no', 'delay in order to obtain more information'.

The discrete evaluation problem with a distinct number of alternatives is very common in public planning. Both cost-benefit analysis and multicriteria analysis deal with these kinds of discrete evaluation analyses. This will be elaborated in the next section. Obviously, the number of alternatives may sometimes be very high. In such cases it is useful to follow a stepwise approach to reduce the number of alternatives (e.g. see Bennema c.s., 1984). For instance, identify first a subset of alternatives which are clearly discriminating. After a first selection of the most relevant project, one may next choose the most desirable project from the set of reasonably relevant projects.

The continuous evaluation problem is concerned with a high number of alternatives. An example is the amount of drinking water needed in a region in a certain year. The demand for drinking water may depend on the number of households, the industrial use, the price, etc. Such continuous policy problems based on multiple criteria (or objectives) can be treated through - what is usually called - multiobjective programming models. This will be discussed in more detail in Section 3.

The ultimate combination of criteria and alternatives gives - in case a discrete multicriteria evaluation is pursued - rise to the following evaluation matrix, which, of course, has to be measured in appropriate units (see Figure 1).

```
          |      ALTERNATIVES          |
          |                            |
          |  1....................N    |
          |                            |
----------+----------------------------|
C     1   |                            |
R     ,   |                            |
I     .   |                            |
T     .   |                            |
E     .   |                            |
R     .   |                            |
I     .   |                            |
A     .   |                            |
      .   |                            |
      I   |                            |
---------------------------------------
```

Figure 1. The structure of an evaluation matrix

The evaluation matrix may contain cardinal (metric) information (e.g. number of jobs), ordinal rankings (e.g., 1,2,3,...) or qualitative information (e.g., good, better, best).

The impact matrix can - without any further information about priorities - be used in several ways. In the first place, one may carry out a dominance analysis by examining whether a certain project (or a set of projects) is better or worse than the remaining ones. In this way the set of relevant projects to be evaluated can be truncated.

Secondly, one may carry out a strength-weakness analysis by identifying for each plan or project n (n=1, ..., N) whether the outcomes of the criteria give a high or a low contribution to the criteria at hand; see Figure 2.

CRITERIA	
FAVOURABLE	UNFAVOURABLE
.	.
.	.
.	.

Figure 2. Strength-weakness analysis

In this way one may easily identify which plans or projects are in agreement with a certain policy criterion.

Thirdly, one may also rank all plans or projects for each separate criterion according to the degree they contribute to that criterion. This is visualised in Figure 3.

CRITERION	RANK ORDER OR PLANS OR PROJECTS
1	plan 1> plan 3> plan 7> ....
.	
.	

Figure 3. Presentation of evaluation information

An interesting new development is the use of computer graphics to improve the presentation of the schemes in Figures 1, 2 and 3 (e.g. see Bertin 1981). By computer graphics we mean the use of computer-drawn or printed images composed of marks or colours. Graphics are based on the assumption that its perceptual properties can correspond to the measurement levels represented in the data to be translated. Although this does not mean that all data properties can be presented by a kind of graphical mark, it may very well improve the information processing of evaluation research towards the decision making process (see also Daru 1985).

As far as the non-monetary values are included in the evaluation method (e.g., intangibles), any choice among alternatives is (implicitly or explicitly) based on priorities regarding the criterion scores of the evaluation matrix of Figure 1. If the political executives do not want to specify in advance priorities - which is usually the case (e.g., see Bennema c.s. 1984) - the analyst's task is rather limited. Then either he or she may apply the above mentioned approaches or priorities have to be assessed. In the latter case, several approaches can be employed.

- Derivation of priorities on the basis of ex post analysis of decisions taken in the past. Clearly, this approach is not useful for unique decision problems.
- Derivation of priorities on the basis of official documents and statements. This approach is sometimes very useful to gather information regarding general issues and policy objectives, but in general it does not lead to precise preferences about the criteria under consideration.
- Direct assessment of priorities on the basis of interviews or questionnaires among the participants in the planning process. This approach is especially fruitful to obtain information about the divergence in opinions. However, it is often very difficult to arrive at adequate numerical priority statements, because the ability of respondents to express preferences in a consistent way varies with the time, place and formulation of planning problems at hand (see also Voogd 1983). Besides, many policy makers do not like to express their preferences directly.

- 'Fictitious' assessment of priorities on the basis of consistent policy scenarious reflecting hypothetical but otherwise reasonable priorities for the policy criteria at hand. This is often a very useful and practical method, because it does not commit directly the responsible policy makers, whereas on the other hand, the consequences of such fictitious policy priorities can easily be traced. Such scenarios may also be derived from official documents.

It is evident that in most choice situations the information about policy preferences is fairly weak, so that usually only qualitative weighting schemes can be created. There are several ways to deal with qualitative weights in multicriteria evaluation (e.g., see Nijkamp c.s. 1984).

The first approach is to calculate the extreme quantitative weights which are in accordance with the postulated qualitative ordering. For example, if the following ordinal priorities are expressed: $w_1 \geqq w_2 \geqq w_3$, the quantitative weights will always have values between the following extreme metric weights: (1,0,0), (½,½,0), and (1/3,1/3,1/3). By applying a suitable multicriteria technique for each extreme weight set, an impression can be obtained about the possible divergence in the final outcome of the evaluation. However, this does not reveal much insight into the most likely intermediate solution (see also Rietveld 1982).

The use of extreme weights can be quite cumbersome if priorities are expressed in a rather detailed way, i.e. with many 'ordinal levels'. A better approach may then be to select a large number of random quantitative weights, which fulfil the ordinal priority ranking. For each random weight set a solution can be obtained, which can be used to update a frequency table which expresses the probability that an alternative will have a first position, second position, third position, and so on. The information on this probability table can finally be aggregated to a most probable final ranking of the alternatives for the given ordinal priority set.

A third approach is to calculate the most probable quantitative weight set (i.e. expected weights) directly, i.e. without using a random approach. By assuming that the 'real' quantitative weights are uniformly distributed over the area delimited by the extreme weights, one can find analytical expressions for the expected metric weight values. It appears that the expected values are a convex function of the corresponding ranks (see Rietveld 1982).

2 DISCRETE MULTICRITERIA METHODS

2.1 The heterogeneity of evaluation problems

Any evaluation method for judging the desirability of public plans or projects should be logically and consistently connected with the nature of the problem concerned. Every decision or choice problem in public planning has its own characteristics, which should be taken into account when a systematic evaluation is pursued. Each type of evaluation problem may require a specific method. Consequently, there is no unambiguous method with a universal validity.

Depending on the characteristics of the planning process and on the precision of the data used, several kinds of problems can be recognised. A very important subdivision concerns the distinction between discrete versus continuous evaluation problems. In the case of discrete problems, the alternatives are a priori known and (very often) subject to debate; in the case of continuous problems, the precise alternatives are not known beforehand. This distinction has already been discussed in the preceding section.

Another important subdivision is the classification of soft versus hard evaluation problems. Soft problems are mainly defined by qualitative or ordinal information on impacts or characteristics of alternatives and/or on weights, whereas hard problems are based on quantitative (i.e. cardinal) information. This subdivision can even be refined by distinguishing also a third kind of category, viz. mixed evalusation problems, which include both qualitative and quantitative information.

The decision making structure may also influence the evaluation approach. A subdivision can be made between multi-person (or multi-committee) and single-person (or single-committee) evaluation problems. In the case of multi-person or multi-committee problems one has to take into account the impossibility to arrive at precise and acceptable group tradeoffs, because of the dynamics of preferences and the strong 'bargaining' characteristics of such decision making processes. A single-person or single-committee problem offers more possibilities for a systematic tradeoff analysis; however, also under these circumstances (implicit) political aims may dominate the evaluation (see Voogd 1983 for a more extensive discussion).

Evaluation problems may need different kinds of outcomes, e.g., some problems imply that a number of acceptable alternative solutions have to be identified, whereas other problems concern the selection of one ultimate alternative. In the first case one aims at the identification of a subset of alternatives, e.g. a set of non-dominated solutions. These are the solutions for which the value of one policy objective cannot be improved without reducing the value of the competing criteria (or objectives). Also other subset delimitations can be used in practice. In public planning this kind of problem often occurs, e.g. if a decision has to be made concerning the approval of a number of projects for premiums, etc. In the second case one aims at finding one single alternative which is considered as satisfactory given the preferences used.

Some evaluation problems must be solved immediately (single step problem), whereas other problems may be treated in a process-like approach (multi-step problem). In the second case the 'learning function' of evaluation is more stressed. Evaluation is seen as a process during which one may add successively more information so that the ultimate solution is identified in a series of sequential steps.

2.2 Discrete methods

There are many different discrete evaluation methods currently in use (see Nijkamp 1979a; Nijkamp and Spronk 1979; Kmietowicz and Pearman 1981; Rietveld 1980; Voogd 1983). A major step in all these methods is to construct an evaluation matrix as explained in Section 1.3 In order to aggregate the information of the evaluation matrix usually a weighting scheme is necessary which expresses the relative importance of the various scores. This is already discussed in Section 1.4.

In the past, cost-benefit analysis has been the most commonly used method for evaluating discrete alternatives. This approach is especially applied to the abovementioned 'single-step' evaluation problems. However, many projects or plans are concerned with outcomes or consequences which cannot be treated in terms of prices, and this makes the cost-benefit approach quite inappropriate for complex public decision making (see Nijkamp 1977, for an extensive criticism). Related methods such as cost-effectiveness analysis (see, among others Seiler 1968), the planning-balance-sheet method (cf. Lichfield c.s. 1975), and the shadow project approach (cf. Klaassen 1973) are significant improvements over traditional cost-benefit analysis for complex planning purposes, but provide no satisfactory solution to the problem of judging incommensurate and intangible outcomes.

There are many discrete multicriteria methods, both for 'hard' and 'soft' evaluation problems. The following hard data methods will be considered here: the expected value method (Schimpeler and Greco 1968; Schlager 1968; Kahne 1975), the discrepancy analysis technique (Nijkamp 1979a), the goals-achievement method (Hill 1973), and the concordance approach (Guigou 1974; Roy 1972; van Delft and Nijkamp 1977).

The expected value method assigns quantitative weights to the criteria and treats these weights as 'quasi-probabilities' which must add up to 1. Thus the expected value of the outcomes of each alternative plan can be calculated by multiplying the value obtained for each criterion by its appropriate weight and then summing the weighted values for all criteria. Essentially, the expected value method calculates the weighted average of all (standardised) criterion scores in the evaluation matrix. This method implies a rather rigid approach since it assumes a perfect linear substitution of the values of the various criteria, which is seldom true in practical applications.

Another method for 'hard' evaluation problems is discrepancy analysis. This approach attempts to rank the alternatives according to their discrepancy from a (hypothetical) optimum alternative. This optimum alternative achieves a set of predefined goals. Statistical correlation coefficients can then be used to identify the alternative most similar to the reference alternative. Although this method can be very attractive in combination with computer graphics, it should be used with care because the various discrepancies in the outcomes of an alternative plan or project cannot be made sufficiently explicit.

A very well known and often applied approach in planning practice concerns the goals-achievement method. This method links each criterion to a quantitative achievement level or target value. Evaluation essentially involves taking the achievement score for each criterion, and aggregating these to give a total achievement score for each alternative plan. The values are aggregated using a weighted summation procedure similar to that described above for the expected value method. Hence, a similar criticism holds for this approach. However, this approach can be quite attractive for evaluation problems which need to be treated with very simple and straightforward methods, e.g., in approach procedures for governmental premiums, etc.

The concordance approach is also widely used. This method is based on a pairwise comparison of alternatives, thus using only the metric interval characteristics of the various scores in the evaluation matrix. The basic idea is to measure the degree to which the scores and their associated weights confirm or contradict the dominant pairwise relationships among the alternatives. The differences in weights and the differences in evaluation scores are usually analysed separately. This approach uses the available information reasonably well and is especially appropriate for dealing with problems where subsets of acceptable alternative solutions have to be found.

In recent years, much attention has been paid to the development of evaluation techniques which are capable of dealing in a consistent way with 'qualitative' or 'soft' evaluation problems. Many operational soft discrete multicriteria methods are now available. The following approaches will be discussed here: the eigenvalue method (Saaty 1977; Lootsma 1980), the extreme expected value method (Kmietowicz and Pearman 1981; Rietveld 1980), the permutation method (Paelinck 1977), the frequency approach (van Delft and Nijkamp 1977; Voogd 1981), the geometric scaling approach (Nijkamp and Voogd 1979, 1981), and the mixed data approach (Voogd 1983). The latter two approaches are especially designed to deal with 'mixed' qualitative-quantitative evaluation problems.

The eigenvalue approach involves the pairwise comparison of alternatives. This comparison is made by using a nine-point scale, where the value 1 means that the alternatives being compared are of equal importance while the other nine implies that one is much more important than the other. A matrix is constructed for each criterion, in which the alternatives are compared in a pairwise fashion with respect to that criterion. The criteria themselves are then compared in a similar way, resulting in a separate pairwise criteria matrix. Next, the information in each matrix is aggregated using an eigenvalue procedure. This involves the calculation of quantitative evaluation scores and weights, which are then used in a weighted summation procedure to determine an aggregated appraisal score for each alternative plan. This approach therefore has the same drawbacks as the expected value method discussed earlier. However, the most fundamental criticism of this approach is that it is impossible for the user to relate the values of the criterion weights to the values obtained for the various alternatives. In other words, the weighting is independent of the characteristics of the plans or projects under consideration, which is incorrect from a theoretical point of view.

The extreme expected value method can be regarded as an extension of the expected value method discussed above. It is still assumed that the scores achieved by each plan with respect to each criterion have quantitative properties, but in addition it is postulated that the probabilities (weights) are only known in a qualitative sense, i.e., only their ordinal properties are given. In essence, the aim of this approach is to determine the alternative with the maximum or minimum expected value. This is done by transforming the discrete problem into a linear programming problem, with the ordinal probabilities as constraints. Some elementary operations lead to maximum and minimum expected values for the alternatives under consideration, which may be used to arrive at a final assessment. However, as has been elaborated by Rietveld (1982), this assessment should not be made solely on the basis of the extreme values, but should also take into account certain expected values for alternatives generated for intermediate values of the probabilities (see also the discussion on the treatment of ordinal weights in Section 1.3).

The permutation method is based on a comparison of all possible final rankings of alternatives in order to find the best 'final' ranking. For each hypothetical final ranking a score is calculated which measures how well this final ranking corresponds to the (ordinal) values registered by each alternative plan or project for each criterion. Instead of the original set of alternatives we now have a new set of alternative configurations of rankings. Then, by using a weighted summation procedure involving the extreme values of the ordinal weights, an appraisal score for each permutation is calculated. Given the extreme weight set used, the best final ranking of alternatives can thus be determined. Due to the permutation principle, the use of this approach is limited to problems involving a few alternatives, although a more heuristic extension to deal with many alternatives is possible. This method suffers from the same limitations as other methods which utilise the weighted summation principle. In addition, a fundamental and serious point of criticism is that the users have to relate the weights to rather abstract permutation scores, instead of to scores which reflect the characteristics of alternatives.

The frequency approach is also based on the pairwise comparison of alternatives. The basic idea of this method is to transform the available ordinal information into information on a 'lower' (i.e., binary) scale, which is then treated as a frequency statistic. This approach also has the disadvantage that it may become rather cumbersome if a large number of alternatives and criteria are involved.

The geometric scaling approach is based on the principles of nonmetric multidimensional scaling. The basic idea of this approach is to transform a large amount of ordinal data into a small amount of quantitative (cardinal) data, such that the new cardinal configuration is as close as possible (i.e., has a maximum goodness-of-fit) to the ordinal data. One limitation of this elegant approach is that it requires a fairly complicated computational algorithm. In addition, evaluation problems treated by this method should have a sufficient number of degrees of freedom to allow geometric scaling. This implies that unless sufficient ordinal information is available, no metric data can be extracted.

Most of the soft multicriteria methods mentioned above have already been used in planning practice, despite the fact that they have only recently been developed. However, one serious and persistent criticism of these techniques is that only the ordinal characteristics of the available quantitative information are utilised. Therefore, the most recent research in this field has concentrated on the development of methods capable of dealing with 'mixed data', i.e., evaluation matrices containing both quantitative scores and qualitative rankings. Nijkamp and Voogd (1981) have developed a mixed data procedure based on the geometric scaling approach which obviously suffers from the same limitations as the simpler version mentioned above. Another set of methods has been developed by Voogd (1983), which involve the construction of two measures: one dealing only with ordinal information and the other with cardinal information. By making various assumptions, the information from these measures can be aggregated into one appraisal score for each alternative. Thus different mixed data methods have been constructed using different sets of assumptions.

2.3 Conclusion

The preceding subsection shows that a whole series of discrete multicriteria methods is now available, each method having its own particular advantages and disadvantages and making its own individual assumptions. It illustrates that there is no universal method for solving every type of plan or project evaluation.

Besides, there always remains uncertainty regarding the applicability of a method, due to its implicit and explicit assumptions. Not all methods give the same results, which can be overcome in practice by performing some kind of sensitivity analysis on the methodological assumptions of the discrete evaluation methods (see Voogd 1983).

3 CONTINUOUS MULTICRITERIA METHODS

3.1 Interactive evaluation

It has been set out in Section 2.1 that evaluation problems can be classified into various categories. A major subdivision of evaluation problems is into 'discrete' and 'continuous' problems. Continuous problems refer to situations where the number of alternative plans or projects is - in principle - infinite, or at least very high. Examples are, for instance, the number of hectares of agricultural land to be cultivated in a rural development program; the capacity of a new hospital in relation to future urban development; the capacity of a municipal waste disposal centre, and so on. Such continuous evaluation problems do not lead to a surveyable number of discrete alternatives, so that the methods described in the preceding section cannot be applied here. Consequently, alternative methods stemming from multiobjective programming theory have to be employed.

As has been mentioned several times in the preceding sections, it is impossible to specify preferences or tradeoffs between criteria if no information is given about the characteristics (impacts) of the alternatives under consideration. For example, the question whether 'environment' must be judged more important than 'employment' is meaningless and cannot be answered if no information is given about the units of measurement. This implies that a 'one-step' continuous evaluation (see Section 2.1) is almost impossible, since it will always be necessary to have a feedback from the results to the normative information used (tradeoffs, preferences, norms, etc.). This calls for some kind of an 'interactive approach'.

Interactive procedures are based on an information exchange between the analyst and the participants in the planning process who guide the evaluation (hereafter called 'the decision committee). The basic feature of such procedures is that the analyst suggests a certain provisional feasible compromise solution to the decision committee, while next this committee may respond to this suggestion by indicating which policy objectives in this provisional solution are unsatisfactorily fulfilled. This provisional solution may be calculated by means of one of the continuous methods to be discussed in the next subsection.

Thus, instead of presenting directly a final solution, the analyst has to develop a learning procedure in order to reach in a limited number of steps a satisfactory final compromise solution. Consequently, the first compromise solution is only a trial solution which has to be presented to the decision committee as a frame of reference for judging alternative efficient solutions. The easiest way to carry out such an interactive procedure is to ask the committee which values of the policy objectives are satisfactory and which are unsatisfactory (and hence have to be improved).

This can easily be done by using a checklist which includes all values of the first compromise solutions of the policy objectives, see Figure 4.

	SATISFACTORY	
VALUES OF PROVISIONAL COMPROMISE SOLUTIONS	YES	NO
Policy criterion 1		
Policy criterion 2		
⋮		
Policy criterion I		

Figure 4. Checklist for compromise solutions

Suppose now that a number of criteria are judged as unsatisfactory by the decision committee. This implies that a new solution has to be identified which is such that these unsatisfactory criteria lead to a better performance. Consequently, all solutions which have a worse performance may be eliminated. After such a truncation of the set of feasible solutions a new provisional compromise solution may be calculated which can be dealt with in the same way, until finally a convergent satisfactory solution has been reached. The steps of such an interactive procedure are presented in the flow-chart of Figure 5.

Interactive procedures have several benefits. They provide information to the decision committee in a stepwise way, they can easily be included in a dynamic decision environment, they lead to an active role of all participants involved, and an a priori specification of preferences or weights is not strictly necessary, although they can be inferred ex post. A limitation of this approach is that the final solution can depend on the procedure followed and especially on the starting solution. In addition, for several continuous evaluation methods there is no guarantee that the compromise solution can be obtained within a finite number of interactive cycles, unless it is assumed that the decision committee is acting in a consistent way. Besides, it is assumed that a committee which includes and represents different interests can arrive at general conclusions about the content of Figure 4.

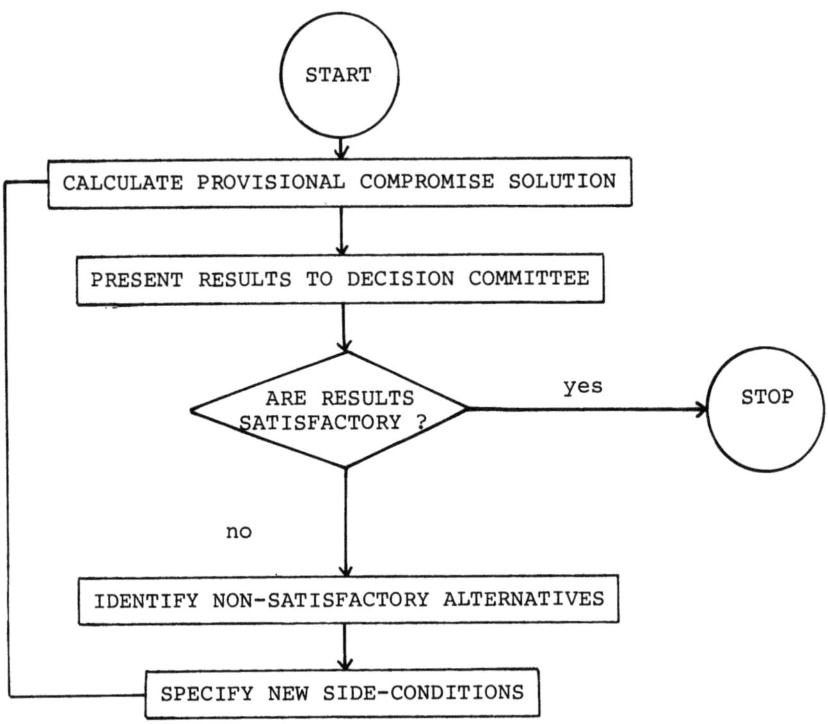

Figure 5. Brief flow-chart of an interactive procedure

3.2 Continuous methods

Much attention has been given in the past to the development of continuous evaluation methods (see among others Nijkamp and Spronk 1979). Especially 'hard' evaluation problems (see Section 2.1) have been investigated, which resulted in a variety of optimisation methods. The following methods will be considered here: utility function approaches (Farquhar 1977; Fishburn 1970);penality models (Theil 1968), goal programming (Lee 1972; Charnes and Cooper 1977; Spronk 1981), min-max approaches (Nijkamp and Rietveld 1976; Rietveld 1980), reference point approaches (Keeney and Raiffa 1976; Zeleny 1974, 1976a, b; Thiriez and Zionts 1976; Starr and Zeleny 1977; Nijkamp 1979b; Wierzbicki 1979) and hierarchical models (Nijkamp 1977; Rietveld 1980).

Utility methods start from the assumption that the entire set of relevant criteria or objectives can be translated through a weighting procedure into one 'utility function'. Such a utility function reflects all tradeoffs and priorities (weights) attached to the successive criteria. Then this utility function has to be optimised given the constraints of the evaluation problem concerned.

The utility approach is a theoretical instrument which has often been used in many neoclassical optimisation problems. It is an elegant approach, but it has also obvious drawbacks. For instance, it presupposes complete prior quantitative information about all weights and tradeoffs among the whole range of feasible values of all criteria.

Penalty models assume the existence of a set of desired achievement levels ('ideal values') for the criteria under consideration. Any discrepancy between an actual criterion value and an ideal value incurs a penalty calculated through some kind of a penalty function. Evidently, the main difficulty in applying this kind of model is lack of information about appropriate penalty functions. For algorithmic reasons (ease of differentiation) often a quadratic function is used; however, this implies the introduction of an additional 'weight' to the deviations, which can be very debatable.

Goal programming models are one of the most frequently used continuous evaluation methods. They are essentially a subclass of penalty models, for which the penalty function is defined as the weighted sum of the respective over and underachievements of a criterion value with respect to the a priori specified achievement level for that particular criterion. The alternative that minimises the penalty function is considered to be the most attractive option. This approach is especially developed for use in an interactive procedure, so that the users can learn about the problem and modify their aspirations (i.e., achievement levels) accordingly.

Min-max approaches are based on the use of a matrix representing the payoffs between conflicting objectives as well as their feasible ranges.

In a similar way as in game theory, one may next calculate the equilibrium solution from the payoff matrix. This equilibrium solution reflects the best compromise choice for the evaluation problem. A drawback is again that there are several ways to arrive at an equilibrium solution so that there is no guarantee that the compromise solution is unique. Here again, an interactive procedure may be helpful. This approach is especially appropriate when it is necessary to take into account different views of a problem in some explicit way. Each view is represented by a criterion function (or objective function) and the information given in a payoff matrix may then be used to help the decision committee to arrive at a compromise solution.

Reference point approaches are based on the concept of an ideal point (or utopian point). This ideal point is defined as a vector whose elements are the maximum values of the individual criterion functions. The closer the criterion values of an alternative is to the values of the ideal point, the better the alternative. The compromise solution is defined as the alternative in the set of efficient solutions for which the distance to the ideal solution is minimal. An efficient solution (Pareto solution) is a solution for which the value of one criterion (or objective) cannot be improved without reducing the value of a competing criterion (or objective). It should be noted that there are also reference point approaches which are formulated in a goal programming framework, where the reference point represents a set of aspiration levels. This approach is only appropriate if the reference points can be modified during the course of the analysis. It should therefore, also be used in an interactive way.

Finally, hierarchical models can be mentioned. These are based on the assumption that all criteria or objectives can be ranked according to their degree of importance. Optimisation is then carried out in a stepwise fashion, so that higher-ranking functions are optimised before those of lower ranks. A tolerance factor (or relaxation factor) can be specified for each function (except the most important), indicating the maximum deviation from the optimum considered acceptable by the decision committee.

The continuous methods described above all deal with 'hard' evaluation problems. 'Soft' continuous approaches, however, did not receive much attention in the past. Apart from some work in the field of fuzzy sets (see Chang 1968; Bellman and Zadeh 1970; Capocelli and De Luca

1973) hardly any elaborative work can be reported on qualitative continuous evaluation methods. An interesting contribution however, can be found in Leung (1983).

3.3 Conclusion

For global and macro decision problems, hard continuous evaluation methods have reached a stage of sufficient maturity; hence they can be and actually are applied in a wide variety of policy analyses. They are especially appropriate in planning processes which involve some kind of 'capacity' determination, e.g., the capacity of drinking water supply, of municipal waste disposal centres, and so forth.

Continuous methods may also be used to scan problems and to identify the main alternative lines of action. However, this task involves very often mostly only qualitative information. Further research in this area is therefore certainly justified, also given the qualitative nature of many decision problems in practice.

REFERENCES

Bennema, S., 't Hoen, H., van Setten, A. and Voogd, H., 'Multicriteria evaluation for regional planning: Some practical experiences', Papers of the Regional Science Association, Batey, P.W.J. (ed), 1984 (forthcoming).

Bertin, J., Graphics and Graphic Information Processing, De Gruyter, Berlin/New York, 1981.

Chadwick, G., A Systems View of Planning, Pergamon, London, 1971.

Charnes, A. and Cooper, W.W., 'Goal programming and multiple objective optimisation', European Journal of Operations Research, 1, 1977, pp. 39-54.

Daru, R., 'Evaluation by graphics', in: Faludi, A. and Voogd, H. (eds), Evaluation of Complex Policy Problems, Delftsche Uitgeversmaatschappij, Delft 1985 (forthcoming).

Faludi, A., 'Critical rationalism and planning methodology', Werkstukken van het Planologisch en Demografisch Instituut, 40, University of Amsterdam, 1981.

Farquhar, P.H., 'A survey of multiattribute utility theory and applications', in: Starr, M.K. and Zeleny, M. (eds), Multiple Criteria Decision Making, North Holland, Amsterdam, 1977, pp. 59-90.

Fishburn, P.C., Utility Theory for Decision Making, Wiley, New York, 1970.

Guigou, J.L., Analyse des Données et Choix à Critères Multiples, Dunod, Paris, 1974.

Hill, M., 'Planning for multiple objectives', Monograph Series, no. 5, Regional Science Research Institute, Philadelphia, 1973.

Kahne, S., 'A contribution to decision making in environmental design', Proceedings of the IEEE 1975, 1975, pp. 518-528.

Keeney, R.L. and Raiffa, H., Decision Analysis with Multiple Conflicting Objectives, Wiley, New York, 1976.

Klaassen, L.H., 'Economic and social projects with environmental repercussions: a shadow project approach', Regional and Urban Economics, vol. 3, 1, 1973, pp. 37-48.

Kmietowicz, Z.W. and Pearman, A.D., Decision Theory and Incomplete Knowledge, Gower, Aldershot, 1981.

Lee, S.M., Goal Programming for Decision Analysis, Auerbach, Philadelphia, 1972.

Leung, Y., 'Urban and regional planning with fuzzy information', in: Chatterjee, L. and Nijkamp, P. (eds), Urban and Regional Policy Analysis in Developing Countries, Gower, Aldershot, 1983.

Lichfield, N., Kettle, P. and Whitbread, M., Evaluation in the Planning Process, Pergamon Press, London, 1975.

Lindblom, C.E., The Policy-Making Process, Englewood Cliffs, New Jersey, 1968.

Lootsma, T.A., 'Saaty's Priority Theory and the nomination of a senior professor in Operations Research', European Journal of Operational Research, 4, 1980, pp. 380-388.

Nijkamp, P. and Rietveld, P., 'Multi-objective programming models, new ways in regional decision-making', Regional Science and Urban Economics, 6, 1976, pp. 253-274.

Nijkamp, P., Theory and Application of Environmental Economics, North Holland, Amsterdam, 1977.

Nijkamp, P., Multidimensional Spatial Data and Decision Analysis, Wiley, Chichester, 1979a.

Nijkamp, P.,'A theory of displaced ideals',Environment and Planning A, 11, 1979b., pp. 1165-1178.

Nijkamp, P. and Spronk, J., 'Analysis of production and location decisions by means of multicriteria analysis', Engineering and Process Economics, 4, 1979, pp. 285-302.

Nijkamp, P. and Voogd, H., 'The use of psychometric techniques in evaluation procedures', Papers of the Regional Science Association, 42, 1979, pp. 119-138.

Nijkamp, P. and Voogd, H., 'New multicriteria methods for physical planning by means of multidimensional scaling techniques', in: Haimes, Y. and Kindler, J. (eds), Water and Related Land Resource Systems, Pergamon Press, Oxford, 1981, pp. 19-30.

Nijkamp, P., Rietveld, P. and Voogd, J., 'A survey of qualitative multiple criteria choice models', in: Nijkamp, P., Leitner, H. and Wrigley, N. (eds), Measuring the unmeasurable, Martinus Nijhoff, The Hague, 1984, pp. 425-450.

Paelinck, J., 'Quantitative multicriteria analysis - applications to airport location', Environment and Planning A, 9 (8), 1977, pp. 883-895.

Rietveld, P., Multiple Objective Decision Methods and Regional Planning, North Holland, Amsterdam, 1980.

Rietveld, P., 'Using ordinal information in decision making under uncertainty', Research Memorandum 1982-12, Department of Economics, Free University, Amsterdam, 1982.

Roy, B., 'Decision avec critères multiples', Metra 11, 1972, pp. 121-151.

Saaty, T.L., 'A scaling method for priorities in hierarchical structures', Journal of Mathematical Psychology, 15, 1977, pp. 234-281.

Schlager, K., 'The rank-based expected value method of plan evaluation', Highway Research Record, 238, 1968, pp. 153-158.

Schimpeler, C.C. and Grecco, W.L., 'The expected value method, an approach based on community structures and values', Highway Research Record, 238, 1968.

Seiler, K., Introduction to Systems Cost-Effectiveness, Wiley, New York, 1968.

Simon, H.A., Administrative Behaviour: A Study of Decison-Making Processes in Administration Organization, Free Press, New York, 1965.

Spronk, J., Interactive Multiple Goal Planning for Capital Budgeting and Financial Planning, Martinus Nijhoff, Boston/The Hague, 1981.

Starr, M.K. and Zeleny, M. (eds), Multiple Criteria Decision Making, North Holland, Amsterdam 1977.

Theil, H., Optimal Decision Rules for Government and Industry, North Holland, Amsterdam, 1968.

Thiriez, H. and Zionts, S. (eds), Multiple Criteria Decision Making, Springer, Berlin, 1976.

Van Delft, A. and Nijkamp, P., Multicriteria Analysis and Regional Decision-Making, Martinus Nijhoff, The Hague/Boston, 1977.

Voogd, H., 'Qualitative multicriteria evaluation methods for development planning', The Canadian Journal of Regional Science, 4, 1981, pp. 73-87.

Voogd, H., Multicriteria Evaluation for Urban and Regional Planning, Pion, London, 1983.

Wierzbicki, A.P., 'The use of reference objectives in multiobjective optimisation; theoretical implications and practical experience', WP-79-66, International Institute for Applied Systems Analysis, Laxenburg, 1979.

Zeleny, M., Linear Multiobjective Programming, Springer, Berlin, 1974.

Zeleny, M., Multiple Criteria Decision Making, Springer, Berlin, 1976a.

Zeleny, M., 'The theory of the displaced ideal', in: Zeleny, M. (ed), Multiple Criteria Decision Making, Springer, Berlin, 1976b, pp. 153-206.

6 Multiple Criteria Mathematical Programming: an Overview and Several Approaches

S. Zionts

I INTRODUCTION

Multiple Criteria Decision Making (MCDM) refers to making decisions in the presence of multiple, usually conflicting, objectives. Multiple criteria decision problems pervade all that we do and include such public policy tasks as determining a country's policy, developing a national energy plan, as well as planning national defense expenditures, in addition to such private enterprise tasks as new product development, pricing decisions, and research project selection. For an individual, the purchase of an automobile or a home exemplifies a multiple criteria problem. Even such routine decisions as the choice of a lunch from a menu, or the assignment of job crews to jobs constitute multiple criteria problems. All have a common thread - multiple conflicting objectives.

In this study, we discuss some of the important aspects of solving such problems, and present some methods developed for solving multiple criteria mathematical programming problems. We also discuss some applications of the methods.

In multiple criteria decision making there is a decision maker (or makers) who make the decision, a set of objectives that are to be pursued and a set of alternatives from which one is to be selected. We shall presently define and question this framework. For now, however, we define some terminology.

Goals, Criteria, Objectives, Attributes, Constraints, and Targets: Their relationships.

In a decision situation we have goals, criteria, objectives, attributes, constraints and targets, in addition to decision variables. Although goals, criteria, objectives, and targets have essentially the same dictionary definitions, it is useful to distinguish among them in a decision making context. Let us define these terms, as they are popularly used in the MCDM field and see how they interrelate.

Criterion: A criterion is a measure of effectiveness of performance. It is the basis for evaluation. Criteria may be further classified as goals or targets and objectives.

Goal, target: A goal (synonymous with target) is something that is either achieved or not. For example, increasing sales of a product by at least 10 per cent during one year over the previous year is a goal. If a goal cannot be or is unlikely to be achieved, it may be converted into an objective.

Objective: An objective is something to be pursued to its fullest. For example, a business may want to maximise its level of profits or maximise the quality of service provided or minimise customer complaints. An objective generally indicates the direction of change desired.

Attribute: An attribute is a measure that gives a basis for evaluating whether goals have been met or not given a particular decision and that provide a means of evaluating the levels of various objectives.

Decision Variable: A decision variable is one of the specific decisions made by a decision maker. For example, the planned production of a given product is a decision variable.

Constraint: A constraint is a limit on attributes and decision variables that may or may not be stated mathematically. For example, that a plant can be operated at most twelve hours per day is a constraint.

2 STRUCTURING A MCDM SITUATION

Most problems have, in addition to multiple conflicting objectives, a hierarchy of objectives. For example, according to Manheim and Hall (1967), the objectives for evaluating passenger transportation facilities serving the Northeast Corridor of the US in 1980 was 'The Good Life'. This superobjective was subdivided into four main objectives:

i. Convenience
ii. Safety
iii. Aesthetics
iv. Economic Considerations

These in turn are divided into subobjectives, and so on, forming a hierarchy of objectives.

Some of the objectives, such as economic considerations, have attributes that permit a precise performance measurement. Others, such as aesthetics, are highly subjective. Not wanting to convert the word subjective into a noun, we may, therefore, have a subjective objective. Further, the number of objectives may be large in total.

To adequately represent the objectives, we must choose appropriate attributes. Keeney and Raiffa (1976) indicate five characteristics the selected attributes of the objectives should have:

i. Complete: They should cover all apsects of a problem.
ii. Operational: They can be meaningfully used in the analysis.
iii. Decomposable: They can be broken into parts to simplify the process.
iv. Nonredundant: They avoid problems of double counting.
v. Minimal: The number of attributes should be kept as small as possible.

I recommend that at most the magic number of about 7 (see Miller (1956)) objectives be used. Such a limitation tends to keep a problem within the realm of operationality. What happens if there are more than about 7 objectives? First, use constraints to limit outcomes of objectives about which you are sure or about which you feel comfortable about setting such limits. Since constraints must be satisfied at any price, you should not make constraints 'too tight'. Further, it is useful to check whether feasible alternatives still exist after adding each constraint or after adding very few constraints. An alternative is to treat some of the objectives as goals or targets. We attempt to satisfy the goals. If we cannot, we treat them as objectives. We try to get as close to achieving them as possible. We shall go into the idea of doing this mathematically later. Structuring a problem properly is an art, and there is no prescribed way of setting up objectives, goals and constraints.

3 A SCENARIO OF MANAGEMENT DECISION MAKING

A scenario of management decision making is generally assumed by most researchers:

i. A decision maker (DM) makes a decision.
ii. He chooses from a set of possible decisions.
iii. The solution he chooses is optimal.

This scenario, though approximately correct, is overly simplified.

To criticise the scenario, the decision maker, if an individual (as opposed to a group), seldom makes a decision in a vacuum. He is heavily influenced by others. Further, in any instances, groups not individuals make decisions. Second, the set of possible decisions is not given. The set of solutions must be somehow generated. The process of determining the set of alternatives may require more effort than choosing among the alternatives. Third, what is meant by an optimal solution? Since it is not possible to simultaneously maximise all objectives in determining a solution, a more workable definition is needed. A typical definition of optimality is not particularly workable: An optimal decision is one that maximises a decision maker's utility (or satisfaction). In spite of the limitations of the decision scenario, it is widely used; hopefully its limitations are recognised. Some limitations are recognised. Some limitations of the scenario are being relaxed in recent work in the area: for example, considering decision making groups instead of individuals.

4 SOME MATHEMATICAL CONSIDERATIONS OF MULTIPLE CRITERIA DECISION MAKING

The general multiple criteria decision making problem may be formulated as follows:

$$\begin{aligned} &\text{'Maximise'} && F(x) \\ &\text{subject to:} && G(x) \leq 0 \end{aligned} \qquad (1)$$

where x is the vector of decision variables, F(x) is the vector of objectives to be 'maximised'. In some cases it will be convenient to have an intervening vector y where $F(x) = H(y(x))$. For example, y may be a vector of stochastic objectives which is a function of x. In that case, H would be a vector of function of the stochastic objectives.

In some cases F will have some components that are ordinal. Attributes such as quality and convenience of location may only be measurable on an ordinal scale. Further, some objectives may be measured only imperfectly. The word maximise is in quotation marks because maximising a vector is not a well-defined operation. We shall define it in several ways in what follows.

The constraints $G(x) \leq 0$ are the constraints that define the feasible solution space. They may be stated explicitly and if mathematical, be either linear or nonlinear. Alternatively, the alternatives may be stated explicitly by listing them as members of a discrete set. It is frequently convenient to assume that the solutions to the constraints can be used to generate a convex set, although that is not necessary.

The formulation of the multiple criteria decision making problem (1) is one that I believe includes virtually all of the approaches developed, as well as the various multiple criteria problems. It is clearly too general, because only very specific forms of problem (1) can be solved in practice. A linear version of problem (1) is as follows:

'Maximise' Cx

subject to: $Ax \leq b$

$x_j \geq 0$, if needed, may be included in the constraints $Ax \leq b$. This particularisation of problem (1) is one on which a substantial amount of study has been made. It is referred to as the <u>m</u>ultiple <u>o</u>bjective <u>l</u>inear <u>p</u>rogramming problem (MOLP) because it is a linear programming problem with multiple objectives. The following theorem, provided in different forms, is found in several places in the multiple criteria literature.

<u>Theorem:</u> Maximising a positive weighted sum of objectives $\lambda'F$ $(= \sum_i \lambda_i F_i)$ over a set of feasible solutions yields a nondominated solution.

<u>Proof:</u> Let the problem be 'Maximise' $F(x)$ subject to $G(x) \leq 0$. Suppose the maximum of $\lambda'F$ where λ is a vector having all positive components is achieved at x^*. Assume that x^* is dominated by a feasible solution x_0. That is, $F(x_0) \geq F(x^*)$ with at least one strict inequality. But then we have $\lambda'F(x_0) \geq \lambda'F(x^*)$ contrary to the hypothesis, thereby proving the theorem.

The theorem does not say that for every nondominated solution there exists a set of weights for which the nondominated solution maximises the weighted sum. As we shall see, that need not be the case.

5 THE OBJECTIVE FUNCTIONS

Let us now consider the objective functions more carefully. The objective functions may all be assumed to be maximised, without loss of generality, because any objective that is to be minimised can be minimised can be minimised by maximising the value of its negative. Accordingly, we shall henceforth refer to objectives to be maximised.

What do we do if we have any goals or targets (as defined earlier?). If they are simultaneously achievable, we simply add constraints that stipulate the specified value be met and not consider them further. Thus, the achievement of the goals is transformed into a admissible solution satisfying all of the constraints. There is an interesting duality between objectives and constraints, in that the two are closely related.

If the goals are not all simultaneously achievable, simply adding constraints as above will lead to no feasible solution to the multiple criteria problem. What must be done in such a situation is to relax some of the goals, or to change goals to objectives as described earlier: to minimise the difference between the goal and the outcome. Although I generally regard this process as somewhat of an art, several of the methods to be considered do find a solution that is 'close' in some sense to a goal vector.

We now consider what is meant by the word 'maximise'. Unlike unidimensional optimisation, in which only one objective is to be maximised, with multiple objectives we are concerned with simultaneously maximising several objectives. Such a maximisation is not defined. There are two definitions of 'maximise' that we can define. We may regard them as opposite ends of the spectrum, although there appear to be a few discrete points on the spectrum.

From the perspective of the greatest generality, a workable definition of 'maximise' is to find all nondominated solutions to a problem and then choose one of them.

Definition: Dominance

Solution 1 dominates solution 2 if $F(x_1) \geq F(x_2)$ with strict inequality holding for at least one component of F.

A solution is said to be nondominated if no other solution dominates it. It seems eminently reasonable to limit the choice of alternatives to nondominated solutions. The idea of finding all nondominated solutions is than plausible: one can presumably considerably reduce the number of alternatives. However as we shall see, for certain classes of problems, the numbers of nondominated alternatives will be enormous - too large to be of practical interest.

On the other hand, there may be some instances where we do not want to eliminate dominated solutions. For example, a dominated solution may be sufficiently close to a nondominated solution that we may decide to make a choice based on some secondary criteria not used in the analysis. We may then very well choose the dominated solution based on the secondary criteria. Alternatively, some of the objectives may not be measurable very precisely. Improved measurements may only be obtained at a cost. In such a sotuation we may not want to exclude dominated alternatives from further analysis. As a concrete example for both, suppose a prospective automobile purchaser is choosing among cars on the basis of price, economy, sportiness, and comfort. Suppose further that a foreign-made car appears somehow to be the best choice, but that there is a domestically-produced automobile that is its equal in all respects except that the price is slightly higher. The decision maker may nonetheless decide to purchase the domestic automobile because of its better availability of spare parts. In the second instance, suppose that the same purchaser is considering two domestically-produced automobiles. We assume as before that the cars are the same for all criteria but one - price. Car A has a lower list price than Car B. However, in the purchase of most automobiles, one can obtain discounts. On haggling with the respective dealer, our purchaser may subsequently find that he can purchase Car B for less than Car A. Hence, if he had excluded Car B because of dominance (on the basis of list price) he would have made a mistake.

The reader may feel that in the first case we should have added spare parts availability to our criteria. Though this could have been done, we may generally use criteria such as this as secondary to resolve close cases. Similarly, it can be argued in the second example that the price variable is transaction price and not list price. Therefore, our selected car is not dominated. Nonetheless, it is difficult to accurately measure transaction price!

At the other end of the spectrum, we define 'Maximise' in terms of utility function: a unique transformation from the objectives to a scalar measure of performance.

Definition: Utility Function

A utility function is a scalar function $u(F(x))$ such that x_1 is preferred to (is indifferent to) x_2 if and only if $F(x_1) \geq F(x_2)$. Because of our statement of problem (1), we have at an optimal solution (for any feasible change) $\nabla u \leq 0$ where ∇u is the gradient or the vector of partial derivatives of u with respect to the components of F. What $\nabla u \leq 0$ means is that the utility cannot be increased by moving in any feasible direction. Depending on the method to be considered, we will either estimate a utility function u or approximate it locally. In either case, we will use the function or its approximation to identify a most preferred solution.

6 A TYPOLOGY OF MULTIPLE CRITERIA DECISION MAKING MODELS

Quite naturally, different writers have proposed different decision making typologies. Typically, the typologies reflect the writers' biases, etc. No doubt, my typology is guilty of this limitation as well. My typology reflects my interpretation of the world of MCDM models. The main dimensions of my typology are:

i. The nature of outcomes - stochastic versus deterministic.
ii. The nature of the alternative generating mechanism - whether the constraints limiting the alternatives are explicit or implicit.

These dimensions are indicated in tabular form in Figure 1. The left-hand column includes the implicit constraint models. When the constraints are implicit or explicit and nonmathematical, the alternatives must be explicit. One of a list of alternatives is then selected. The decision analysis problem is included in the implicit constraint category. When the constraints are explicit and mathematical, then the alternative solutions are implicit and may be infinite in number of the solution space is continuous and consists of more than one solution. Problems in the explicit constraint category are generally regarded as mathematical programming problems involving multiple criteria.

More dimensions may be added to the typology. In addition to implicit constraints versus explicit constraints, and deterministic outcomes versus stochastic outcomes, we can identify other dimensions as well. We may classify the number of decision makers as a dimension: one decision maker versus two or more decision makers. We may classify the number of objectives, the nature of utility functions considered, as well as the number of solutions found (one solution versus all non-dominated solutions). I have chosen only two dimensions because they seem to be the most significant factors.

	Implicit Constraints (Explicit Solutions)	Explicit Constraints (Implicit Solutions)
Deterministic Outcomes	Choosing Among Deterministic Discrete Alternatives or Deterministic Decision Analysis	Deterministic Mathematical Programming
Stochastic Outcomes	Stochastic Decision Analysis	Stochastic Mathematical Programming

Figure 1. A Multiple Criteria Decision Method Typology

In our presentation we consider only problems having explicit constraints: mathematical programming problems. Because most of the work has been done on deterministic problems, the bulk of our presentation is on deterministic mathematical programming problems.

In virtually all of the work on multiple criteria decision making, the spirit of the model employed is not necessarily to determine the best decision (though that is desirable!), but to help the decision making in arriving at his decision. This is what Roy (1977) refers to as 'decision aid'. It is also what Keeney and Raiffa (1976) refer to as 'getting your head straightened out'. Before we consider some of the methods in more detail, we present two examples. The first is useful in illustrating some concepts; the second will be used in its presented form and in variations to illustrate the various methods.

Two Examples

Consider the following problem, which we shall refer to as Example 1:

$$
\begin{aligned}
\text{Maximise } f_1 &= -x_1 + 2x_2 \\
f_2 &= 2x_1 - x_2 \\
\text{subject to: } x_1 &\leq 4 \\
x_2 &\leq 4 \\
x_1 + x_2 &\leq 7 \\
-x_1 + x_2 &\leq 3 \\
x_1 - x_2 &\leq 3 \\
x_1, x_2 &\geq 0
\end{aligned}
$$

The plot of the feasible solution is shown in Figure 2, the maximum solutions indicated (e for f_1, and b for f_2) for each of the objectives. In that figure, we have also identified all of the feasible extreme point solutions as o and a through n. In Figure 3, we have plotted the values of the objective functions for this problem. Each of the feasible solutions in Figure 2 has a corresponding point in Figure 3. For example, solution b represented as $x_1 = 4$ and $x_2 = 1$ has objective function values $f_1 = -2$ and $f_2 = 7$ and is so plotted in Figure 2. The nondominated solutions are shown as the heavy broken line b, c, d, e. An optimal solution presumably will be found along that line, since any point not on that line is either dominated (below and/or to the left) or infeasible (above and/or to the right).

Since x_1 and x_2 are the decision variables, we refer to a graph in terms of x_1 and x_2 such as Figure 2 as a graph in decision or activity space. The corresponding space is referred to as the decision or activity space. Variables f_1 and f_2 are the objectives; therefore, we refer to a graph in terms of f_1 and f_2 such as Figure 3 as a graph in objective function space. The corresponding space is referred to as the objective function space. Our example, for convenience of plotting, consists of two variables and two objectives. In general, the number of objectives and variables will not be the same. Usually the number of variables greatly exceeds the number of objectives.

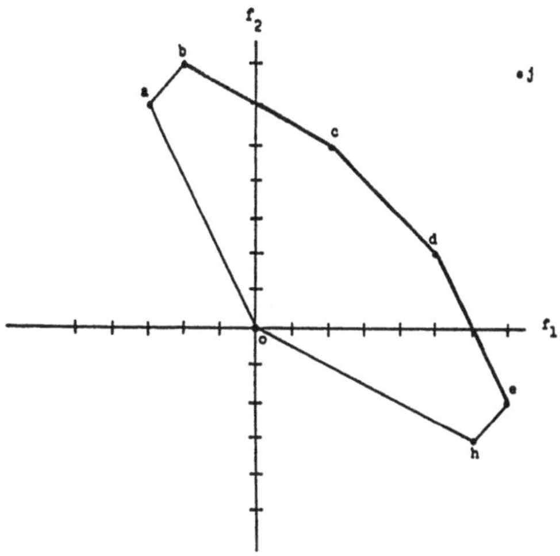

Figure 2. The feasible region of example one and the two objectives f_1 and f_2

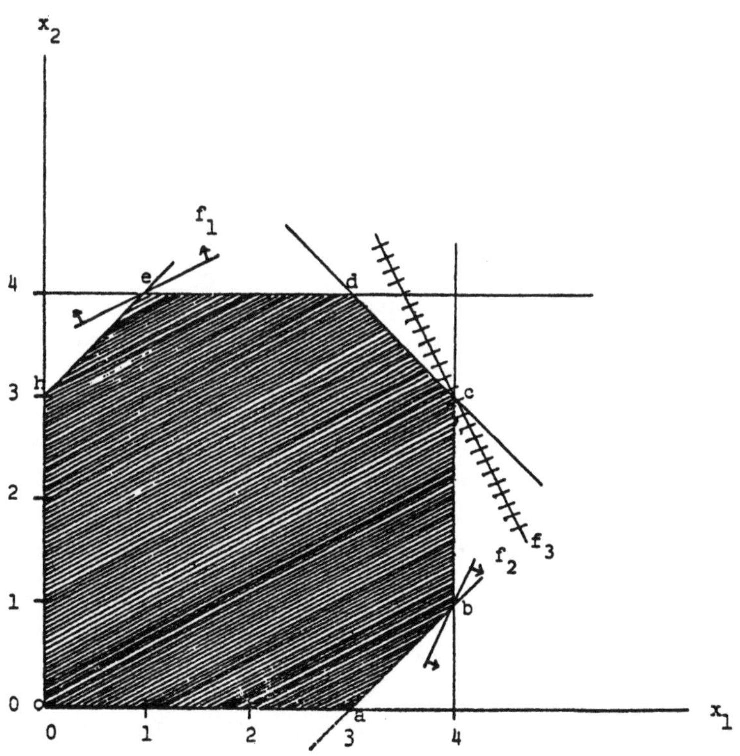

Figure 3. A plot of the first example problem in objective function space: in terms of the values of the objective functions

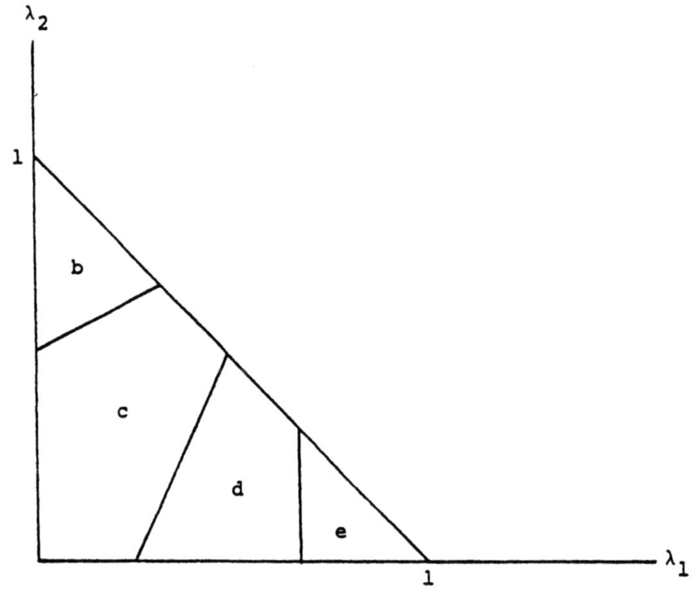

Figure 4. A plot indicating the values of λ_1 and λ_2 ($\lambda_3 = 1 - \lambda_1 - \lambda_2$) for the three-objective extension of example 1

We may make the first example more complicated by adding a third objective: $f_3 = 2x_1 + x_2$. See the cross-hatched line in Figure 2. The objective function f_3 is maximised at point c; the plot of the feasible solutions in decision variable space does not change otherwise. To make a plot in objective function space with three objectives, we would have to add a third dimension to Figure 3. Rather than do that, we first reconsider Figure 3 with two objectives. Denoting as a weighted objective function $\lambda_1 f_1 + \lambda_2 f_2$, we can see that (assuming $\lambda_1 + \lambda_2 = 1$) for $\lambda_1 > 2/3$ solution e is optimal. For $\lambda_1 = 2/3$ both solutions d and e (as well as the solutions on the line between them) are optimal. For $1/2 < \lambda_1 < 2/3$, solution d is optimal. Similarly, for $1/3 < \lambda_1 < 1/2$, solution c is optimal, and for $0 < \lambda_1 < 1/3$, solution b is optimal. Because $\lambda_2 = 1 - \lambda_1$, we could plot the regions along a straight line. Adding a third objectives gives us a weighted objective function $\lambda_1 f_1 + \lambda_1 f_2 + \lambda_3 f_3$. Now using the restriction $\lambda_3 = 1 - \lambda_1 - \lambda_2$ we may draw the regions in which each solution is optimal. See Figure 4. The solutions with $\lambda_3 = 0$ (i.e., $\lambda_1 + \lambda_2 = 1$) are still valid; they appear along the line $\lambda_1 + \lambda_2 = 1$. Other solutions are indicated accordingly.

Now consider a more complicated example, Example 1.

$$2x_1 + x_2 + 4x_3 + 3x_4 \leq 60 \quad (\text{slack } x_5)$$

$$3x_1 + 4x_2 + x_3 + 2x_4 \leq 60 \quad (\text{slack } x_6)$$

$$x_1, x_2, x_3, x_4 \geq 60$$

Three objectives are to be maximised:

$$u_1 = 3x_1 + x_2 + 2x_3 + x_4$$

$$u_2 = x_1 - x_2 + 2x_3 + 4x_4$$

$$u_3 = -x_1 + 5x_2 + x_3 + 2x_4$$

The problem has nine basic feasible solutions which are listed below for convenience (all omitted variables are zero):

1.	$x_1 = 18$,	$x_3 = 6$,	$u_1 = 66$,	$u_2 = 30$,	$u_3 = -12$
2.	$x_4 = 20$,	$x_6 = 20$,	$u_1 = 20$,	$u_2 = 80$,	$u_3 = 40$
3.	$x_2 = 15$,	$x_5 = 45$,	$u_1 = 15$,	$u_2 = -15$,	$u_3 = 75$
4.	$x_2 = 6$,	$x_4 = 18$,	$u_1 = 24$,	$u_2 = 66$,	$u_3 = 66$
5.	$x_1 = 12$,	$x_4 = 12$,	$u_1 = 48$,	$u_2 = 60$,	$u_3 = 12$
6.	$x_2 = 12$,	$x_3 = 12$,	$u_1 = 36$,	$u_2 = 12$,	$u_3 = 72$
7.	$x_3 = 15$,	$x_6 = 45$,	$u_1 = 30$,	$u_2 = 30$,	$u_3 = 15$
8.	$x_1 = 20$,	$x_5 = 20$,	$u_1 = 60$,	$u_2 = 20$,	$u_3 = -20$
9.	$x_5 = 60$,	$x_6 = 60$,	$u_1 = 0$,	$u_2 = 0$,	$u_3 = 0$

The first six solutions are nondominated, the last three are dominated. Figure 5 indicates which solutions are adjacent extreme point solutions of which other solutions (i.e., they differ by precisely one basic variable).

In order to plot the problem solutions in activity space we need to plot a 4-dimensional graph! More reasonable is plotting the objectives in three dimensions. However, instead we present the plot for the weights λ_1 and λ_2 (and λ_3) as we did for Example 1.(See Figure 6.)

Any solutions which have a common edge in Figure 6 are adjacent. (See Figure 5.) However, some solutions are adjacent (e.g. 3 and 4), yet do not have a common edge. We shall say more about this later.

Solution	is adjacent to Solutions
1	5, 6, 7, 8
2	4, 5, 7, 9
3	4, 6, 8, 9
4	2, 3, 5, 6
5	1, 2, 4, 8
6	1, 3, 4, 7
7	1, 2, 6, 9
8	1, 3, 5, 9
9	2, 3, 7, 8

Figure 5. Adjacency of basic feasible solutions of example 2

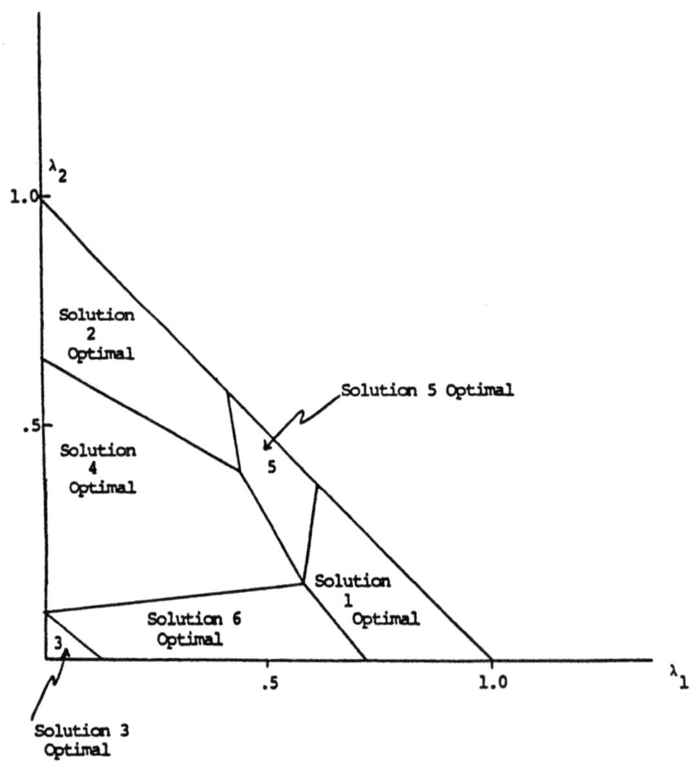

Figure 6. A plot of λ values and the corresponding optimal solutions

7 METHODS INVOLVING EXPLICIT CONSTRAINTS

When constraints are written explicitly, the solutions are implicit. If the constraints are expressed mathematically, it may be possible to solve for solutions using mathematical programming techniques. Each constraint limiting possible actions is described mathematically by an equation or inequality. Further, where the constraints and objectives are linear or piecewise linear, the computational power of linear programming methods may be used.

Some Naive Methods of Solving Multiple Criteria Mathematical Programming Methods

There are several naive methods for solving multiple criteria mathematical programming problems. By calling the methods naive, I do not mean to denigrate them. They are simple in concept, though in general not very good. Sometimes naive methods such as these do prove to be effective, or are useful in that they provide a stepping stone in developing more effective methods. As we shall see, many of these ideas have been refined into effective methods.

i Setting levels of all objectives

The first of the naive methods to be considered is that of specifying or setting levels of all objectives, and then solving for a feasible solution. Let the problem be as follows:

$$\text{'Maximise'} \quad Cx$$
$$\text{subject to} \quad Ax \leq b, \; x \geq 0$$

Then this approach is to specify a vector d such that $Cx = d$. The object then is to find a feasible solution to the set of constraints

$$Cx = d$$
$$Ax \leq b, \; x \geq 0$$

The problem can be solved as a linear programming problem, and there are three possible outcomes as illustrated in Figure 7 for a two-objective problem. The feasible region is indicated. The three possible outcomes are as follows:

a. No feasible solution
b. A dominated solution
c. A nondominated solution.

These are illustrated in Figure 7. If the objectives are set too high, there is no feasible solution (e.g., point a). If the objectives are not set high enough, a feasible solution that is dominated (e.g., solution b) will be found. Almost certainly one of these two outcomes will occur. Only in rare circumstances would simply selecting a vector yield an efficient (or nondominated) solution. Given two points such as a and b, however, we can sometimes use a binary search for a nondominated solution on the line segment connecting them (e.g., line segment ab; the nondominated solution would be point e). That this does not necessarily happen is illustrated by feasible point k and infeasible point ℓ; there is no efficient point on the line segment joining them.

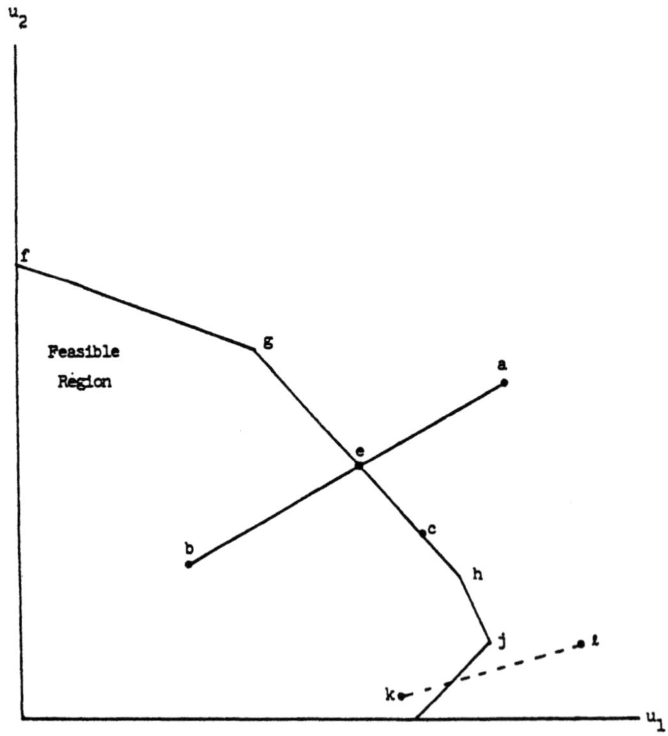

Figure 7. A graph of a simple two-dimensional example

Even if we had a method for finding an efficient solution, we would not necessarily know which solution is best. Methods that set levels of all objectives but overcome some of the limitations include goal programming and a method that has been developed by Wierzbicki (1979). These are discussed in later sections. See also the step method (Bayonoun et al. 1971).

ii Setting minimal levels of all but one objective

A second naive approach is to set minimum levels for all but one objective and to maximise the remaining objective. Mathematically this amounts to solving a linear programming of the following form:

$$\begin{aligned} \text{Maximise} \quad & C_1 x \\ \text{subject to} \quad & C_2 x \geq d_2 \\ & C_3 x \geq d_3 \\ & \vdots \\ & C_p x \geq d_p \\ & Ax \leq b, \quad x \geq 0 \end{aligned}$$

where $d_2, \ldots, d_p$ are the minimum levels of objectives 2, ..., p and $C_1, C_2, \ldots, C_p$ are the p objective function vectors. We have chosen to maximise the first objective without loss of generality. The result will certainly be a nondominated solution [1]. For our example problem of Figure 7, there are infinitely many solutions along the line segments fg, gh and hj. Presumably, one (or more) of these solutions is preferred to the others. Which of these solutions is most preferred by the decision maker? That is not clear. A method that employs this approach has been developed by Haimes and Hall (1974).

iii Finding all efficient extreme point solutions

Multiple Objective Linear Programming (MOLP) to find all nondominated or efficient solutions has been widely proposed as another approach. The concept of vector maximum and its early consideration by researchers (see for example, Charnes and Cooper (1961)) has been around for a long time. Only in the early 70s was it considered seriously as a computational procedure. Evans and Steuer (1973), and Yu and Zeleny (1975) generated and solved problems of several sizes to obtain all nondominated extreme point solutions of:

$$\begin{array}{ll} \text{'Maximise'} & Cx \\ \text{subject to} & Ax = b \\ & x \geq 0 \end{array}$$

The results of finding all nondominated extreme point solutions for multiple objective problems are not good, except for two-objective problems. For two-objective problems, parametric programming may be used to solve for all efficient solutions. For more than two objectives, there are in general far too many nondominated extreme point solutions. Basically, the methods consider the linear programming problem

$$\begin{array}{ll} \text{'Maximise} & \lambda' Cx \\ \text{subject to} & Ax = b \\ & x \geq 0 \end{array}$$

where the vector of weights $\lambda > 0$. For every nondominated extreme point solution, there exists a convex cone in λ space, that is a cone in which $\lambda'(C_N - C_B B^{-1}N) \leq 0$, using the usual linear programming notation (C_N and C_B are the nonbasic and basic partitions, respectively, of C, B is the basis, and N is the complement of B with respect to A). The methods for finding all nondominated extreme point solutions essentially enumerate the the convex cones in λ space. The idea was that all efficient solutions could be computed, and the decision maker could choose from them. Since there are in general far too many, the approach is not workable in practice. Steuer's contracting cone method, described in a later section, partially overcomes this problem.

iv Using weights to combine objective functions

The idea of using weights seems to be a attractive one. It involves averaging or blending the objectives into a composite objective and then maximising the result. The difficulty is in specifying weights. It is incorrect to say that if the weight for one objective is larger than that of another, that the first objective is more important than the second and vice versa. Further, the weights depend upon the units in which the objectives are measured. For example, equal weights have a rather unequal effect if one objective is to maximise GNP measured in billions of dollars and to maximise the fraction of the population who are above the poverty levels as measured by a number between zero and one. The second objective will in that case have virtually no effect. Therefore, the problem is that of specifying the weights to be used, or, for a nonlinear function, specifying the function. The Zionts-Wallenius method (considered below) extends and uses this approach.

Overcoming the Problems of the Naive Approaches

Several of the naive approaches have appealing characteristics, which no doubt led to their development. To overcome some of the problems with the methods, further development was done on these methods. We now consider the results.

i Goal programming

The concept of goal programming, effectively a method for setting all objectives, was introduced by Charnes and Cooper (1961), and extended by Ijiri (1965) and Lee (1972), among others. Goal programming involves the solution of linear programming problems (alghough other mathematical programming forms such as integer programming have also been formulated in a goal programming context) with several goals or targets. Generally, goal programming assumes a linear constraint set of the (matrix) form:

$$Ax = b$$
$$x \geq 0$$

where x is the vector of decision variables. Denoting an objective as $c_i'x$, there are several possible forms, all of which can be written as:

$$h_i \leq c_i'x \leq u_i$$

where h_i is the desired lower bound on objective i, and u_i is the desired upper bound. The bound constraints are not 'hard' in that they can be violated as we shall now see. First add variables s_i and t_i and rewrite the bound constraints as

$$c_i'x - s_i \leq u_i, \quad i=1, \ldots, p$$
$$c_i'x + t_i \geq h_i, \quad i=1, \ldots, p$$

where p is the number of objectives or goals. Now, using matrix notation with $c_i = (c_{i1}, c_{i2}, \ldots, c_{ip})'$, $s = (s_1, s_2, \ldots, s_p)'$, $t = (t_1, t_2, \ldots, t_p)'$, $k = (k_1, k_2, \ldots, k_p)'$, $q = (q_1, q_2, \ldots, q_p)'$, $u = (u_1, u_2, \ldots, u_p)'$ and $h = (h_1, h_2, \ldots, h_p)'$ we wish to

$$\begin{aligned} \text{Minimise} \quad & k's + q't \\ \text{subject to} \quad & Cx - s \le u \\ & Cx + t \ge h \\ & Ax = b \\ & x, s, t \ge 0 \end{aligned}$$

where k and q are vectors of weights to measure the violations of the bound constraints. If desired, several different s and t variables may be used for each goal with different values of k and q as well as upper bounds on the s and t variables. The effect of this is to allow for piecewise-linear nonlinear penalties in the failure to achieve goals. As outlined, the relationships yield convex sets. For more information on these nonlinearities as well as nonconvex nonlinearities, see Charnes and Cooper (1977).

The bound constraints may be of several different forms. If $u_i = h_i$, the goal is a desired fixed level that is sought. (In that case, we need only one goal constraint $c_i x - s_i + t_i = u_i$ $(=h_i)$.) If $u_i > h_i$, the goal is a range. See Figure 8. The penalties may be symmetric or not. If u_i is infinite (or h_i negatively infinite), the corresponding constraint may be omitted. A goal may, therefore, operate as a threshold plus an objective, that is a threshold that is desired, plus an objective that is operable given the threshold is attained. Thus, the formulation possibilities with goal programming are indeed general.

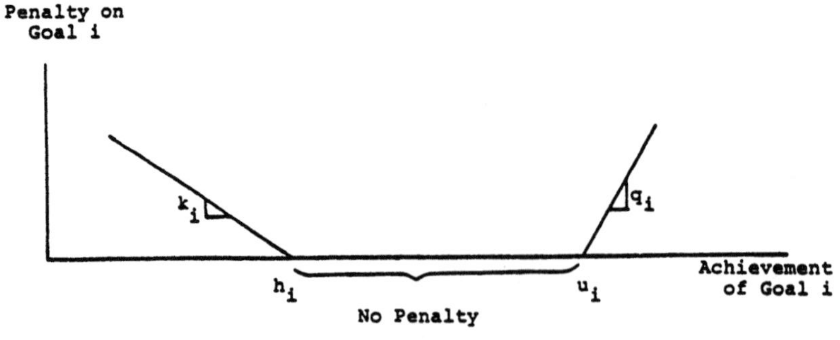

Figure 8. A goal that is a range

Instead of minimising a weighted sum of deviations from goals, goal programming may be used to minimise the maximum deviation from a set of goals. This is done by changing the formulation by adding the constraints.

$$q_i s_i \leq z$$

$$k_i t_i \leq z$$

and changing the objective to minimise z. The effective objective is then to minimise $(\max(q_i s_i, k_i t_i))$, the maximum weighted deviation from a goal.

Another variation of goal programming employs preemptive priorities instead of numerical weights. Let some subset of weights have much greater values than another subset of weights so that any finite multiple of the weights of the latter set is always less than any of the weights of the former set. The effect is to first minimise the weighted sums for the highest preemptive priority group. Then constraining that weighted sum to be equal to its minimum value, the next highest preemptive priority group sum is minimised, and so no, for as many preemptive priority groups as there may be.

Where goal programming falls flat is in the selection of the goals as well as the specifications of the weights, that is the vectors k and q. The selection of goals should not be a difficult problem, although it is important for the decision maker to be aware of tradeoffs which face him. The weights must be selected by the user, and goal programming does not have much to say about the choice of weights. About the only device that is offered in terms of weights is preemptive priorities, which we have already considered. Nonetheless, goal programming has been fairly widely sued in practice because of the ease of specifying a goal vector, and the ease of understanding what is going on. We solve as a goal programming problem Example 2 of Section 1, minimising the absolute sum of (negative) deviations only from the goal (66, 80, 75). The formulation is as follows:

$$\begin{aligned}
\text{Minimise} \quad & t_1 + t_2 + t_3 \\
\text{subject to} \quad & 3x_1 + x_2 + 2x_3 + x_4 + t_1 \geq 66 \\
& x_1 - x_2 + 2x_3 + 4x_4 + t_2 \geq 80 \\
& -x_1 + 5x_2 + x_3 + 2x_4 + t_3 \geq 75 \\
& 2x_1 + x_2 + 4x_3 + 3x_4 \leq 60 \\
& 3x_1 + 4x_2 + x_3 + 2x_4 \leq 60 \\
& x_1, x_2, x_3, x_4, t_1, t_2, t_3 \geq 0
\end{aligned}$$

The optimal solution to the above problem is $x_2 = 6$, $x_4 = 18$, $t_1 = 42$, $t_2 = 14$, $t_3 = 9$ (all other variables are zero) or $u_1 = 24$, $u_2 = 66$, $u_3 = 66$. Changing the objective function to Minimise $3t_1 + t_2 + t_3$ changes the solution to $u_1 = 66$, $u_2 = 30$, $u_3 = -12$, to illustrate another set of weights.

If we now add to the formulation $t_1 \leq z$, $t_2 \leq z$, and $t_3 \leq z$ and change the objective to minimise z we have an example of minimising the maximum deviation from each goal. We obtain the solution $x_1 = 4.86$, $x_2 = 5.014$, $x_3 = 2.38$, $x_4 = 11{,}24$, $t_1 = t_2 = t_3 = t_4 = z = 29.40$, or $u_1 = 36.6.$, $u_2 = 50.6$ and $u_3 = 45.6$.

We now illustrate an example using preemptive priorities. Let us assume that our first priority is to get u_1 to 50, our second priority is to get u_2 to 50, and our third priority is to get u_3 to 50.

We formulate the problem as follows:

$$\begin{aligned}
\text{Minimise} \quad & P_1t_1 + P_2t_2 + P_3t_3 && (P_1 >> P_2 >> P_3) \\
& 3x_1 + x_2 + 2x_3 + x_4 + t_1 \geq 50 && (u_1 \geq 50) \\
& x_1 - x_2 + 2x_3 + x_4 + t_2 \geq 50 && (u_2 \geq 50) \\
& -x_1 + 5x_2 + x_3 + 2x_4 + t_3 \geq 50 && (u_3 \geq 50) \\
& 2x_1 + x_2 + 4x_3 + 3x_4 \leq 60 \\
& 3x_1 + 4x_2 + x_3 + 2x_4 \leq 60 \\
& x_1, x_2, x_3, x_4, t_1, t_2, t_3 \geq 0
\end{aligned}$$

Our subsequence of solutions is as follows, omitting the identity matrix from the tableaux.

	x_1	x_2	x_3	x_4	t_1	t_2	t_3	
x_7	-3	-1	-2	-1	-1	0	0	-50
x_3	-1	1	-2	-4	0	-1	0	-50
x_9	1	-5	-1	-2	0	0	-1	-50
x_5	2	1	4	3	0	0	0	60
x_6	3	4	1	2	0	0	0	60

Tableau 1

Variables x_7, x_8 and x_9 are the slack variables on the objective function constraint, and x_5 and x_6 are the slack variables for Example 2. By making the three partial pivots indicated in Tableau 1 (see Karwan and Zionts (1980)),we have the feasible solution indicated in Tableau 2.

	x_1	x_2	x_3	x_4	x_7	x_8	x_9		
t_1	3	1	2	1	-1	0	0	50	→
t_2	1	-1	2	4	0	-1	0	50	
t_3	-1	5	1	2	0	0	-1	50	
t_5	2	1	4	3	0	0	0	60	
t_6	3	4	1	2	0	0	0	60	
	↑								

Tableau 2

Focussing on the first objective u_1 and its row t_1, we choose the most positive entry 3. The minimum ratio is also in the t_1 row, which means we immediately have $u_1 = 50$, as in Tableau 3.

	t_1	x_2	x_3	x_4	x_7	x_8	x_9	
x_1	.33	.33	.67	.33	-.33	0	0	16.67
t_2	-.33	-1.33	1.33	3.67	.33	-1	0	33.33 →
t_3	.33	5.33	1.67	2.33	-.33	0	-1	66.67
t_5	-.67	.33	2.67	2.33	.67	0	0	26.67
x_6	-1	3	-1	1	1	0	0	10

Tableau 3

At this point we drop variable t_1 since our first goal has been attained. Now we focus on u_2 and use the t_2 row. Its largest entry is in the x_4 column and the minimum ratio is in the t_2 row, which means we are about to attain our second priority goal $u_2 = 50$, as in Tableau 4.

	x_2	x_3	t_2	x_7	x_8	x_9	
x_1	.45	.55	-.09	-.36	.09	0	13.64
x_4	-.36	.36	.27	.09	-.27	0	9.09
t_3	6.18	.82	-.64	-.55	.64	-1	45.45
x_5	1.18	1.82	-.64	.45	.64	0	5.45
x_6	[3.36]	-1.36	-.27	.91	.27	0	.91 →
	↑						

Tableau 4

At this point we drop variable t_2 since our second goal has now been attained. Next we focus on u_3 and use the t_3 row. We bring in x_2, replacing x_6 leading to Tableau 5.

	x_6	x_3	x_7	x_8	x_9	
x_1	-.14	.73	-.49	.05	0	13.51
x_4	.11	.22	.19	-.24	0	9.19
x_3	-1.84	3.32	-2.22	.14	-1	43.78
x_5	-.35	[2.30]	.14	.54	0	5.14 →
x_2	.30	-.41	.27	.08	0	.27
		↑				

Tableau 5

We next, continuing with u_3 and using the t_3 row as our objective, introduce x_3 in place of x_5 yielding Tableau 6.

	x_6	x_5	x_7	x_8	x_9	
x_1	-2.35	-.32	-.53	-.12	0	11.88
x_4	.14	-.09	.18	-.29	0	8.71
t_3	-1.33	-1.45	-2.41	-.65	-1	36.35
x_3	-.15	.44	.06	.26	0	2.24
x_2	.24	.18	.29	.18	0	1.18

Tableau 6

At this point t_3 can be reduced no further; hence Tableau 6 gives us the optimal solution $t_1 = 0$ or $u_1 = 50$, $t_2 = 0$ or $u_2 = 50$, and $t_3 = 36.35$ or $u_3 = 13.65$, with $x_1 = 11.88$, $x_2 = 1.18$, $x_3 = 2.24$ and $x_4 = 8.71$. If the variables x_7, x_8 and x_9 were basic, they would indicate the excess achievement of the corresponding goal. Sang Lee (1972) refers to the above procedure in slightly different form as the simplex method of goal programming.

ii Scalarising functions and the method of Wierzbicki

Wierzbicki (1979) has developed a method which may be thought of as a method for setting levels of all objectives. It assumes that all objectives are to be maximised, and employs a scalarising function to find an efficient solution. Referring to our naive version, the chosen levels of objectives are almost certainly infeasible or dominated. The scalarising method of reference point approach, as it is also called (see Kallio, Lewandowski and Orchard Hays (1980)), finds the closest efficient solution to the chosen point. It is inteded to be used in a simulation-type mode by the decision maker.

Although there are a wide variety of scalarisation functions that could be used, one that seems quite effective is one which can be represented in a linear programming context. Let $\bar{u}_i$ be the target level for objective i. The objective is to maximise

$$\left\{\min(\rho \min_i\{C_i x - \bar{u}_i\} \sum_i (C_i x - \bar{u}_i)) + \varepsilon(C_i x - \bar{u}_i)\right\}$$

where the parameter $\rho \geq p$ the number of objectives and ε is a nonnegative vector. This objective function is achieved by a similar representation to that in goal programming for the minimisation of the maximum deviation from a set of goals. Here, however, we maximise the minimum of (1) a constant times the minimum overachievement of a goal, and (2) the sum of overachievements of goals, averaged together with a weighted overachievement of goals. As in the case of goal programming, the function and parameters are somewhat arbitrary. However, the purpose of this method is to be used as an efficient solution generator, one that can be used to generate a sequence of efficient solution points. It is rather similar to goal programming and has been programmed to solve problems having as many as 99 objectives with as many as 1000 constraints.

iii Steuer's Contracting Cone Method

Steuer's Contracting Cone Method (Steuer and Schuler (1976) and Steuer and Wallace (1978)), see also Steuer (1977), is a refinement to the generation of all nondominated solutions that generate only a relatively small number of nondominated extreme point solutions. It does this by selecting a convex cone in λ space that is large initially and includes sets of weights corresponding to many nondominated extreme point solutions. Rather than generating all of them, however, he generates only a very small number of extreme point solutions, and questions the decision maker regarding their relative attractiveness. He then uses the responses to contract the cone. When the cone becomes sufficiently small, the method generates all of the nondominated extreme point solutions in the cone for final consideration by the decision maker.

Assuming that there are p objectives, Steuer's method generates 2p + 1 trial solutions each time. The vectors generated are [2]:

	Values in General	Initial Values
λ_1	= the first extreme vector	= (1,0,0,...,0)
λ_2	= the second extreme vector	= (0,1,0,...,0)
⋮		
λ_p	= the pth extreme vector	= (0,0,0,...,1)
λ_{p+1}	$= (1/p\ (\lambda_1 + \lambda_2 + \ldots + \lambda_p)$	= (1/p,1/p.1/p.....,1/p)
λ_{p+2}	$= (\lambda_2 + \lambda_3 + \ldots + \lambda_p + \lambda_{p+1})/p$	$= (1/p^2, r, r, r, \ldots, r)$
λ_{p+3}	$= (\lambda_1 + \lambda_3 + \lambda_4 + \ .. + \lambda_p + \lambda_{p+1})/p$	$= (r, 1/p^2, r, r, \ldots, r)$
λ_{p+4}	$= (\lambda_1 + \lambda_2 + \lambda_4 + \ .. + \lambda_p + \lambda_{p+1})/p$	$= (r, r, 1/p^2, r, \ldots, r)$
⋮		
λ_{2p+1}	$= (\lambda_1 + \lambda_2 + \ldots + \lambda_{p-1} + \lambda_{p+1})/p$	$= (r, r, r, \ldots, r, 1/p^2)$
	where	$r = (p + 1)/p^2$

The first p vectors are the extreme vectors of the cone, the p + 1st is the mean or centre of gravity of the first p vectors, and each of the others is the mean or centre of gravity of p - 1 extreme vectors and the p + 1st vector. For each of the weight vectors λ, a linear programming problem is solved maximising $\lambda'Cx$, and the decision maker is presented with the 2p + 1 solutions. He is asked to choose which of the solutions he likes most, or if he is ready to look at all of the extreme point solutions in the cone. In the latter case, all extreme point solutions in the cone are found and presented to the decision maker for a final choice. Otherwise, the cone is contracted about the selected extreme point solution in the following way:

1. If the chosen solution is one that corresponds to one of the first p vectors above, then the first p vectors (the extreme vectors) for the next iteration are the vectors corresponding to the chosen solution, say λ_1, and the average of that vector with each of the other p - 1 extreme vectors, for example:

	Value in General	Value for the Second Iteration
λ_1'	λ_1 =	$(1,0,0,\ldots,0)$
λ_2'	$= .5\lambda_1 + .5\lambda_2$ =	$(.5,.5,0,\ldots,0)$
λ_3'	$= .5\lambda_1 + .5\lambda_3$ =	$(.5,0,.5,\ldots,0)$
$\vdots$		
λ_p'	$= .5\lambda_1 + .5\lambda_2$ =	$(.5,0,0,\ldots,0,.5)$

where the primes indicate the new trial weights.

2. If the chosen solution is the centre solution corresponding to vector λ_{p+1}, then the first p vectors (the extreme vectors) for the next iteration are the average of each extreme vector and the mean vector, as follows:

	Value in General	Value for the Second Iteration
λ_1'	$= (\lambda_1 + \lambda_{p+1})/2$	$= (.5 + .5/p,.5/p,.5/p,\ldots,.5/p)$
λ_2'	$= (\lambda_2 + \lambda_{p+1})/2$	$= (.5/p..5 + .5/p,.5/p,\ldots,.5/p)$
λ_3'	$= (\lambda_3 + \lambda_{p+1})/2$	$= (.5/p,.5/p,.5 + .5/p,\ldots,.5/p)$
$\vdots$		
λ_p'	$= (\lambda_p + \lambda_{p+1})/2$	$= (.5/p,.5/p,.5/p,\ldots,.5/p,.5 + .5/p)$

3. If the chosen solution is an off-centre solution corresponding to one of the vectors $\lambda_{p+2},\ldots,\lambda_{2p+1}$, say λ_{p+2}, which has the maximum Euclidean distance from λ_1 from any off-centre vector, then the first p vectors (the extreme vectors) for the next iteration are the average of the all but the most distant single extreme vector, e.g. $\lambda_2,\ldots,\lambda_p$, together with each of the p extreme vectors, as follows:

	Values in General	Values for the Second Iteration
λ_1'	$=.5\ _1 + .5\sum_{j=2}^{p+1} \lambda_j/p$	$= (.5 + .5/p^2,.5r,.5r,\ldots,.5r)$
λ_2'	$=.5\ _2 + .5\sum_{j=2}^{p+1} \lambda_j/p$	$= (.5/p^2,.5 + .5r,.5r,\ldots,.5r)$
λ_3'	$=.5\ _3 + .5\sum_{j=2}^{p+1} \lambda_j/p$	$= (.5/p^2,.5r,.5 + .5r,\ldots,.5r)$
$\vdots$		
λ_p'	$=.5\ _p + .5\sum_{j=2}^{p+1} \lambda_j/p$	$= (.5/p^2,.5r,.5r,\ldots,.5 + .5r)$

In other words, the new extreme vectors consist of the average of the chosen vector and the old extreme vectors.

In each of the three cases, the components $\lambda'_{p+1},\ldots,\lambda'_{2p+1}$ are found from $\lambda'_1,\ldots,\lambda'_p$ in the same way as $\lambda_{p+1},\ldots,\lambda_{2p+1}$ are calculated from $\lambda_{p+1},\ldots,\lambda_{2p+1}$.

The process is repeated until the decision maker asks for all efficient solutions defined in a cone to make a final decision. The effect of contracting the cone is to reduce the volume of the cone to $(1/2)^p$ of what it was at each contraction. This fraction could be adjusted to a larger or smaller fraction, if desired. To illustrate how the cone contracts as we have described, consider a three objective problem. Figure 9 illustrates such a cone section with $\lambda_1 + \lambda_2 + \lambda_3 = 1$. If we contract the cone about one the the original p extreme vectors (λ_1), we have diagram shown in Figure 9a. If we contract the cone about the centre of gravity (the mean - λ_4), we have the diagram shown in Figure 9b. Finally, if we contract the cone about one of the off-centre solutions (λ_5), we have the diagram shown in Figure 9c.

The procedure is appealing, but heuristic in nature. It does not always find the optimal solution. Consider the following problem, contrived from Example 2.

$$\begin{aligned}
\text{Maximise } u_1 &= 66x_1 + 20x_2 + 15x_3 + 24x_4 + 29.6x_5 + 36x_6 \\
u_2 &= 30x_1 + 80x_2 - 15x_3 + 66x_4 + 69.6x_5 + 12x_6 \\
u_3 &= -12x_1 + 40x_2 + 75x_3 + 66x_4 + 29.6x_5 + 72x_6 \\
\text{subject to } & x_1 + x_2 + x_3 + x_4 + x_5 + x_6 \le 1 \\
& x_1,\ldots,x_6 \ge 0
\end{aligned}$$

Suppose that the true set of weights is $\lambda_1 = .5205$, $\lambda_2 = .4$, $\lambda_3 = .0795$. The optimal solution is then $x_5 = 1$, all other x's zero. To help simplify calculations, we have plotted values of λ_1 and λ_2 ($\lambda_3 = 1 - \lambda_1 - \lambda_2$) and the associated optimal solutions in Figure 10. Solution j optimal means $x_j = 1$, and all other x's are zero.

Using Steuer's method, we have the following trial vectors, and the corresponding optimal solutions which maximise the objective function for the given vectors.

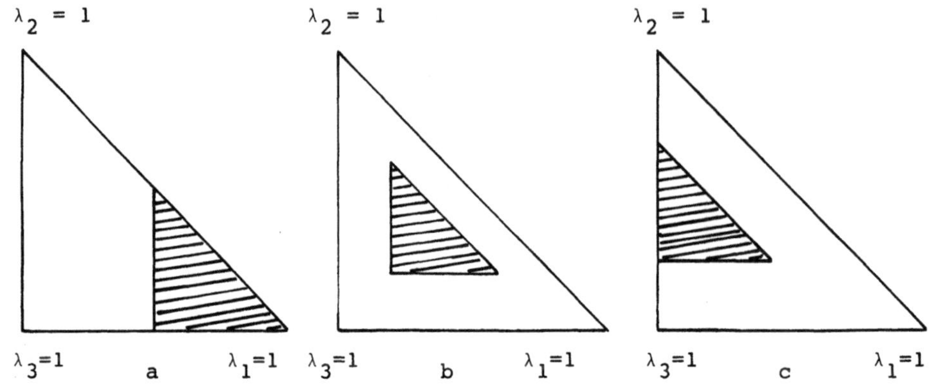

Figure 9.

An illustration of the three cases of contracting cones.

Case a The solution corresponding to $\lambda_1 = 1$, $\lambda_j = 0 (j \neq 1)$, is preferred.

Case b The solution corresponding to $\lambda_j = 1/p$, $j = 1, \ldots, p$, is preferred.

Case c The solution corresponding to $\lambda_1 = 1/p^2$, $\lambda_j = (p + 1)/p^2$, $j \neq 1$ is preferred.

λ^1 = (1 0 0) = Solution 1

λ^2 = (0 1 0) = Solution 2

λ^3 = (0 0 1) = Solution 3

λ^4 = (1/3 1/3 1/3) = Solution 4

λ^5 = (1/9 4/9 4/9) = Solution 5

λ^6 = (4/9 1/9 4/9) = Solution 6

λ^7 = (4/9 4/9 1/9) = Solution 7

Of the five solutions found in the first iteration, solution 2 is the most preferred. If trial vector λ^2 is selected for contraction, the restricted region of Figure 4.5, bounded by $\lambda_1 = 0$, $\lambda_2 = .5$, and $\lambda_1 + \lambda_2 = 1$, will not include any points with solution 5 optimal. If trial vector λ^7 is selcted for contraction, the restricted region of Figure 4.5 will be bounded by $\lambda_1 = .25$, $\lambda_2 = .25$, and $\lambda_1 + \lambda_2 = 1$. In that case, none of the trial vectors will yield solution 5, and of the two that yield solution 2, contracting about one of them will not include any solutions containing solution 5. Thus three-fourths of the possible choices in the first two iterations will not lead to solution 5, and the remaining one depends on subsequent choices.

Though not suggested by Steuer, this problem may be alleviated by breaking ties arbitrarily, and then, once the optimal solution has supposedly been found, generate all adjacent efficient extreme points. If none of these are preferred to the supposed optimum, it is indeed optimal. Otherwise, further investigation must be made. For the example, solution 5 is an adjacent efficient extreme point of solution 2. Generally, however, a solution such as the one we have here will be ever so slightly better than the one found by the method.

The method has the capability of generating all of the efficient solutions in a convex cone of weights λ. It seems attractive because the cone can be contracted until it is as small as the user wishes. The disadvantages are that the decision maker must choose among as many as 2p + 1 alternatives each iteration, as opposed to a smaller number. as shown in the contrived example, the optimal solution is not necessarily obtained. A way of overcoming that problem is indicated although that suggested way could prove cumbersome in some instances.

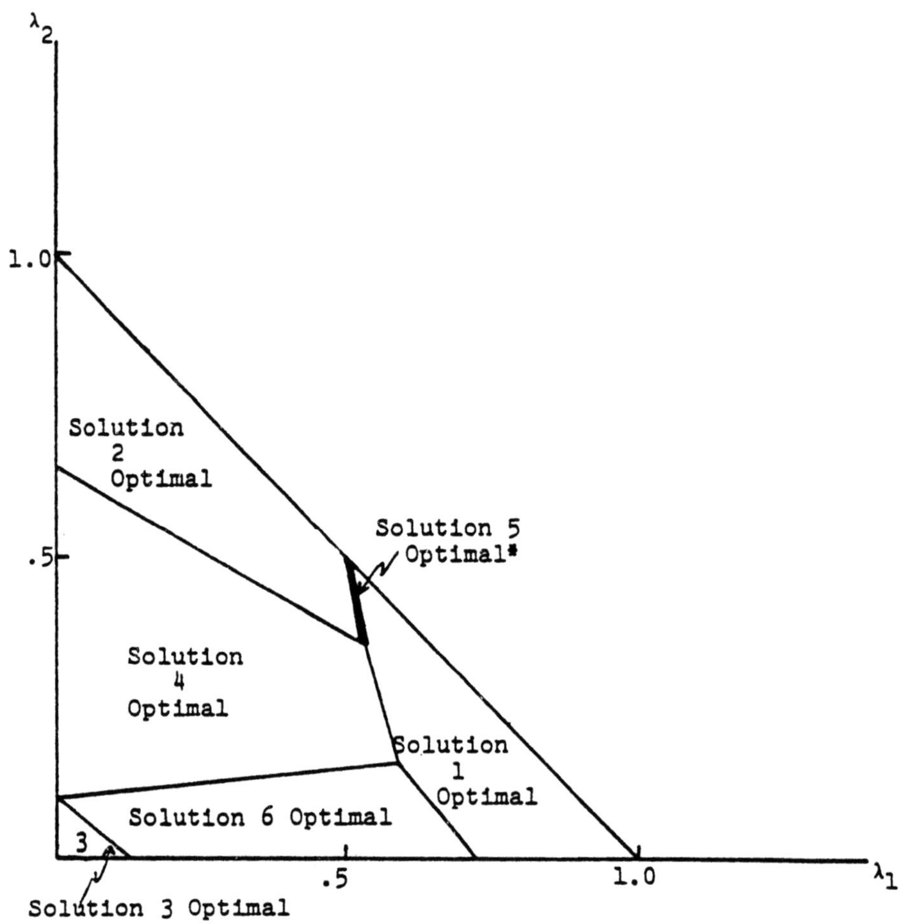

Figure 10. A plot of λ values and the corresponding optimal solutions

* This set has a nonempty though relatively small interior

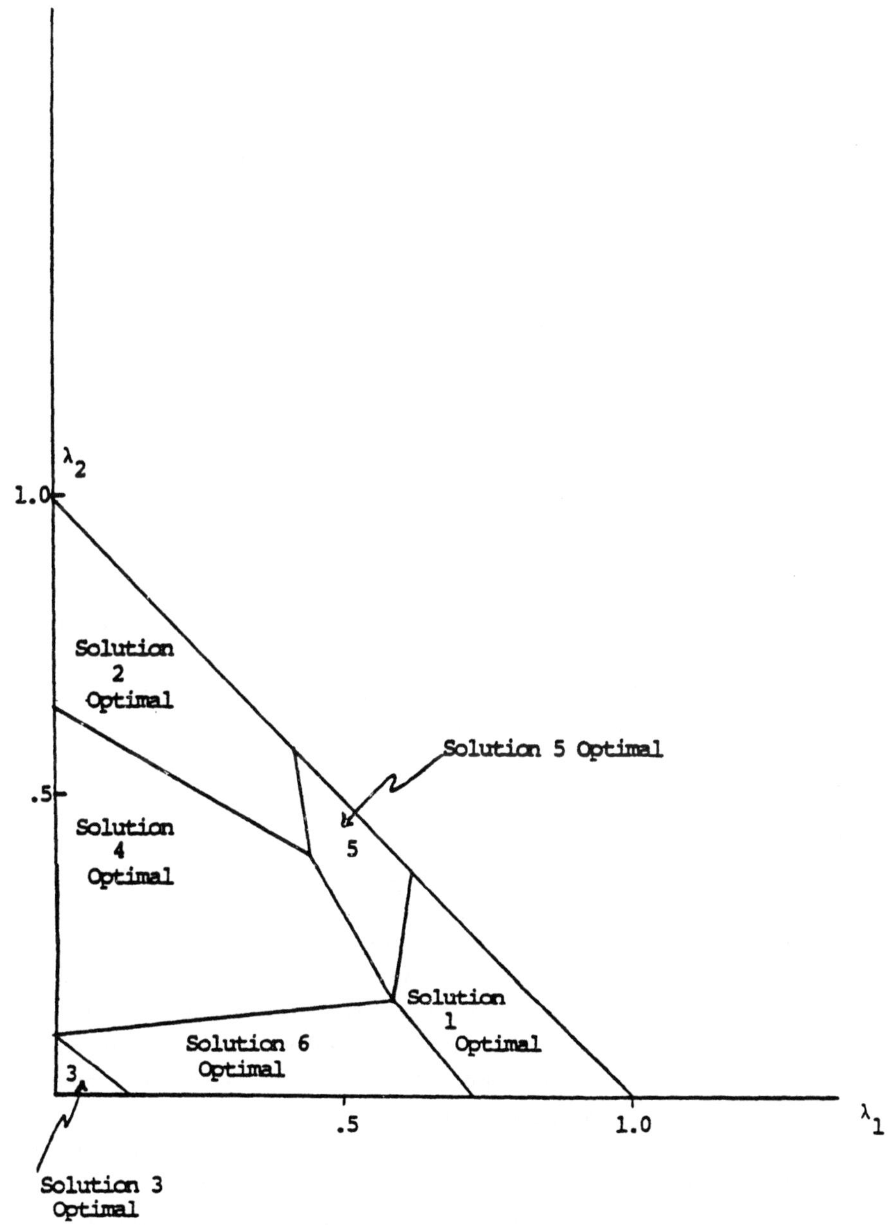

Figure 11. A plot of λ values and the corresponding optimal solutions

A more reasonable though less interesting example is the original Example 2. We plot the λ values and the regions of corresponding optimal solutions in Figure 11. Assuming a 'true' set of weights of $\lambda_1 = .58$, $\lambda_2 = .21$, and $\lambda_3 = .21$, solution 5 is optimal. Steuer's set first set of weights and their solutions are as follows:

λ_1	λ_2	λ_3	Solution
1	0	0	1
0	1	0	2
0	0	1	3
1/3	1/3	1/3	4
1/9	4/9	4/9	4
4/9	1/9	4/9	6
4/9	4/9	1/9	5

The cone will be contracted in the region of solution 5, and will certainly find the optimal solution, particularly since all feasible optimal extreme point solutions have been already listed above. Regarding performance, Steuer and Schuler (1976) report favourable experience in applications to forestry management problems.

iv The Zionts-Wallenius Method

A method for multiple objective linear programming which uses weights is one developed by Zionts and Wallenius (1976,1983). In that framework a numerical weight (arbitrary initially) is chosen for each objective. Then each objective is multiplied by its weight, and all of the weighted objectives are then summed. The resulting composite objective is a proxy for a utility function. (The manager need not be aware of the combination process.) Using the composite objective, solve the corresponding linear programming problem. The solution to that problem, an efficient solution, is presented to the decision maker in terms of the levels of each objective achieved. Then the decision maker is offered some trades from that solution, again only in terms of the marginal changes to the objectives. The trades take the form, "Are you willing to reduce objective 1 by so much in return for an increase in objective 2 by a certain amount, an increase in objective 3 by a certain amount, and so on?" The decision maker is asked to respond either yes or no, or I don't know to the proposed trade. The method then develops a new set of weights consistent with the responses obtained, and a corresponding new solution. The process is then repeated, until a best solution is found.

The above version of the method is valid for linear utility functions. However, the method is extended to allow for the maximisation of a general but unspecified concave function of objectives. The changes to the method from that described above are modest. First where possible the trades are presented in terms of scenarios, e.g., "Which do you prefer, alternative A or alternative B?" Second, each new nondominated extreme point solution to the problem is compated with the old, and either the new solution, or one preferred to the old one is used for the next iteration. Finally, the procedure terminates with a neighbourhood that contains the optimal solution. Experience with the method has been good. With as many as seven objectives on moderate linear programming problems (about 300 constraints) the maximum number of solutions is about ten, and the maximum number of questions is under 100.

We describe the general concave (GC) version in some detail. The linear problem form may, of course, be solved as a special case, though the GC method does not reduce to the linear method in that case.

We repeat the formulation of the problem for convenience.

$$\text{Maximise} \quad g(Cx)$$
$$\text{subject to} \quad Ax \leq b,\ x \geq 0$$

The underlying concave utility function g is assumed to have continuous first derivatives. We present the algorithm as a sequence of steps.

1. Choose an arbitrary initial vector of weights, $\lambda > 0$.
2. Solve the linear programming problem

$$\text{Maximise} \quad \lambda' Cx$$
$$\text{subject to} \quad Ax \leq b,\ x \geq 0$$

   The result is a nondominated extreme point solution x^*. If this is the first time through this step, go to step 3. Otherwise, ask whether solution x^* is preferred to the old x^* solution. If yes, discard the old solution and go to step 3. If no, replace x^* by x^o and go to step 3.

3. Find all adjacent efficient extreme point solutions to x* consistent with prior responses. If there are none, drop the oldest set of responses and repeat step 3. Otherwise go to step 4.

4. (This step is simplified over what is used. See Zionts and Wallenius (1933) for more information.) Ask the decision maker to choose between x* and an adjacent efficient extreme point solution. Do not repeat any questions previously asked. If the objective function values of the solutions are too close or if he has preferred x to an adjacent solution, ask the decision maker about the tradeoffs between the two solutions. He may indicate which solution he prefers, or indicate that he cannot choose between the two. If he prefers no alternatives or tradeoff go to step 5. Otherwise mark a solution preferred to x* as x^o and go to step 6.

5. If all previous responses have been deleted, stop: if the decision maker does not like any tradeoffs from x*, the optimal solution is x*. Otherwise, to find the optimal solution, the method terminates and a search method (not part of this method) must be used in which case previous responses have not been deleted, delete the oldest set of responses and go to step 3.

6. Find a set of weights $\lambda > 0$ consistent with all previous responses. If there is no feasible set, delete the oldest response and repeat step 6. When a feasible set of weights is achieved, go to step 2.

To find the adjacent efficient extreme points in step 3, consider the tradeoffs offered $(w_{1j},\ldots,w_{pj})$ by moving to the adjacent extreme point solution j. Then, consider the following linear programming problem:

$$\text{Maximise} \quad \sum_{i=1}^{p} w_{ik}\lambda_i$$

$$\text{subject to} \quad \sum_{i=1}^{p} w_{ij}\lambda_i \leq 0 \qquad j\in N,\ j\neq k \tag{A}$$

$$\lambda_i \geq 0\ , \qquad i=1,\ldots,p$$

where N is the set of nonbasic variables corresponding to solution on x*. No convex combination of tradeoffs dominates the null vector, for otherwise solutions x* would not be efficient.

Definition: Given two efficient extreme point solutions x_a and x*, solution x_a is an adjacent efficient extreme point solution of x* if and only if all convex combinations of x^* and x_a are efficient solutions.

Theorem: The optimal solution to problem (A) is zero if and only if solution k offering the tradeoff vector $w_{1k},\ldots,w_{pk}$ is not an efficient vector of the set of vectors w_j, $j \in N$.

$$\sum_{i \neq k} \mu_i w_{ij} \geq w_{kj} \qquad j=1,\ldots,p$$

$$\mu_i \geq 0$$

Attributing a null minimising objective function and writing a dual linear programming problem we have:

$$\text{Maximise} \quad \sum_{j=1}^{p} w_{kj} \lambda_j$$

$$\text{subject to} \quad \sum_{j=1}^{p} w_{ij} \lambda_j \leq 0 \quad i \neq k$$

$$j \geq 0$$

By linear programming duality, if one solution has a finite optimum, so does the other, and both have objective functions of zero, QED.

Corollary: If problem (A) has a positive infinite solution, then solution k offering the tradeoff vector $w_{1k},\ldots,w_{pk}$ is an efficient vector of the set of vectors w_j, $j \in N$.

The method does not explicitly solve problem (A) for every value of k. What it does is to choose one value of k and to solve (A) for that value of k. At each iteration, a sequence of tests for other values of k are made which in general eliminate solving problems for subsequent values of k. When the status of the optimal solution for the current objective is known, another value of k, whose status is not yet known, is selected for optimisation.

As an example, we consider Example 2. As a 'true' set of weights we use $\lambda_1 = .58$, $\lambda_2 = .21$, and $\lambda_3 = .21$. Our solution procedure begins with $\lambda_1 = \lambda_2 = \lambda_3 = 1/3$. Refer to Figure 11 for further insight. The initial solution is solution 4. First the decision maker is asked to compare solutions 4 and 2, he should prefer 4. Considering 4 versus 5, he should prefer 5. Considering 4 versus 6, he should prefer 4. A consistent set of weights [3] is $\lambda_1 = .818$, $\lambda_2 = .182$, $\lambda_3 = 0$, and the new solution is solution 1. The decision maker is asked to choose between 1 and 5; he should prefer 5. A set of consistent weights is .594, .160, .246. They yield solution 5. A final question is asked: between 5 and 2. Since he should prefer 5, there are no further questions to ask; solution 5 is optimal.

The Zionts-Wallenius method is extended to integer programming in Zionts (1977b), which is implemented and tested in Villareal (1979). See also Villareal, Karwan and Zionts (1980a, 1980b) and Karwan, Zionts and Villareal (1983). Other methods of multiple criteria integer programming are summarised in Zionts (1979).

The Zionts-Wallenius method has been used by several organisations and has met with success. For example, Wallenius, Wallenius and Vartia (1978) describe an application to macroeconomic planning for the Government of Finland. They used an input-output model of the Finnish economy with four objectives chosen by the Finnish Economic Council chaired by the Prime Minister. The objectives were:

1. the percentage change in gross domestic product
2. unemployment
3. the rate of inflation as measured by consumer prices
4. the balance of trade

They first tried using the Geoffrion, Dyer and Feinberg (1972) appeoach using an improvement prescribed by Dyer (1973). Although the method worked, the users found the estimation of the marginal rates of substitution difficult. Then the Zionts-Wallenius method was used. Results were obtained that were quite satisfactory.

One criticism of the Zionts-Wallenius approach is that at termination we may not always have an optimal solution. However, the termination of the procedure indicates when this does occur. In such instances, we will have an extreme point solution that is preferred to all adjacent efficient extreme point solutions. A search procedure will then have to be used to find the optimal. See, for example, Deshpande (1980).

v The Geoffrion, Dyer and Feinberg Method

The next mathematical programming method to be discussed, that of Geoffrion, Dyer and Feinberg (1972), is in the spirit of a weighting method. However, it is a gradient type method which allows for a nonlinear program. The method begins with a decision that satisfies all of the constraints. Then information is elicited from the decision maker indicating how he would like to alter the initial levels of the various objectives. More specifically, he is asked to indicate how much of a reference criterion he is willing to give up in order to gain a fixed amount of one of the other criteria. The responses are elicited for every criterion except the reference criterion.

To illustrate, suppose that one has three objectives:

1. to maximise return on investment
2. to maximise growth in sales
3. to minimise borrowing.

Given a starting feasible solution and taking return on investment as our reference criterion, the decision maker would be asked two questions to consider from that solution:

1. What percentage growth in sales must you gain in order to give up a 1% return on investment?
2. What decrease in borrowing must you achieve in order to give up a 1% return on investment?

His responses can be used to determine the direction of change in objectives most desired.

That direction is them used as a objective function to be maximised, and the solution (the new solution) maximising the objective is found. Then a one-dimensional search is conducted with the decision maker from the previous solution to the new solution. The decision maker is asked in a systematic manner to choose the best decision along the direction. Using the best decision as a starting point, a new direction is elicited from the decision maker as above and the process is repeated until the decision maker is satisfied with the solution.

We would like to give an example of the Geoffrion, Dyer and Feinberg method. However, if we assume a linear utility function, and provide correct tradeoff information, the method requires only one iteration. If we assume a nonlinear utility function or consider a linear utility function and do not provide correct tradeoff information, more iterations are required. We choose to assume a nonlinear utility function. We use Example 2; our utility function is:

$$\text{Maximise} \quad U = -(u_1 - 66)^2 - (u_2 - 80)^2 - (u_3 - 75)^2$$

$$\begin{aligned} \text{subject to} \quad u_1 &= 3x_1 + x_2 + 2x_3 + x_4 \\ u_2 &= x_1 - x_2 + 2x_3 + 4x_4 \\ u_3 &= -x_1 + 5x_2 + x_3 + 2x_4 \\ & 2x_1 + x_2 + 4x_3 + 3x_4 \leq 60 \\ & x_1, x_2, x_3, x_4 \leq 0 \end{aligned}$$

We start with the solution $u_1 = u_2 = u_3 = x_1 = x_2 = x_3 = x_4 = 0$ ('true' objective function value -16,381). The partial derivatives are $\frac{\partial u}{\partial u_1} = -1(u_1 - 66)$, $\frac{\partial u}{\partial u_2} = -2(u_2 - 80)$, and $\frac{\partial u}{\partial u_3} = -2(u_3 - 75)$. For the initial solution the vector of partial derivatives is 132, 160, 150, normalised as .299, .362, .339. We solve the linear programming problem using this set of weights to combine objectives. From Figure 4.5 we see the solution with that set of weights is solution 4 (24 66 66). We then choose the best solution on the line segment between objective function value -2041). We find this by searching along the line segment between the two solutions. The new normalised objective function vector at (24 66 66) is .646 .215 .138, and the solution for that set of weights is solution 5 (48 60 12). The maximum solution on the line segment between (26.6 64.8 61.2) and (48 60 12) is (27.4 63.7 59.5) (with true objective function value -1999). At this point we begin to alternate between maximising solutions four and five until the solution converges. The first few solutions and the optimum are summarised in Table 1. The optimal solution is approximately $x_1 = 1.5$, $x_2 = 5.25$, $x_4 = 17.25$ with objective function values (27.0 65.25 59.25).

An application of the method to the operation of an academic department on a university campus is described based on data from the 1970-1971 operations of the Graduate School of Management, University of California, Los Angeles. A linear programming model of the problem was developed and used to formulate annual departmental operating plans. Six criteria for evaluation were stated, including number of course sections offered at various levels, the level of teaching assistance used, and faculty involvement in various nonteaching activities. The decision variables under the control of the department were the number of course sections offered at different levels, the number of regular and temporary faculty hired, and the number of faculty released from teaching. The starting point for the analysis was the previous year's operating position, and the resulting solution suggested an important reallocation of faculty effort from teaching to other activities. The method was used without significant difficulty, and the results were adopted by the department.

Table 1.

	Solution		Objective Function Value	Maximising Solution		
1	0	0	-16,381	24	66	66
2	24	66	- 2,041	66	30	-12
3	26.6	61.2	- 2,005	48	60	12
4	27.4	59.5	- 1,999	24	66	66
5	27.0	60.3	- 1,993	48	60	12
6	27.34	59.52	- 1,992.15	24	66	66
7	27.092	60.002	- 1,991.8	48	60	12
.						
.						
.						
∞	65.25	59.25	- 1,991.8	{24 48	66 60	66} 12}

The problems in the method are the evaluation of the gradient and the choice of a solution along the line segment in the search procedure.

7 STOCHASTIC PROBLEMS WITH EXPLICIT CONSTRAINTS

Little work has been done in the case of stochastic problems using explicit constraints, probably because problems are generally sufficiently complex in a deterministic or deterministically equivalent world, without considering any probabilistic effects. Further, even in the deterministic domain there is no plethora of application experience. Certain obvious cases suggest themselves, such as those in which expected value of objectives is to be maximised and an additive utility function is appropriate. Some of the linear programming models under uncertainty, such as the resource models, would appear to lead to straightforward multiple objective programming models.

D.L. Keefer (1978a, 1978b) has developed a procedure and has solved several problems by using a result of Keeney (1974) which states that for three or more objectives, if for some objective i, objectives i and j (for every j) are preferentially independent of their complement and objective i is utility independent of its complement, the utility function is either linear $u(r) = \Sigma k_i u_k / r_i$ or multiplicative (see Keeney and Raiffa 1976). He has fitted utility functions and solved several problems. The problems have had a resulting nonlinear utility function and linear constraints. A few small problems have been solved using Keefer's approach. Because of the nonlinearity and nonconcavity of the utility functions Keefer encountered, locally optimal solutions are obtained.

8 CONCLUSION

This presentation was designed as an introduction to the multiple criteria decision problem, with a presentation to some of the methods that have been developed to solve the multiple objective mathematical programming problem. Our treatment was, of necessity, brief. For further information on the methods presented refer to the references. For additional information on these methods and new developments in the field, refer to the various journals in management science. We have mentioned some applications of the methods. The methods are proving useful in helping people to solve multiple criteria decision problems.

NOTES

[1] Ralph Steuer has pointed out that solutions to such problems may be in some cases weakly dominated.
[2] Instead of using zeroes in the vector, we use some sufficiently small positive numbers. However, for simplicity of presentation use zeros here.
[3] We do not use zero weights: λ_3 would be equal to come arbitrary small positive number.

REFERENCES

Benayoun, R., de Montgolfier, J., Tergny, J. and Larichev, O, 'Linear programming with multiple objective functions: step method (STEM)' Mathematical Programming, 1, 1971, pp. 366-375.

Charnes, A. and Cooper, W.W., Management Models and Industrial Applications of Linear Programming, John Wiley and Sons, New York, 1961.

Charnes, A. and Cooper, W.W., 'Goal programming and multiple objective optimization - Part 1', European Journal of Operations Research, 1, 1977, pp. 39-54.

Deshpande, D., 'Investigations in multiple objective linear programming - theory and an application', Unpublished Doctoral Dissertation, School of Management, State University of New York at Buffalo, 1980.

Dyer, J., 'A time-sharing computer program for the solution to the multiple criteria problem', Management Science, 19, 1973, pp. 1379-1383.

Evans, J.P. and Steuer, R.E., 'Generating efficient extreme points in linear multiple objective programming: two algorithms and computing experience', in Cochrane and Zeleny (1973), pp. 349-365.

Geoffrion, A.M., Dyer, J.S. and Feinberg, A., 'An interactive approach for multicriterion optimization with an application to the operation of an academic department', Management Science, 19, 1972, pp. 357-368.

Haimes, Y.Y. and Hall, W.A., 'Multiobjectives in water resources systems analysis: the surrogate worth tradeoff method', Water Resources Research, 10, 1974, pp. 615-623.

Ijiri, Y., Management Goals and Accounting for Control, North Holland Publishing Co., Amsterdam and Rand McNally, Chicago, 1965.

Kallio, M., Lewandowski, A. and Orchard-Hays, W., 'An implementation of the reference point approach for multiobjective optimization', Working Paper no. 80-35, International Institute for Applied Systems Analysis, Laxenburg, Austria, 1980.

Karwan, M.H., Zionts, S. and Villareal, B., 'An improved interactive multicriteria integer programming algorithm', Working Paper no. 530, School of Management, State University of New York at Buffalo, Revised February 1983.

Karwan, M.H. and Zionts, S., 'On finding starting feasible solutions for some specifally structured linear programming problems', Working Paper no. 445, School of Management, State University of New York at Buffalo, 1980.

Keefer, D.L., 'Allocation planning for R&D with uncertainty and multiple objectives', IEEE Transactions on Engineering Management', EM-25, 1978a, pp. 8-14.

Keefer, D.L., 'Applying multiobjective decision analysis to resource allocation planning problems', in Zionts (1978), pp. 299-320.

Keeney, R.L., 'Multiplicative utility functions', Operations Research, 22, 1974, pp. 22-34.

Keeney, R.L. and Raiffa, H., Decisions with Multiple Objectives: Preferences and Value Tradeoffs, John Wiley and Sons, New York, 1976.

Lee, S.M., Goal Programming for Decision Analysis, Auerbach, Philadelphia, 1972.

Manheim, M.L. and Hall, F., 'Abstract representation of goals: A method for making decisions in complex problems', in: Transportation: A Service, Proceedings of the Sesquicentennial Forum, New York Academy of Sciences American Society of Mechanical Engineers, New York, 1967.

Miller, G., 'The magical number seven plus or minus two: some limits on our capacity for processing information', Psychological Review, 63, 1956, pp. 81-97.

Roy, B., 'Partial preference analysis and decision aid: the fuzzy outranking relation concept', in Bell, Keeney and Raiffa (1977).

Steuer, R.E., 'Multiple objective linear programming with interval criterion weights', Management Science, 23, 1977, pp. 305-316.

Steuer, R.E. and Schuler, A.T., 'An interactive multiple objective linear programming approach to a problem in forest management', Working Paper No. BA2, College of Business and Economics, University of Kentucky, 1976.

Steuer, R.E. and Wallace, M.J. Jr., 'An interactive multiple objective wage and salary administration procedure', in Lee, S.M. and Thorp, C.D. Jr. (eds), Personnel Management: A Computer-Based System, Petrocelli, New York, 1978, pp. 159-176.

Villareal, B., Multicriteria Integer Linear Programming, Doctoral Dissertation, Department of Industrial Engineering, State University of New York at Buffalo, 1979.

Villareal, B., Karwan, M.H. and Zionts, S., 'An interactive branch and bound procedure for multicriterion integer linear programming', in Fandel and Gal, 1980a.

Villareal, B., Karwan, M.H. and Zionts, S., 'A branch and bound approach to interactive multicriteria integer linear programming', Paper presented at the Joint National Meeting TIMS/ORSA, Washington, DC, 1980b.

Wallenius, H., Wallenius, J. and Vartia, P., 'An approach to solving multiple criteria macroeconomic policy problems and an application', Management Science, 24, 1978, pp. 1021-1030.

Wierzbicki, A.P., 'The use of reference objectives in multiobjective optimization', Working Paper 79-66, International Institute for Applied Systems Analysis, Laxenburg, Austria, 1979.

Yu, P.L. and Zeleny, M., 'The set of all nondominated solutions in the linear cases and a multicriteria simplex method', Journal of Mathematical Analysis and Applications, 49, 1975, pp. 430-468.

Zionts, S., 'Integer linear programming with multiple objectives', Annals of Discrete Mathematics, 1, 1977, pp. 551-562.

Zionts, S. and Wallenius, J., 'An interactive programming method for solving the multiple criteria problem', Management Science, 22, 1976, pp. 652-663.

Zionts, S. and Wallenius, J., 'An interactive multiple objective linear programming method for a class of underlying nonlinear utility functions', Management Science, vol. 29, no. 5, May 1983, pp. 529-529.

7 Mathematics of the Multiple Objective Programming Problem - a Tutorial

H. Isermann

1 MULTIPLE OBJECTIVE DECISION MODELS

1.1 The efficiency principle

The constitutive conponents of a multiple objective decision model are:

1. a set X of potential or feasible alternatives,
2. $K > 1$ objective functions $z_k : X \to \mathbb{R}$ with $k = 1, \ldots, K$,
3. K binary preference relations $R_K (k = 1, \ldots, K)$.

The set of potential or feasible alternatives comprises at least two objects, actions, items of choice, etc. from which a selection of one or more alternatives is to be made or their ranking is to be performed with respect to given objectives.

Each alternative $x \in X$ can be characterised by a set of attributes, i.e. physical or physiological characteristics identifiable with the alternatives more or less independently of a particular decision maker (DM). The DM (an individual or a group) who is faced with the selection of one or more alternatives from X at some point of time will consider a finite subset of attributes relevant with respect to the formulation and achievement of his objectives. Each objective reflects one or more of these relevant attributes and thus defines a particular dimension of the DM's evaluation system. The objective function $z_k = z_k(x)$ measures the contribution of the alternative $x \in X$ with respect to the k-th dimension of valuation $(k = 1, \ldots, K)$ on the basis of the levels of the respective attributes associated or implied by the alternative x.

Associated with each objective function $z_k(x)$ is a binary preference relation R_k on $Z_k := (z_k(x) \mid x \in X)$, where $z_k(x^1) R_k z_k(x^2)$ means that the DM rates $z_k(x^1)$ at least as high as $z_k(x^2)$ for $x^1, x^2 \in X$. By means of this weak preference relation R_k a strong preference relation P_k can be defined:

$z_k(x^1)P_k z_k(x^2) \leftrightarrow z_k(x^1)R_k z_k(x^2)$ and not $(z_k(x^2)R_k z_k(x^1))$.

$z_k(x^1)P_k z_k(x^2)$ is equivalent to: The DM rates $z_k(x^1)$ at least as high as $z_k(x^2)$ but he does not rate $z_k(x^2)$ at least as high as $z_k(x^1)$. Hence $z_k(x^1)P_k z_k(x^2)$ reads: The DM rates $z_k(x^1)$ higher than $z_k(x^2)$ $(x^1, x^2 \in X)$. Each of the considered K objectives is thus represented by an objective function $z_k = z_k(x)$ and a binary preference relation R_k which specifies the aspired extent of $z_k(x)$.

In order to illustrate some possible realisations of the binary preference relation R_k let us assume that with respect to the k-th dimension of valuation the DM rates $z_k(x^1)$ at least as high as $z_k(x^2)$, if and only if $z_k(x^1) \geqq z_k(z^2)$ $(x^1, x^2 \in X)$, i.e.

$$z_k(x^1)\ R_k z_k(x^2) \leftrightarrow z_k(x^1) \geqq z_k(x^2) \qquad x^1, x^2 \in X .$$

Then the preference relation R_k implies the objective to <u>maximise</u> objective function $z_k(x)$ over X. If with respect to the j-th dimension of valuation the DM rates $z_j(x^1)$ at least as high as $z_j(x^2)$ if and only if $z_j(x^1) \leqq z_j(x^2)$ $(x^1, x^2 \in X)$, i.e.

$$z_j(x^1)R_j z_j(x^2) \leftrightarrow z_j(x^1) \leqq z_j(x^2) \qquad x^1, x^2 \in X .$$

R_j implies the objective to <u>minimise</u> objective function $z_j(x)$ over X. In many decision situations a DM expresses a decision behaviour pattern wherein he constructs for some or each dimension of valuation a goal or target value which relates to the attainment of specific performance levels. These goals may be aspiration levels internally arrived at (see e.g. Becker and Siegel 1958, Simon 1967, Stedry 1962), or maybe goals imposed by superiors, the market or the social environment (see e.g. Becker and Green 1962, Chapman and Volkmann 1939, McGregor 1957). This satisficing behaviour can also be represented by a binary preference relation: Let us assume that with respect to the i-th dimension of valuation a DM has determined a goal $\bar{z}_i$, which he tries to attain from below. We further assume that to all $x \in X$ with $z_i(x) \geqq \bar{z}_i$ the DM is indifferent, but if for some $x^1, x^2 \in X$ $z_i(x^1) < \bar{z}_i$ and $z_i(x^2) < \bar{z}_i$ holds the DM prefers that alternative which induces a smaller underachievement of the goal $\bar{z}_i$. Then this preference pattern with respect to the i-th dimension of valuation can be represented by R_i: The DM rates $z_i(x^1)$ at least as high as $z_i(x^2)$ if and only if

$$\min\ \{z_i(x^1),\ \bar{z}_i\} \geqq \min\ \{z_i(x^2),\ \bar{z}_i\} \qquad (x^1, x^2 \in X) \text{ i.e.}$$

$$z_i(x^1)\ R_i z_i(x^2) \leftrightarrow \min\{z_i(x^1),\ \bar{z}_i\} \geqq \min\{z_i(x^2),\ \bar{z}_i\}\quad x^1,x^2 \in X.$$

Is the DM in a position to specify the objective functions which are relevant with respect to his valuation system and the associated preference relations, then on the basis of this partial information on the DM's valuation system a subset of efficient alternatives an be separated from the set of alternatives. In this context an alternative $x^* \in X$ is called efficient with respect to X, the K objective functions $z_k(x)$ and the respective preference relations R_k if and only if there is no $x' \in X$ such that

$$z_k(x')\ R_k z_k(x^*) \qquad (k = 1, \ldots, K)$$

and

$$z_k(x')\ P_k z_k(x^*) \qquad \text{for at least one } k \in (1, \ldots, K)$$

holds.

Example 1

In order to illustrate the efficiency concept let us consider a finite set of six alternatives and three objective functions.

Alternative	$z_1(x)$	$z_2(x)$	$z_3(x)$
x^1	30	15	1
x^2	20	45	3
x^3	10	10	4
x^4	15	30	3
x^5	25	15	1
x^6	20	40	2

If the DM prefers with respect to each $z_k(x)$ (k=1, 2, 3) higher values to lower values then the alternatives x^1, x^2 and x^3 are efficient with respect to X, $z_k(x)$ and the here assumed preference relations R_k (k = 1,2,3).

Now, let the assumed preference relations R'_k (k = 1, 2, 3) be such that for each $z_k(x)$ lower values are preferred to higher values. Then the alternatives x^3, x^4, x^5 and x^6 are efficient with respect to X, $z_k(x)$ and the preference relations R'_k.

If a DM specifies for each $z_k(x)$ a target value which is to be attained from below, say $\bar{z}_1 = 40$, $\bar{z}_2 = 40$ and $\bar{z}_3 = 2$, then the alternatives

x^1, x^2 and x^6 are efficient with respect to X, $z_k(x)$ and the here assumed preference relations R_k^* (k = 1, 2, 3).

The efficiency property of an alternative is a relative property: Another composition of the set of alternatives or the pursued objective functions or an alteration of at least one preference relation R_k may entail that an efficient alternative becomes nonefficient and vice versa. Let us call an alternative $\hat{x}$ compromise alternative, if the DM does not prefer any z(x) ($x \in X$) to $z(\hat{x})$. As a compromise alternative has to be an efficient alternative - otherwise the partial information about the DM's valuation system on which the efficiency concept is based is not correct - the efficient alternatives are the nominees for the compromise alternative.

1.2 The linear multiple objective program

In the sequel we shall be concerned with multiple objective decision models which can be represented in the form of a multiple objective linear programming problem. The K scalar-valued objective functions $z_k(x)$ are linear, $z_k(x) = c_k x$, and the set X of feasible alternatives is described by a system of linear inequalities,

$$X = (x \in \mathbb{R}^N \mid Ax \leqq b,\ x \geqq 0) \ .$$

For each of the K considered objective functions $z_k(x)$, (k = 1, ...,K), $z_k(x^1)\ R_k z_k(x^2)$ holds if and only if $z_k(x^1) \geqq z_k(x^2)$ holds, which implies that the DM wants to maximise each of the considered K objective functions. Then the underlying multiple objective linear programming problem is as follows:

$$\text{"max"} \left\{ \begin{array}{ll|l} z_1(x) = & c_1 x & \\ \vdots & \vdots & x \in X \\ z_K(x) = & c_K x & \end{array} \right\}$$

Alternatively, the problem can be formulated in a more compact mode:

$$\text{"max"} \ (z(x) = Cx \mid x \in X)$$

where $z(x) = (z_1(x), \ldots, z_K(x))^T$, C is the KxN criterion matrix whose rows are formed by the 1xN vectors c_k (k = 1, ..., K), and "max" is the notation for finding all efficient solutions (in a maximising sense).

Example 2

Consider the linear multiple objective program

$$\text{"max"} \begin{pmatrix} z_1(x) \\ z_2(x) \end{pmatrix} = \begin{pmatrix} 1 & 2 \\ 4 & 1 \end{pmatrix} \begin{pmatrix} x_1 \\ x_2 \end{pmatrix}$$

$$\begin{aligned} \text{s.t.} \quad x_1 + 3\,x_2 &\leqq 42 \\ x_1 + x_2 &\leqq 20 \\ 2\,x_1 + x_2 &\leqq 30 \\ x_1 + \quad &\geqq 3 \\ x_2 &\geqq 2 \end{aligned}$$

The set X of this linear multiple objective program is a polyhedron with five extreme points $x^1, \ldots, x^5$ (cf. Figure 1).

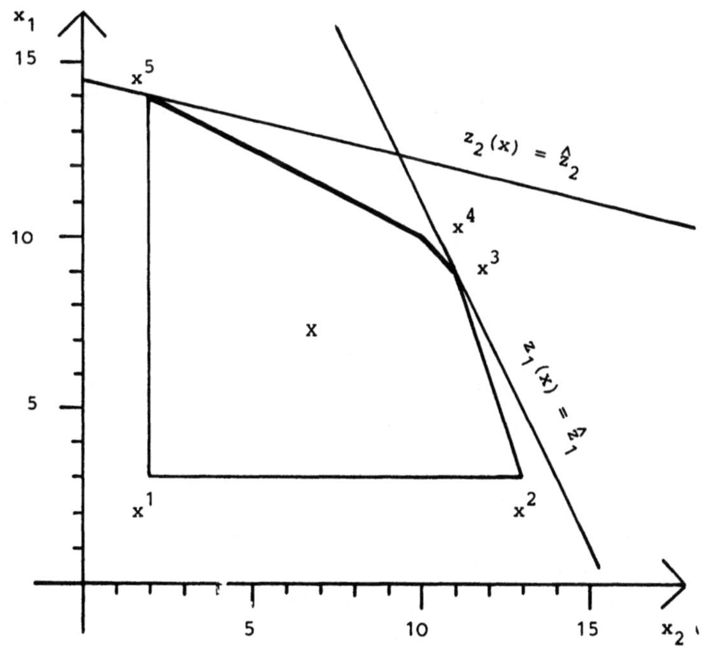

Figure 1. The set of alternatives X (Decision Space)

The heavy boundary of X denotes the set of efficient solutions X_E. All other solutions in X are inferior to those in X_E.

Observe that $z(x) = (z_1(x), \ldots, z_K(x))^T$ maps the N-dimensional set X into its K-dimensional image $z(X) = Z$. It is often useful to explain some concepts in terms of the value space Z rather than the decision space X.

If we compute for each $x \in X$ the respective values of the two objective functions $z_1(x)$ and $z_2(x)$ we obtain the polyhedron $Z = (z(x) \mid x \in X)$ depicted in Figure 2.

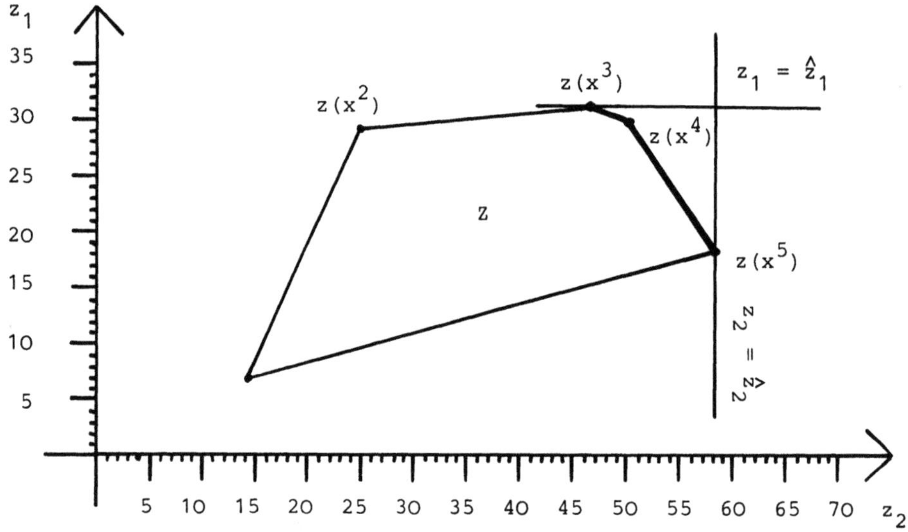

Figure 2. Mapping of X from Fig. 1 into the value space Z

In the course of an actual decision process the DM needs information. As a first information we may offer him the maximal and minimal value of each scalar-valued objective function $z_k(x)$ $(k = 1, \ldots, K)$ over the efficient set X_E.

In Figure 1 observe that z_1 is maximised at point $x^3 = (9, 11)^T$, achieving value $z_1(x^3) = 31$; objective function $z_2(x)$ reaches its maximum at point $x^5 = (14, 2)^T$, and the value $z_2(x^5) = 58$. From the (individually) maximal values of $z_1(x)$ and $z_2(x)$ over X we can form the vector $\hat{z} = (31, 58)^T$ which is called the <u>ideal point</u>. If there exists some $\hat{x} \in X$ with $z(\hat{x}) = \hat{z}$ then the underlying multiple objective linear programming problem has a <u>perfect solution</u> at which all scalar-valued objective functions $z_k(x)$ are maximised simultaneously.

In our example $z_1(x)$ achieves its minimal value over X_E at x^5 with $z_1(x^5) = 18$, and $z_2(x)$ achieves its minimal value over X_E at x^3 with $z_2(x^3) = 47$. Recall that at x^3 the maximal value of $z_1(x)$ and at x_5 the maximal value of $z_2(x)$ is obtained. If the linear multiple objective program comprises more than two scalar-valued objective functions, then a special solution method (see Isermann and Steuer 1984) had to be applied in order to determine the minimum values of the scalar-valued objective functions over the efficient set X_E.

In our example $z_1(x)$ ranges over X_E from 18 to 31 and $z_2(x)$ ranges over X_E from 47 to 58.

1.3 Decision-oriented information in multiple objective programming - a survey

The primary function of an analyst is to support the DM in his decision process. As there are many ways to select a compromise solution from the set of efficient solutions, the kind of information required by the DM varies with the kind of decision process adopted in order to determine a compromise solution.

A first step may be to determine the set of efficient solutions X_E or some subset of X_E, e.g. the set of efficient basic solutions for a linear multiple objective program. In some decision problems the DM may be able to select from X_E or from a subset of X_E a compromise solution. We shall briefly outline in Section 2 an algorithm by which the set X_E can be generated. Moreover, by applying subroutines of the algorithm local information about the interrelations of the objective functions can be provided.

In many situations, the determination of X_E does not prove to be an adequate way of supporting the DM in his decision process. However, in order to discriminate among the efficient alternatives, additional information about the DM's valuation system is necessary. If the DM is able and willing to specify his valuation system in such a way that it can be represented by a compromise objective function, then a compromise model may be applied to determine a compromise alternative. Some of these compromise models will be presented in Section 3.

An approach which seems to be adequate for most decision situations is offered by the interactive procedures. Typical of the interactive procedures is the dialogue between the DM and a computer (analyst). In the course of this dialogue information is exchanged: The DM provides some relevant information about his valuation system. The computer (analyst) processes this information and generates on the basis of the available information about the DM's valuation system at least one efficient solution, which is presented to the DM. If the DM accepts a presented solution as a compromise solution, the dialogue terminates. Otherwise the DM is asked to provide additional information about his valuation system in order to continue the search for a compromise solution.

2 OUTLINE OF A SOLUTION METHOD FOR THE LINEAR MULTIPLE OBJECTIVE PROGRAM

2.1 A solution method for the linear multiple objective program with K = 2

In order to determine all efficient solutions for a linear multiple objective program with two scalar-valued objective functions the following parametric program may be solved:

Let λ^0 be the minimum value of $z_2(x)$ over the efficient set, then all optimal solutions for the parametric linear program

$$\begin{aligned} \text{s.t.} \quad & \max z_1(x) \\ & Ax \leqq b \\ & x \geqq 0 \\ & z_2(x) \geqq \lambda \qquad \text{with } \lambda^0 \leqq \lambda < +\infty \end{aligned}$$

are efficient solutions for the respective linear multiple objective program. We shall illustrate this solution method for the linear multiple objective program of Example 2.

Example 3

We have to solve the following linear parametric program

$$\max z_1(x) = x_1 + 2x_2$$

s.t.

$$\begin{aligned} x_1 + 3x_2 &\leqq 42 \\ x_1 + x_2 &\leqq 20 \\ 2x_1 + x_2 &\leqq 30 \\ x_1 &\geqq 3 \\ x_2 &\geqq 2 \\ 4x_1 + x_2 &\geqq \lambda \qquad \text{with } 47 \leqq \lambda < +\infty \end{aligned}$$

This linear parametric program has three optimal basic solutions which can be depicted from the following simplex tableaux.

ρ	x_1	x_2	x_3	x_4	x_5	x_6	x_7	x_8	$x_B(\lambda)$	
7			1/2	-1/2			1		9	
6			-1/2	3/2		1			6	
5			1/2	-5/2	1				1	$\lambda = 47$
1	1		-1/2	3/2					9	
2		1	1/2	-1/2					11	
8			-3/2	11/2				1	$47 - \lambda$	
Δz_ℓ			1/2	1/2					31	
7				4/3			1	1/3	$74/3 - r/3$	
6				-1/3		1		-1/3	$-29/3 + r/3$	
5				-2/3	1			1/3	$50/3 - r/3$	$47 \leqq \lambda \leqq 50$
1	1			-1/3				-1/3	$-20/3 + r/3$	
2		1		4/3				1/3	$80/3 - r/3$	
3			1	-11/3				-2/3	$-94/3 + 2r/3$	
Δz_ℓ				7/3				1/3	$140/3 - \lambda/3$	
7					2		1	1	$58 - \lambda$	
6					-1/2	1		-1/2	$-18 + r/2$	$50 \leqq \lambda \leqq 58$
4				1	-3/2			-1/2	$-25 + r/2$	
1	1				-1/2			-1/2	$-15 + r/2$	
2		1			2			1	$60 - \lambda$	
3			1		-11/2			-5/2	$-123 + 5r/2$	
Δz_ℓ					7/2			3/2	$105 - 3r/2$	

A graphical display of the values of the two objective functions over the efficient set may be a way to impart the information about the interrelations of the objective functions to the DM (cf. Figure 3).

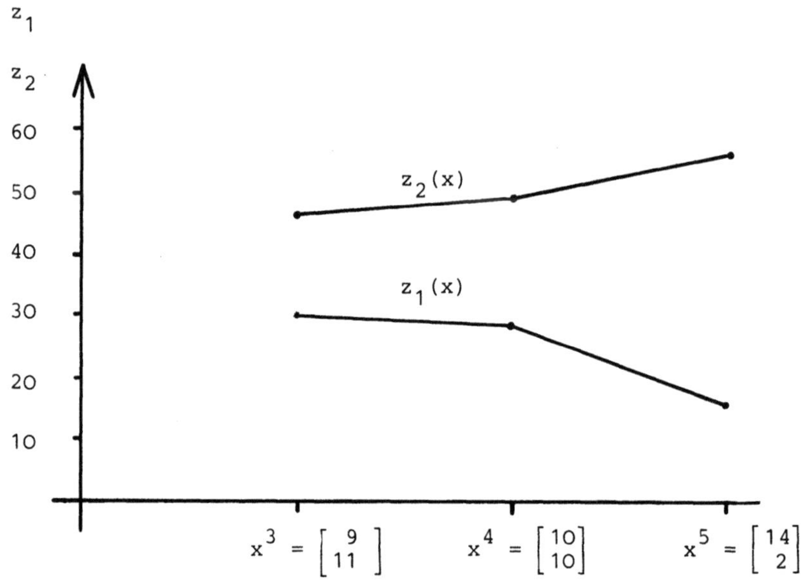

Figure 3. Values of the objective functions over the efficient set

2.2 Outline of a solution method for the linear multiple objective program with K > 2

Several solution methods for linear multiple objective programs with more than two scalar-valued objective functions also apply an adopted parametric programming routine. Consider the linear K-parametric program

$$\begin{aligned} & \max\ t^T C x \\ \text{s.t.}\quad & Ax \leqq b \\ & x \geqq 0 \end{aligned}$$

with $t \in \Lambda$ and $\Lambda = (t \in \mathbb{R}^K \mid t > 0,\ \sum_{k=1}^{K} t_k = 1)$.

The following efficiency theorem for the linear multiple objective program holds (see e.g. Isermann 1974): If $\hat{x}$ is an optimal solution for the K-parametric program for some $\hat{t} \in \Lambda$ then $\hat{x}$ is an efficient solution for the respective linear multiple objective program. If x^* is an efficient solution for a linear multiple objective program, then there exists a $t^* \in \Lambda$ such that x^* is an optimal solution for the respective linear K-parametric program with $t = t^*$.

If X is bounded an initial efficient basic solution for the linear multiple objective program can be determined if we solve the respective K-parametric program for some $t^1 \in \Lambda$. Let us denote the initial efficient basic solution by x^1. Before continuing with the solution procedure let us first introduce the adjacency property of efficient basic solutions. Let x^i and x^j be efficient basic solutions for a linear multiple objective objective program, then x^i and x^j are said to be adjacent, if (i) and (ii) hold:

(i) x^i and x^j have m-1 basic variables in common
(ii) each x^0 which can be represented as a convex combination of x^i and x^j is efficient.

Let J be the index set of all efficient basic solutions. The set of all x^j $(j \in J)$ and the existing adjacency relations among the efficient basic solutions can be represented by the solution graph $G = (E, L)$. G is an undirected graph with
$E = (x^j \mid j \in J)$ being the set of nodes and
$L = ((x^i, x^j) \mid x^i, x^j \in E,\ x^i \text{ and } x^j \text{ are adjacent})$
being the set of edges of G. The solution graph of a linear multiple objective program is finite and connected. Thus in order to determine all efficient basic solutions we merely need a procedure to identify all efficient basic solutions which are adjacent to an efficient basic solution x^j.

Let ρ_j be the index set of the basic variables of x^j. The multiple objective simplex tableau has the following form:

ρ_j	x_1	x_2	$\cdots$	x_n	
j_1	y_{11}	y_{12}	$\cdots$	y_{1n}	y_1
$\vdots$	$\vdots$	$\vdots$		$\vdots$	$\vdots$
j_i	y_{i1}	y_{i2}	$\cdots$	y_{in}	y_i
$\vdots$	$\vdots$	$\vdots$		$\vdots$	$\vdots$
j_m	y_{m1}	y_{m2}	$\cdots$	y_{mn}	y_m
	Δz_1^1	Δz_2^1	$\cdots$	Δz_n^1	$z_1(x^j)$
	$\vdots$	$\vdots$		$\vdots$	$\vdots$
	Δz_1^k	Δz_2^k	$\cdots$	Δz_n^k	$z_k(x^j)$
	$\vdots$	$\vdots$		$\vdots$	$\vdots$
	Δz_1^K	Δz_2^K	$\cdots$	Δz_n^K	$z_K(x^j)$
	$\sum_{k=1}^{K} t_k^j \Delta z_1^k$	$\sum_{k=1}^{K} t_k^j \Delta z_2^k$		$\sum_{k=1}^{K} t_k^j \Delta z_n^k$	

Instead of presenting the formal set-up of the further solution procedure we shall provide the necessary details of the algorithm by means of an example.

<u>Example 4</u>

In order to illustrate the solution procedure we consider the following multiple objective linear program :

$$\text{"max"} \quad z(x) = \begin{pmatrix} z_1(x) \\ z_2(x) \\ z_3(x) \end{pmatrix} = \begin{pmatrix} 2x_1 & & - x_3 \\ -x_1 & + 3x_2 & - x_3 \\ -2x_1 & - x_2 & + 4x_3 \end{pmatrix}$$

s.t.

$$\begin{aligned} x_1 + x_2 + x_3 &\leqq 3 \\ 2x_1 + x_2 + 2x_3 &\leqq 4 \\ x_1 - x_2 &\leqq 4 \\ x_1, x_2, x_3 &\geqq 0 \end{aligned}$$

The corresponding K-parametric linear program reads

$$\max z(x,t) = t_1(2x_1 - x_3) + t_2(-x_1 + 3x_2 - x_3) + t_3(-2x_1 - x_2 + 4x_3)$$

s.t.

$$\begin{aligned} x_1 + x_2 + x_3 &\leqq 3 \\ 2x_1 + x_2 + 2x_3 &\leqq 4 \\ x_1 - x_2 &\leqq 4 \\ x_1, x_2, x_3 &\geqq 0 \end{aligned}$$

with $t_1, t_2, t_3 > 0$ and $t_1 + t_2 + t_3 = 1$.

We determine an initial efficient basic solution x^1 by solving the above parametric linear program with $t^1 = (6/11, 2/11, 3/11)$. $(x^1 = (1, 2, 0, 0, 0, 5)^T$ with $z(x^1) = (2, 5, -4)^T$ is the initial efficient basic solution. The respective multiple objective simplex tableau reads

ρ_1	x_1	x_2	x_3	x_4	x_5	x_6		
2	0	1	0	2	-1	0	2	
1	1	0	1	-1	1	0	1	
6	0	0	-1	3	-2	1	5	
	0	0	3	-2	2	0	2	
	0	0	0	7	-4	0	5	
	0	0	-6	0	-1	0	-4	
$\Delta z_\ell(t^1)$	0	0	0	2/11	1/11	0		$t^1 = ({}^6/11, {}^2/11, {}^3/11)$
$\Delta z_\ell(t')$	0	0	0	0	5/25	0		$t' = ({}^{14}/25, {}^4/25, {}^7/25)$
$\Delta z_\ell(t'')$	0	0	0	5/15	0	0		$t'' = ({}^8/15, {}^3/15, {}^4/15)$

Recall that for $t = t^1$ x^1 is not a unique optimal solution for the above parametric linear program. We obtain by pivoting in the third column ($y_{23} = 1$ is pivot element) the basic solution $x^2 = (0,2,1,0,0,6)^T$ with $z(x^2) = (-1, 5, 2)^T$. x^2 as well as x^1 are optimal for the parametric linear program for $t = t^1$. Thus x^1 and x^2 are adjacent.

In order to check if by pivoting in the fourth column of our current multiple objective simplex tableau an efficient basic solution can be determined which is adjacent to x^1 we have to answer the question if for some $t \in \Lambda$ x^1 as well as the feasible basic solution obtained by pivoting in the fourth column are optimal solutions for the above parametric linear program. In order to answer the latter question we try to solve the linear system (cf. Isermann (1977) for more details).

$$
\begin{array}{rrrll}
-2t_1 & +\ 7t_2 & & = 0 & (\ell' = 4) \\
3t_1 & & -\ 6t_3 & \geqq 0 & (\ell = 3) \\
2t_1 & -\ 4t_2 & -\ t_3 & \geqq 0 & (\ell = 5) \\
t_1 & +\ t_2 & +\ t_3 & = 1 & \\
 & & t_k & > 0 & (k = 1,2,3).
\end{array}
$$

which is formed by the reduced cost coefficient of our current multiple objective simplex tableau.

$t' = (14/25,\ 4/25,\ 7/25)$ is a solution for this system. Hence by pivoting in the fourth column ($y_{14} = 2$ is pivot element) we obtain the basic solution $x^2 = (2,0,0,1,0,2)^T$ with $z(x^3) = (4, -2, 4)^T$, x^3 as well as x^1 are optimal for the parametric linear program for $t = t'$. Hence x^1 and x^3 are adjacent efficient basic solutions.

From our current multiple objective simplex tableau we can extract an additional information: For $t = t'$ not only x^1, x^2 and x^3 but all convex combinations of x^1, x^2, x^3 are optimal solutions for our parametric linear program and thus efficient solutions for our multiple objective linear program.

In order to check if by pivoting in the fifth column of our current multiple objective simplex tableau an efficient basic solution can be determined which is adjacent to x^1 we try to solve the linear system

$$\begin{aligned}
2t_1 - 4t_2 - \ \ t_3 &= 0 \quad (\ell' = 5)\\
3t_1 \qquad\quad - 6t_3 &\geqq 0 \quad (\ell = 3)\\
-2t_1 + 7t_2 \qquad\quad &\geqq 0 \quad (\ell = 4)\\
t_1 + \ \ t_2 + \ \ t_3 &= 1\\
t_k &> 0 \quad (k = 1,2,3)
\end{aligned}$$

which is formed by the reduced cost coefficients of our current multiple objective simplex tableau.
$t'' = (8/15,\ 3/15,\ 4/15)$ is a solution for this system. By pivoting in the fifth column ($y_{25} = 1$ is pivot element) we obtain the efficient basic solution $x^4 = (0,3,0,0,1,7)^T$ with $z(x^4) = (0,\ 9,\ -3)^T$. x^4 is adjacent to x^1. Moreover, we learn from our current multiple objective simplex tableau that all convex combinations of x^1, x^2 and x^4 are efficient solutions for our multiple objective linear program.

One further efficient basic solution can be determined: If we depart e.g. from the multiple objective simplex tableau corresponding to x^2 $x^5 = (0,0,2,1,0,4)^T$ with $z(x^5) = (-2,\ -2,\ 8)^T$ is obtained. Figure 4 contains the solution graph of the multiple objective linear program of Example 4.

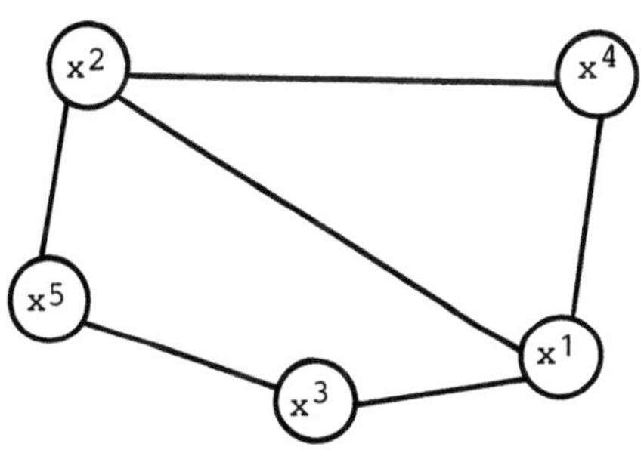

Figure 4. Solution graph of the multiple objective linear program of Example 4

The efficient set of this multiple objective linear program is

$$X^E = X_E^1 \cup X_E^2 \text{ with}$$

$$X_E^1 = \{x \mid x = \lambda_1 x^1 + \lambda_2 x^2 + \lambda_3 x^3 + \lambda_5 x^5 ;$$
$$\lambda_1, \lambda_2, \lambda_3, \lambda_5 \geqq 0,\ \lambda_1 + \lambda_2 + \lambda_3 + \lambda_5 = 1\} .$$

$$X_E^2 = \{x \mid x = \lambda_1 x^1 + \lambda_2 x^2 + \lambda_4 x^4 ;$$
$$\lambda_1, \lambda_2, \lambda_4 \geqq 0, \lambda_1 + \lambda_2 + \lambda_4 = 1\}$$

Note, that e.g. each $x = \lambda_3 x^3 + \lambda_4 x^4$ with $\lambda_3, \lambda_4 > 0$ and $\lambda_3 + \lambda_4 = 1$ is not an efficient solution. A comprehensive presentation of the illustrated solution procedure is found in Isermann (1977). Other solution procedures are discussed in Steuer (1985).

In a decision process the DM may be interested in adjacent efficient basic solutions and the adapted values of the objective functions in order to evaluate them in comparison with the efficient solution at hand. The multiple objective simplex tableau offers comprehensive information about the value-implications if one wants to move away from the current efficient basic solution. In order to illustrate this point we shall consider the multiple objective simplex tableau with the efficient basic solution x^1. We already know that by pivoting in the third, fourth or fifth column of this tableau efficient basic solutions can be determined which are adjacent to x^1. Therefore, we shall call the nonbasic variables x_3, x_4 and x_5 efficient variables. If we raise e.g. x_5 to some positive level ε the current values of the objective functions could change in the following way: the current value of z_1 would decrease by 2ε; the current values of z_2 and z_3 would increase by 4ε and 1ε , respectively. The vector $\bar{c}^5 = (-2, 4, 1)^T$ which is composed of the reduced cost coefficients of the fifth column multiplied by -1 will be called the tradeoff-vector of the nonbasic variable x_5. As x_5 is an efficient variable $\bar{c}^5$ is an efficient tradeoff-vector. $\bar{c}^5$ specifies the rates of exchange among the considered three objective functions and thus offers a direction of movement in the decision space which leads from the current value $z(x^1)$ to a set of values of $z(x)$ to which efficient solutions can be associated. Thus if e.g. the DM is not satisfied with the objective function values of the current efficient solution x^1, the efficient tradeoff-vector $\bar{c}^3 = (-3, 0, 6)^T$, $\bar{c}^4 = (2, -7, 0)^T$ and $\bar{c}^5 = (-2, 4, 1)^T$ offer a direction of movement in the decision space from which the DM may select a direction which is of interest to him. A full discussion of the information potential of efficient tradeoff-vectors is e.g. found in Isermann (1977a, p. 256).

3 DETERMINING COMPROMISE SOLUTIONS BY MEANS OF COMPROMISE MODELS

If the DM is able and willing to specify his valuation system in such a way that the valuation system can be represented by a compromise model then - under these assumptions - the optimal solution for the compromise model is the compromise solution to which no other feasible solution is preferred by the DM.

However, compromise models may also be effectively utilised in the course of an interactive decision process. Here the compromise model may be considered a tool which generates on the basis of partial information about the DM's valuation system candidates for the compromise solution which the DM may reject or accept in the course of the decision process.

3.1 Compromise models with a scalar-valued preference function

In these models it is assumed that the DM's valuation system can be represented by a scalar-valued preference function ϕ which is to be maximised. By means of the mapping $\phi: Z \rightarrow \mathbb{R}$ to each $z(x) \in Z$ a real-valued scalar $\phi(z(x)) \in \mathbb{R}$ is associated such that the natural order of the real numbers $(z(x))$ represents the DM's ordering of the objective functions' values $z(x)$, i.e. for any two $z(x'), z(x'') \in Z$ we have:

$z(x'')$ is not preferred to $z(x')$	$\leftrightarrow$	$\phi(z(x')) \geqq \phi(z(x''))$
$z(x')$ is preferred to $z(x'')$	$\leftrightarrow$	$\phi(z(x')) > \phi(z(x''))$
DM is indifferent between $z(x')$ and $z(x'')$	$\leftrightarrow$	$\phi(z(x')) = \phi(z(x''))$.

If the preference function $\phi(z(x))$ is known, except for the maximisation of $\phi(z(x))$, the decision problem is solved. The compromise solution is an optimal solution for the compromise model

$$\max\ (\phi(z(x)) \mid x \in X)\ .$$

A sufficient condition that <u>each</u> optimal solution for this compromise model is an efficient solution for the respective multiple objective program is the following: $\phi(z(x)$ is with respect to $z \in Z$ a monotonously <u>increasing</u> function (cf. e.g. Kosmol 1973).
The function

$$\psi(z(x)) = t_1 z_1(x) + t_2 z_2(x) + t_3 z_3(x)$$

is monotonously increasing with respect to $z \in \mathbb{R}^3$ as long as $t_1, t_2, t_3 > 0$. If e.g. $t_1 = 0$ and $t_2, t_3 \geqq 0$, $\psi(z(x))$ is a monotonously <u>nondecreasing</u> preference function. If the preference function is monotonously nondecreasing at least one optimal solution for the above compromise model is an efficient solution for the respective multiple objective program.

A preference function of the form $\phi(z(x)) = \sum_{k=1}^{K} t_k z_k(x)$ where $t_k > 0$ is the weight associated with the k-th objective function is rather common but involves several implications the DM might not be aware of. A comprehensive discussion of the underlying assumptions of an additive preference function is e.g. found in von Winterfeldt and Fischer (1975). In order to illustrate the compensating effect of this preference function consider the preference function $\psi(z(x)) = 3z_1(x) + 2z_2(x)$ and the following alternatives with their objective function values.

	$z_1(x)$	$z_2(x)$	$\psi(z(x))$
x^1	2000	3000	12000
x^2	-1000	7500	12000
x^3	4000	0	12000
x^4	- 999	7500	12003
x^5	4000	1	12002

The assumed preference function implies that starting with $z(x^1) = (2000, 3000)^T$ the DM is indifferent

(i) with respect to any decrease of the value of the first objective function as long as the value of the second objective function is increased according to the proportion 3:2.

(ii) with respect to any increase of the value of the first objective function as long as the value of the second objective function is decreased according to the proportion 3:2.

Let $X = (x^1, x^2, x^3, x^4, x^5)$ be the set of alternatives. The here assumed preference function implies that x^4 with $z(x^4) = (-999, 7500)^T$ is the compromise solution. If for some reason x^4 has to be eliminated from X then - according to the compromise model - x^5 with $z(x^5) = (4000, 1)^T$ is the compromise solution.

With respect to finite sets of alternatives a preference function on the basis of positive weights leads to a further implication: There are efficient solutions which are never selected as compromise solutions. In order to illustrate this point, we consider a set of three efficient alternatives:

	$z_1(x)$	$z_2(x)$
x^1	11	3
x^2	6	7
x^4	2	11

Let the DM prefer $z(x^2)$ to $z(x^1)$ as well as $z(x^3)$. If we want to determine weights t_1 and t_2 which reflect this ordering, we do not succeed: From $z(x^2)$ is preferred to $z(z^1)$ follows:

$$6t_1 + 7t_2 > 11t_1 + 3t_2 \Rightarrow -5t_1 + 4t_2 > 0 .$$

From $z(x^2)$ is preferred to $z(x^3)$ follows

$$6t_1 + 7t_2 > 2t_1 + 11t_2 \Rightarrow 4t_1 - 4t_2 > 0 .$$

However, $-5t_1 + 4t_2 > 0$ and $4t_1 - 4t_2 > 0$ imply $4t_1 > 5t_1$ and thus a contradiction to $t_k > 0$ $(k = 1, 2)$. Thus there are no positive weights such that x^2 will be selected as a compromise alternative.

3.2 Compromise models with specified target values for the objective functions

The basis of these compromise models is a vector of target values $\bar{z} = (\bar{z}_1, \ldots, \bar{z}_k)^T$ and a dispreference function φ which is to be minimised. It is assumed that the DM evaluates each alternative x according to the deviation of z(x) from $\bar{z}$. Let

$$w(x) = \bar{z} - z(x) .$$

By means of the mapping φ: $w(X) \to \mathbb{R}$ to each $w(x) \in w(X)$ a real-valued scalar $\varphi(w(x)) \in \mathbb{R}$ is associated that the natural order of the real numbers $\varphi(w(x))$ represents the DM's ordering of the deviations of z(x) from $\bar{z}$, i.e.

for any two $w(x'), w(x'') \in w(X)$ we have:

$w(x'')$ is not preferred to $w(x')$	$\leftrightarrow$	$\varphi(w(x')) \leqq \varphi(w(x''))$
$w(x')$ is preferred to $w(x'')$	$\leftrightarrow$	$\varphi(w(x')) < \varphi(w(x''))$
DM is indifferent between $w(x')$ and $w(x'')$	$\leftrightarrow$	$\varphi(w(x')) = \varphi(w(x''))$.

If $\bar{z}$ and the dispreference function $\varphi(w(x)$ are known, except for the minimisation of $\varphi(w(x))$ the decision problem is solved. The compromise solution is an optimal solution for the compromise model

$$\min(\varphi(w(x)) \mid x \in X,\ z(x) + w(x) = \bar{z})$$

In many situations the ideal point $\hat{z}$ is selected as vector of target values for the above compromise model. Under this condition and the additional assumption that $\varphi(w(x))$ is with respect to $w(x) \in w(X)$ a monotonously <u>increasing</u> function, each optimal solution for the above compromise model is an efficient solution for the respective multiple objective program.

The dispreference function $\varphi(w(x)$ is often established by weighting the underachievement of the target values. Such a compromise model is illustrated in the following.

Example 5

We consider the multiple objective linear program of Example 4. The ideal point for this problem is $\hat{z} = (4, 9, 8)^T$. Let w_k measure the underachievement of the k-th objective function with respect to $\hat{z}_k$ (k = 1, 2, 3) and the weights specified by the DM: $t_1 = 5$, $t_2 = 0.5$ and $t_3 = 3$. Then the compromise model has the following form:

$$\begin{array}{llr}
\min & \varphi = 5w_1 + 0.5w_2 + 3w_3 & \\
\text{s.t.} & x_1 + x_2 + x_3 & \leqq 3 \\
& 2x_1 + x_2 + 2x_3 & \leqq 4 \\
& x_1 - x_2 & \leqq 4 \\
& 2x_1 - x_3 - w_1 & = 4 \\
& -x_1 + 3x_2 - x_3 - w_2 & = 9 \\
& -2x_1 - x_2 + 4x_3 - w_3 & = 8 \\
& x_1, x_2, x_3, w_1, w_2, w_3 & \geqq 0
\end{array}$$

The optimal solution for this compromise model is the efficient basic solution $\hat{x} = x^5 = (0,0,2,1,0,4)^T$ with $z(\hat{x}) = z(x^5) = (-2, -2, 8)^T$ and $\hat{w} = (6, 11, 0)^T$.

Instead of minimising the weighted sum of deviations the DM might be interested in minimising the maximal deviation from $\hat{z}_k$ $(k = 1, \ldots, K)$. This compromise model has the form

$$\min\{\max\{w_k \mid z_k(x) + w_k = \hat{z}_k \quad (k=1, \ldots, K)\} \mid x \in X\} .$$

We introduce the nonnegative variable v such that

$$v \geqq \hat{z}_k - z_k(x) \quad \text{for all } x \in X \ (k=1, \ldots, K).$$

Then each optimal solution for the above compromise model is also optimal for

$$\min \varphi' = v$$

s.t.

$$z_k(x) + v \geqq \hat{z}_k \qquad (k = 1, \ldots, K)$$

$$x \in X$$

Note that the dispreference function $\varphi' = v$ is not monotonously increasing with respect to $w(x)$. In order to make sure that each optimal solution is also an efficient solution, we minimise instead of φ'

$$\varphi = v - \varepsilon \sum_{k=1}^{K} z_k(x)$$

with ε being a very small but positive scalar.

Example 6

We shall consider the multiple objective linear program

$$\text{"max" } z(x) = \begin{pmatrix} x_1 \\ 0.5x_1 + 0.5x_2 \\ 3x_2 \end{pmatrix}$$

s.t. $x_1 + x_2 \leqq 10$

$x_1, x_2 \geqq 0.$

The ideal point for this problem is $\hat{z} = (10, 5, 30)^T$.

If we want to minimise the maximal deviation from $\hat{z}_k$ $(k = 1, 2, 3)$ we have to solve the linear program

$$\begin{array}{lrcl} & \min & = & v - 10^{-10}\,(1.5x_1 + 3.5x_2) \\ \text{s.t.} & x_1 + x_2 & \leqq & 10 \\ & x_1 + v & \geqq & 10 \\ & 0.5x_1 + 0.5x_2 + v & \geqq & 5 \\ & 3x_2 + v & \geqq & 30 \\ & x_1, x_2, v & \geqq & 0\,. \end{array}$$

The optimal solution for this compromise model is

$$\tilde{x} = (2.5,\ 7.5)^T \text{ and } \tilde{v} = 7.5$$

Thus the minimised maximal underachievement of the target value is 7.5. From $z(\tilde{x}) = (2.5,\ 5,\ 22.5)^T$ we learn that with respect to the first and third objective functions, the underachievement of the target value is 7.5. With respect to the second objective function, the target value $\hat{z}_2 = 10$ is reached by $\tilde{x}$.

Note that in Example 5 we have $z_1(\tilde{x}) = 0.25\hat{z}_1$, $z_2(\tilde{x}) = \hat{z}_2$ and $z_3(\tilde{x}) = 0.75\hat{z}_3$. If we want to minimise the <u>relatively</u> minimal underachievement of the target values, we normalise each constraint in the form

$$z_k(x) + v \geqq \hat{z}_k \qquad (k = 1, \ldots, K)$$

to

$$z_k(x)/\hat{z}_k + v \geqq 1 \qquad (k = 1, \ldots, K)$$

<u>Example 7</u>

We shall consider the multiple objective linear program of Example 6. The compromise model which minimises the relatively maximal underachievement of the target values is:

$$\min \varphi = v - 10^{-10} (1.5x_1 + 3.5x_2)$$

s.t.

$$\begin{aligned} x_1 + \quad x_2 \quad &\leq 10 \\ 0.1x_1 \quad + v &\geq 1 \\ 0.1x_1 + 0.1x_2 + v &\geq 1 \\ 0.1x_2 + v &\geq 1 \\ x_1, x_2, v &\geq 0 . \end{aligned}$$

The optimal solution for this compromise model is $x^* = (5, 5)^T$ and $v^* = 0.5$. From $z(x^*) = (5, 5, 15)^T$ we learn: $z_1(x^*) = 0.5\hat{z}_1$, $z_2(x^*) = \hat{z}_2$ and $z_3(x^*) = 0.5\hat{z}_3$.

REFERENCES

Becker, S. and Green, D. Jr., 'Budgeting and employee behaviour', The Journal of Business, 35, 1962, pp. 392-402.

Becker, S. and Siegel, S., 'Utility of grades: level of aspiration in a decision theory context', Journal of Experimental Psychology, 55, 1958, pp. 81-85.

Chapman D.W. and Volkmann, J., 'A social determinant of the level of aspiration', Journal of Abnormal Psychology, 34, 1939, pp. 225-238.

Isermann, H., 'Proper efficiency and the linear vector maximum problem', Operations Research, 22, 1974, pp. 189-191.

Isermann, H., 'The enumeration of the set of all efficient solutions for a multiple objective linear program', Operations Research Quarterly, 28, 1977, pp. 711-725.

Isermann, H., 'The relevance of duality in multiple objective linear programming', TIMS Studies in the Management Sciences, 6, 1977a, pp. 241-262.

Isermann, H. and Steuer, R., Payoff Tables and Minimum Criterion Values Over the Efficient Set, Coll. Bus. Admin., University of Georgia, Athens, 1984.

Kosmol, P., 'Zur vektorwertigen Optimierung', Operations Research-Verfahren XV, 1973, pp. 77-84.

McGregor, D., 'An uneasy look at performance appraisal', Harvard Business Review, 35, 1957, no. 3.

Simon, H.A., Models of Man, Wiley, New York, 1967.

Stedry, A., 'Aspiration levels, attitudes and performance in a goal-oriented situation', Industrial Management Review, 3. no. 2, 1962.

Steuer, R., Multiple Criteria Optimization, Wiley, New York, 1985.

Winterfeldt, D. von and Fischer, G.W., ' Multi-attribute utility theory: models and assessment procedures', in: Wendt, D. and Vlek, C. (eds), Utility, Probability and Human Decision Making, R. Reidel, Dordrecht, 1975, pp. 47-85.

8 Decision Concepts for Organisations

G. Fandel

1 INTRODUCTION

When, in the beginning of the fifties Simon (1952/53), for the first time, systematically tried to analyse decisions in organisations with a view to concluding from this the necessary quantitative solution instruments, it had rashly been expected that the formal foundations of an organisation theory with respect to business administration would be created very soon. In view of the developments which have taken place in the meantime in the fields of game and bargaining theory, and considering the knowledge obtained from the theory of multiple criteria decision making, it seems reasonable today to make another attempt to find out how far quantitative economic concepts of this kind can be used for or contribute to the formulating and solving of decision problems in organisations. Thus, cooperative games with or without side payments as well as non-cooperative games come into consideration. As to the application of the theory of bargaining to decision problems in organisations, two qualitatively different procedures have been developed, namely the approaches based on the game theory and the concessive models of bargaining formulated on the basis of spontaneous elements of behaviour.

2 DESCRIPTION OF THE DECISION SITUATIONS IN ORGANISATIONS

For the formal description of the decision problems in organisations let

$\mathbb{N}$	be the set of the natural numbers,
$\mathbb{R}$	be the set of real numbers,
n	$\in [N] = \{1, \ldots, N\}$ be the decision makers - units or persons - in the organisation, $N \in \mathbb{N}$ and $N \geq 2$,
$A \subset \mathbb{R}^N$	be the set of decision alternatives $a = (a_1, \ldots, a_N)$ of an organisation, and

$U \subset \mathbb{R}^N$ be the set of utility vectors $u = (u_1, \ldots, u_N)$ of the organisation which develop as a mapping of A under the individual utility functions $u_n = u_n(a)$, $n \in [N]$, of the decision makers, that is to say $U = u(A)$.

In order to obtain a reasonable economic and mathematical formulation of the problem let us further assume that the set of decision alternatives A is convex, bounded and closed, and that the utility functions u_n, $n \in [N]$, are concave, continuous and different from each other, that is to say, $u_n \neq u_{n'}$ is true for $n, n' \in [N]$ and $n \neq n'$ in particular. Without loss of generality we further suppose that every decision maker n controls one and only one decision component a_n of a vector a, where $a_n \in A_n$ and $a \in A = A_1 \times \ldots \times A_N$; A_n designates the set of decision alternatives of the n-th decision maker.

Then the decision problem in organisations consists in choosing alternatives $a \in A$ or, which is equivalent, in determining utility vectors $u \in U$ that the decision makers of the organisation will regard as solutions to their decision process. The common decision rule of the organisation members determines the choice of such $a \in A$ or $u \in U$. This rule can at the same time serve to characterise the solution approach used. In this connection, the notion of decision rule means an operation $Q: \mathbb{R}^N \to \mathbb{R}^N$, which for each utility set $U \subset \mathbb{R}^N$ chooses a subset $L_Q \subseteq U$, and thus for each decision set $A \subset \mathbb{R}^N$, a subset of decision alternatives A_Q with $u(A_Q) = L_Q$. $L_Q = \{u' \in U \mid u = Q[u'(a)], a \in A\}$ can be designated as set of the Q-optimal solutions to the organisational decision problem.

For practical reasons the solution L_Q of the decision problem is to fulfil the following requirements:

$$L_Q \neq \emptyset \,, \tag{A1}$$

that is to say, there must exist at least one solution to each decision problem

$$L_Q \subset U \,, \tag{A2}$$

that is to say, only such utility vectors will be suitable for solutions which can be obtained by corresponding feasible decision alternatives.

Designate $M(U) = \{u \in U | u \geq \bar{\bar{u}}\}$, where the utility vector $\bar{\bar{u}}$ indicates the utility level $\bar{\bar{u}}_n = \max_{a_n} \min_{\bar{a}_n} u_n(a_n, \bar{a}_n)$ $\bar{a}_n = (a_1, \ldots, a_{n-1}, a_{n+1}, \ldots, a_N)$ $(a_n, \bar{a}_n) \in A$ and $n \in [N]$ which the individual decision makers can at least obtain within the organisation, then let

$$L_Q \subset M(U) \ . \qquad \text{(A3)}$$

Thus postulate (A3) requires the solutions to be individually rational (Luce, Raiffa 1958, pp. 192-193).

Let $P(U) = \{u \in U | w \geq u \wedge w \in U \Rightarrow w = u\}$ be the set of all Pareto-optimal utility vectors of U. Then, the solution is to satisfy the condition

$$L_Q \subset P(U) \qquad \text{(A4)}$$

that is to say, consider efficient results only.

$$L_Q \text{ is a one-element set} \qquad \text{(A5)}$$

insures the uniqueness of the solution.

The conditions (A1)-(A5) allow a comment on the quality of the solution proposals still to be presented, that means, a comment with respect to their contribution to the optimal decison in organisations. In this connection, existence, feasibility and individual rationality of the solution are quite obvious postulates derived from plausibility assumptions. From the economic point of view, the requirement of the Pareto-optimality corresponds to the use of synergic effects which can emerge in organisations due to the joint effort of several members. Under the conditions (A1)-(A4) the necessity of a unique solution results from the fact: if there exist several Pareto-optimal solutions, then some decision makers will profit more from one result vector than from another, and vice versa, so that with interests conflicting, a final solution to the decision problem has not yet been found. Furthermore, uniqueness is necessary for a stable or equilibrated decision behaviour of the persons involved (Harsanyi 1963, p. 219; Friedman 1971, p. 7).

3 ORGANISATION-THEORETIC NOTIONS OF SOLUTION

The organisation-theoretic notions of solutions which have been historically developed in the literature are attributable to the effort to restrict the utility set U already ex ante by eliminating obviously bad result vectors, without at the same time determining unique solutions or even definitely establishing the decision rule of the organisation.

a) Simon (1952-53, p. 42 ff.) designates the set

$$L_\Omega = V(U) = \{u \in U | u(a) \geq \bar{u},\ a \in A\} \ .$$

as viable solutions.

Here $\bar{u}_n$, $n \in [N]$, indicates the utility of the n-th decision maker, which he can also obtain without being a member of the organisation for example by joining another organisation. The decisions made by the organisation must at least yield these utility levels in order to ensure the existence of the organisation. The fulfilment of the postulates (A1)-(A5) by the viable solutions is dependent on the special location of $\bar{u}$ and is realised if and only if $\bar{u} \in P(U)$ holds, hence is located on the efficient border of U. Generally, however, the viable solutions, if they exist, will be neither Pareto-optimal nor unique so that, as a rule, this notion of solution is not sufficient for determining an optimal decision in the organisation. The solutions which will be considered in the following are always assumed to be viable.

b) The Pareto-optimal solutions result from

$$L_\Omega = P(U) \ ,$$

hence are described by the efficient border of the utility set U. Unless for special problem structures this border consists of one point only, the Pareto-optimal solutions will violate the postulate of uniqueness (A5), and, as a rule, not definitely solve the organisational decision problem.

c) By individually maximal solutions Simon (1952-53, p. 42 ff.) understands

$$L_\Omega = I(U) = \bigcup_{n=1}^{N} I_n(U) \text{ with } I_n(U) = \{u \in U | u_n = \max_{a \in A} u_n(a)\},\ n \in [N]$$

that is, they comprise all result vectors which imply a maximal utility for one decision maker. Evidently, the individually maximal solutions need not be Pareto-optimal, that is to say, the notion of solution underlying I(U) is generally incompatible with postulate (A4). Furthermore, with interests of the organisation members conflicting, I(U) normally is no one-element set, so that in this case also the uniqueness postulate (A5) is violated. Thus, I(U) is not generally acceptable as a solution to the organisational decision problem.

d) A solution may be called organisationally maximal if

$$L_Q = \{\hat{u}=u(a),\ a \in A\} \text{ with } \hat{u}_n = \max_{a \in A} u_n(a) \text{ for all } n \in [N]$$

that is to say, if there exist decision alternatives which maximise the utility of all organisation members simultaneously. The existence of such a solution is very strongly dependent on the particular problem structure and, therefore, cannot generally be assumed, so that (A1) need not be fulfilled. If, however, there exists an organisationally maximal solution, then it fulfils all postulates (A1)-(A5). But in this case, analogous to a perfect solution (Geoffrion 1965, p.2) in decision situations with multiple objectives, there no longer exists an organisational decision problem.

The properties of the organisation-theoretic notions of solution dealt with are sometimes unsatisfactory with respect to the requirements (A1)-(A5), which can mainly be ascribed to the fact that they largely dispense with the formulation of a decision behaviour common to all organisation members. Approaches taking this requirement into account in different ways will be discussed more thoroughly in the following section.

4 GAME- AND BARGAINING-THEORETIC CONTRIBUTIONS TO THE SOLVING OF ORGANISATIONAL DECISION PROBLEMS

4.1 Game-theoretic solution approaches

a) For two-person cooperative games without side payments Nash (1953, p. 136 ff.) has indicated an axiomatically founded solution which can be extended to N persons and is then characterised as follows:

$$L_Q = \{u^* \in U \mid \prod_{n=1}^{N} (u_n^* - t_n) = \max_{a \in A} \prod_{n=1}^{N} [u_n(a) - t_n],\ t\ U\} .$$

In this expression $t \in U$ designates a disagreement vector - which is not Pareto-optimal - from the interior of U; t may be given definitely by the rules of the game, or be determinable by threat strategies

(Harsanyi 1963, p. 195 ff.) of the players. The optimal solutions u* are then characterised by the fact that they maximise the product of all utility increases with respect to the disagreement vector $t \in U$ for the decision makers involved.

Obviously, this so-called cooperative Nash solution satisfies the requirements (A1) and (A2), as well as postulate (A3) after construction of t. On account of the strictly monotonically increasing and strictly convex goal precept which follows from the underlying axioms the u* are Pareto-optimal and with the possible unique choice of the disagreement vector $t \in U$ also unique, that is to say, they satisfy the conditions (A4) and (A5). Thus, as a whole, the cooperative Nash concept is well suited for solving organisational decision problems. Furthermore, it has the properties which are desirable for utility-theoretic considerations, that the solution u* is invariant with respect to linear utility transformations, symmetric with respect to the decision makers and independent of irrelevant alternatives.

b) For the solving of N-Person cooperative games with side payments and transferable utilities Shapley (1953) has formulated the value $\varphi(v)$ of a game. Being defined on the characteristic function v which describes the game it assigns the payoff $\varphi_n(v)$ to each of the decision makers $n \in [N]$ at the end of the game. In this connection $v: P[N] \to \mathbb{R}$ is a mapping of the power set of N into the real numbers, and for each coalition $\bar{S}$, $\bar{S} \in P([N])$ or $\bar{S} \subseteq \bar{N}$, $\bar{S}v(\bar{S})$ indicates the common payoff under transferable utilities, which it can obtain by the maximin strategy at the expense of the coalition $\bar{N}-\bar{S}$ of the other players:

$$v(\bar{S}) = \max_{a^{\bar{S}}} \min_{a^{\bar{N}-\bar{S}}} \sum_{n \in \bar{S}} u_n(a^{\bar{S}}, a^{\bar{N}-\bar{S}}), \text{ for all } \bar{S} \subseteq \bar{N},\ a = (a^{\bar{S}}, a^{\bar{N}-\bar{S}}) \in A; \qquad (1)$$

$\bar{N}$ designates the coalition consisting of all decision makers of the organisation. Because of the axiomatic requirements which, according to Shapley, the mathematical structure of φ has to satisfy it can be shown that there exists a unique function φ describing the value of the game for each player $n \in [N]$ and reading as follows:

$$\varphi_n(v) = \sum_{\bar{S} \subseteq \bar{N}} \frac{(S-1)!(N-S)!}{N!} [v(\bar{S}) - v(\bar{S} - \{n\})], \qquad (2)$$

$$n \in [N], \quad S = ||\bar{S}|| \text{ and } N = ||\bar{N}|| .$$

The solution corresponding to the Shapley value can be formally represented as follows:

$$L_Q = \{u^* \in U \mid u^* = \varphi(v)\} .$$

With regard to expression (1) existence and uniqueness of the solution u* follow directly from formula (2). Pareto-optimality of u* is guaranteed by the axiomatic construction of φ, since the maximal payoff which can jointly be obtained for all players will be distributed fully to them due to the solution vector u*, that is to say $\sum_{n=1}^{N} u_n^* = v(\bar{N})$ holds. u* continues to be individually rational since the the function φ satisfies the conditions $\varphi_n(v) \geq v(\{n\})$ for all $n \in [N]$. The feasibility of u* is ascribable to the classification of the considered game by admitted side payments and transferable utilities, since the utility set is then characterised by

$$U = \{u \mid \sum_{n=1}^{N} u_n \leq v(\bar{N})\} \tag{3}$$

and $u^* \in U$ holds because of Pareto-optimality. Thus, in case of a possible equivalent mapping of the organisational decision problem by the game situation discussed here, all requirements (A1)-(A5) for its solution are satisfied, so that in this sense the Shapley value can serve as a concept of solution. Its workability in real cases, however, is questionable due to the fact that it can only be used for solving games with transferable utilities in which side payments take place. Under practical aspects these assumptions are critical and clearly limit the efficiency of the Shapley value with respect to the solution of decision problems in organisations.

c) Shapley himself has indicated a way which allows the extending of his solution idea to cooperative games without side payments; thus it is made more attractive for the application to organisational decision problems. As opposed to the concept of value of the game this proposal is referred to as evaluation of a game (Shapley 1964; Shapley, Shubik 1969). The starting point for deriving the Shapley evaluation once more is the characteristic function v which, however, is now given by the mapping $v: P([N]) \to \mathbb{R}^S$, $S \in [N]$, since there are no side payments. It assigns to each coalition $\bar{S} \subseteq \bar{N}$ a subset $v(\bar{S}) \subset \mathbb{R}^S$, $S = \|\bar{S}\|$, of feasible payoff vectors. The sets $v(\bar{S})$ are subsets of the utility set $U = v(\bar{N}) \subset \mathbb{R}^N$, that is to say $v(\bar{S}) \subseteq v(\bar{N})$ for all $\bar{S} \subseteq \bar{N}$; they are assumed to be convex, closed and nonempty. Its vectors

$u^{\bar{N}}=(u_n)_{n\in\bar{S}}\in v(\bar{S})$ result from the projection of corresponding $u\in U$ into $\mathbb{R}^S$, and consequently contain just as many components as there are members in the coalition $\bar{S}$. In order to extend the Shapley approach represented in b) to game situations of this kind the following procedure is taken for determining the Shapley evaluation.

1. By rescaling the utility function of the decision makers by a vector

$$\lambda = (\lambda_1, \ldots, \lambda_N) \geq 0 , \quad \lambda \neq 0 , \tag{4}$$

the utility set $U=v(\bar{N})$ of the cooperative game without side payments will be transformed into the utility set $U'=v'(\bar{N})=\{u' | u'=(\lambda_1 u_1, \ldots, \lambda_N u_N)=>\lambda,u<, u\in U\}$ of another cooperative game without side payments, where

$$v'(\bar{S})=\{u'^{\bar{S}} | u'^{\bar{S}}=>\lambda^{\bar{S}},u^{\bar{S}}<, u^{\bar{S}}\in v(\bar{S})\}, \bar{S}\subseteq\bar{N} \text{ and } \lambda^{\bar{S}}=(\lambda_n)_{n\in\bar{S}} \tag{5}$$

holds.

2. The cooperative game without side payments with the transformed characteristic function v' is now treated as a corresponding cooperative game with side payments and transferable utilities. The latter then possesses the characteristic functions $v''(S)$.

3. On the basis of v'' compute the Shapley value

$$\varphi(v'')=\tilde{u} \tag{6}$$

according to (2).

4. If now $\tilde{u}\in U'=v'(\bar{N})$ holds, that is to say, if there exists a $u^*\in U=v(\bar{N})$ with the property

$$\varphi(v'')=\tilde{u}=>\lambda, u^*<,$$

then $\tilde{u}$ - and consequently u^* - can be obtained also without drawing on side payments. $u^*\in U$ which, after rescaling the utility functions, corresponds to $\tilde{u}\in U'$ on returning to the original cooperative game without side payments is to be regarded as the solution of this game, that is to say, let

$$L_Q = \{u^*\in U | >\lambda,u^*< = \varphi(v'')\} .$$

$\lambda \cdot u^*$ is referred to by Shapley as the evaluation of a game if and only if λ and u^* satisfy the requirements (4) and (7).

The Shapley evaluation $\lambda \cdot u^*$ fulfils the existence postulate (A1) for any finite N-person cooperative game without side payments (Shapley 1964); according to its construction the appropriate solution vector u^* will then also obey the requirements (A2)-(A4). As opposed to the Shapley value, in this case the uniqueness is dependent on the possible unique choice of the scaling vector λ, so that the fulfilment of (A5) cannot be generally ensured. Precisely this deficiency, however, gives rise to the strongest objections as regards the practical use of the Shapley evaluation for solving organisational decision problems. An additional difficulty is the fact that the relative utility positions of the decision makers shift in the solution vector u^* when the relative utility weights are changed by the choice of λ (Fandel 1979, p. 52). Therefore, in higher-dimensional problems it is hardly any longer possible to predict in which way solution u^* will behave in case of variation of λ if there exist several evaluations $\lambda \cdot u^*$ for a cooperative game without side payments.

d) Extending the minimax criterion developed for two-person zero-sum games Nash (1951) designates the set of equilibrium decisions a^* in common N-person non-cooperative games as their solution. This so-called non-cooperative Nash solution formally reads as follows for the considered decision situation in organisations:

$$L_Q = \{u^* \in U \mid u^* = u(a^*),\ a^* \in A, \text{ and } u_n(a^*) = \max_{a_n \in A_n} u_n(a_n, \bar{a}_n^*) \text{ for all } n \in [N]\}.$$

Nash has shown that each non-cooperative game of this kind possesses at least one equilibrium vector $a^* \in A$. Such equilibria are at the same time feasible and individually rational. As opposed to these positive statements with respect to the postulates (A1)-(A3) the requirements (A4) of Pareto-optimality and (A5) of uniqueness cannot normally be ensured for the non-cooperative equilibria (Luce, Raiffa 1958, pp. 106 ff.; Shubik 1960). Therefore, the non-cooperative Nash concept cannot generally be considered to be a satisfactory approach to the solution of organisational decision problems.

e). In order to come from non-efficient equilibria in non-cooperative games to such equilibria with Pareto-optimal utility vectors Friedman (1971) starts from the formulation of a supergame consisting of the infinite periodical repetition of a given normal game. To deal with it, a new class of non-cooperative supergame equilibria is introduced by definition, first assuming that the normal game possesses only a (non-efficient) equilibrium $c \in A$. In this connection for each decision maker $n \in [N]$ a supergame strategy σ'_n on the basis of a decision vector $a' \in A$ which strictly dominates the normal equilibrium c with respect to the utility - that is to say, for which $u(a') >> u(c)$ holds - may be constructed as follows:

$$\begin{aligned} &\sigma'_n = (a_{n1}, a_{n2}, \ldots, a_{nt}, \ldots) \text{ with} \\ &a_{n1} = a'_n \\ &a_{nt} = \begin{cases} a'_n, \text{ if } a_{n'\tau} = a'_{n'}, \ n \neq n', & \tau = 1, \ldots, t-1, \ t > 1, \\ c_n \text{ otherwise} . \end{cases} \end{aligned} \tag{8}$$

Allowing (8) the supergame strategy $\sigma^{a'} = (a', a', \ldots)$ represents a non-cooperative equilibrium if it fulfils the condition

$$\sum_{t=1}^{\infty} \alpha_n^{t-1} u_n(a') > u_n(\bar{a}'_n, b_n) + \sum_{t=2}^{\infty} \alpha_n^{t-1} u_n(c) \text{ for all } n \in [N]. \tag{9}$$

α_n designates the discount rate of the decision maker n; it is constant for all periods t. $u_n(\bar{a}'_n, b_n) = \max\{u_n(\bar{a}'_n, a_n) | a_n \in A_n\}$, $n \in [N]$, indicates the maximal yield which he can achieve at the expense of all other players by deviating once from a'. Since condition (9) after splitting, applying the sum formula and regrouping is equivalent to

$$u_n(a') > u_n(c) + (1-\alpha_n)[u_n(\bar{a}'_n, b_n) - u_n(c)] \equiv u_n^+(a'), \ n \in [N], \tag{10}$$

the class of the non-cooperative supergame equilibria can now be described in the utility space by the following set $U_G^{\sigma'} \subset U$:

$$U_G^{\sigma'} = \{u \in U | u(a') >> u^+(a') \text{ and } u(a') >> u(c), \ a' \in A\}. \tag{11}$$

If (10) is transformed into (12)

$$\frac{\alpha_n}{1-\alpha_n} [u_n(a') - u_n(c)] > u_n(\bar{a}'_n, b_n) - u_n(a'), \quad n \in [N], \tag{12}$$

it can be seen that the supergame strategy $\sigma^a = (a, a, \ldots)$, resulting from the infinite repetition of a strategy $a \in A$ of the normal game dominating the equilibrium c belongs to $U_G^{\sigma'}$, if for each decision maker the single net gain obtainable by deviating from a - right side of the inequation (12) - is smaller than the cash value of the permanent utility losses to be expected on account of the reaction of the partners - left side of the inequation (12). According to (8) any other supergame strategy σ_n for player n is weakly dominated either by $\sigma_n'=(a_{n1}, a_{n2}, \ldots)$ or $\sigma_n''=(b_n, c_n, c_n, \ldots)$.

Now, in order to particularly mark a Pareto-optimal σ^{a*} in the sense of (8) as solution among the equilibria of the supergame, Friedman proposes that the temptation to deviate from a* is to be equally large for all players, that means

$$L_Q=\{u^*\in U \mid u^*=u(a^*)\in P(U_G^{\sigma'}) \text{ and } v_n(a^*)=v_{n'}(a^*) \text{ for all } n, n'\in[N]\}$$

The temptation to deviate $v_n(a^*)$ is defined by:

$$v_n(a^*) = \frac{u_n(\bar{a}_n^*, b_n) - u_n(a^*)}{u_n(a^*) - u_n(c)}, \quad n\in[N] . \tag{13}$$

The existence of such a decision alternative a* is not generally guaranteed since the set $U_G^{\sigma'}$ - and thus also L_Q - can become empty according to condition (10) in case of small discount rates (that is high time preferences) of the decision makers. For sufficiently high discount rates, however, the fulfilment of postulate (A1) can be ensured. In this case a* will also satisfy the requirements (A2)-(A4). The uniqueness of the solution, however, cannot be guaranteed at the same time (Friedman 1971, p. 8 ff.), which means that on account of a possible violation of (A5) the Friedman concept can be used for solving the organisational decision problem in special cases only.

4.2 Bargaining-theoretic solution approaches

a) The N-person bargaining model developed by Harsanyi (1963) is based on the idea to generalise the cooperative Nash solution (Nash 1950 and 1953) which has been conceived for two-person decisions. As opposed to the determination of solutions described in 4.1.a) the N-person decision on the Harsanyi model, however, must first be decomposed into a set of two-person subgames between all possible pairs n and n' from [N] according to the mathematical concept of the theory of bargaining. Allowing for their interdependence the resulting subgames will then have to be formulated so mutually consistently with respect to the partial conditions of solution that subsequently, the total solution of the organisational decision problem can be composed of them in the form of an equilibrium strictly taking two-person subgames as a basis.

Let the function $f(u)=0$ describe the efficient border $P(U)$ of the utility set U in parametric form, and let it be differentiable. With the analytic properties of the cooperative Nash solution for the two-person decision problem the optimal total solution to the general N-person bargaining problem

$$L_Q=\{u^*\in U \mid u^*= u^{\bar{N}}\}$$

which in the Harsanyi model has successively been composed of the solutions to two-party subgames can then be characterised by the following system of necessary conditions (Harsanyi 1963, pp. 214-215):

$$f(u^{\bar{N}}) = 0 \tag{14.1}$$

$$c_n=f_n(u^{\bar{N}}) = \partial f/\partial u_n|u^{\bar{N}}; \quad n\in\bar{N} ; \tag{14.2}$$

$$u_n^{\bar{S}}=u_n(a^{\bar{S}o}, a^{\bar{S}'0}) ; \quad n\in\bar{S}, \bar{S}\subset\bar{N}, \bar{S}'=\bar{N} - \bar{S} \tag{14.3}$$

$$t_n^{\bar{S}} = \sum_{\substack{\bar{R}\subset\bar{S}\\ n\in\bar{R}}} (-1)^{s-r+1} u_n^{\bar{R}}; \quad n\in\bar{S}; \bar{S}\subseteq\bar{N}, s=||\bar{S}||>1, r=||\bar{R}|| ; \tag{14.4}$$

$$c_n(u_n^{\bar{N}}-t_n^{\bar{N}}) = c_{n'}(u_{n'}^{\bar{N}}-t_{n'}^{\bar{N}}) \text{ for all } n, n'\in\bar{N} ; \tag{14.5}$$

$$\sum_{n\in\bar{S}} c_n u_n^{\bar{S}} - \sum_{n'\in\bar{S}'} c_{n'} u_{n'}^{\bar{S}'}$$

$$= \sum_{n\in\bar{S}} c_n u_n(a^{\bar{S}o}, a^{\bar{S}'o}) - \sum_{n'\in\bar{S}'} c_{n'} u_{n'}(a^{\bar{S}o}, a^{\bar{S}o}) \tag{14.6}$$

$$= \max_{a^{\bar{S}}\in A^{\bar{S}}} \min_{a^{\bar{S}'}\in A^{\bar{S}'}} [\sum_{n\in\bar{S}} c_n u_n(a^{\bar{S}},a^{\bar{S}'}) - \sum_{n'\in\bar{S}'} c_{n'} u_{n'}(a^{\bar{S}},a^{\bar{S}'})],$$

$$\bar{S}, \bar{S}'\subset\bar{N}, A^{\bar{S}} = \times_{n\in\bar{S}} A_n ;$$

subject to: $c_n(u_n^{\bar{S}} -t_n^{\bar{S}})=c_k(u_k^{\bar{S}}-t_k^{\bar{S}}), \quad n,k\in\bar{S};$

$$c_{n'}(u_{n'}^{\bar{S}'}-t_{n'}^{\bar{S}'})=c_l(u_l^{\bar{S}'}-t_l^{\bar{S}'}), \quad n',l\in\bar{S}'.$$

Conditions (14.1), (14.2), (14.5) and (14.6) are expressive of the fact that for a consistent construction of the bargaining result according to the cooperative Nash concept, the criteria of optimality of the total solution must be of prime importance for all two-person or two-party subgames, too. According to (14.3) the utility of the decision maker n in the coalition $\bar{S}$ is dependent on the choice of optimal threat strategies $a^{\bar{S}o}$ and $a^{\bar{S}'o}$ by the two coalitions $\bar{S}$ and $\bar{S}'$. When he joins this coalition his disagreement payoff, however, according to (14.4) will consist of the cumulated utility increases achieved by him in all subcoalitions $\bar{R}\subset\bar{S}$ of which he was a member previously.

The optimal solution $u^{\bar{N}}$ of the problem (14.1)-(14.6) which, in its formulation, tries to make the most perfect use of the Nash axioms for two-person cooperative games with respect to the theory of bargaining in general fulfils the requirements (A1)-(A4). Difficulties, however, in unrestrictedly accepting $u^*=u^{\bar{N}}$ as optimal solution to the organisational decision problem may arise from the fact that the disagreement payoffs are variable on account of threat strategies, so that the solution $u^{\bar{N}}$ need not necessarily be unique. This violation of (A5) is however, avoidable by presetting $t_n^{\bar{S}}$.

Other bargaining-theoretic approaches on the basis of the cooperative Nash concept have been formulated by Lemaire (1973), Miyasawa (1964) and Isbell (1960). Further game-theoretically founded solution proposals with regard to the bargaining problem which start out from systems of axioms different from those of Nash may be found in Krelle (1975).

b) As an alternative to such game-theoretically founded approaches of the theory of bargaining Contini and Zionts (1968) have conceived a concessive bargaining model in which the solution to the organisational decision problem is simultaneously determined by agreement of all group members. This agreement is reached under threat of an imposed solution $y\in U$ by means of a process of concession which is continuous with respect to time and leads to the solution

$$L_Q=\{u^*\in U \mid u^*\geq z(t)\geq y\} .$$

Here z(t) designates the decision makers' aspiration levels at time t, declining in the course of the process of concession. At the beginning let $z(0)=\hat{u}$, that is to say, let the aspiration levels tally with the individual utility maxima of the organisation members at time t=0. The concession behaviour of the decision makers which is achieved by the threat of an imposed solution is described by the following system of conditions:

$$dz_n(t)/dt = \begin{cases} k_n(t)<0, \text{ if } L_Q=\emptyset \text{ and } z_n(t)>y_n, \\ 0 \text{ otherwise,} \end{cases} \qquad n\in[N]. \tag{15}$$

Consequently, every decision maker is ready to make concessions only as long as no feasible solution has been found and his aspiration level remains above the payoff which would be yielded to him in case of the imposed solution. If one of the conditions does no longer apply, then the concession rate $k_n(t)$ will become equal to zero.

In order to ensure according to the postulate (A1) the existence of a solution, that is to say $L_Q\neq\emptyset$, the functions $k_n(t)$ are subjected to the following additional sufficient conditions that for every $k_n(t)$ there exists a t_n', $0\leq t_n'<\infty$, with

$$-\int_0^{t_n'} k_n(\tau)d\tau = \hat{u}_n-y_n, \quad n\in[N]. \tag{16}$$

Thus, even if the condition $L_Q=\emptyset$ in (15) is neglected the concession path $z(t)$ for a finite $t'=\max\{t_n'|n\in[N]\}$ would at any rate have at least to lead to the imposed solution $y\in U$ as stationary solution. With the existence the feasibility requirement (A2) is at the same time fulfilled by the solution u^*. The individual rationality (postulate (A3)) of u^*, however, is not automatically given; it is rather dependent on the clever choice of the imposed solution y. Sufficient for the guarantee of individually rational solutions is $y \geq \bar{\bar{u}}$. Pareto-optimality and uniqueness of the solution u^*, as well, cannot be generally ensured without additional conditions. Contini and Zionts have shown that (A4) and (A5) are fulfilled if the utility set is strictly convex. It is also sufficient if for the location of the imposed solution $y\in U$ $\eta(y)\cap R(U)\subseteq P(U)$ holds with $\eta(y)=\{u\in\mathbb{R}^N|u\geq y\}$ and and $R(U)$ as border of the utility set U (Fandel 1979, p. 115).

It is evident that the concessive bargaining model developed by Contini and Zionts can be used for solving the organisational decision problem on certain additional conditions only, the existence of which must always be separately examined. Nevertheless, this concept with its spontaneous elements of behaviour - expressed in concession rates - may by all means be regarded as a practice-oriented alternative to the axiomatically founded solution approaches. The question, however, in how far the concession rates of the decision makers can rationally be accounted for, remains still be to answered. This problem will be treated in the next section concluding this article.

4.3 On the rationalising of the concession behaviour

It is unsatisfactory, that so far there are only two-person concepts available for rationally elaborating the concession behaviour characterised according to (15) (Fandel 1979, p. 120 ff.). Their ability to give information about the solution of the organisation decision problem is limited correspondingly; yet, they indicate possibilities of development with respect to elaborating the rational foundations of the concessive bargaining models under the aspect of their usefulness in practice.

Most of the approaches can be reduced to the idea of the bargaining theorem developed by Zeuthen (1930, Chapter 4). According to this theorem the concession behaviour for jointly determine a Pareto-optimal solution vector $u^* \in P(U)$ depends on the subjective probabilities of conflict which can maximally be accepted by the two bargaining partners; the former result from the Pareto-optimal proposals and counterproposals which are made by the two players in the course of the process of concession. At the beginning let u^1 and u^2, $u^1 \neq u^2$, be the proposal and counterproposal of the first and the second decision maker, respectively. Let $\bar{u} \in U$ represent the disagreement or conflict point, and let $U' = \{u \in U | u \geq \bar{u}\}$. Then the following conclusions can be drawn with respect to the first decision maker:

1. He can definitely achieve the utility u_1^2 if he accepts the counterproposal u^2 of the second decision maker (action 1).
2. If, however, he rejects u^2 persisting in his proposal u^1 (action 2) the expected value of his utility will be $\bar{u}_1\pi + u_1^1(1-\pi)$ where π indicates the probability that the decision maker 2 will risk a conflict.

The subjective conflict probability p_1 which is maximally acceptable for decision maker 1 and with which he is just able to keep up his proposal then results from the indifference between the two actions indicated, that is to say, if one has

$$u_1^2 = \bar{u}_1 \, p_1 + u_1^1(1-p_1) \quad \text{or} \quad p_1 = (u_1^1 - u_1^2)/(u_1^1 - \bar{u}_1) \, . \qquad (17)$$

Correspondingly, for the second decision maker, one obtains:

$$p_2 = (u_2^2 - u_2^1)/(u_2^2 - \bar{u}_2) \ .$$

According to Zeuthen now a concession is made by the decision maker $n \in \{1,2\}$ for whom

$$p_n \leq p_{n'} \ ; \ p_n, \ p_{n'} > 0 \quad \text{and} \quad n, \ n' \in \{1,2\}, \ n \neq n' \tag{19}$$

holds, that is to say, by that decision maker who is not able to cope with a greater probability of conflict than his bargaining partner. The concession consists of a new proposal (e.g. $\hat{u}^2$ instead of u^2) which causes the probability of conflict maximally endurable to become greater again than that of the contrahent, thus forcing the latter to make concessions for his part. This process is iteratively continued until a common agreement solution $u^* \in P(U')$ is obtained. If, allowing for the expressions (17) and (18) condition (19) is transformed into the equivalent inequation

$$(u_n^n - \bar{u}_n)(u_{n'}^n - \bar{u}_{n'}) \leq (u_n^{n'} - \bar{u}_n)(u_{n'}^{n'} - \bar{u}_{n'}); \ n, n \in \{1,2\}, \quad n \neq n' \tag{20}$$

for N=2, it can be seen that the rationalising of the concession behaviour in the bargaining theorem by Zeuthen is identical to the axioms of the cooperative Nash solution (see section 4.1.a)). The embedding of a concession behaviour thus rationalised in the system (15) of the bargaining model by Contini and Zionts is quite obvious now if there the process is discretised by proposals and counter-proposals $u^n(t) \in P(U')$, $n \in \{1,2\}$, at times t, $t=0,1,2,\ldots$ Using the old symbols we then have : $y = \bar{u}$, $z_n(0) = \hat{u}_n = \max\{u_n \mid u \in U'\} = u_n^n(0)$ and

$$z_n(t+1) - z_n(t) = \begin{cases} k_n(t) < 0, \ \text{if } L_Q = \emptyset \text{ and } \prod_{r=1}^{2} [u_r^n(t) - \bar{u}_r] \leq \prod_{r=1}^{2} [u_r^{n'}(t) - \bar{u}_r] \\ 0 \ \text{otherwise,} \end{cases}$$

with $\quad n, n' \in \{1,2\} \quad$ and $n \neq n'$ (15')

$k_n \quad u_n^n(t+1) - u_n^n(t)$ and

$u^n(t+1)$ with the property that n $\quad u \in P(U')$

exists with $u_n > u_n^n(t+1)$ and

$$\prod_{r=1}^{2} (u_r - \bar{u}_r) > \prod_{r=1}^{2} [u_r^n(t+1) - \bar{u}_r] \ ,$$

$n \in \{1,2\} \quad$ and $\quad t \in \{0, 1, 2, \ldots\}$.

The extension of the thus described rational concession behaviour according to (20) or (15') to N persons, N>2, is obvious, but it can no longer formally be concluded from the bargaining theorem by

Zeuthen (condition 19). The above remarks show, however, that the combination of game-theoretic axioms and concessive bargaining models which are based on spontaneous elements of behaviour may yield valuable suggestions for the solving of organisational decision problems.

REFERENCES

Contini, B. and Zionts, S., 'Restricted bargaining for organisations with multiple objectives', Econometrica, 1968, pp. 397-414.

Fandel, G., Optimale Entscheidungen in Organisationen, Berlin-Heidelberg-New York, 1979.

Fandel, G. and Wilhelm, J., 'Zur Entscheidungstheorie bei mehrfacher Zielsetzung', Zeitschrift für Operational Research, vol. 20, 1976, pp. 1-21.

Friedman, J.W., 'A non-cooperative equilibrium for supergames', Review of Economics Studies, 1971, pp. 1-12.

Geoffrion, A.M., A Parametric Programming Solution to the Vector Maximum Problem, with Applications to Decisions under Uncertainty, Stanford, California, 1965.

Harsanyi, J.C., 'A simplified bargaining model for the n-person cooperative game', International Economic Review, 1963, pp. 194-220.

Isbell, J.R., 'A modification of Harsanyi's bargaining model', Bulletin of the American Mathematical Society, 1960, pp. 70-73.

Krelle, W., 'A new theory of bargaining, applied to the problem of wage determination and strikes', Wirtschaftstheoretische Abteilung, no. 70, Institut für Gesellschafts- und Wirtschaftswissenschaften der Universität Bonn, Bonn, 1975.

Lemaire, J., 'A new value for games without transferable utilities', International Journal of Game Theory, vol. 2, 1973, pp. 205-213.

Luce, R.D. and Raiffa, H., Games and Decisions, New York, 1958.

Miyasawa, K., 'The n-person bargaining game', in: Dresher, M., Shapley, L.S. and Tucker, A.W. (eds), Advances in Game Theory, Princeton, New Jersey, 1964, pp. 547-575.

Nash, J.F., 'The bargaining problem', Econometrica, 1950, pp. 155-162.

Nash, J.F., 'Noncooperative games', Annals of Mathematics, 1951, pp. 286-295.

Nash, J.F., 'Two person cooperative games', Econometrica, 1953, pp. 128-140.

Shapley, L.S., 'A value for n-person games', in: Kuhn, H.W. and Tucker, A.W. (eds), Contributions to the Theory of Games, Vol. II, Princeton, New Jersey, 1953, pp. 307-317.

Shapley, L.S., 'Values of large market games: status of the problem', Memorandum RM-3957-PR, The Rand Corporation, Santa Monica, California, February 1964.

Shapley, L.S. and Shubik, M., 'Pure competition, coalition power and fair division', International Economic Review, 1969, pp. 337-362.

Shubik, M., 'Games decision and industrial organisation', Management Science, 1960, pp. 455-474.

Simon, H.A., 'A comparison of organisation theories', The Review of Economic Studies, 1952-53, pp. 40-48.

Thiriez, H. and Zionts, S. (eds), Multiple Criteria Decision Making, Berlin-Heidelberg-New York, 1976.

Zeuthen, F., Problems of Monopoly and Economic Warfare, London, 1930.

Zionts, S. (ed), Multiple Criteria Problem Solving, Berlin-Heidelberg-New York, 1978.

9 Theories of Risk and MCDM

G. Colson

1 INTRODUCTION

1.1 The limits of our study

Since the concept and the measures of risk are largely spread over different research fields, this paper does not pretend to be a survey of the treatment of risk through the MCDM literature for two reasons. First, we think that existing theories of risk suffer from a lack of generality because uncertainty and risk are too narrowly conceived. Second, maybe because of this lack of generality, few papers or books specifically deal with risk in MCDM and we think that the existing literature on MCDM under the conditions of risk is still in its infancy.

So, our main purpose is to build a new grid of analysis of uncertainty and risk in the literature, with a special regard to MCDM. The scope of this paper is limited to general individual risk. This means that group decisions and the study of various components of risk are explicitly beyond our scope. In fact, we exclude many topics: for instance, utility theory variations, behavioural decision theory, applied psychometric methods like conjoint measurement and multidimensional scaling, or the probability risk theory as is used by actuaries. References on these specialised topics can be found for instance in Farquhar's paper (1977).

Our readings were mainly in Finance, Management Science and, more specifically, the 'Decision Aid' literature. Moreover, we only intend to present examples of quotations in those fields.

More details on this study, for instance, on the relationship between risk and time, are to be found in our thesis (1982).

1.2 Our starting positions about uncertainty, risk, information and their measures:

- Uncertainty is produced by everything which is a cause of unknowledge of the decision maker as far as it is related to his decision problem.

- The unknowledge - we prefer that word to ignorance which is more specifically used (see Arrow and Hurwicz 1972, Cohen and Jaffray 1980, 1982) - is issued from an intervention of hazard or from ambiguity (also called imprecision), or from a restrained perception of the decision problem complexity [1] or from any combination of these three main factors of uncertainty.

- Ambiguity comes from the fact that the observed reality is imperfectly perceived, conceived and then expressed by the decision maker (see Bouchon 1983, 1984, Dubois 1983, Roy 1977, 1978, Roy and Vincke 1981).
  So, fuzziness is only a component of ambiguity as is here defined (Gupta and Sanchez 1982a, 1982b, Kickert 1978, Zadeh 1978, Zionts 1981.

The third factor of uncertainty (the imperfect reduction of complexity) is not measurable since the actual complexity [1] is unknown. Of course, its non measurability does not justify that this important uncertainty component should be bypassed in any risk analysis [2]. However, since its analysis is not always specific to the decision problem at hand, we shall not explicitly consider this third factor in our overview of MCDM literature dealing with risk in the broadest sense proposed hereabove.

- Uncertainty is a necessary, but not a sufficient condition, of risk. Risk is a combination of uncertainty and value, increasing with each of these arguments and becoming null with one of them.

- The uncertainty measures summarise the uncertainty under one or more forms (hazard, ambiguity, complexity). Examples are probability measure, membership function in fuzzy sets theory, entropy and so on.

  The valued information measures add a valuation to the assessment

or to the objective measurement of uncertainty.
Examples are bayesian risk, EVPI, EVSI in decision theory. Here, two cases are to be considered.

1. A value function is used and the measure is strictly a measure of the value of information.
2. By using a von Neumann-Morgenstern utility function, the bayesian measures of risk become risk measures.

- Thus three elements are needed for making a complete risk measure
  - the assessment or the objective measurement of uncertainty,
  - a valuation (of outcomes),
  - the consideration of the decision maker's attitude to risk.

  Examples are utility function of von Neumann-Morgenstern, Pratt (1964), Arrow index, bayesian risk when utility is used and so on.

2 THE THREE APPROACHES TO RISK IN THE LITERATURE

We group the risk treatments into three main approaches:

- the Expected Utility approach (EU)
- the Penalisation of Deviations from a Target (PDT)
- the Time and Stochastic Dominances (TSD).

1. The main risk approach: the von Neumann-Morgenstern (1967) Expected Utility (EU) approach, is neither validated by evidence nor similar to actual decision processes (Allais and Hagen 1979, McCord and de Neufville 1983, Moscarola 1980, Rivett 1975, Roy 1977, Roy and Vincke 1981, Starr and Zeleny 1977, Stigum and Wenstøp 1983, Tversky 1977, Vincke 1981). Furthermore, the decision maker is much too constrained by the procedure of this approach. However, the Expected Utility approach is still the most seductive tool as far as the stochastic component of risk is concerned. The explicit consideration of risk attitudes (aversion, proneness) and of attributes of interdependence, and the approximate transparency of the approach are its main qualities. An aesthetic mathematical deduction of apparently simple and convincing axioms on behaviour explains the seduction of the EU approach among economists. In Finance, this approach is a natural extension of a single usual criterion: the expected terminal wealth. Few financial authors acknowledge that the firm does not always pursue this single

objective through its numerous financial targets (Spronk 1981, 1982).

2. Most risk measures (R) are presented under the form of a <u>function of penalisation of deviations from a target</u>.

i) <u>For the unidimensional case</u>, (Stone 1973) proposes its generalised risk measure:

$$r_\alpha\ (\gamma(F),\ \eta(F),F)\ \equiv \int_{-\infty}^{\gamma} |x-\eta(F)|^\alpha\ dF(x) \qquad (1)$$

where $F(x) \equiv P(\tilde{x} < x)$ is the distribution function for outcomes x;
$\gamma(F)$ is the upper limit of outcomes - f.i. a fractile,
$\eta(F)$ is a (variable) upper target - f.i. the mean,
α is a weighting parameter for the deviations.

A special case is the generalised risk measure by Fishburn (1977):

$$\rho_\alpha(t,F) \equiv \int_{-\infty}^{t} (t-x)^\alpha\ dF(x)\ , \qquad \alpha \geq 0\ , \qquad (2)$$

wihere t is a <u>fixed</u> upper target.

This Fishburn measure is useful to define <u>a degree (α) of the risk measure</u>, which is also the degree of the polynome of the associated utility function, if any. Let us observe with Fishburn the following implications:

$\alpha = 0 \Rightarrow F(t) = P(\tilde{x} < t)$, so we get the 'ruin threshold' criterion associated with a one-step utility function.

$0 < \alpha < 1 \Rightarrow$ a risk-seeking behaviour for outcomes below the target,

$\alpha > 1 \quad \Rightarrow$ a risk-aversion behaviour for these same outcomes,

$\alpha = 2 \quad \Rightarrow \rho_2 = S^-$, the lower semi-variance - the variance can be obtained from (1) with $\alpha = 2$, $\gamma \to \infty$ and $\eta(F) = E$ (the mean).

$\alpha = \infty \quad \Rightarrow$ we obtain the 'maximum of losses' criterion.

ii) <u>An expected Return - Risk approach</u> (ER) is frequently used in Finance: this bicriteria approach consists either in maximising E for a given R or in minimising R for a given E. As a special case, the Mean-Variance (EV) approach can be issued from the EU approach under unrealistic conditions - normality of outcomes or quadratic utility. While this well known and commonly used EV approach has been justified also being an approximation or a limit of the more rigorous EU approach (Merton and Samuelson 1974, Samuelson 1970, Samuelson and Merton 1974), the EV approach is less criticised in the intertemporal continuous model (Merton 1975, Merton, forthcoming), although the associated EU approach is to be revisited in this intertemporal context (Kreps and Porteus 1978).

We note with Colson and Zeleny (1979, p. 16) that the multimoment approach (mean, variance, skewness, ..) proposed by the financial literature is indeed a partial decomposition of the stochastic dominance approach.

Other MODM techniques will be discussed in the next section.

3. Stochastic Dominance (SD) (see Bawa 1975, 1977, Hadar and Russell 1969, Hanoch and Levy 1969) is theoretically seductive but is not a practical tool. The pairwise comparison of distributions requires the complete knowledge of the whole distributions, which is not easy when only the family of distribution is known and stable. Several algorithms exist (Bawa 1975, Whitmore and Findlay 1978), but the admissible subsets are generally too large to be useful. Anyway, data requirement is huge.

   Binary or convex Time Dominance (TD) (Ekern 1981) is a fine theoretical tool. Unfortunately, the introduction of 'stochastic' uncertainty into TD seems poor.

All these three approaches are linked (Colson 1982) so that the behavioural criticisms against EU attain the latter two approaches.

3 RISK IN MULTIPLE CRITERIA DECISION METHODS

Until recent advances in non-compensatory approaches (Fishburn 1976, Vansnick 1984), only the MultiAttribute Utility Theory (MAUT) deserved the term of theory, since other MADM or MODM [3] methods are not yet organised in a theory. This is the reason why we shall begin with the MAUT. For other MCDM methods, only the stochastic and the ambiguity factors of uncertainty will be reviewed.

3.1 The Maut (see Farquhar 1977, Keeney 1972, 1982, Keeney and Raiffa 1976)

The MAUT takes into account the stochastic component of uncertainty and casually the ambiguity component as far as data imprecision can be subjectively assessed by a decision maker. We even claim that MAUT is the only MCDM model in which the risk attitudes are clearly introduced. This allows useful risk measures although they are unidimensional (with some exceptions (Richard 1975)).

The MAUT opponents argue with all the usual attacks against the EU approach in the unidimensional case. Further criticisms are relevant for the multidimensional case. MAUT defenders know that a direct assessment of joint utilities is such a heavy task to be implemented by a decision maker. Therefore, they propose useful decompositions of the joint utility function based upon a qualitative structuration of preferences under uncertainty. The ideal decomposition is the additive form where only unidimensional utility assessments are needed. Other main forms are the multiplicative form and the multilinear one. For these latter usual forms, few joint assessments are needed. Recently, Bell (1979) found interpolation methods using grids which approximate joint utility functions when a useful decomposition is unavailable. More on utility decompositions can be found in the survey by Farquhar (1977),

Keeney and Raiffa (1976, p. 349) acknowledge the awkwardness of the assessment procedures: necessity of asking extreme value questions, awkward calculus of components and coefficients, no fast feedback to the decision maker of his choices' implications, no updating procedure. According to SRI (Stanford Research Institute), the main practical difficulties of implementation concern the assessment of attitudes to risk and of probability distributions, chiefly when random variables are correlated.

In short, opponents mainly reproach MAUT for its lack of fitting, its distance from any actual decision process (which is replaced by a compelled evaluation process where ambiguity is sometimes arbitrarily suppressed), its cardinal index (Roy 1977, Roy and Vincke 1981, Starr and Zeleny 1977). Moreover, the practical appeal of the method is counteracted by its practical unableness to resolve the interdependence of random variables.

The components of risk aversion, appearing in the utility assessments, are pathological for two of them according to Bell (1981). The first one is not pathological: it is the classical influence of the decreasing marginal value of money. The two other components are, in his opinion, the anxiety of facing uncertainty, and the differences of losses when two lotteries with the same missed prize produce unequal terminal wealths. See also Dyer and Sarin (1982).

3.2 Other MCDM methods

Numerous other MCDM methods do not supply such a convincing modelling of randomness and of attitudes to risk as MAUT does. On the contrary, other risk components are sometimes better dealt with by these methods.

i) Randomness in uncertainty

a) Approach by Wilhelm (1975)
Jochem Wilhelm studied the conditions under which a MCDM approach under conditions of uncertainty can follow the classical method of the vector maximisation used by MCDM under conditions of certainty. He defines the set of objective risks as the criteria covariances matrix. He concludes (p. 103) that the vector maximisation is valuable as long as criteria are stochastically independent. This latter hypothesis of independence corresponds with the hypothesis of decision maker indifference to objective risks. This hypothesis requires that all criteria covariances were null (p. 54). When this hypothesis is too strong, Wilhelm (p. 54, pp. 103-104) states a quadratic approach which is obviously inspired by the quadratic portfolio selection model by Markowitz. Wilhelm also defines attitudes to objective risks in a classical manner by presenting a quadratic utility model (pp. 85-88). Then he states - how to be surprised? - that using such a quadratic model requires a cardinal utility function while the deterministic model (which one?) bears an ordinal structure for data (p. 92).

The generalisation by Wilhelm of MCDM for dealing with uncertainty definitely remains unclear and not convincing at all.

b) Fandel and Wilhelm (1976, p. 224) distinguish three approaches for solving MCDM problems under conditions of uncertainty.
1. If the state (θ_j) space is finite with dimension k, one will build for p criteria, pk objective functions, with

$f_{ij}(d) = f_i(d, \theta_j)$, $i = 1$ to p, where d is a decision. The extended MCDM problem $(D, F \equiv \{f_{ij}\} | d \in D)$ is solved in 'certainty'.

2. Dinkelback and Isermann (1973) suggest computing the certainty-equivalent, f_{ci}, for each random function $f_i(d,\tilde{\theta})$ and then to solve the problem (D,F_c) in 'certainty'.

By using the expected values of the random functions, the classical form of CCP is found again (Näslund 1967).

3. The last quoted approach is the simultaneous consideration of objectives by the MAUT, allowing stochastic and preferential interdependencies for criteria.

c) According to Leclercq (1979), Stochastic Programming (SP) (Kall 1976, Vajda 1972) belongs to MCDM by nature.

The general model has been proposed by Kall (1976). Let us follow Leclercq (1982, pp.33-34):

"Let $(\Omega, \sigma, P_\omega)$ denote a probabilised space and A, b, c respectively one random matrix (dimension m by n) and two random vectors (dimension m and n) defined on the triplet.

Let also D denote a closed set of R^{+n} and f a function from $\Omega * R^n$ to R^t. Stochastic linear programming studies the following problem: search a strategy, in fact a probability measure P_d on the Borel set D such that $f(Ad - b, c'd)$ is maximised with respect to a relation order defined on R^t.

In the most frequent cases f can be written using an integral on $\Omega * D$:

$$f(Ad - b, c'd) = \int_{\Omega * D} g(c'd, Ad - b)\, dP_\omega\, dP_d\ .$$

Like in game theory, we will say that P_d is a pure strategy or decision when the probability distribution is such that $\exists\ z \in D : P_d(\{z\}) = 1$. This case is known as 'order 0'.

Some other problems give up the independence hypothesis P_d and P_ω and search a strategy $d = d(A, b, c)$ (often the shape $d = Gb$ is used where G is a n by m unknown matrix); they belong to the general 'order 1' family of problems.

Two kinds of problems can be studied: decision (Here and Now) problems and description (Wait and See) problems. In 'wait and see' problems, the decision d is taken after the realisation of the random events and, for instance, the distribution of the objective functions must be found. In 'here and now' problems, the decision d must be taken before the knowledge of the realised values of the random variables."

Even in simple cases, the solutions for those SP require a "tremendous amount of work". Let us quote three special cases where a deterministic equivalent problem has been defined:

- the Chance Constrained Programming (CCP) by Charnes and Cooper (1959, 1977),
- the Stochastic Programming with Recourse (SPR),
- the Interactive Multiple Stochastic Programming (IMSP) by Leclercq (1982).

Let us recall, with Hogan, Morris and Thomson (1981) that a problem SPR can be written under the following form:

$$\max \{E_\theta\, u\, [f(\theta,d)] \mid d \in D\}, \qquad \theta \in \Theta \subset \mathbb{R}_m\,, \quad D \subset \mathbb{R}_n\,,$$

where d is the vector of decisions taken under the conditions of risk since θ is an events vector, the observed outcome is a function f, u is a utility function and E the expected value.

Each time a value of θ is observed, a recourse action is taken which will change f.

The authors claim that nearly all actual decision problems under risk can be featured under the form of SPR (p. 699). They also quote several authors who consider CCP as mathematically equivalent to SPR. According to the CCP form (p. 700), one can write:

$$z^c = \min_d \{E_d[cd] \mid P(a_i d \geq b_i) \geq \alpha_i,\ i=1 \text{ to } m;\ d \in D\},$$

where d, a_i, $c \in \mathbb{R}_n$ and $b_i \in \mathbb{R}$ and $\alpha_i \in [0,1]$, P is the probability.

The associated SPR problem should be:

$$z^R = \min_d \{E_{A,b,c} [L(d,A,b,c)] \mid d \epsilon D\},$$

where A is a matrix with rows a_i; $b \epsilon \mathbb{R}_m$; L is a loss function.

According to Charnes and Cooper (1959), CCP is applicable to "Temporal planning in which uncertain elements are present, but in which management is successful in controlling variables with which to influence outcomes..." Blau (1974) discovered that CCP leaves a negative EVPI, in contradiction to bayesian statistical decision theory. Gartska (1980) shows that mathematically equivalent CCP and SPR are not economically equivalent, due to different penalty structures of their programmes so that $EVPI^R > EVPI^C = 0$. The expected value of information is lost by transferring from SPR form to equivalent CCP. Hogan, Morris and Thomson justify this loss (1981, p. 703) by noting:

"... chance constrained are suggested as applicable when costs of deviations from goals cannot be adequately quantified or are not in commensurate units for inclusion in the objective function ... To require that this convenient approach to computing a solution also measures $EVPI^R$ is too much to expect. If costs of goal deviations cannot be adequately quantified then $EVPI^R$ is also not quantifiable."

Finally, the three authors conclude that CCP is seriously deficient as a model and is not a very good computing tool.

IMSP is an approach without utility function, where the objective(s) take one of the following shapes:

(E) : max E(c'd) (mean); (V) : min V(c'd) (variance);

(P) : max P(c'd) $\geq$ s) (probability); $\begin{cases} \text{(K) : max s (threshold),} \\ \text{s.t. P(c'd)} \geq \text{s)} \geq \alpha \text{ given.} \end{cases}$

Some of these shapes can be combined into EV, EP, EK problems. The P problem is formally easier when the decision maker wishes to maximise the probablity of realisation of the constraint: max P(Ad $\leq$ b). Indeed, this case produces an interesting uniformity of the treatment of constraints and objectives.

Finally, observe that nearly all those SP methods pertain to the second approach of risk: to define a 'function of penalisation of deviations from a multidimensional target', with risk measures of degree nul. This latter point makes those methods questionable from a behavioural point of view.

ii) Ambiguity in MCDM

a) Fuzzy sets approach by Jean-Marie Blin (1977)

J.M. Blin intends to show (p. 134):
"that the problems raised by the multiplicity of evaluation criteria are intrinsically fuzzy set problems and that many of the proposed solution procedures are simply methods to 'defuzzify' the problem.

Blin pleads for keeping some fuzziness in the concepts in order for the decision maker to be made comfortable in using them (p. 137) and in order to avoid two defaults of the notion of efficiency.

First, this latter notion produces two stages in the research for a unique solution so that MCDM conception seems hybrid. Then, efficiency is myopic in the sense that every dominated solution, even very close to the efficient frontier, is excluded from any further consideration.

Now to build a fuzzy efficient set allows the inclusion of all these bordering decisions with different membership degrees.

The membership function $\mu_E(d)$ of a decision $d \varepsilon D$ to the fuzzy efficient set E is as follows:

$$\mu_E(d) = \operatorname*{Min}_i \lambda_i(d)\ \mu_i(d)\ , \ i = 1,2,\ldots, (p+q)$$

$$\sum_{i=1}^{p} \lambda_i(d) = 1 \text{ and } \lambda_i(d) = 1 \text{ for } i > p\ ,$$

where $\mu_i(d)$ is the membership function for d for the criterion function ($i \leq p$) on for the constraint ($i > p$), $\lambda_i(d)$ is the membership function used for weighting the ith criterion.

Then Blin shows a formal equivalence between the membership functions and MCDM methods. Thus, the principle of fuzzification allows generation and study of several MCDM methods [4].

Using another technique, Zeleny and Colson also get, in portfolio selection, a 'probable' efficient frontier so that portfolios inside this frontier are probably, but not surely dominated (Colson and Zeleny 1979).

b) Ambiguity in weighting criteria

By comparison with MAUT, the main problem of MCDM methods, less formalised or more decision oriented, is how to discover a weighting or preempting process for criteria which do not compel at all the decision maker to make choices but only uses naturally available information.

Hence, MCDM methods have been classified according to the required level of information and to the kind of casually interactive procedures for weighting. (See Hwang and Masud 1979.) For instance, the method of Geoffrion, Dyer and Feinberg (1972) allows an interactive research of tradeoffs between criteria depending on an implicit utility function.

The method by Zionts and Wallenius (Zionts 1981, Zionts and Wallenius 1976) assumes a linear aggregation function for criteria, where weights are progressively found out, the weights set being implicitly the same during the procedure. The research procedures for weights through a sequence of compromises have already been quoted (Starr and Zeleny 1977). So, the interval programminq (Steuer 1977), the multiparametric decomposition (Gal and Nemoda 1972) is resting upon the same idea that the decision maker cannot assess an unambiguous value for each weight, but only intervals or spaces where those weights can vary.

Finally, weights are implicitly imposed by choosing a proximity measure in the ideal solution approaches - that is the solution optimising all objective functions. Among these approaches, the method STEM by Benayoun and Tergny (1972) proposes an interactive process for revealing weights which are included in the proximity measure. Zeleny even proposes a theory of displaced ideals (Zeleny 1974, pp. 167-182, 1977).

All these MCDM methods, quoted hereabove, leave an uneasiness about weighting. Indeed, even for interactive methods, there is a doubt about the final set of weights due to the dependence of this set on the path used through the interactive process. The choice of the method seems not to be neutral with regard to the preference elicitation. The doubt grows when using methods with ordinal data and cardinal weights.

The discomfort about weighting is strongly reduced by using the method ORESTE proposed by Roubens whose suggestion is to substitute a semi-order on criteria to the knowledge of weights. So, the preference relations between criteria is expressed under an ordinal manner (Roubens 1980, p. 59). However, as quoted by the author himself, the method ORESTE still requires the decision maker to choose three parameters (α : a substitution rate between criteria, β : a non-indifference threshold, λ : a non-comparability threshold). Using works by Kemeny (1959), Barbut (1966), Jacquet-Lagrèze (1978), Barthelemy (1979) among others, Roubens (1981, 1982) proposed then a purely ordinal multicriteria method:

"... to summarise a family of total weak orders (B_1, ..., B_k) of a finite set X : (a,b,c..) by a solution of:

$$\min_{B} \sum_{k} d(B,B_k) \text{ provided that: } d(B,B_k) \leq d(B,B_{k+1}),\ k;1,\ldots K-1,$$

where B may be an order, a weak order, a semi-order, and d is the distance of the symmetrical difference ($d(A,B)=|A \cup B|-|A \cap B|$). The optimal weak order is called median order (order or semi-order). Constraints are designed for obtaining a total structure closer to weak order B_k than to weak order B_{k+1}, since the weight of the criterion k is smaller than the weight of the criterion k+1." (Roubens 1982, pp. 1-9)

Note with this author (Roubens 1982, p. 2) that the method QUALIFLEX by Paelinck (1976) indeed consists of getting 'a median order associated with each weights set and consistent with a total weak order on the set of criteria'.

c) <u>Ambiguity (= imprecision) and extended notions for rankings and criteria</u>

In his various works, Bernard Roy tried to extend the MCDM methodology and to get it closer to actual decision problems. one of his main arguments is to take into account imprecision of data and of preferences with preserving respect of the decision maker. So, preference modelling is nowadays oriented towards processing less and less imprecise structures while the criterion notion becomes fuzzier. Roubens (1980) or Roy and Vincke (1981) state relationships between preference structures (orders, weak orders and semi-orders) and the kind of criterion (true, pre, semi or pseudo-criterion).

"Pseudo-criterion is a function g whose discriminating power is characterised by two thresholds q(g) and p(g) in the following way: $\forall$ a, bεA (the opportunity set):

$$aIb \Longleftrightarrow -q(g(a)) \leq g(a) - g(b) \leq q(g(b)),$$
$$aQb \Longleftrightarrow q(g(b)) < g(a) - g(b) \leq p(g(b)),$$
$$aPb \Longleftrightarrow p(g(b)) < g(a) - g(b),$$

$$\frac{q(g(b)) - q(g(a))}{g(b) - g(a)} \geq -1$$

$$\frac{p(g(b)) - p(g(a))}{g(b) - g(a)} \geq -1"$$

(See Roy and Vincke 1981, p. 215)

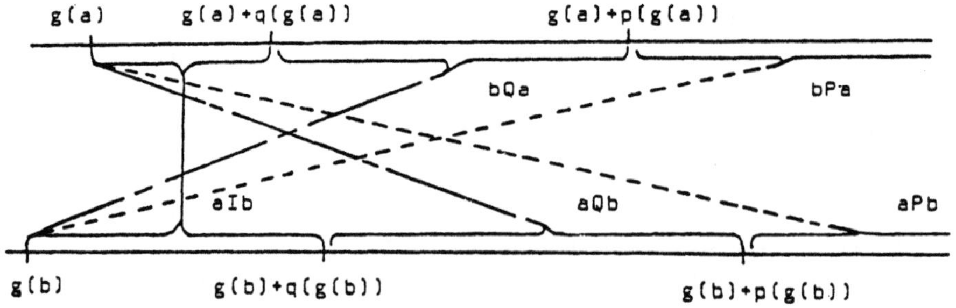

<u>Figure 1.</u> Preferences and Indifference Relationships for a Pseudo-Criterion

P is a strict preference, I is the indifference due to a lack of significance of values difference for criterion g. Q is a weak preference due to a hesitation indifference and strict preference.

If p=q=constant, the pseudo-criterion becomes a quasi-criterion with a constant threshold. Hence, it has been shown by Scott and Suppes (1958) that the binary relation (P,I) is a semi-order for a finite A. If p=q=0, the usual criterion, i.e. the true criterion is found again while (P,I) becomes a total weak order.

In methods ELECTRE I and II, outranking lies upon true criteria while ELECTRE III uses a fuzzy outranking based on pseudo-criteria, and it is unnecessary to determine a total weak order (see Roy 1978).

Let us note here that the literature about outrankings (the concept owed to B. Roy) is a quickly expanding research field (Siskos et al. 1983). Observe also that the main concepts of 'discordance' and 'concordance' of the Electre methods have been revisited by Dujmovĭc (1974).

An interesting new avenue is proposed with 'the aggregation-desaggregation logic' followed by Jacquet-Lagrèze and Siskos (1982). It seems to me close to the decision maker practice, while it realises a compromise between a priori global preferences and individual preferences on each criterion.

3.3 Conclusions

Only MAUT provides a convincing modelling of the 'random' components of the risk and of the risk attitude, provided that criticisms against the maximum EU principle and difficulties in the MAUT assessment were outcast.

The stochastic programming with recourse is useful in dealing with randomness and ambiguity for measuring penalties of objectives deviations. Chance Constrained Programming, available for temporal planning under uncertainty, presents conceptual problems.

Standing in contrast to these awkwardly implemented devices, most multicriteria methods intend to be easier, and closer to the decision maker. Beyond axiomatic and convergence problems in these methods, the ambiguity is mostly introduced into them in the sense of data or preferences imprecision or in the sense of fuzziness. Here, we ask: is it opportune to compel ambiguity into a mathematical form at the expense of its richness of meaning?

4 CONCLUSIONS AND EXTENSIONS

From our readings of the risk literature, it seems that uncertainty and risk concepts should be more general. First, the risk evaluation needs an uncertainty assessment and a valuation of decision outcomes. The uncertainty concept must be extended to everything which is a factor in the 'unknowledge' of the decision maker or of the explorer, and not to be limited, as mainly done in the literature, to only its random component. So, we have proposed the addition of the component of ambiguity, specific to imperfect human perception, and a component issued from the unavoidable imperfect reduction of the badly known complexity of the decision problem or of the observed phenomenon. The risk measure makes more than a valuation of risk, it also takes into account risk attitudes. It is just this consideration of decision maker attitudes which makes the difference between a risk measure and a measure of valued information (like EVPI).

Other extensions or better foundations of the risk measure are still to be done. Some new avenues have been proposed (Colson 1982).

First, vector measures of risk are useful each time risk components are not aggregable into the form of a general risk.

Although there exist multidimensional measures of risk-aversion or of risk-proneness (see, for instance, Richard 1975), literature is poor in vector measures of risk. As far as we know, our propositions with those of Zeleny (Colson 1981, Colson and Zeleny 1979, 1980, Zeleny 1978) are a first attempt to measure and to deal with vector risk. Note that the multimoment approaches in portfolio selection are indeed the decomposition of one objective: the stochastic dominance and could be outcast as being a multicriteria approach (Colson and Zeleny 1979).

Finally, let us observe that Finance (Spronk 1981, 1982) and risk management (Chevalier and Hirsch 1978, 1978a, 1981) literature, among others, open the door for these vector measures of risk.

Second, the dynamic risk appears with uncertain time distribution and evolution of returns, with changes in decision environment and alterations of decision maker preferences. From a theoretical point of view, we suggest building on a stochastico-temporal approach producing stochastic dominance and time dominance as peculiar cases. However, unless strong hypotheses on decision maker preferences exist, this approach could be less effective than its two well-known peculiar cases.

Third, we have already suggested building a bipolar theory of risk based upon the so-called bipolar hypothesis [5] (Colson 1981). This 'conflicting' new theory has produced two interesting results up till now:

i) the bipolar hypothesis allows inserting again the speculative attitudes of investment in finance analysis.

ii) as a special case: the Prospect Ranking Vector (PRV) model by Colson and Zeleny (1979, 1980) provides rankings of uncertain prospects under the conditions of imperfect knowledge about the decision maker's attitudes to risk and his returns assessments [6]. A special issue of this PRV model is a generalisation of the classical mean minimum variance analysis, which is conservative, to a new tricriteria approach: to maximise mean and upper semi-variance (S^+), and to minimise lower semi-variance (S^-).

Fourth, the decision instability is a time specific feature of risk (Colson 1983, Talpaz et al. 1983). So, it seems useful to define a risk of decision change (Colson 1982). On the other hand, the desire of decision flexibility appears in Microeconomics with Marshak and Nelson (1962), and Koopmans (1964), while this idea is introduced in decision analysis by Merkhoffer (1975, 1977). Observe that the versatility criterion of Werczberger (1979, 1981, 1982) is a probability measure for the risk of change in a multidimensional case. This latter criterion is inspired by 'the comparative hypervolum' criterion by Charnetski (1978).

To encompass these two components of risk perception through time (the decision change risk and and the decision inflexibility risk), we suggest another bipolar hypothesis: 'every man's attitude to risk through time takes into account two opposite bents of human nature: the desire of change and the desire of stability, and this produces a bipole in the perception of dynamic risk".

Many papers no longer consider the decision as being an event abstracted from environment and from time. More general and concrete studies are evolving from outcome-oriented approaches toward process-oriented approaches. Limiting ourselves to a better understanding of general individual risk, one of our suggestions is to link it at an imperfect progress through a personal decision process (Colson 1982). Of course, such an individual approach is not consistent with a frequent occurrence of many actors in the process. Now, recent enquiries (Moscarola 1980) have revealed such a diversity of decision processes in organisations that their common features are not easily found while a taxonomy of decision processes may be an unattainable objective.

NOTES

[1] 'Complexity' is here accepted in its broadest sense. See for instance, Casti (1979) and Gottinger (1983).

[2] As pointed out by Chapman and Cooper (1983), risk analysis is more and more concerned with the choice of a good model. Furthermore, O.R. methods move towards the use of situation-specific methods where the modelling risk may be greater and unknown.

[3] See (Hwang and Masud 1979, Hwang and Yoon 1981, Starr and Zeleny 1977) for the classical distinction between MultiAttribute Decision Methods (MADM) and MultiObjective Decision Methods (MODM).

[4] Of course, many authors work on fuzzy MCDM. See, for instance, Ignizio and Daniels 1983, Zionts 1981).

[5] The bipolar hypothesis is that 'every man's attitude toward risk is ex ante (i.e. before the decision making) characterised by both a speculative pole and a conservative pole. Ex post, the predominant attitude of risk aversion or risk proneness depends on the situation and on the decision maker.

[6] The imperfect knowledge of returns probabilities begins to be investigated in several studies.

REFERENCES

Allais, M. and Hagen, D., Expected Utility Hypothesis and the Allais Paradox, D. Reidel Publ. Co., Dordrecht, Holland, 1979.

Allen, T.C. and Duval, L., 'A theoretical and practical approach to risk management', Article 1, Panorama of the risk management process, Risk and Insurance Management Society, New York, 1971.

Arrow, K.J. and Hurwicz, L., 'An optimality criterion for decision making under ignorance', in: Carter, C.F. and Ford, J.L. (eds), Uncertainty and Expectations in Economics, Basil Blackwell and Mott Ltd., Oxford, 1972.

Ball, B.C. Jr., 'Managing risk in the real world', EJOR, 14, 3, 1983, pp. 248-261.

Barbur, M., 'Note sur les ordres totaux à distance minimum d'une relation binaire donnée', Math. et Sci. Humaines, 17, 1966, pp. 47-48.

Barthelemy, J.P., Propriétés Métriques des Ensembles Ordonnées. Comparaison et agrégation de relations binaires, Thèse doctorat d'état de Mathématiques, Université de Besançon, 1979.

Bawa, V.S., 'Optimal rules for ordering uncertain prospects', Journal Financial Economics, 2, 1975, pp. 95-121.

Bawa, V.S., 'Mathematical programming of admissible portfolios', Manag. Sci., 22, 1977, pp. 779-785.

Bawa, V.S., Lindenberg, E.B. and Rafsky, L.C., 'An efficient algorithm to determine stochastic dominance admissible sets', Manag. Sci., 25,7, 1979, pp. 609-622.

Bell, D.E., 'Multiattribute utility functions: decompositions using interpolation', Manag. Sci., 25, 8, 1979, pp. 744-753.

Bell, D.E., 'Components of risk aversion', in: Brans (ed), Operational Research 81, July 20-24, Hamburg, North Holland, 1981, pp. 235-242.

Benayoun, S.M., Montgolfier, J. de, Tergny, J. and Larichev, O., 'Linear programming with multiple objedtive functions step method (STEM)', Math. Prog., 1, 3, 1972, pp. 336-375.

Blau, R.A., 'Stochastic programming and decision analysis: an apparent dilemma', Manag. Sci., 21, 1974, pp. 271-276.

Blin, J.M., 'Fuzzy sets in multiple criteria decision making', in: Starr and Zeleny (eds), TIMS Studies in Management Sciences, 6, 1977, pp. 129-146.

Bouchon, B., 'Questionnaires in a fuzzy setting', in: Kapzyk, J. and Yager, R.R. (eds), Management Decision Support Systems using Fuzzy Sets and Possibility Theory, Verlag TUV Rheinland, 1983.

Bouchon, B., 'Décisions basées sur des informations floues', in: Colson, G. and Teghem (eds), XIX Meeting of the European Working Group on Multiple Criteria Decision Aid, 15-16 March, 1984, Working papers of EIASM.

Casti, J., Connectivity, Complexity and Catastrophe in Large-Scale Systems, IIASA, 7, Wiley, New York, 1979.

Chapman, J.R. and Cooper, D.F., 'Risk analysis: testing some prejudices', EJOR, 14,3, 1983, pp. 238-247.

Charnes, A. and Cooper, W., 'Chance constrained programming', Manag. Sci., 1959, pp. 73-79.

Charnes, A. and Cooper, W., 'Goal programming and multiple objective optimisations - Part I', EJOR, 1, 1977, pp. 39-54.

Charnetski, J.R., 'Multi-attribute decision making with partial information: the comparative hypervolum criterion', Nav. Res. Log. Quarterly, 25, 1978, pp. 279-288.

Chevalier, A. and Hirsch, G., 'Risk management in financial decisions: a critical survey', ESCP, presented at Corporate Finance Workshop at the European Institute for Advanced Studies in Management, Brussels, December 7, 1978.

Chevalier, A. and Hirsch, G., 'La gestion des risques: un impératif primordial de la fonction financière', Cahiers d'Etudes et de Recherches, Series Recherches, 78-1, 1978a.

Chevalier, A. and Hirsch, G., 'The assessment of political risk in the investment decision', J. of Op. Res. Soc., 1981, pp. 599-610.

Cohen, M. and Jaffray, J.Y., 'Rational behavior under complete ignorance', Economètrica, 48-5, 1980, pp. 1281-1299.

Cohen, M. and Jaffray, J.Y., 'Experimental results on decision making under uncertainty', in: Henn, R. et al. (eds), Methods of Operations Research, 44, Oelgeschlager, Gunn and Hain, 1982.

Colson, G.E., 'Le risque d'inversion de la décision bayesienne et ses proxy-mesures', 1979, September. Reprint in" GRAAL, 8304, Université de Liège, 1983a.

Colson, G.E., 'La théorie bipolaire du risque: applications en sélection des investissements et en sélection de portefeuilles (conséquences de l'hypothèse bipolaire sur l'équilibre individuel et l'équilibre de marché)', September 1980. Reprint in: GRAAL, 8305, Université de Liège, 1983b.

Colson, G.E., 'Le bipolarisme de degré zéro (son application au choix d'investissement sous conditions d'information partielle: le modèle Prospect Ranking Vector', September 1981. Reprint in: GRAAL, 8306, Université de Liège, 1983c.

Colson, G.E., 'Toward a bipolar theory of risk', EJOR, 6, 4, 1981a, pp. 352-359.

Colson, G.E., Contributions à lEtude des Mesures d'Information et de Risque, PhD Thesis, Université de Liège, 1982.

Colson, G.E. and Teghem, J. Jr., Multiple Criteria Decision Aid in an Uncertain Context, Proceedings of the XIX Meeting of the European Working Group on Multiple Criteria Decision Aid, 15-16 March 1984, Working Papers of EIASM, Brussels, 1984.

Colson, G.E. and Zeleny, M.,'Uncertain prospects ranking and portfolio analysis under the conditions of partial information', in: Mathematical Systems in Economics', 44, Oelgeschlager, Gunn and Hain, Cambridge Mass., 1979.

Colson, G.E. and Zeleny, M., 'Multicriterion concept of risk under incomplete information', Co. and OR, 7, 1-2, 1980, pp. 125-143.

Dinkelbach, W. and Isermann, H., 'On decision making under multiple criteria and under incomplete information', in: Cochrane and Zeleny (eds), Multiple Criteria Decision Making, Columbia, South Carolina, 1973.

Dubois, D., Modèles Mathématiques de l'Imprécis et de l'Incertain en Vue d'Applications aux Techniques d'Aide à la Décision, Thèse d'Etat, Grenoble, 1983.

Dujmović, J.J., 'Weighted conjunctive and disjunctive means and their application in system evaluation', Publikacije Elektrotechnićkog, Matematika I Fizika, no. 461-497, 1974, pp. 147-158.

Dyer, J.S. and Sarin, R.K., 'Relative risk aversion', Manag. Sci., 28, 8, 1982, pp. 875-886.

Ekern, S., 'Time dominance efficiency analysis', J. Finance, 36, 5, 1981, pp. 1023-1034.

Fandel, G. and Wilhelm, J., 'Rational solution principles and information requirements as elements of a theory of multiple criteria decision making', in: Thiriez, H. and Zionts, S. (eds), Multiple Criteria Decision Making, Jouy and Josas, France, 1975, and Springer Verlag, 130, 1976, pp. 215-231.

Farquhar, P.H., 'A survey of multiattribute utility theory and applications', in: Starr, M.K. and Zeleny, M. (eds), Multiple Criteria Decision Making, TIMS Studies in the Management Sciences, 6, North Holland, 1977, pp. 59-89.

Fishburn, P.C., 'Non-compensatory preferences', Synthese, 33, 1976, pp. 393-403.

Fishburn, P.C., 'Mean-risk analysis with risk associated with below-target returns', Am. Econ. Rev., 67, 2, 1977, pp. 116-126.

Fishburn, P.C., 'A survey of multiattribute/multicriterion evaluation theories', in: Zionts, S. (ed), Multiple Criteria Integer Problem Solving, Proceedings, Buffalo, NY (USA), Lecture Notes in Economics and Mathematical Systems, Springer Verlag, 155, 1978, pp. 181-224.

Gal, T. and Nedoma, J., 'Multiparametric linear programming', Manag. Sci., 18, 7, 1972, pp. 406-422.

Gartska, S.J., 'The economic equivalence of several stochastic programming models', in: Demster (ed), Stochastic Programming, Academic Press, New York, 1980, pp. 83-91.

Geoffrion, A.M., Dyer, J.S. and Feinberg, A., 'An interactive approach for multicriterion optimization, with an application to the operation of an academic department', Manag. Sci., 19, 4, 1972, pp. 357-368.

Gottinger, H.W., 'Coping with complexity', Theory and Decision Library 33, D. Reidel, Martinus Nijhoff, 1983.

Grauer, M. and Wierzbicki, A. (eds), Multiple Objective and Stochastic Optimization, IIASA, Laxemburg, 1982.

Gupta, M.M., Ragade, R.K. and Yager, R.R., Advances in Fuzzy Set Theory and Applications, North Holland, Amsterdam, 1979.

Gupta, M.M. and Sanchez, E. (eds), Approximate Reasoning in Decision Analysis, North Holland, 1982a.

Gupta, M.M . and Sanchez, E. (eds), Fuzzy Information and Decision Processes, North Holland, 1982b.

Hadar, J. and Russell, W.R., 'Rules for ordering uncertain prospects', Am. Econ. Rev., 59, 1969, pp. 25-34.

Hanoch, G. and Levy, H., 'The efficiency analysis of choices involving risk', Rev. of Econ. Studies, 36, 1969, pp. 335-346.

Hogan, A.J., Morris, J.G. and Thompson, H.E., 'Decision problem under risk and Chance Constrained Programming: dilemma in the transition', Manag. Sci., 27, 6, 1981, pp. 698-716.

Hwang, C.L. and Masud, A.S.M., Multiple Objective Decision Making Methods and Applications (a state-of-the-art survey), Springer Verlag, 164, 1979.

Hwang, C.L., Paidy, S.R. and Yoon, K., 'Mathematical programming with multiple objectives: a tutorial', Co. and OR, 7, 1-2, 1980, pp. 5-31.

Hwang, C.L. and Yoon, K., Multiple Attribute Decision Making, Methods and Applications, Springer Verlag, 1981.

Ignizio, J.P. and Daniels, S.C., 'Fuzzy multicriteria integer programming via fuzzy generalized networks', FSS, 10, 3, 1983, pp. 261-270.

Jacquet-Lagrèze, E., 'Représentation de quasi-ordres et de relations probabilistes transitives sous forme standard et méthodes d'approximation', Math. et Sci. Humaines, 63, 1978, pp. 5-24.

Jacquet-Lagrèze, E. and Siskos, J., 'Assessing a set of additive utility functions of multicriteria decision making', the UTA Method, EJOR, 10, 1982, pp. 151-164.

Kall, P., 'Stochastic linear programming', Lecture Notes in Econometrics and Operations Research, 21, Springer Verlag, Berlin, 1976.

Keeney, R.L., 'An illustrated procedure for assessing multiattribute utility functions', Sloan Manag. Rev., Fall, 1972, pp. 37-50.

Keeney, R.L., 'Decision analysis: an overview', Operations Research, 30, 1982, pp. 803-838.

Keeney, R.L. and Raiffa, H., Decision with Multiple Objectives: Preferences and Value Trade-offs, Wiley, New York, 1976.

Kemeny, J.G., 'Mathematics without numbers', Daedalus, 88, 1959, pp. 577-591.

Kickert, W.J.M., Fuzzy Theories on Decision Making: A Critical Review, Martinus Nijhoff, 1978.

Kmietowicz, Z.W. and Pearman, A.D., Decision Theory and Incomplete Knowledge, Gower, Aldershot, UK, 1981.

Knight, F.H., Risk, Uncertainty and Profit, University of Chicago Press, London, 1971, (1st Edition 1921).

Koopmans, T.C., 'On the flexibility of future preferences', in: Shelly and Brian (eds), Human Judgments and Optimality, Wiley, New York, 1964.

Kreps, D.M., 'A representation theorem for "preference for flexibility"', Econometrica, 47, 3, 1979, pp. 565-571.

Kreps, D.M. and Porteus, E.L., 'Temporal resolution of uncertainty and dynamic choice theory', Econometrica, 46, 1, 1978, pp. 185-200.

Leclercq, J.P., Résolution de Programmes Linéaires Stochastiques par des Techniques Multicritères, Thèse de Doctorat, Faculty of Science, University of Namur, 1979.

Leclercq, J.P., 'Stochastic programming: an interactive multicriteria approach', EJOR, 10, 1982, pp. 33-41.

Marshak, T. and Nelson, R., 'Flexibility, uncertainty and economic theory', Metroeconomica, ap-December, 1962, pp. 42-58.

McCord, M. and Neufville, R. de, Exploration of Fundamental Deficiencies of Expected Utility Theory, Draft paper (January) - presented at XVth Journées EURO, aide à la décision multicritère, Namur, 18-19 March 1982.

Merkhoffer, M.W., Flexibility and Decision Analysis, PhD Thesis, Department of Engineering Economic Systems, Stanford University, 1975.

Merkhoffer, M.W., 'The value of information given decision flexibility', Manag. Sci., 23, 7, 1977, pp. 716-727.

Merton, R.C., 'Theory of finance from the perspective of continuous time', J. of Fin. and Quant. Analysis, 10, 1975, pp. 659-674.

Merton, R.C., 'On the mathematics and economic assumptions of continuous-time models', in: Sharpe, W. (ed), Financial Economics: Essays in Honor of Paul Cootner, North Holland, Amsterdam (forthcoming).

Merton, R.C. and Samuelson, P.A., 'Fallacy of the log-normal approximation to optimal portfolio decision-making over many periods', J. of Fin. Econ., 1, 1974, pp. 67-94.

Moscarola, J., 'Le processus de décision dans les organisations', Enseignement et Gestion, Nouvelle Série, 15, Autumn, 1980, pp. 5-18.

Näslund, B., Decisions Under Risk, Stockholm, 1967.

Paelinck, J.H.P., 'Qualitative multiple criteria analysis, environmental protection and multiregional development', Papers of the Regional Science Association, 36, 1976, pp. 59-74.

Pratt, J.W., 'Risk aversion in the small and in the large', Econometrica, 32, 1964, pp. 122-136.

Richard, S.F., 'Multivariate risk aversion, utility independence and separable utility functions', Manag. Sci., 22, 1, 1975, pp. 12-21.

Rivett, B.H.P., 'Behavioural problems of utility theory', in: White and Bowen (eds), Theories of Decision in Practice, Hodder and Stoughton, 1975, pp. 21-27.

Roubens, M., 'Analyse et agrégation des préférences: modélisation, ajustment et résumé de données relationnelles', Rev. Belge de Stat., d'Info. et de Rech. Op., 20, 2, 1980, pp. 36-67.

Roubens, M., 'Preference relations on actions and criteria in multiple criteria decision making', EJOR, 10, 1981, pp. 51-55.

Roubens, M., 'Médiane et méthodes multicritères ordinales', article présenté aux XV° journées EURO aide à la décision multicritère, 18-19 March, Namur, published in Rev. Belge de Stat., d'Info. et de Rech. Op., 22, 2, 1982, pp. 21-35.

Roy, B., 'A conceptual framework for a prescriptive theory of decision aid', in: Starr and Zeleny (eds), TIMS Studies in the Management Sciences, 6, North Holland, 1977, pp. 179-210.

Roy, B., 'ELECTRE III: un algorithme de classement fondé sur une représentation floue des préférences en présence de critères multiples', Cahiers Centre Etudes Recherche Opérationnelle, 20, 1, 1978, pp. 2-23.

Roy, B. and Vincke, Ph., 'Multicriteria analysis: survey and new directions', EJOR, 8, 3, 1981, pp. 207-218.

Samuelson, P.A., 'The fundamental approximation theorem of portfolio analysis in terms of means, variances and higher moments', Rev. of Econ. Studies, 37, 1970, pp. 537-542.

Samuelson, P.A. and Merton, R.C., 'Generalized mean-variance tradeoffs for best perturbations corrections to approximate portfolio decisions', J. Finance, 29, 1, 1974, pp. 27-40.

Scott, D. and Suppes, P., 'Foundational aspects of theories of measurement', J. Symbolic Logic, 23, 1958, pp. 113-128.

Siskos, J., Washer, G. and Winkels, H.M., 'A bibliography on outranking approaches (1966-1982)', Cahiers du LAMSADE, 45, Paris, March 1983.

Spronk, J., Interactive Multiple Goal Programming: Applications to Financial Planning, Martinus Nijhoff, Boston, 1981.

Spronk, J., 'Goals and constraints in financial planning', in: Grauer, and Wierzbicki (eds), Multiple Objective and Stochastic Optimization, IIASA, Laxemburg, 1982.

Starr, M.K. and Zeleny, M., 'MCDM - state and future of the arts', in: Starr and Zeleny (eds), TIMS Studies in the Management Science, 6, North Holland, 1977, pp. 5-29.

Steuer, R.E., 'Multiple objective linear programming with interval criterion weights', Manag. Sci., 23, 3, 1977, pp. 305-316.

Stigum, B.P. and Wenstøp, F. (eds), Foundations of Utility and Risk Theory with Applications, Theory and Decision Library 37, D. Reidel, Martinus Nijhoff, 1983.

Stone, B.K., 'A general class of three-parameter risk measures', J. of Finance, 28, 1973, pp. 675-685.

Talpaz, H., Harpaz, A. and Penson, J.P., 'Risk and spectral instability in portfolio analysis', EJOR, 14, 1983, pp. 262-269.

Tavernier, G., 'Risk managers: ready for anything', Int. Manag., 32, 7, 1977, pp. 22-25.

Tehranian, H., 'Empirical studies in portfolio performance using higher degrees of stochastic dominance', J. of Finance, 35, 1980, pp. 159-171.

Tell, B., 'The effect of uncertainty on the selection of a multiple criteria utility model', in: Roubens, M. (ed), Advances in Operations Research, North Holland, 1977, pp. 497-504.

Teghem, J. Jr. and Kunsch, P.L., 'Application of multi-objective stochastic linear programming to power systems planning', in: Colson, G. and Teghem, J. (eds), XIX Meeting of the European Working Group on Multiple Criteria Decision Aid, proceedings in EIASM papers, 15-16 March 1984.

Tversky, A., 'On the elicitation of preferences: descriptive and prescriptive considerations', in: Bell, D.E., Keeney, R.L. and Raiffa, H. (eds), Conflicting Objectives in Decisions, IIASA, Wiley, New York, 1977, pp. 209-222.

Vajda, S., Probabilistic Programming, Academic Press, New York, 1972.

Vansnick, J.C., 'Strength of preferences: theoretical and practical apsects', in: Brans, J.P. (ed), Operational Research 1984, North Holland (forthcoming).

Vansnick,J.C., 'Inter-criteria information in multiple criteria decision making, the non-compensatory approach', in: Colson, G. and Teghem, J. Jr. (eds), XIX Meeting of the European Working Group on Multiple Criteria Decision Aid, proceedings in EIASM papers, 15-16 March 1984.

Vedder, J.N., 'Multiattribute decision making under uncertainty using bounded intervals', in: Cochrane, J.L. and Zeleny, M. (eds), Multiple Criteria Decision Making, University of South Carolina Press, Columbia, 1973, pp. 93-107.

Vincke, Ph., 'Preference modelling: a survey and experiment', in: Brans, J.P. (ed), Operations Research 81, Actes du congrès IFORS 81, North Holland, Hamburg, 1981, pp. 341-354.

Neumann, J. von and Morgenstern, O., Theory of Games and Economic Behavior, Princeton University Press, Princeton, 1944, (2nd Edition 1947, 3rd Edition 1967).

Walsten, Th. and Budescu, D.V., 'Encoding subjective probabilities (state-of-the-art)', Manag. Sci., 29, 2, 1983, pp. 151-173.

Werczberger, E., 'The versatility model in decision making under uncertainty with regard to goals and constraints', working paper 53 presented at the 9th meeting of EURO Working Group on Multicriteria decision Making in Amsterdam, 6 April 1979, pp. 1-20.

Werczberger, E., 'The versatility model in decision making under uncertainty with regard to goals and constraints', in: Nijkamp, P. and Spronk, J. (eds), Multiple Criteria Analysis: Operational Methods, Gower, Aldershot, 1981, pp. 187-199.

Werczberger, E., 'Multiperson multitarget decision making using the versatility criterion', working paper 66, presented at the Fifth International Conference on MCDM, Mons, 9-13 August, 1982.

Whitmore, G.A. and Findlay, M.C., Stochastic Dominance: An Approach to Decision Making under Risk, Health, Lexington, Mass., 1978.

Wilhelm, J., Objectives and Multi-Objective Decision Making under Uncertainty, Springer Verlag, 112, Berlin, 1975.

Yu, P.L., 'Cone convexity, cone extreme points and nondominated solutions in decision problems with multi-objectives', J. Optimization Theory and Applications, 14, 3, 1974, pp. 319-377.

Zadeh, L.A., 'Fuzzy sets as a basis for a theory of possibility', Fuzzy Sets and Systems, 1, 1978, pp. 3-28.

Zeleny, M., Linear Multiobjective Programming, Springer Verlag, 95, New York, 1974.

Zeleny, M., 'Adaptive displacement of preferences in decision making', in: Starr and Zeleny (eds), TIMS Studies in the Management Science, 6, 1977, pp. 147-157.

Zeleny, M., 'Multidimensional measure of risk: prospect ranking vector (PRV)', in: Zionts, S. (ed), Multiple Criteria Problem Solving, Springer, New York, 1978, pp. 529-548.

Zeleny, M., 'Satisficing, optimization and risk in portfolio selection', in: Derkunderen, F. and Crum, R. (eds), Financing Issues and Corporate Project Selection, Martinus Nijhoff, Boston, 1980.

Zionts, S., 'A multiple criteria method for choosing among discrete alternatives', EJOR, Vol 7/2, 181, pp. 143-147.

Zionts, S. and Wallenius, J., 'An interactive programming method for solving the multiple criteria problem', Manag. Sci., 22, 1976, pp. 652-663.

Zimmermann, H.J., 'Using fuzzy sets in operational research', EJOR, 13, 3, 1983, pp. 201-216.

10 Data Structures and Complexity of Algorithms for Discrete MCDM Methods

J. Fichefet

1 INTRODUCTION

It appears that microcomputers will play a more and more important part in the use of multiple criteria decision aid methods. It is thus interesting to evaluate the impact of the implementation design on response time. In this respect, one of the most valuable means is the concept which has been called 'time complexity' of algorithms. This time complexity is rather dependent on the data structures used to represent and to manipulate the objects involved in the algorithms.

This paper intends to illustrate this point of view for discrete MCDM methods and has been divided into two parts.

Part I recalls some basic definitions and results concerning binary relations, preference relations and graph theory, and defines the concept of complexity of algorithms. Part I also examines two basic data structures (lists and stacks) and their possible use in order to represent graphs inside a computer. A basic algorithm, called depth-first search, is also described and concerns a visiting plan for all vertices and arcs of a digraph.

It seems clear that all data structures (Aho et al. 1974, Aho et al. 1983, Reingold et al. 1977) are a priori of great interest in the field of MCDM methods and that a choice had to be made in this paper. That is the reason why we decided to organise Part II around the basic data structures and the depth-first search algorithm described in Part I. We thus came to present algorithms which are of interest in preference modelling and MCDM and are concerned with such problems as: determining the transitive closure and the strong components of a weak preference relation, finding quasi-orders compatible with a preference relation, testing particular properties and determining the choice set of a preference relation. All algorithms are presented with a pseudo-language which is hoped to be self-evident.

Part I : Generalities

1.1 Basic definitions and notations concerning relations, preference relations and directed graphs

1.1.1 Binary relations

Let A be a set. The cardinality of A will be denoted by $|A|$. A binary relation S on A is a subset of the Cartesian product A x A, i.e. a set of ordered pairs (a,b) such that a and b are in A. We shall write, for a,b∈A :

$$a \; S \; b \quad \text{if and only if } (a,b) \in S,$$
$$\sim a \; S \; b \quad \text{if and only if } (a,b) \notin S.$$

A binary relation S on A may satisfy one or more of the following properties:

- reflexivity if a S a for all a∈A,
- irreflexivity if ~a S a for all a∈A,
- symmetry if a S b ⇒ b S a for all a,b∈A,
- antisymmetry if a S b ⇒~ b S a for all a,b∈A such that a ≠ b,
- asymmetry if a S b ⇒~ b S A for all a,b∈A. Thus asymmetry implies irreflexivity and antisymmetry,
- transitivity if a S b and b S c ⇒ a S c for all a,b,c∈A,
- completeness if for all a,b∈A : a ≠ b ⇒ a S b or b S a,
- strong completeness if a S b or b S a for all a,b∈A. A strong complete relation is reflexive and complete.

  A binary relation can satisfy several of these properties simultaneously. Table 1 gives the most usual relation types. Let us note that:
- a quasi-order is also called a pre-order,
- a total order is also called a complete order, or a linear order, or a simple order.

When S is an equivalence relation on A, then the set

$$a^* = (b \in A : a \; S \; b)$$

is called the (S-) equivalence class containing a while a is called a representative of a*. The collection of all equivalence classes is named the quotient of A by S and will be denoted by A/S. This quotient is a partition of A : every element of A is in one and only one equivalence class.

Table 1.

Relation property / Relation type	re-flex-ive	symme-tric	transi-tive	asymme-tric	antisym-metric	complete	strongly complete
Equivalence	x	x	x				
Quasi-order	x		x				
Weak order			x				x
Total order			x		x		x
Strict total order			x	x		x	
Partial order	x		x		x		
Strict partial order			x	x			

1.1.2 Directed graphs

A directed graph or digraph $G = (V,E)$ consists of a finite set V of vertices and a set E of arcs or directed edges. An arc is an ordered pair of vertices (x,y) where x is the initial endpoint and y is the terminal endpoint.

When $(x,y) \in E$, we say that x and y are adjacent vertices, y is a successor of x, x is a predecessor of y and arc (x,y) is from x to y. An arc of G of the form (x,x) is called a loop.

The out-degree (in-degree) of a vertex x is the number of arcs which have x as initial (terminal) endpoint and are not loops, and will be denoted by $d^+(x)(d^-(x))$.

The adjacency matrix of digraph $G = (V,E)$ is a $|V| \times |V|$ matrix M where the element $M(x,y)$ corresponding to vertices $x,y \in V$ is equal to 1 when (x,y) is an arc and equal to 0 otherwise.

A path in a digraph is a sequence of vertices $(x_0, x_1, x_2, \ldots, x_q)$ such that $(x_{i-1}, x_i) \in E$ for $i=1,2,\ldots,q$. This path is from x_0 to x_q

and passes through vertices x_1, x_2, ..., x_{q-1}, and ends at x_q. Arcs (x_{i-1}, x_i), for i=1,2,...,q, are said to be on the path. The length of a path is the number of arcs on the path. When a path is from a vertex to the same vertex, it is called a cycle. A digraph is acyclic when it contains no cycle.

A vertex x is an ancestor of vertex y if there is a path from x to y. In this case, vertex y is a descendant of vertex x. The transitive closure of digraph G = (V,E) is a digraph $\hat{G}$ = (V,F) such that (x,y)∈F in $\hat{G}$ if there exists a path (≠ loop) from x to y in G. Let G = (V,E) be a digraph, A⊆V and F⊆E. The subgraph of G induced by A is the digraph $G_A = (A, E_A)$ such that

$$E_A = ((x,y) \in E \mid x \in A \text{ and } y \in A) ,$$

while the partial graph of G generated by F is the digraph (V,F) whose vertex set is V and whose arc set is F. A partial subgraph of G is the subgraph of a partial graph of G.

Let G = (V,E) be a digraph and S be the equivalence relation on V such that x S y if and only if x = y or there is a path from x to y and a path from y to x. The subgraphs $G_i = (V_i, E_i)$ of G induced by the S - equivalence classes V_i are called the strongly connected components or the strong components of G. A digraph with only one strong component is said to be a strongly connected digraph.

A rooted tree, or an arborescence, is a digraph with a designated vertex called a root such that there is a unique path from the root to any other vertex. It is clear that a rooted tree is acyclic and has only one root.

What A is a finite set, let us note that a binary relation S on A can be looked upon as a directed graph G = (A, S) and vice versa, for a S b if and only if (a,b) is an arc of G. We shall thus speak of a reflexive digraph, and so on.

In particular, a digraph G = (V,E), whose adjacency matrix is M, is said to be:

- symmetric if, for all x,y∈V,

$$(x,y) \in E \Rightarrow (y,z)\ E, \text{ or } M(x,y) = M(y,x) = 1,$$

- antisymmetric if, for all $x,y \in V$ and $x = y$,

$$(x,y) \in E \Rightarrow (y,x) \notin E, \text{ or } M(x,y) + M(y,x) \leq 1.$$

- transitive if, for all $x,y,z \in V$,

$$(x,y) \in E \text{ and } (y,z) \in E \Rightarrow (x,z) \in E, \text{ or } M(x,y) + M(y,z) - M(x,z) \leq 1,$$

- complete if, for all $x,y \in V$ and $x \neq y$,

$$(x,y)\ E \Rightarrow (y,x) \in E \text{ or } M(x,y) + M(y,x) \geq 1.$$

1.1.3 Preference relations

Let A be a finite set of alternatives or actions among which a choice must be made, and W be a binary relation of weak preference on A with the meaning that a W b if and only if 'action a is at least as good as action b'. Corresponding to W, we can define relations of 'strict preference' P, of 'indifference' I and of 'incomparability' R on the set A:

$$a\ P\ b \text{ if and only if } a\ W\ b \text{ and } \sim b\ W\ a,$$
$$a\ I\ b \text{ if and only if } a\ W\ b \text{ and } b\ W\ a,$$
$$a\ R\ b \text{ if and only if } \sim a\ W\ b \text{ and } \sim b\ W\ a.$$

Clearly, P is asymmetric whereas I and R are symmetric. Conventionally, we shall take W and I as reflexive, and R as irreflexive. We shall define:

- a nondominated action as an action $a \in A$ such that no other action $b \in A$ such that b P a. The set of all nondominated actions will be denoted by N(A,W) and called the nondominated set;
- a best action as an action $a \in A$ such that a W b for all $b \in A$. The set of all best actions will be called the choice set and denoted by C(A,W).

Let us note that a best action of A is also nondominated but not vice versa so that $C(A,W) \subseteq N(A,W)$. Moreover, C(A,W) or N(A,W) may be empty.

When weak preference W is a quasi-order, it can be easily shown (Sen 1970) that:

1. indifference I is transitive and is thus an equivalence relation;
2. a P b and b I c $\Rightarrow$ a P c;
3. a I b and b P c $\Rightarrow$ a P c;
4. strict preference P is transitive and is thus a strict partial order;
5. the nondominated set N(A,W) is not empty;
6. if the choice set C(A,W) is not empty, then C(A,W) = N(A,W).

When weak preference W is a weak order, then R is empty and properties (1) - (6) hold and also:

7. $C(B,W) \neq \emptyset$ for every nonempty subset B of A (see Sen 1970);
8. $C(A,W) = N(A,W) \neq \emptyset$ as a consequence of (7) and (6);
9. if W* is the binary relation defined on the quotient A/I by

$$a^* \ W^* \ b^* \quad \text{if and only if} \quad a \ W \ b \ ,$$

   then W* is a total order on A/I. In other words, strict preference P is a strict total order on the set of I - equivalence classes of A.

Weak preference W is said to be quasi-transitive when the corresponding strict preference relation P is transitive. When W is quasi-transitive and strongly complete, it can be shown that the hereabove property (7) still holds.

Weak preference W is said to be an interval order (see Golumbic 1980, Roberts 1979) when it is strongly complete and the corresponding strict preference P is a Ferrers' relation, i.e.

$$a \ P \ b \text{ and } c \ P \ d \Rightarrow a \ P \ d \text{ or } c \ P \ b \text{ for all } a,b,c,d \in A.$$

Weak preference W is said to be a semiorder (see Golumbic 1980, Jacquet-Lagreze 1978, Roberts 1979) when it is an interval order and P is semi-transitive, i.e.

$$a \ P \ b \text{ and } b \ P \ c \Rightarrow a \ P \ d \text{ or } d \ P \ c \text{ for all } a,b,c,d \in A.$$

As a Ferrers' relation is transitive, interval order and semiorder are strongly complete and quasi-transitive so that property (7) holds again for them.

Let us finally point out that a weak preference W on A can be represented by means of a digraph whose vertex set is A and in which:

- there is an arc from a to b, and none from b to a, when a P b,
- a and b are the endpoints of two arcs of opposite direction when a I b.

1.2 Basic data structures

1.2.1 The abstract data type 'list'

Mathematically, a list is a linearly ordered set

$$t_1, t_2, \ldots, t_n$$

of elements of a given type (boolean, integer, ...) where $n \geq 0$.
The number n of its elements is called its length. An empty list is a list which has no elements ($n = 0$).

In order to represent a list inside a computer, we must choose a data structure, for example, schematically:

- an array representation, in which the elements are arranged in order in fixed contiguous memory locations,
- a linked representation, in which the elements are not arranged contiguously but are linked by pointers.

a) Array representation

If a_1 is the address of the first element t_1 and if n is the number of locations required to store a single element of the list, then the address of element t_i is:

$$a_i = a_1 + (i-1)p \ .$$

The advantage of such a representation is that it allows for direct access to any element of the list.

Inconvenients are that:

- inserting a new element between t_i and t_{i+1} requires shifting $t_{i+1}, t_{i+2}, \ldots, t_n$ to the right by p locations;
- deleting an element t_i requires shifting $t_{i+1}, \ldots, t_n$ to the left by p locations;
- when insertions must be done, it is necessary to put a bound on the length to which the list will grow.

b) Linked representation

In this representation, a pointer P_i is associated with each element

t_i and records the location at which the next element t_{i+1} and pointer P_{i+1} (i = 1, ..., n-1) are stored (see Figure 1). A <u>nil</u> pointer is associated with t_n. A <u>header</u> holds no element of the list but contains a pointer P_0 to the first element t_1.

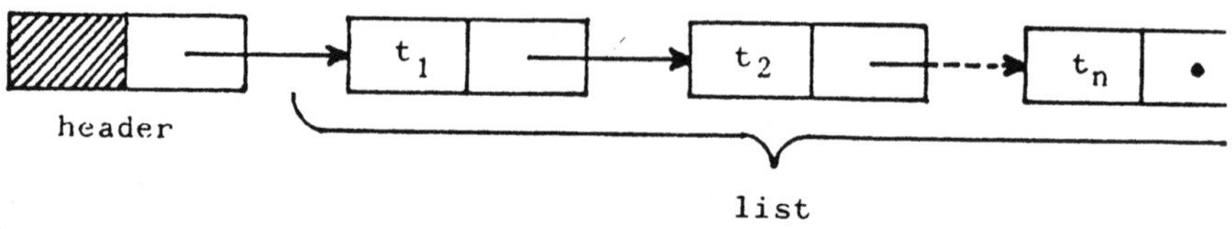

Figure 1.

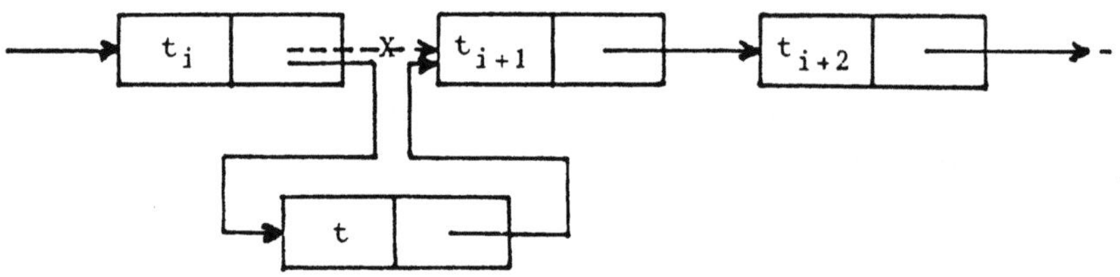

Figure 2.

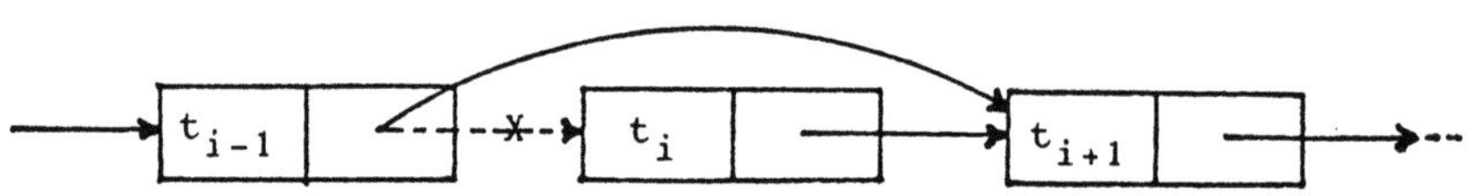

Figure 3.

With linked representation, insertions and deletions are facilitated:

- when inserting a new element t to the list between t_i and t_{i+1}, it is only necessary to create a memory zone for t and its pointer, and to position two pointers: the pointer of t to the location where t_{i+1} and P_{i+1} are stored and the pointer of t_i to the location of t (see Figure 2).
- deleting an element t_i consists in recording the location of (t_{i+1}, P_{i+1}) in the pointer P_{i-1} (see Figure 3). Again, no shifting is necessary.

These two operations involve two special mechanisms: the first one in order to liberate memory locations when inserting, and the second one (garbage collection) for recovery of unused space when deleting frequently.

Disadvantages of the linked representation are a waste of space for pointed implementation and a loss of performance when random access to the elements of the list is frequent, for access to elements other than the first is necessarily indirect and inefficient. It is thus clear that the choice between array and linked representation must be envisaged with great care and depends on the circumstances of utilisation.

Let us note that the linked representation described above is called a <u>singly-linked</u> list and that other linked representations can be used, such as a doubly-linked list, circular list (Aho et al. 1974, Aho et al. 1983, Meyer and Baudoin 1978, Reingold et al. 1977).

1.2.2 Stacks

A <u>push down stack</u> or <u>stack</u> for short, is a particular form of a list in which insertions and deletions occur only at the right end, called the <u>top</u> of the stack. In a high level programming language for instance, a stack S could be implemented as a one-dimensional array STACK and an integer variable t to keep track of the top of the stack, the empty stack corresponding to t = 0.

Insertion of an element x at the top, designated by S ⇐ x, and deletion of the top with setting the value of x to be the element at the top, designated by x ⇐ S, could be described as follows:

```
S ⇐ x                              x ⇐ S

    t ← t+1                            if t = 0 then
    if t > n then                         |underflow
          |overflow
    else                               else
          |STACK (t) ← x                  |x ← STACK (t)
                                          |t ← t-1
```

1.3 The design of efficient algorithms

When having recognised that a problem is <u>computable</u> (i.e. can be solved with algorithms) and when faced with a choice among algorithms that solve the problem, several points of view can be taken into account, for example (Aho et al. 1983):

a) Choose an algorithm that is easy to understand, code and debug,
b) Choose an algorithm that makes efficient use of the computer's resources, especially one that runs as fast as possible.

In respect of point of view a), computer scientists have worked and are still working on a <u>theory of programming</u>. Related to this is the concept of <u>program correctness</u>: does the program representing the algorithm terminate with a correct answer for every input to the problem?

Here we shall be concerned only with point of view b). In this respect let us note that the running time of a program depends on factors such as:

- the input to the program,
- the quality of the code generated by the compiler used to create the object program,
- the nature and speed of the instructions on the machine used to execute the program,
- the intrinsic 'complexity' of the algorithm underlying the program.

These factors show that the running time of an algorithm cannot be expressed in standard time units such as seconds. It is the reason why computer scientists make a distinction between:

- the practical complexity of an algorithm, which is an exact measure of the running time on a particular model of machine, and
- the theoretical complexity of an algorithm, in which the units of the running time are left unspecified, and which rather considers the running time as being the number of instructions executed on an idealised machine.

Hereafter, we shall be concerned only with theoretical complexity and write complexity, for short. We shall also use the big-oh and big-omega notation with the following meaning.

Let n be the input 'size' of a particular algorithm and T(n) be the corresponding running time. We shall say that T(n) is O(f(n)) when there is a positive constant c such that $T(n) \leq cf(n)$ for all but some finite (possibly empty) set of non-negative values for n, so that f(n) is an upper bound on the growth rate of T(n). Similarly, we shall write that T(n) is $\Omega(g(n))$ when there exists a constant d such that $T(n) \geq dg(n)$ infinitely often (for an infinite number of values of n).

Let us insist on the fact that the big-oh notation implies some loss of information. As an example, let us consider, for a similar problem, two algorithms whose running times are $T_1(n)$ and $T_2(n)$ respectively. At first sight, it might seem that:

- both algorithms have the same 'efficiency' because $T_1(n)$ and $T_2(n)$ are both $O(n^2)$. But it might happen that the proportionality constants, hidden in the big-oh, are such that, for example, $T_1(n) = 100\,n^2 + 2000n + 900$ and $T_2(n) = 300\,n^2 + 1000\,n + 100$, so that

$T_1(n) = T_2(n)$ for $n = 1$ and 4 only;

- the first algorithm is more efficient than the second one because, for example, $T_1(n)$ is $O(n)$ and $T_2(n)$ is $O(n^2)$. But a second examination could reveal that $T_1(n) > T_2(n)$ for all values of n considered in practice (example: $T_1(n) = 2000\ n$ and $T_2(n) = n^2 + n$ so that $T_1(n) > T_2(n)$ for $0 < n < 1999$).

However, complexity analysis has a main advantage because it gives an idea of the increase in problem size that can be achieved with an increase in computer speed. As an example, suppose two algorithms A_1 and A_2 whose time complexities are $O(n^2)$ and $O(\log_{10} n)$ respectively. If $n = n_1$ and $n = n_2$ are the maximum sizes of problems that can now be treated with A_1 and A_2 respectively, then the maximum sizes will be respectively $10\ n_1$ with A_1 and $n_2 100$ with A_2 for a computer which will run 100 times faster.

Let us finally remark that, when T(n) is O(f(n)) for an algorithm, then this algorithm is said to be:

- a <u>linear time algorithm</u> when f(n) is a linear function,
- a <u>polynomial time algorithm</u> when f(n) is some polynomial function,
- an <u>exponential time algorithm</u> in the other cases, even for example when $f(n) = n^{\log n}$ which is not usually regarded as an exponential function.

The concept of problem complexity will not be considered here. The interested reader can learn more in Garey and Johnson (1979).

1.4 Representing digraphs inside a computer

A number of different representations are possible (Reingold et al. 1977) but we will be concerned here solely with representations derived from the adjacency matrix of a digraph.

We shall suppose here that the vertex set of digraph G = (V,E) is V = {1, ..., n} and that |E| = m. The most popular representation of G is the adjacency matrix itself, i.e. the matrix M whose elements M(i,j) are 1 or true when there is an arc from i to j, and o or false otherwise. This n x n matrix can be considered as a list $t_1, t_2, \ldots, t_n$ in which each t_i is a list of n elements consisting of the i-th column of the matrix. It is thus clear that the space requirement for the matrix representation will be $\Omega(n^2)$. If p is the number of locations required to represent an element M(j,i), then the list t_i begins at location $a_i = a_1 + (i-1)pn$ so that the location of M(j,i) is

$$a_i + (j-1)p = a_1 + [(i-1)n + (j-1)]p$$

and accessing an element of the adjacency matrix takes a constant time O(1).

The adjacency matrix representation will therefore be useful with algorithms which frequently examine the presence of given arcs. The main disadvantage of the adjacency matrix representation is the $\Omega(n^2)$ space requirement which might preclude good running times of algorithms for sparse digraphs (i.e. in which the number of arcs is much less than n^2). It is the reason why the adjacency lists representation is also considered.

The adjacency list for a vertex i which will be denoted by Adj(i), is a list, in some order, of all successors of i. Digraph G can be represented by the adjacency lists of all its vertices, with a $\Omega(n+m)$ space requirement.

Figure 4(b) is a singly-linked representation of the digraph in Figure 4(a), while Figure 4(c) represents an implementation of Figure 4(b): HEAD (i) is a pointer to the adjacency list for vertex i. Figure 4(d) is an array representation of the adjacency lists for the same digraph: again HEAD (i) is a pointer to the adjacency list for vertex i, which is stored in INFO while SUC (i) is the number of vertices contained in Adj(i) and serves to calculate HEAD (i+1). Of course, SUC is optional but might be useful in algorithms where SUC (i) must be known.

Let us finally point out that no representation is best for all operations that can be performed on a digraph.

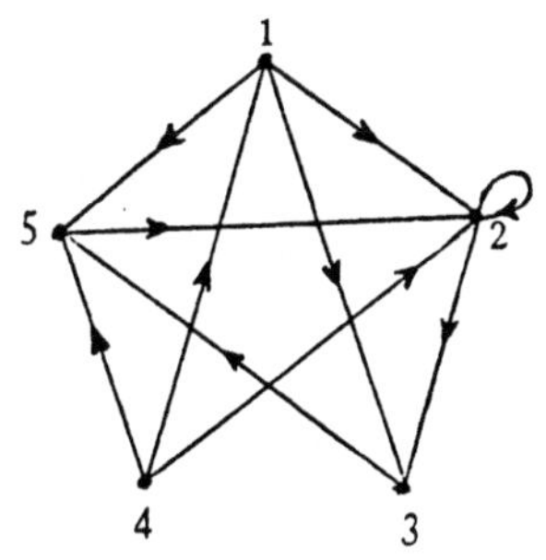

(a)

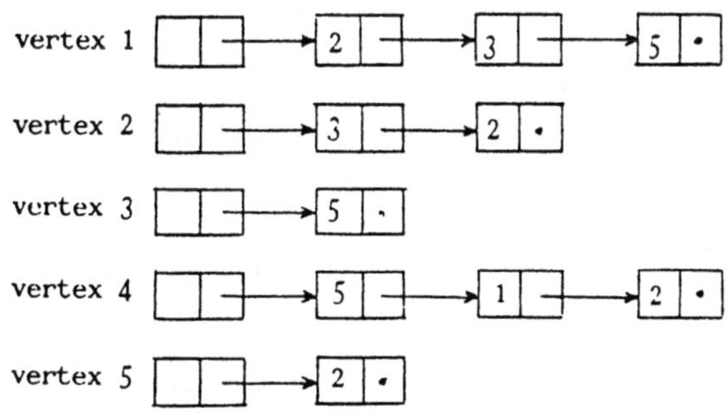

Headers (b)

	1	2	3	4	5
HEAD	1	4	6	7	10

	1	2	3	4	5	6	7	8	9	10
INFO	2	3	5	3	2	5	5	1	2	2
LINK	2	3	.	5	.	.	8	9	.	.

(c)

	1	2	3	4	5
HEAD	1	4	6	7	10
SUC	3	2	1	3	1

	1	2	3	4	5	6	7	8	9	10
INFO	2	3	5	3	2	5	5	1	2	2

(d)

<u>Figure 4.</u>

1.5 Depth-first search of directed graphs

Visiting all vertices and arcs is a key feature for some algorithms on digraphs. Depth-first search constitutes such a visiting plan and can be described as follows.

Let G = (V,E) be a digraph on which each vertex is initially marked unvisited. Then:

1. Select a vertex v∈V as a start vertex and mark it visited;
2. Visit each unvisited successor of v in turn, using depth-first search recursively;
3. When all descendants of v have been visited, the visit process of v has been fulfilled;
4. If unvisited vertices are still existing in the digraph, then select an unvisited vertex as a new start vertex;
5. Repeat this process until no vertex in V remains unvisited.

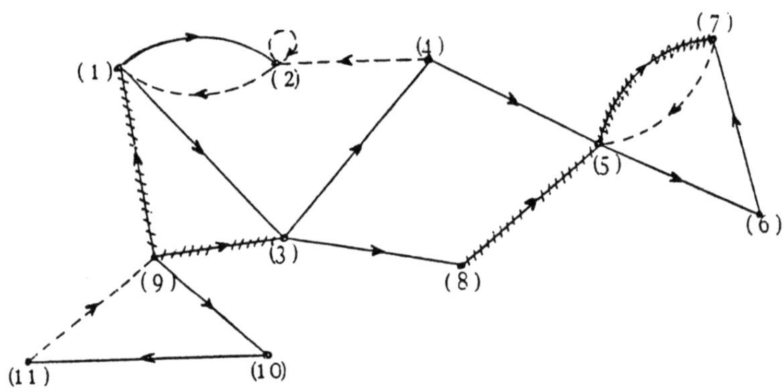

Figure 5.

Figure 5 is an example of such a depth-first search (for the moment, do not make any distinction between the different kinds of arcs suggested by the figure): the numbers in parentheses give the order according to which the vertices have been visited, starting from 1. Algorithm 1 describes the recursive procedure for depth-first search. The digraph G = (V,E) is supposed to be represented by the adjacency list Adj(v) for all vertices v∈V. A one-dimensional array num is used in order to indicate whether a vertex has been previously visited (num(v) ≠ 0) or not (num(v) = 0).

Algorithm 1

```
 1.      i ← 0
 2.      for each v∈V do
 3.         |num(v) = 0
 4.      for each v∈V do
 5.         if num(v) = 0 then
 6.         |DFSEARCH (v)
         procedure DFSEARCH (v)
 7.         |i ← i + 1
 8.         |num(v) ← i + 1
 9.         |for each w∈ Adj(v) do
10.         |   |if num(w) = 0 then
11.         |   |   |DFSEARCH (w)
```

Theorem 1. Algorithm 1 is a linear time algorithm and requires $O(|V| + |E|)$ time.

Proof - Statements 1,3,5,6,7,3,10,11 can each be done in constant time $O(1)$ so that lines 2-3 and lines 5-6 are both done in $O(|V|)$ time and lines 9-11 take $O(|Adj(v)|)$ time. Therefore, the entire procedure DFSEARCH (v) requires $O(|Adj(v)|)$ time and, by reason that DFSEARCH is called once for each vertex, the time complexity of the algorithm is

$$O(|V|) + O(\sum_{v \in V} |Adj(v)|) = O(|V| + |E|).$$

Let us now come back to Figure 5 and note, on the one hand that the numbers associated with the vertices correspond to the numbering of vertices accomplished by algorithm 1 thanks to array num, and that, on the other hand, all arcs have been traversed when all the vertices have been visited. Four types of arcs appear after traversal, as indicated in Table 2. A loop is always a back arc. The tree arcs, together with their endpoints, form a depth-first spanning forest and each of them is located in a rooted tree of the forest, whose root is always chosen in lines 4-6 of algorithm 1.

Table 2.

Type arc	Representation	Goes		Depth-first search numbering
		from a	to	
Tree arc	 v w	visited vertex v	an unvisited vertex w	num(w) = 1 + num(last visited vertex)
Back arc	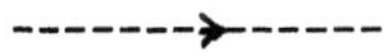 v w	visited vertex v	an ancestor w[1] of v	num(v) ≥ num(w)
Forward arc	 v w	visited vertex v	a descendant[1] w≠v of v	num(v) < num(w)
Cross arc	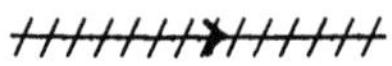 v w	visited vertex v	a vertex w that is neither an ancestor nor a descendant of v[1]	num(v) > num(w)

[1] Here, the words ancestor and descendant refer to an already visited vertex and to the orientation of the visiting process

Part II : Computer Algorithms Related to Discrete Multiple Criteria Decision Methods

II.2 Notations

The following notations will be used hereafter:

A	: a finite set of alternatives or actions, with $n = \|A\|$,
$C_1, C_2, \ldots, C_q$	: relevant criteria or points of view for evaluation purposes of all actions in A,
W	: an individual or a global (corresponding to $C_1, \ldots, C_1$) weak preference relation defined on A,
P, I, R	: strict preference, indifference and incomparability relations corresponding to W,
G = (A,E)	: weak preference digraph corresponding to W, with $m = \|E\|$,
G(P), G(I)	: the strict preference and indifference digraphs for Pand I,
W_i, P_i, I_i, R_i	: weak preference, strict preference, indifference and incomparability relations associated with criterion C_i,
G_i, $G(P_i)$, $G(I_i)$	: the digraphs corresponding to W_i, P_i and I_i respectively.

II.2 Transitive closure of a weak preference relation

Given a weak preferenee relation W on A and the corresponding digraph G = (A,E), let us define the following relations on A:

$a \tilde{W} b$ if and only if there is a path from a to b in G,

$a \hat{W} b$ if and only if there is a path $\neq$ loop from a to b in G,

$a \hat{P} b$ if and only if there is a path from a to b in G(P).

Notice that:

- the digraph representing $\hat{W}$ is the transitive closure $\hat{G} = (A,F)$ of G,
- the digraph representing $\tilde{W}$ can be obtained from $\hat{G}$ by adding a loop at each vertex,
- when W is a quasi-order, then $W = \tilde{W}$,
- when W is quasi-transitive, then P is transitive and $P = \hat{P}$,

- the digraph representing $\hat{P}$ is the transitive closure $\hat{G}(P)$ of $G(P)$,
- when a $\hat{W}$ a, then there exists a cycle ($\neq$ loop) containing a in G (voting or Condorcet's paradox).

Thus knowing how to determine the transitive closure of a digraph is useful in order to recognise weak preference relations that are quasi-orders or quasi-transitive relations.

Let us show how it can be done for digraph G, supposing that G is represented by its adjacency matrix M. It is easy to prove by induction that $M^r(a,b) = 1$ if and only if there is a path of length r from a to be in G, where M^r denotes the rth-boolean power of M. Then, the adjacency matrix of digraph $\hat{G}$ is:

$$\hat{M} = M \oplus M^2 \oplus \ldots \oplus M^n ,$$

where $\oplus$ denotes boolean addition. As the time complexity for matrix multiplication is $O(n^3)$, the calculation of $\hat{M}$ with the above formula can be performed in $O(n^4)$ operations. However, a more interesting time complexity can be attained, as indicated by the following theorem.

Theorem 2 : Let us suppose that the actions in A are numbered from 1 to n. Let $(M_k;\ k = 0,1,\ldots,n)$ be the sequence of matrices defined by:

$$M_0(i,j) = M(i,j) ,$$

$$M_k(i,j) = M_{k-1}(i,j) \oplus [M_{k-1}(i,k) \otimes M_{k-1}(k,j)] , \quad i,j,k=1,\ldots,n$$

where $\otimes$ denotes boolean multiplication. Then $M_n = \hat{M}$.

Proof: Let us prove by induction that $M_k(i,j) = 1$ if and only if there is a path from $i \in A$ to $j \in A$ using only intermediate vertices in $\{1,2,\ldots,k\} \subseteq A$. This is certainly true for $k = 0$. Let us show that, if it is true for $k = r-1$, it is also true for $k = r$. But

$$M_r(i,j) = M_{r-1}(i,j) \oplus [M_{r-1}(i,r) \otimes M_{r-1}(r,j)]$$

is equal to 1 only if:

- either $M_{r-1}(i,j) = 1$, and then there is a path from i to j using only intermediate vertices in $1,2,\ldots,r-1$.
- or $M_{r-1}(i,r) = M_{r-1}(r,j) = 1$, and then there are paths from i to r and from r to j, and from i to j as a consequence, using only intermediate vertices in $(1,2,\ldots, r-1)$.

Let us note that, for k = 1, ..., n :

$$M_k(i,j) = \begin{cases} M_{k-1}(i,j) & \text{if } M_{k-1}(i,k) = 0 , \\ M_{k-1}(i,j) \oplus M_{k-1}(k,j) & \text{if } M_{k-1}(i,k) = 1 , \end{cases}$$

and that:

- $M_{k-1}(i,j)$ enters into the computation only for $M_k(i,j)$,
- $M_{k-1}(r,j)$ is used to compute rows other than the ith-row, but $M_k(k,j) = M_{k-1}(k,j)$ by the hereabove formula.

Therefore, it is possible to perform the computation of $M_n = \hat{M}$ with one copy T of the adjacency matrix M, as indicated in algorithm 2 known as Warshall's algorithm. The output of the algorithm is $T = \hat{M}$. Time complexity is clearly $O(n^3)$.

Algorithm 2

```
for i = 1 to n do
    for j = 1 to n do
        |T(i,j) ← M(i,j)
for k = 1 to n do
   |for i = 1 to n do
   |    |if T(i,k) = 1 then
   |    |   |for j = 1 to n do
   |    |   |    |T(i,j) ← T(i,j) ⊕ T(k,j)
```

II.3 Determining the strong components of a weak preference relation

By definition, the strong components of a weak preference relation W on A are the strong components of the corresponding digraph G = (A,E) and W is said to be strongly connected when G is a strongly connected digraph.

Let $G_i = (A_i, E_i)$, i=1, ..., q, be the strong components of G. In each G_i two actions are always on a cycle. The relation W_r defined on the set $C = \{A_1,...,A_q\}$ by:

$A_i W_r A_j$ if and only if there exists $a \in A_i$ and $b \in A_j$ such that a W b

is called the <u>reduced relation</u> from W and digraph $G_r = (C,W_r)$ is called the <u>reduced digraph</u> from G.

Determining the reduced digraph corresponding to a weak preference relation is a problem encountered, for example, in discrete multiple criteria decision methods such as outranking methods (Benayoun et al. 1966, Roy 1969, Roy and Bertier 1971, Roy, 1971). It is therefore interesting to know an efficient algorithm in order to find the strong components of a digraph.

Let us assume that the adjacency matrix $\hat{M}$ of the transitive closure $\hat{G}$ of digraph G is known and that

$$\hat{M}(a,b) = \hat{M}(b,a) = 1 \text{ and } \hat{M}(a,a) = \hat{M}(b,b) = 1 .$$

That means that a and b are on the same cycle. As a consequence, the rows corresponding to a and b in $\hat{M}$ are identical and a and b are in the same strong component of G. Conversely, when a and b are in the same strong component of G, then the rows corresponding to a and b in $\hat{M}$ are identical.

On the other hand, vertex a all alone is a strong component of G if and only if $\hat{M}(a,a) = 0$. Therefore, Warshall's algorithm can be the basis of a $0(n^3)$ time complexity algorithm for determining the strong components of G = (A,E). However, Tarjan has shown that it is possible to find a linear time algorithm using depth-first search.

In order to illustrate the basic ideas of Tarjan's algorithm, let us come back to the digraph G = (A,E) in Figure 5. The depth-first spanning forest H = (A,F) that appears from this figure contains two rooted trees and is represented in Figure 6, while the four strong components $G_i = (A_i, E_i)$ of G are represented in Figure 7.

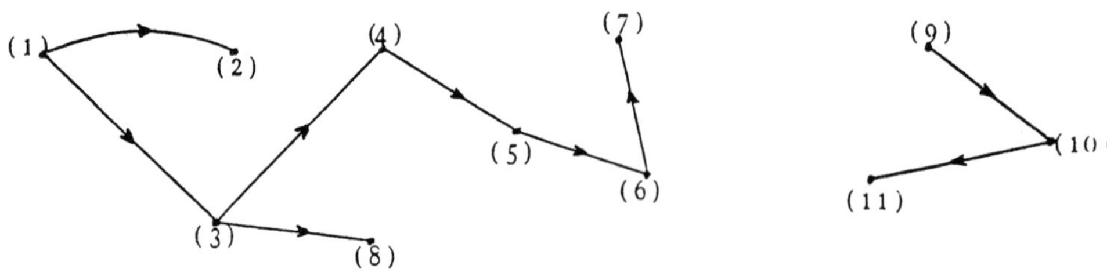

Figure 6.

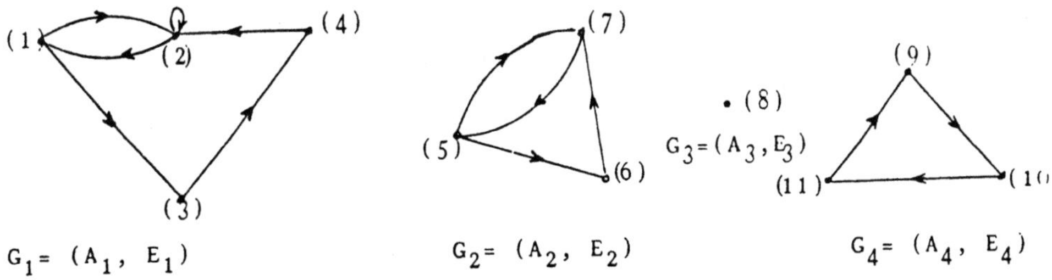

Figure 7.

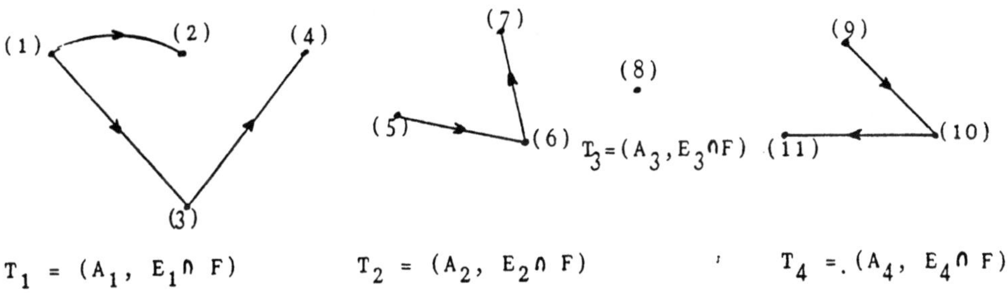

Figure 8.

From H and the G_i's, let us define the digraphs $T = (A_i, E_i \cap F)$ as indicated in Figure 8. In this example, each digraph T_i is a rooted tree, and it can easily be shown (Aho et al. 1974, Reingold et al. 1977) that this is true in general.

Theorem 4: Let $G_i = (A_i, E_i)$ be a strong component of a digraph $G = (A,E)$ and $H = (A,F)$ be a depth-first spanning forest for G. Then digraph $T_i = (A_i, E_i \cap F)$ is a rooted tree whose root will be called the root of the strong component G_i.

Let $\{num(a) \mid a \in A\}$ be a depth-first numbering of the vertices of digraph G and C(a) be the set of vertices $b \in A$ such that b can be reached from $a \in A$ with a path contained in G and composed of zero or more tree arcs followed by at most one back arc or one cross arc, and such that the root of the strong component containing b is an ancestor of a. Let us also consider the numbering $\{link(a) \mid a \in A\}$ defined by:

$$link(a) = \min(\{num(a)\} \cup \{num(b) \mid b \in C(a)\}.$$

Recall that the numbers in parentheses in Figures 5 to 8 are a depth-first numbering of the vertices of digraph G in Figure 5. The associated link-numbering is presented in Table 3. It appears in this example that link(a) = num(a) when a is the root of a strong component of G and that link(a) < num(a) otherwise. In fact, this is always true (Aho et al. 1974).

Theorem 5: Let G = (A,E) be a digraph, {num(a)| a∈A} be a depth-first numbering of the vertices and {link(a)| a∈A} be the associated link-numbering. A vertex a∈A is the root of a strong component of G if and only if link(a) = num(a).

Table 3.

num(a)	1	2	3	4	5	6	7	8	9	10	11
link(a)	1	1	2	2	5	5	5	8	9	9	9

Theorems 4 and 5 are key results in order to determine the strong components of a digraph G = (A,E) in an algorithmic way. Algorithm 3 shows that the link values and the strong components are easily calculated during a depth-first search. G is supposed to be represented by the adjacency lists of the vertices. During execution of algorithm 3, the vertices of G are inserted at the top of a stack S in the order they are visited. As often as a root is encountered, all vertices of the corresponding strong component are on top of the stack and are deleted from the stack. On reaching vertex a∈A the first time, link(a) is set to the depth-first numbering num(a) of a. If a back arc or a cross arc (a,b) is traversed (notice that back arcs which are loops can be ignored), and b is in the same strong component as some ancestor of a, then link(a) is set to the minimum of its current value and num(b). If a tree arc (a,b) is traversed, then the rooted subtree with root b is recursively traversed and link(b) calculated; on return at a, link(a) is set to the minimum of its current value and link(b).

In order to know whether b is in the same strong component as some ancestor of a, a test is made to see whether b is still on stack or not. This can be done by using a boolean array indicating whether or not a vertex is on S. If b is still on stack S, the root of the strong component containing b is an ancestor of a.

Formal proof of algorithm 3 can be found in Aho et al. (1974). The time complexity is O(n+m) since:

- the time complexity of the portions of the algorithm, other than procedure STRONG, is O(n);
- one call of procedure STRONG(a), exclusive of recursive calls to STRONG, requires a constant time plus a time proportional to the number of successors of a;
- procedure STRONG is called only once at each vertex, and each vertex is placed on the stack and removed from the stack only once;
- thus, all calls to procedure STRONG together require a time proportional to n+m.

Algorithm 3

```
i ← 0
S ←   empty stack
for   each a∈A do
      | num(a) ← 0
for   each a∈A do
      | if num(a) = 0 then
      |       STRONG(a)

procedure   STRONG(a)
      | i ← i + 1
      | num(a) ← i
      | link(a) ← i
      | S ⇐ a
      | for each b∈Adj(a) do
      |     | if num(b) = 0 then
      |     |    | [(a,b) is a tree arc]
      |     |    | STRONG(b)
      |     |    | link(a) ← min(link(a), link(b))
      |     | else
      |     |    | if num(b) < num(a) and b is on stack S then
      |     |    |    | [(a,b) is a back arc or a cross arc and b
      |     |    |    |  is in the same strong component as a, since
      |     |    |    |  b∈Adj(a) and b on stack S means that b is
      |     |    |    |  in the same strong component as some ances-
      |     |    |    |  tor of a]
      |     |    |    | link(a) ← min(link(a), num(b))
      |     | if link(a) = num(a) then
      |     |    |     [a is the root of a strong component]
      |     |    | while the top c on S satisfies num(c)≥num(a)
      |     |    |    | do add c to the current strong component
      |     |    |    | delete c from stack S
```

II.4 Finding quasi-orders compatible with a preference relation

Let W be a weak preference relation on a set A of actions and G = (A,E) be the corresponding digraph. A quasi-order Q compatible with W is in fact a numbering $\{nu(a) \mid a \in A\}$ of vertices of G such that:

(i) $nu(a) > 0$ is an integer for all $a \in A$;

(ii) vertices with the same numbers are the Q-equivalence classes;

(iii) $a,b \in A$, $a \neq b$ and $a\ W\ b \Rightarrow nu(a) < nu(b)$.

The problem of finding a quasi-order compatible with a weak preference relation is related, for example, to outranking methods (Roy and Bertier 1971):

- W is an outranking relation on A,
- the reduced digraph from G is determined;
- one searches for a quasi-order compatible with the reduced relation from W.

It can be easily shown (Roy 1969) that:

Theorem 6: A quasi-order Q compatible with W exists if and only if G is acyclic (loops excepted).

In computer science, the construction of a numbering such as the one described hereabove is known as the topological sort of the vertices of an acyclic digraph (Aho et al. 1974, Aho et al 1983, Meyeŕ and Baudoin 1978, Reingold et al. 1977) and a linear time algorithm due to Tarjan is known. Topological sort is a problem of concern when a large project is divided into a collection of smaller tasks, some of which having to be performed in certain specified orders so that the entire project may be completed. In multiple criteria decision aid methods, it is important to know whether a compatible quasi-order is unique or not, and, in case of non-uniqueness, to study some 'extreme' compatible quasi-orders. It can be shown (Golumbic 1980, Roy, 1969) that:

Theorem 7: When W is complete ($R = \emptyset$), the following statements are equivalent:

(i) G is acyclic (loops excepted, so that $I = \{(a,a) \mid a \in A\}$,

(ii) G is transitive and antisymmetric (i.e. G is a transitive tournament),

(iii) the vertices can uniquely be linearly ordered $(a_1, a_2, \ldots, a_n)$

in such a way that a_i has in-degree $d^-(a_i) = i+1$ in G for all i,

(iv) the linear order$(a_1, a_2, \ldots, a_n)$ is such that $(a_i, a_j) \in E$ if and only if $i < j$.

In other words, when W is acyclic and complete, there is a unique quasi-order compatible with W and which is a total order on A. When W is acyclic and not complete ($R \neq \emptyset$), there are several quasi-orders compatible with W and, in particular, two extreme quasi-orders with respective numberings $\{\inf(a) \mid a \in A\}$ and $\{\sup(a) \mid a \in A\}$ such that, for each quasi-order $\{nu(a) \mid a \in A\}$ compatible with W, we have:

$$\inf(a) \leq nu(a) \leq \sup(a), \quad \text{for all } a \in A,$$

where

$$\inf(a) = 1 + r(a), \quad \sup(a) = \max\{nu(a) \mid a \in A\} - h(a),$$

and r(a) and h(a) are respectively the rank function (Roy 1969) and height function defined on the vertices of digraph G = (A,E) by:

$$r(a) = \begin{cases} 0 & \text{if a is a source (i.e } d^-(a) = 0), \\ 1 + \max\{r(b) \mid b \neq a,\ (b,a) \in E\} & \text{otherwise} \end{cases}$$

$$h(a) = \begin{cases} 0 & \text{if a is a sink (i.e. } d^-(a) = 0), \\ 1 + \max\{h(b) \mid b \neq a,\ (a,b) \in E\} & \text{otherwise ,} \end{cases}$$

Notice that, when W is acyclic and complete, then we have

$$\inf(a) = \sup(a) = 1 + d^-(a) \text{ for all } a \in A \text{ (see theorem 7).}$$

Let us also note that (Roy 1969) a vertex a has rank r (height h) in an acyclic digraph if and only if the maximum number of arcs forming a path to a (from a) is exactly r (exactly h). This propriety suggests adopting one of the algorithms of the all-pairs shortest paths problem (Aho et al. 1983) in order to determine the rank and height of each vertex in G.

For example, let us examine the possible use of Floyd's algorithm (Aho et al. 1983), supposing that the actions in A are numbered from 1 to n and that digraph G is represented by its adjacency matrix M. Envisaged in our context, Floyd's algorithm is based on the following theorem:

Theorem 8: Let M_0 be the matrix defined by

$$M_0(i,j) = \begin{cases} M(i,j) & \text{if } i \neq j \text{ and } (i,j) \in E, \\ 0 & \text{if } i = j \\ -\infty & \text{otherwise} \end{cases}$$

and (M_k; k = 1, ..., n) be the sequence of matrices such that:

$$M_k(i,j) = \max(M_{k-1}(i,j),\ M_{k-1}(i,k) + M_{k-1}(k,j)), \quad i,j,k=1,2,\ldots,n.$$

Then $M_n(i,j)$ is the length of the longest path from i to j.

Since $M_k(i,k) = M_{k-1}(i,k)$ and $M_k(k,j) = M_{k-1}(k,j)$, we can compute M_n with only one copy T of matrix M. Algorithm 4 performs the computation of ranks r(j) and heights h(j) of all vertices and has clearly a $O(n^3)$ running time.

Algorithm 4

```
for i = 1 to n do
  | for   j = 1 to n do
  |     | if i = j then
  |     |    T(i,j) ← 0
  |     | else
  |     |    | if   M(i,j) = 0 then
  |     |    |      T(i,j) ← -∞
  |     |    | else T(i,j) ← 1
for k = 1 to n do
  | for i = 1 to n do
  |     | if  T(i,k) ≠ -∞ then
  |     |    | for j = 1 to n do
  |     |    |     T(i,j) ← max(T(i,j), T(i,k) + T(k,j))
for j = 1 to n do
  |   r(j) ← 0
  |   h(j) ← 0
  |   for i = 1 to n do
  |     | if  T(i,j) > r(j) then
  |     |     |r(j) ← T(i,j)
  |     | if  T(j,i) > h(j) then
  |     |     |h(j) ← T(j,i)
```

However, it is possible to find the heights of the vertices in linear time, supposing that the digraph is represented by the adjacency lists of its vertices and performing a depth-first search of all vertices. In fact, when all successors of a vertex have been visited, it is possible to determine its height by definition.

Algorithm 5 illustrates this computation and has clearly a 0(n+m) time complexity. Algorithm 5 can also be used to determine the ranks of vertices: just enter a digraph which is obtained from G by reversing the orientations of arcs. In this case, a 'height-first search' method (go from each vertex to its predecessors) could also be imagined.

Algorithm 5

```
for   each a∈A do
      |num(a) ← 0
      |h(a) ← n
i ← 0
for   each a∈A do
      |if  num(a) = 0 do
      |      |HEIGHT(a)

procedure   HEIGHT(a)
      |  i ← i + 1
      | num (a) ← i
      |  if Adj(a) = {a} then
      |     | [a has no successor other than a]
      |     | h(a) ← 0
      |else
      |     | for each b∈Adj(a) such that b ≠ a do
      |     |   |   if   num(b) = 0 then
      |     |   |       |HEIGHT(b)
      |     |   |   else
      |     |   |       |if h(b) = n then
      |     |   |       |   [G contains a cycle]
      |     | h(a) ← 1 + max(h(b)|b∈Adj(a)
```

Let us finally mention that methods for approximating binary relations by semiorders have already been proposed (Jacquet-Lagreze 1978).

II.5 Recognising particular properties of weak preference relations

In Section II.2, we have seen that Warshall's algorithm can be useful in order to recognise (in $0(n^3)$ operations) weak preference relations which are quasi-transitive or are quasi-orders. Of course, this algorithm can also be used in order to see if indifference is transitive. Here, we come to other properties of preference relations.

(a) Test that strict preference relation P is acyclic

This can be done again with Warshall's algorithm since a one-element in the adjacency matrix of the transitive closure $\hat{G}(P)$ of digraph G(P) indicates that a cycle passes through the corresponding vertex or action. However, it can also be done in linear time. In fact, depth-first search can be used to determine whether G(P) is acyclic or not:

- if a back arc is encountered during a depth-first search of G(P), then clearly the digraph has a cycle;
- conversely, if G(P) has a cycle, then a back arc will always be encountered in any depth-first search of G(P), as easily verified.

(b) Test that a complete strict preference relation P is a strict total order

The answer is furnished by theorem 7 as it is sufficient to test that G(P) is acyclic. Another method would consist of verifying that there are no duplicates among the in-degrees (or out-degrees) of the vertices. Knowing that P is a strict total order, the linear order indicated in theorem 7 (iii) can be determined easily:

- Put the vertices in an array N(1), ..., N(n) and the corresponding in-degrees in an array D(1), ..., D(n);
- Add 1 to the in-degrees;
- Since all in-degrees are different, bin sorting (Aho et al. 1983) can be used to sort the in-degrees in ascending order. This can be done in 0(n) steps. Visit D(1), D(2), ..., D(n) in turn. If D(i) = j $\neq$ i, swap D(i) and D(j), and N(i) and N(j). If, after swapping, we have D(i) = k $\neq$ j, then swap D(i) and D(k), N(i) and N(k), and so on. Once an in-degree (+1) i is at its place D(91), it is never moved. After completion of all operations, array A gives the ordering of vertices which was wanted.

(c) Other tests concerning recognition of semiorders and interval orders have been proposed in Jacquet-Lagreze (1978). Some problems related to the time complexity of these tests have been solved (see Golumbic 1980, interval graphs).

II.6 Determining the choice set of a weak preference relation. The Lexicographic multiple criteria decision aid method

Let us recall (see Section I.1.3) that the choice set of a weak preference relation W on A exists when W is a weak order, a semiorder or an interval order, for example.

When the array representation of Figure 4(d) is adopted for the digraph corresponding to W, the choice set C(A,W) is easily calculated in 0(n) steps: it suffices to look at each SUC(i), i = 1, ..., n, and to put action i into C(A,W) when SUC(i) = n. Thus the lexicographic multiple criteria decision method can be easily implemented. Let us recall that this method supposes that the criteria C_1, C_2, ..., C_q are linearly ordered (suppose here that C_1 is most important, then C_2, and so on) and determines firstly, the choice set $S_1(A,W_1)$ in respect to weak preference W_1, and secondly, the choice set $S_2(S_1(A,W_1), W_2)$ if $|S_1(A,W_1)| > 1$, and so on.

REFERENCES

Aho, A.V., Hopcroft, J.E. and Ullman, J.D., The Design and Analysis of Computer Algorithms, Addison-Wesley, Reading, Mass., 1974.

Aho, A.V., Hopcroft, J.E. and Ullman, J.D., Data Structures and Algorithms, Addison-Wesley, Reading, Mass., 1983.

Garey, M.R. and Johnson, D.S., Computers and Intractability, W.H. Freeman, San Francisco, 1979.

Golumbic, M.C., Algorithmic Graph Theory and Perfect Graphs, Academic Press, New York, 1980.

Jacquet-Lagreze, E., 'Représentation de quasi-ordres et de relations probabilistes sous forme standard et méthodes d'approximation', Mathématiques et Sciences Humaines, no. 63, 1978, pp. 5-24.

Meyer, B. and Baudoin, C., Méthodes de Programmation, Eyrolles, Paris, 1978.

Reingold, E.M., Nievergelt, J. and Deo, N., Combinatorial Algorithms: Theory and Practice, Prentice-Hall, Englewood Cliffs, NJ, 1977.

Roberts, F.S., Measurement Theory, Addison-Wesley, Reading, Mass., 1979.

Roubens, M. and Vincke, Ph., 'Représentation et ajustement des ordres d'intervalle',EURO Working Group on Multicriteria Decision Aid, 12th Meeting, Bochum University, 9-10 October, 1980.

Benayoun, R., Roy, B. and Sussman, B., 'Electre: une méthode pour guider le choix en présence de points de vue multiples', SEMA, Direction Scientifique, Note de Travail no. 49, Paris, juin 1966.

Roy, B., Algèbre Moderne et Théorie des Graphes. Tome 1, Dunod, Paris, 1969.

Roy, B. and Bertier, P., 'La méthode Electre II: une méthode de classement en présence de critères multiples', SEMA, Direction Scientifique, Note de Travail no. 142, Paris, avril 1971.

Roy, B., 'How outranking relation helps multiple criteria decision making', in Cochrane, J.L. and Zeleny, M. (eds), Multiple Criteria Decision Making, University of South Carolina Press, Columbia, South Carolina, 1973, pp. 179-201.

Sen, A.K., Collective Choice and Social Welfare, Holden-Day, San Francisco, and Oliver & Boyd, Edinburgh, 1970.

11 Data Base Approach for Multicriteria Decision Support Systems (MCDSS)

M. T. Jelassi, M. Jarke and A. Checroun

1 INTRODUCTION

Traditional intuitive methods of decision making are no longer adequate to deal with the complex problems faced by the modern decision maker. The difficulty in addressing these problems is complicated by the interrelations, immediacy and far-reaching implications of actions taken (Donovan 1976). Decision support systems have been developed to provide the information and analysis necessary for the decisions. Personal computers, computer networks, data bases, colour graphics and computer-based models are among the technological developments which are stimulating interest in the use of computers to support decision making (Sprague and Carlson 1982). The characteristics of the problems associated with decision support are different from those to which data base systems and other computational technologies have normally been applied in the past.

In the particular context of multiple-criteria decision making, the data management system should support the following MCDM characteristics:

1) The explicit knowledge about multiple evaluation criteria within the method (rather than only in the head of the decision maker), and the change of the relevant criteria over time.

2) The computational aspect which consists of the search for the efficient solution of the problem at hand; for instance, by computing the objective function, extracting the feasible alternatives and evaluating them.

3) The frequent interaction between the decision support tool and the end user(s) to assess the objectives, and to check the consistency between the decision making process and the user's preferences (Jacquet-Lagreze and Shakun 1983; Jaquet-Lagreze and Siskos 1982).

4) The learning process offered by conversational MCDM, since the decision maker can express his preference by weighting the evaluation criteria, making pairwise judgements, or by simply giving an ordinal ranking of alternatives.

The problems are such that it is likely that the decision maker's perception of the problem will change over time and that the inherent nature of the problem itself may change. Hence, additional technologies, methodologies and approaches are needed to make existing data base and computational systems more effective in addressing problems of such a nature.

2 IMPORTANCE OF DATA BASE MANAGEMENT TO MCDSS

Most applications of data base systems and computer-based information systems have been aimed at operational control or management control in organisations, and therefore the major concerns of such systems have been at low levels, dealing primarily with raw data. With multiple criteria decision support systems, data analysis needs are more important. Furthermore, mechanisms must be included for quickly adapting to the changing nature of problems, for assimilating new data series, and for integrating existing models and programs in the effort to save time and responding to a particular decision maker's request. Hence, computational technology as applied to decision support systems needs a new approach, including a better, faster data base management system (Donovan 1976).

Altshuler and Plagman (1974) have articulated the role of data bases in decision support. They consider some of the questions concerning the structure of the data base in decision support systems (which they call Corporate Level Systems). In particular, they suggest what data about data should be maintained in these systems in order to help solve such recognised problems of decision support systems as validation and open-ended design.

3 REQUIREMENTS FOR MCDSS

In the first part of this section, we will discuss the technical requirements needed to meet the characteristics of the problems that multiple-criteria decision support systems must address. In the second, we will focus on the data base requirements for MCDSS.

3.1 Technical requirements to MCDSS

We recognise the following requirements from the work of Donovan (1976) and others:

1) Data management capability. Because the problems are changing continuously and the answers are needed quickly, the data management capability must have an interactive component that can quickly introduce new data series and validate, protect and query them. Furthermore, the data associated with these problems is constantly changing and must be obtained from many different sources. Since many of the data series exist under different and potentially incompatible data base management systems, and these data series are maintained by people using those systems, it is important to have facilities for integrating data from diverse general purpose data base management systems into such a form that a single-user application program may access them.

2) Analytical capabilities. Coupled with the capabilities of a data base, it is important to have sophisticated computational facilities for analysing the data since the complexity of the problems addressed demand more than raw data. Required capabilities include modelling language, statistical packages and other facilities.

3) Multiple-criteria representation. Depending on the method at hand, the criteria used to evaluate alternatives, and the relationships between these criteria (e.g., weights) are implicit or explicit. The MCDSS must be able to store and present to the user the current system of objectives, as well as apply it to the available alternatives.

4) Transferability. Because of the short time available for responding to the decision maker's needs, it is important that the MCDSS is able to build upon existing work, such as existing models or existing programs. It is also necessary to work with data coming from different sources. Hence, it is valuable to bring up in an integrated framework any programs, computational aids or data series that are applicable, even though these programs and data series may currently be operating on seemingly incompatible computer systems.

5) Reliability, maintainability and capabilities for incorporating new technologies. Software associated with any decision support system must be reliable, maintainable and adaptive to changes in technology.

The transferability requirement is important for two reasons: first as was mentioned above, it allows for the incorporation of existing models, data base systems and other software into an integrated framework quickly; second, it minimises the need to retrain users of existing systems. Support personnel should be able to operate a computational facility using data management tools and languages with which they are familiar. They would not be required to learn new tools, thus saving time and expense.

Primarily in response to the transferability need outlined above, Donovan's emphasis has been to find techniques for accommodating different data base systems and analysis systems in one integrated framework. Rather than force the conversion and transport of application systems to one operating system, Donovan advocates the use of the virtual machine concept, and the networking of virtual machines.

The use of the virtual machine configuration allows different users, working on similar problems, access to the same data base. Each user may be familiar with a different analytical system. The data needed by all users may be maintained by one user. In decision making systems, it is often desirable for different (and often incompatible) application programs (e.g. models) to be able to interact with each other frequently.

3.2 Data base requirements for MCDSS

Among the three components of a multiple-criteria decision support system (i.e. the data, the model and the dialogue management), the data base management system constitutes an important element since it supports the interaction with the decision maker, as well as with the set of multiple-criteria decision methods used in the decision processes (see Figure 1).

We are interested in investigating how to improve data base systems for the goal of supporting decision making. How can we choose the most appropriate data model for use in MCDSS? Should we base our choice on the operations and integrity constraints, or on the representation of the data? what are the data base requirements for MCDSS? Do we need additional data base requirements to the 'traditional' ones in building a MCDSS? If so, what is the degree of their importance? Then, based on these requirements, how can we design the MCDSS data base component? At which level and up to which degree may a DBMS be used to support the dialogue and model management components?

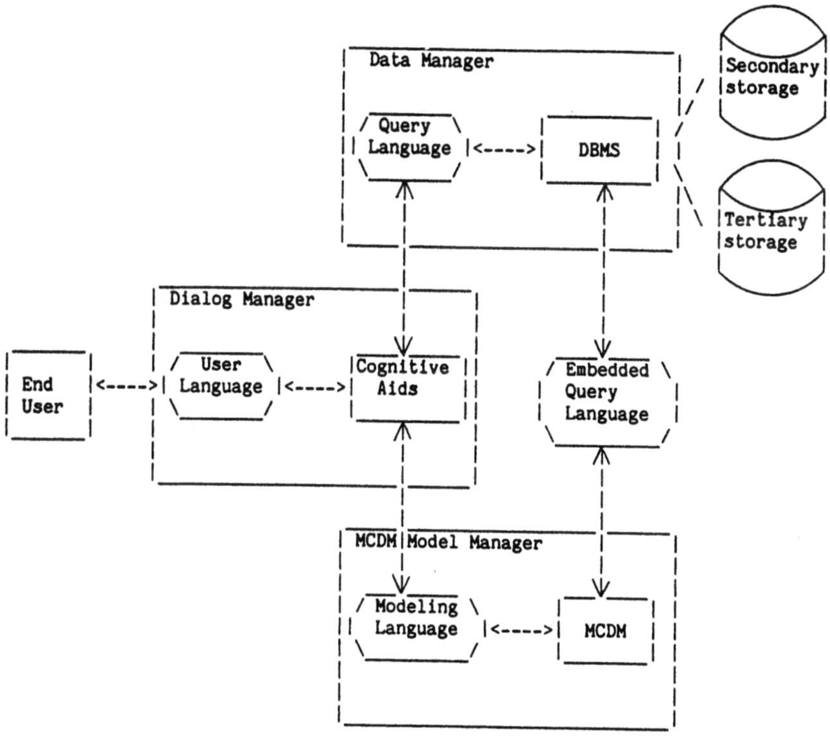

Figure 1. The MCDSS Architecture (adapted from Stohr(1981) and Stohr and White (1982))

Common data base requirements to decision support systems and in particular to MCDSS are:

1) For the data, the DBMS should support different memory aids such as workspaces for intermediate results, libraries for saving workspaces, links among data, and triggers to remind decision makers of operations to be performed or of data that should be considered (Clemons 1981). The amount of data used during the decision making process varies over time, and also varies among decisions and decision makers. Large volumes of data, coming from internal and/or

external sources, are potentially relevant to a decision, but only small volumes are actually needed during the decision process. Since a variety of sources are used, a catalogue of data sources would be a valuable aid. Since decision making insights often come from looking at data in new ways, the DBMS should support establishing relationships and views.

2) Among the operations needed in a decision making environment, data reduction (or abstraction) from large amounts of data involves subsetting, combination, and aggregating of records and fields in a data base. Since minor data errors often vanish in the aggregation process, absolute accuracy may not be required. The most recent data also may not always be required, especially when decisions are based on time series data which cover several years. On the other hand, data reduction does not imply that all data should be aggregates because the decision maker often wants to examine selected detailed data used to create an aggregate value. There may also be a hierarchy of decision levels requiring different degrees of aggregation (Jarke 1982).

3) The decision making process has often a wide time frame. For instance, to perform the forecasting operation (i.e. looking at data from the past and projecting data for the future), several 'historical files' and alternative projections for the 'current files' are necessary. Random access to all of these data is needed since insights or questions based on one set of data lead the decision maker to access data that he did not expect to need, or data that are not related to the data currently being used in terms of storage location or access keys.

4) Since the users of a MCDSS tend to have low programming skills, the data base management system should interface to the user at the external level rather than at the conceptual or internal level (see Interim Report ANSI 1975). That is, the decision maker should be free from having to know details of how data are stored and how operations on the data base are implemented. In addition, the data base component should be integrated with the dialogue and model management components.

5) A key aspect of data base performance for interactive MCDSS is its impact on response time. However, good response time is relative to the time frame of the decision and the time constraints and expectations of the decision makers.

4 DATA MODELS FOR MCDSS

In building the data base management component for MCDSS, there will be an implicit or explicit choice of one or more data models. A data 'model' is a method of representing, organising, storing and handling data in a computer. A data model has three parts (see CODASYL Report 1971):

1) A collection of data structures (lists, tables, relations, hierarchies, and networks). These data structures define the fields and records allowed in the data base.
2) A collection of operations that can be applied (usually by the DBMS) to the data structures. The operations define the allowed manipulations of those fields and records. Retrieval, update, combination and summation are examples of these operations.
3) A collection of integrity rules that define the 'legal' states (set of values) of changes of state (operations on values) for the data structures. In other words, the integrity constraints define what fields and record constraints must be preserved by the operations.

The data model for multiple-criteria decision support systems should not be confused with the modelling component of MCDSS. Although the data base management component may be used by the modelling component, the data model is a model of data storage and/or operations on storage, where the modelling component contains models of decision processes.

There is a rough equivalence among the three 'great' data models (relational, hierarchical and network) in terms of what information can be represented in each. For a given set of data (objects), there is a representation in any of these models. The differences among the models are whether the relationships are explicit or implicit, what operations are possible given the representation, and what constraints are placed on the representation.

The logical view of data has been an important issue in recent years in data base design, because existing commercial systems are based on one of the three major data models (relational, hierarchical and network) (Codd 1980).

4.1 The Relational Data Model

A relational data base can be thought of as a collection of tables. The values in each column of a table stem from a common domain such that - mathematically speaking - a relation is a subset of the Cartesian product of the domains. Relations can map one-one, one-many, and many-many relationships within the same construct. The relation elements - rows of the tables - are usually referred to as tuples. In contrast to the set-theoretic definition of relations, the columns are not identified by their position but by so-called attribute names. Relationships between different tables are usually established through common domains underlying part of their attributes.

Retrieval operations on relations are viewed as the construction of derived relations from existing ones, either by means of a non-procedural description of the desired result or by application of set-oriented algebra operations. While retrieval operations are powerful set-oriented procedures, altering operations such as insert, delete and update are typically performed tuple-at-a-time.

Integrity constraints can be defined as predicates over relations much in the same way as retrieval operations. In particular, a subset of attributes whose values descrive a tuple uniquely can be defined as a primary key for a relation and this property can be enforced by integrity checks when altering operations are attempted. In summary, the strengths of the relational model are that elegant and powerful theoretical foundations are available for this model, and that it is based on a single concept, the table, which is easily understood by human users.

4.2 The Network Data Model

The basic constructs of a network data model are logical record types represented by rectangles that correspond to entity sets and DBTG-set types represented by arrows that correspond to relationship types in the E/R model (CODASYL Report 1971). The most important construct in the network model is the set that relates the owner record type to one or more member record types. In case of many-many relationships, one must create a link record type between the two record types. Record occurrences correspond to entities, data items to attributes, and set occurrences to relationships.

The network model compared with the relational model shows that the former uses predefined access paths through set mechanisms, while the latter does not and all possible routes are dynamically materialised; the former specifies certain integrity constraints to the data structure, while the latter only declares them as adjuncts to the data structure. Four major areas of data definition are structure, physical placement, access path, and integrity and privacy constraints (Michaels 1976). The relational model includes neither physical placement nor access paths, and there is clear separation between structure and constraints, while the network model includes all these four areas of description.

4.3 The Hierarchical Data Model

In this model, the data is represented by a tree structure where each node corresponds to one record (type). The record type at the top of the tree is known as the root, and the elements at the lowest levels, which have no children, are called leaves. No child record type can have more than one parent segment type, whereas in the network structure, as long as the child is in a different set, it can have more than one parent (owner). Therefore, many-many relationships cannot be handled directly in the hierarchical model. A set type represents the relationship between the owner record type and member record type in a network sense, and it is formally declared; but it is implied in the hierarchical model. No child segment occurrence can exist without its parent, while it can be defined in the network data model by a singular set for which the owner is the 'SYSTEM', where the SYSTEM has only one occurrence in the network model.

4.4 Choosing a data model

The choice of a data model depends on the users, the decisions, and on the capacilities of the DBMS that could be used. There is a diverse community of users facing a multiple-criteria decision support system. The MCDSS should therefore provide information to all levels of management in a batch or in an interactive model. The users (including decision makers at all levels, researchers, and analysts) need standard reports and interaction with the data base for data retrieval, modelling or computation in order to solve structured, semi-structured, or unstructured problems.

Codd (1980), McGee (1976), Michaëls (1976) and Ullman (1980) outline several factors for data base evaluation: being easy to use, easy to understand, easy to manipulate, and easy to implement. These factors should be taken into account while designing the MCDSS's data base component.

From these four points of view, the relational model is a very promising approach because of its non-procedural languages, its separation between structural elements and physical elements to maintain data independence, and its simplicity in data structure and data manipulation. In fact, researchers, decision makers, and analysts have found that viewing data in the form of a table (relation) is conceptually simple. Multiple-criteria decision support systems have requirements not only for data manipulation but also for facilities for data analysis.

The network model is more complex than the relational because of its procedural language, its rigid structure and its bundling four areas of data definition into one construct, which makes it lose its data independence.

Where many-many relationships exist, the hierarchical structure is even more complex and rigid than the network structure. The user, as Date (1981) pointed out, is forced to devote more time and effort to solving problems that are introduced by the hierarchical data structure and that are not intrinsic to the questions being asked. Of course, hierarchies are a natural way to model truly hierarchical structures from the real world. From an updating operation point of view, the hierarchical model possesses more undesirable properties than the previous two logical data models.

Generally, the relational model is more appealing in the environment of a DSS, but we are not suggesting that any one model should be dominant (Codd 1970, Michaëls 1976). Because user demands are so diversified, no one model can meet the needs of the large community of users completely for all circumstances (Lee 1983).

5 A DESIGN FOR THE DATA BASE COMPONENT OF MCDSS

The data base requirements for multiple-criteria decision support systems, discussed in Section 3.2 of this paper, pointed out the following key elements which should be considered while designing the data base management component of MCDSS:

1) The characteristics of the data such as the variety of data types, data sources, volume and level of detail, in addition to the wide time frame.
2) The operations which support data manipulation, criteria manipulation, subsetting and aggregation.
3) The interfaces to the other MCDSS components (at the internal level), and to the end user (at the external level).
4) The system's performance in terms of its response time.

In the following secions, we propose some data base management services within the multiple-criteria decision making framework.

5.1 Data definition services

1) A dictionary should exist as a separate component of the data base. It will be used to catalogue the data in the data base by containing descriptions of the criteria, the views, the integrity constraints, and supporting some operations such as adding new entries, deleting entries, retrieving information on the entries, and maintaining multiple indices (e.g. data name, data type, creation date). Integrating data dictionary operations with other functions is very useful. For instance, deleting an item from the dictionary will result in deleting it from the data base.

2) A special property of MCDSS is the 'views capability', i.e. the possibility for the decision maker to see the data in different ways, as, for example, required by the changes in the evaluation criteria used. A view can be defined as a subset, aggregation, or other combination of data, extracted from the data base (Jarke et al. 1984, Rosenthal et al. 1982). We need some operations to determine whether a user is allowed to access customised data structures (data bases, records, or fields) or not. A view is not stored in the data base; it is only part of the conceptual data model, and that is, a view is defined as a query and implemented using the query language (Sprague and Carlson 1982). In order to provide different views of a file, different descriptions may be needed for the same file, and therefore, retained in the data base dictionary.

5.2 Data manipulation services

1) The creation, deletion, and update operations are necessary to maintain the data base. The query operations are used to manipulate and select records and fields from the data base.

2) Concurrency control (Bernstein and Goodman 1981) determines whether several users can access simultaneously the data base (at the field, record, or data base level). If sharing is allowed, the DBMS should provide procedures to prevent users from accessing inconsistent data or getting into 'deadlock'.

3) Access path optimisation (Jarke et al. 1984, Selinger et al. 1979, and Ullman 1980) and file reorganisation (Sockut and Goldberg 1979) are used to increase the performance of the DBMS's operations. To perform these operations, a data independence between the programs and the data is a must. Access path optimisation consists of choosing the order in which records are selected (from the disk) and minimising the number of records that have to be searched. File reorganisation consists of changing the physical arrangement of records on the disk and/or changing the structure of the data base.

4) In addition to the 'classical' operations of a data base management system stated above, a 'staging process' involving a data extraction facility (Carlson 1975, McGee 1976, Walker 1980) is required to meet the decision maker's needs. Its role consists of accessing different kinds of source files, operating on these files, and producing a target file, called the extracted data base.

The rationale for a staging process is:

a) That a variety of source data bases can be interfaced with the MCDSS data base. One example of such a situation, a DSS for supporting container transportation decisions (Jarke 1982) where source data bases are distributed over the world.

b) Accessing an extracted data base is much more efficient than accessing large operational files.

c) Retrieval of data is easier for a decision maker from an extracted data base than if various source files must be accessed.

The differences between extraction and queries are:

a) Description of the source files which may be external to the MCDSS, must be available for the extraction process.

b) While the answer to a query is normally displayed to the user, the result of an extraction operation is loaded into a target data base. The data extraction technique involves aggregating and subsetting from source data bases to form an extracted data base which is used by the other MCDSS's components, i.e., the dialogue and the model management components. With the subsetting operations, the user is able to select fields or records from the source data base using a given criteria. With the aggregation operations, he can sum, count, join or combine several fields or records, using for example one or more common attributes. Aggregation sometimes causes the decision maker to want to examine the detailed data that were used to create the aggregate. Therefore, it may lead to the need for the inverse operation, disaggregation. If aggregation and subsetting requests are often repeated with few or no modifications, a library of aggregation and subsetting operations is useful.

The staging process (McGee 1976), represented in Figure 2, consists of four steps:

a) The reading operation accesses the data bases in the tertiary storage (historical data, external data sources, very large transaction processing (TP) data files), and moves the data into the staging process's working area.

b) The editing operation validates and edits the data, by changing for instance, the item names or the data types.

c) The subsetting and aggregating operations 'reduce' the data, as described above.

d) The loading of the file moves the data from its reduced form to the MCDSS data base (the target storage) which contains the model intermediate results, the criterion values, and the raw data.

Another component of the data management tool for multiple-criteria decision support systems (see Figure 2) is the 'query language facility'. It could be invoked at any time to retrieve quantitative or descriptive information that might be relevant to a particular step in the decision making process. The query operations are invoked by the model and the dialogue management components. They produce, as results of the queries, reports or on-line displays. The query language facility must be integrated with the other operations (e.g. insert, delete, update) invoked via the dialogue component by the decision maker. This integration can be realised by using the input-in-context dialogue in which the user inputs are always given in the context of the previous output from the MCDSS (Sprague and Carlson 1982). The query language facility is used more heavily during the intelligence and choice phases, and used least during design. An end user interface should be part of the query language facility (Stohr et al. 1983) to facilitate the interaction between the decision maker and the MCDSS. In this context, we mean by 'end user' any user who might, or might not, have a prior experience in the computer field, such as a researcher, an analyst, or a decision maker at any level of the organisation (e.g. clerk, manager).

The 'generalised view processor' is a key element of the MCDSS's data manager. It plays the following roles:

a) It processes the translated data base transactions coming from the query facility language;
b) It transforms the raw data coming from the local MCDSS data base, through the DBMS, into preprocessed data; and
c) It interfaces with the staging processor whenever data from the tertiary storage are needed, and with the data dictionary to retrieve the criteria definitions and/or the view definitions (Figure 2).

5.3 Data integrity services

In this category we include:

a) Protection tests (Stonebraker 1975) which check the decision maker's password, and control the access level (field, record or data base level),
b) Recovery operations (Verhofstad 1978) which restore the data base to a consistent state after a hardware or a software failure, and
c) Integrity checks (Stonebraker 1975) which consist of checking data for consistency and accuracy in order to validate new entries.

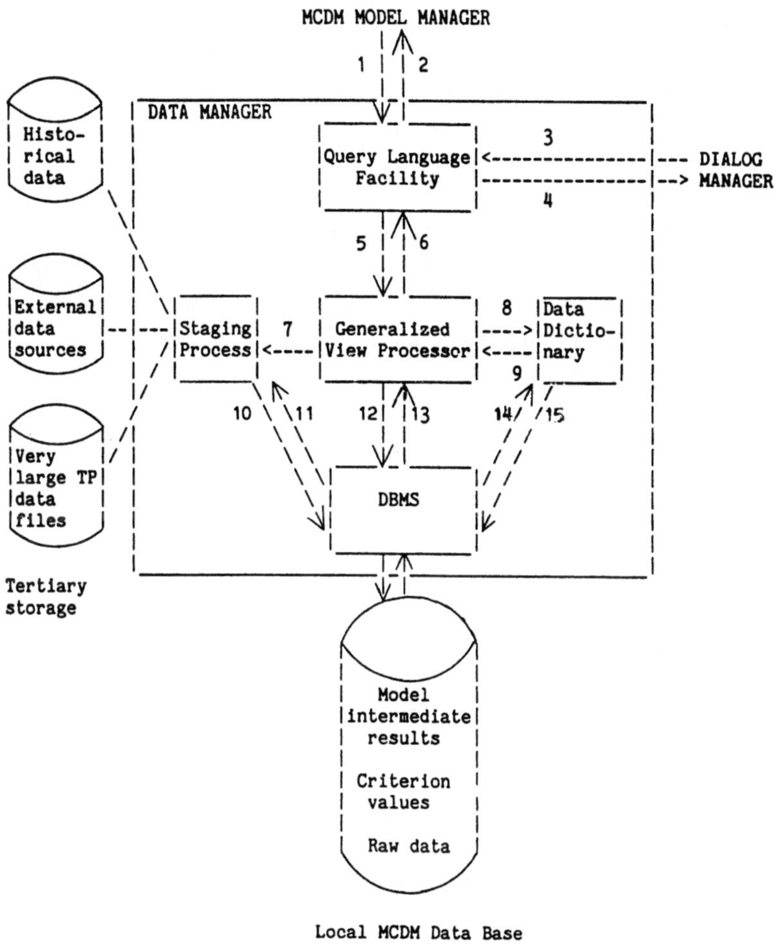

Legend:

1. Query/Insert
2. Data/Definitions
3. Query/Insert/Delete/Update
4. Data/Messages/Definitions
5. Translated transaction
6. Preprocessed data
7. Request
8. Request
9. Criteria definitions/View definitions
10. Load
11. Unload
12. Data base transaction
13. Raw data
14. Request
15. Data/definitions/Integrity constraints

Figure 2. The Data Management Component of the MCDSS

6 CONCLUSIONS

Designing a data base oriented MCDSS represents a new challenge, which requires integrating computer technology, management science and organisational theory.

A decision maker needs two capabilities: data management and modelling. The difference between a conventional DBMS and a DBMS that can support decision making processes is that the latter has to incorporate the capability to handle models and on-line interfaces to data bases (Bennett 1983, Stohr et al. 1980).

The design criterion for such a comprehensive system is that it must handle the interfaces among the users (Stohr et al. 1982), data bases, and models. In addition, user involvement and knowledge of the multiple criteria decision making application to be developed are required in implementing a successful MCDSS.

REFERENCES

Altshuler, G. and Plagman, B., 'User/system interface within the context of an integrated corporate data base', Proceedings AFIPS, 1974 National Computer Conference, vol. 43, AFIPS Press, Montvale, NJ, 1974, pp. 27-33.

ANSI/X3/SPARC Study Group on Data Base Management Systems, Interim ANSI, February 1975.

Bennett, J.L., Building Decision Support Systems, Addison Wesley, Reading, Mass., 1983.

Bernstein, P.A. and Goodman, N., 'Concurrency control in distributed database systems', Computing Surveys, 13, 2, 1981.

Carlson, E.D., 'Using large data bases for interactive problem solving', Proceedings of the International Conference on Very Large Data Bases, ACM, 1975, pp. 499-501.

Clemons, E.K., 'Data base design for decision support', Proceedings of the 14th Hawaii International Conference of Systems Science, 1981.

'CODASYL Data Base Task Group Report, 1971', CODASYL, Association for Computing Machinery, New York, April 1971.

Codd, E.F., 'Data models in data base management', Proceedings of the Workshop on Data Abstraction Data Bases and Conceptual Modeling, ACM Order Number 474800, 1980, pp. 112-114.

Codd, E.F., 'A relational model of data for large shared data banks', Communications of the Association for Computing Machinery, 13, 1970.

Date, C.J., An Introduction to Database Systems, Third Edition, Addison-Wesley, Reading, Mass., 1981.

Donovan, J.J., 'Database system approach to management decision support', ACM Transactions on Database Systems, vol. 1, no. 4, 1976, pp. 344-369.

Jacquet-Lagreze, E. and Shakun, M.F., 'Decision support systems for semi-structured buying decisions', to appear in the European Journal of Operational Research, 1983.

Jacquet-Lagreze, E. and Siskos, J., 'Assessing a set of additive utility functions for multicriteria decision-making, the UTA method', European Journal of Operational Research, vol. 10, no. 2, North-Holland, Amsterdam, 1982, pp. 151-164.

Jarke, M., 'Developing decision support systems: A contained management Example', International Journal of Policy Analysis and Information Systems, Special issue on Decision Support Systems, vol. 6, no. 4, December 1982, pp. 351-372.

Jarke, M. and Koch, J., 'A survey of query optimization in centralized database systems', Working Paper, Center for Research on Information Systems, Graduale School of Business Administration, New York University, November 1982.

Jarke, M. and Vassiliou, Y., 'Coupling expert systems with database management systems', in Reitman, W. (ed), Artificial Intelligence. Applications for Business, Ablex, Norwood, NJ, 1984.

Lee, D.T., 'Database-oriented decision support systems', Proceedings AFIPS, National Computer Conference, AFIPS Press, Montvale, NJ, 1983, pp. 453-465.

McGee, W.C., 'On user criteria for data model evaluation', ACM Transactions on Database Systems, vol. 1, no. 4, December 1976, pp. 370-387.

Methlie, L.B., 'Data management for decision support systems', Data Base, vol. 12, no. 1-2, Fall 1980, pp. 40-46.

Michaels, A.S., 'A comparison of the relational and CODASYL approaches to data-base management', ACM Computing Surveys 8, 1976.

Rosenthal, A. and Reiner, D., 'Querying relational views of networks', Proceedings of the IEEE COMPSAC Conference, Chicago, Illinois, 1982.

Selinger, P., Astrahan, M.M., Chamberlin, D.D., Lorie, P.A., and Price, T.G., 'Access path selection in a relational database management system', Proceedings of the ACM-SIGMOD Conference, Boston, 1979.

Sockut, G.H. and Goldberg, R.P., 'Database reorganization - principles and practice', Computing Surveys, 11, 1979, pp. 371-396.

Sprague, R.H. Jr., and Carlson, E.D., Building Effective Decision Support Systems, Prentice-Hall, Englewood Cliffs, NJ, 1982.

Stohr, E.A. and Tanniru, M.R., 'A database for operations research models', International Journal of Policy Analysis and Information Systems, vol. 4, no. 1, 1980, pp. 105-121.

Stohr, E.A., 'DSS for cooperative decision making', Working Paper, Center for Research on Information Systems, Graduate School of Business Administration, New York University, 1981.

Stohr, E.A. and White, N.H., 'User inferfaces for decision support systems: An overview', International Journal of Policy Analysis and Information Systems, Special issue on Decision Support Systems, vol. 6, no. 4, December 1982, pp. 393-423.

Stohr, E.A. and Ginzberg, M.J., 'Decision support systems: Issues and perspectives', Proceedings of the NYU symposium on Decision Support Systems, Ginzberg, M.J., Reitman, W. and Stohr, E.A. (eds), North-Holland, 1982, pp. 9-31.

Stohr, E.A. and White, N.H., 'Languages for decision support systems', to appear in Management and Office Information Systems, S.K. Chang (ed), Plenum Press, New York, 1983.

Stonebraker, M., 'Implementation of integrity constraints and views by query modification', Proceedings of the ACM-SIGMOD Conference, 1975, pp. 65-77.

Ullman, J.D., Principles of Database Systems, Computer Science Press, 1980.

Verhofstad, J.S.M., 'Recovery techniques for database systems', Computing Surveys 10, 1978, pp. 167-197.

Walker, A., 'On retrieval from a small version of a large database', Proceedings of the Sixth International Conference on Very Large Data Bases, Montreal, 1980, pp. 47-54.

12 Design of Computer Support for Multicriteria and Multiperson Decisions in Regional Water Resources Planning

H. Schaeffers

1 INTRODUCTION: ORGANISATION OF REGIONAL WATER PLANNING AND DECISION MAKING

1.1 General

Decision making for design of regional water resources systems shows a high complexity, due to many interrelations between aspects, decision makers and planning procedures. Aspects are of a technical, a psychological, an ergonomical (human-computer interaction) and an organisational nature. Decision makers are policy makers, planners and designers.

In The Netherlands, planning of regional water resources is embedded in a complex and still changing planning structure, with high and conflicting demands for information processing, coordination and decentralisation. In this structure, long range policies are set at the national level in the so-called Structure Plan for Drinking and Industrial Water Supply (SPWS), prepared by the National Institute for Water Supply (NIWS). The SPWS is meant to guide coordination of drinking and industrial water resources planning in relation to land use policies at several levels of timespan (long range, medium range, short range), aggregation (regional level, project level) and decentralised public decision making (national, regional and local authorities). In the process of coordination, tradeoffs have to be made between conflicting objectives.

The medium range planning of water resources is conducted by the Organisation of Water Companies (OWC) and constrained by the SPWS. Traditionally, regional planning of water resources projects was conducted by the (subregional) Water Companies (WC), organised in the OWC.

In the past, these WC's operated nearly autonomously, the OWC's function being merely limited to 'summing-up' WC plans and to support WC's. In that situation, no 'integral' models were used. Heuristics and experience of decision makers sufficed.

However, the development of the planning and decision making structure, especially policy formation at the national level as a consequence of the desire to use scarce resources (water, budgets) in a more efficient way, presses for more coordination and integrated planning, according to the more or less 'systems view' of planning, adopted in the seventies.

1.2 Decision situations

In Twente, the current decision situation is a transition between a 'past' and a 'future' situation; therefore, for analytical purposes, we consider two idealised situations: past/current (PC) and current/future (CF). Figure 1 summarises the tasks of actors in PC and CF decision situations. The PC decision situation is of a more decentralised nature. The system boundary of the physical system is restricted to a subregion. Projects are connected to one user, facilitating planning of capacity expansions. Tradeoffs are only made between cost and risk, but no attempt is made to find an optimal solution. Damages to agriculture and environment are assessed afterwards, not during the decision process. Risk, quantity and quality are treated as constraints, using standards and simple decision rules. Minimisation of cost and maximisation of autonomy of WC's are the fundamental objectives. In this situation, regional plans consist of 'summed up' subregional plans.

In the CF decision situation, however, more integration of decision aspects is possible. Here, the scale is regional instead of subregional, and objectives as well as types of decision support differ from the PC situation. Projects are connected to multiple users in a network, allowing for more efficient regional-scale plans, but requiring more advanced models and information management. Objectives involve cost, protection against damages (agriculture, environment), risk, quality. Communication processes, involving bargaining and exchange of information between WC's, OWC and NIWS in a Regional Group (RG) are necessary. Here, formal decision aids (simulation and optimisation models integrated with interactive technologies), show a function in providing a medium for communication and resolution of conflicts. At the same time however, a potential for new conflicts arises: models and assumptions can be disclaimed for political-strategic reasons.

Actors	PC Decision Situation	CF Decision Situation
WC's	Project planning in subregions; simple decision rules; submitting plans to OWC.	Participation in regional planning; bargaining, exchange of information with OWC in the Regional Group
OWC	Summing up subregional plans; information procedures	Coordination of subregional planning; information procedures; conflict resolution (in the RG)
Regional Group (RG) (WC's, OWC and NIWS)	-	Conflict resolution, formal decision aids; generation of alternatives (see above)

Figure 1. Actors and tasks in PC and CF decision situations

In Figure 2, a comparison between the PC and CF decision processes is made. In general, activities in the CF process are more complex and involve more actors. In terms of the typology of Mintzberg et al. (1976), the 'political routines' (bargaining, communication) are more explicitly addressed to in the CF situation. This complicates the CF process. Also, generation of CF alternatives is more important in the CF process, presumably as a means to resolve conflicts in the bargaining process between WC's. Another mechanism for conflict resolution is the development of general agreements (ex ante) for instance with respect to water quality, choice of locations, and economic principles in evaluation of investment alternatives.

The more complex organisation of the CF process can be seen as an answer to the 'environment', inducing internal needs for conflict resolution. However, one of the arising paradoxes is that additional research into effects of decisions, e.g. locations of projects, in order to motivate the choice of a location with respect to local or regional decision authorities, gives rise to demands for more research.

Another tendency is the closure between planning and decision making, as a result of the introduction of conflict resolution systems, for instance, leading to guaranteeing implementation of projects that are included in the plan. This closure shows a discrepancy with respect to criteria from a rational decision model (see Alexander 1979).

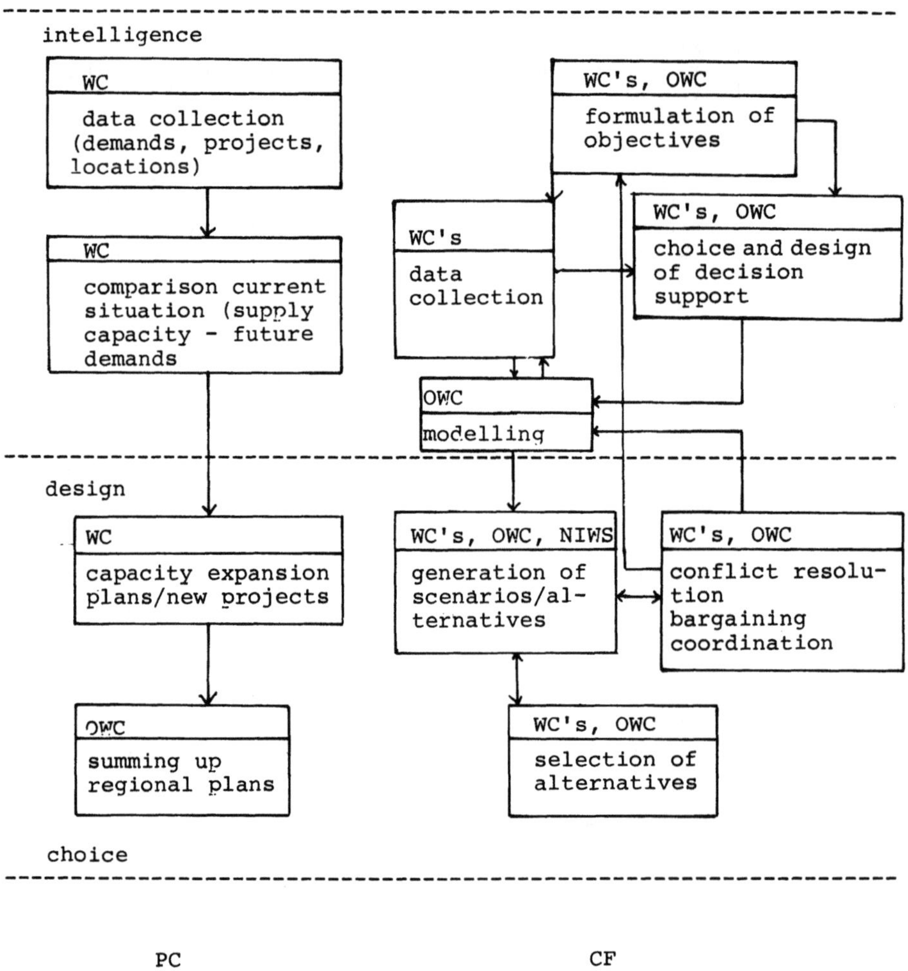

Figure 2. Decision processes in PC (subregional) and CF (regional) planning

We summarise some problems and their consequences for design of decision support:
There are limits to coordination: the complex nature of the planning and decision making structure gives rise to an instrumental view of planning. In that view, problems are formulated in terms of (lack of) 'control'. This systems paradigm does not suffice in coping with the complexity of decision making networks, consisting of interdependent sets of 'actors' at various levels of decision making and decision influencing. A 'political' model of decision making (see Allison 1971) would be more adequate, allowing actors to have different objectives, priorities and perceptions of the decision situation, and allowing for processes such as agenda-setting and bargaining (see also Kunreuther et al. 1982). A related problem is the need for communication between organisations, groups and persons involved in the decision making process. For instance, the danger of loss of autonomy is one reason for limited communication between WC's, especially where political disagreements exist. This situation shows an analogy to a sequential prisoners' dilemma game (see Axelrod 1984). Of interest here is the function of a decision support system to support cooperation. A third problem concerns the decision support needed in a changing decision situation, involving conflicting objectives and interests. Conditions have to be formulated which guide acceptance of decision support in interorganisational policy groups while maintaining normative emphasis. Also, the nature and function of user participation in the design must be discussed.

Use of formal models to be integrated in a decision support system will probably be dependent upon its flexibility. As mentioned earlier, decision activities show a high closure. Also, the decision process is dynamic. Application of formal models would restructure the decision problem, thus limiting their acceptance. Here, the problem is the use of formal models as a tool for learning in a strategic environment.

Several criteria for acceptance of plans show a political nature: for instance, minimisation of conflicts between actors involved. An objective function, relating effects of decisions to actions, often cannot be specified in advance. Here, simulation seems an acceptable modelling strategy, but inferior solutions are produced. The integration of multiobjective optimisation models in conflict situations remains to be investigated. Several of these topics will be addressed in the following case study.

2 CASE STUDY

We describe the process of design of decision support for the problem of planning of regional water resources in Twente, The Netherlands (see Schaffers 1984). Figure 3 shows the context of this study. Methodologically, several problems arise with respect to validity. Only suggestions for hypotheses can be generated as a result of the one-shot nature of this case study. Also, iterative design is difficult to evaluate.

A first step in the decision has been the development of software to be used in human-computer experiments. Three different decision situations have been dealt with. These will be summarised as follows:

- (small) group decision making, semi-structured problem
- (large) group decision making, ill-structured problem
- (individual) decision making, semi-structured problem.

The technique of gaming has been used to simulate the external environment.

These experiments suggested several limitations in using man-computer interaction for the solution of planning problems, requiring further research. In the group decision making cases, different standards with respect to rationality arose, compared to the normative views of decision making. Conflict, vote-trading and strategies in priority setting do have functional properties, and can be disturbed by methods that impose structure on group processes. A risk of using a formal method is its potential for generating conflict when diverging opinions can be expected. These experiences have been used in the case study.

2.1 Design process

The design problem is ill-structured; information with respect to causal relations, objectives and priorities, even the physical structure of the regional water resources network, was scarcely available at the beginning of the design process. The modelling process has been organised as a communication process between designers and, as potential users, representatives of relevant organisations at different policy levels (managers of regional WC's, representatives of the OWC, the NIWS, and the Ministry of Health and Environmental Management (HEM).

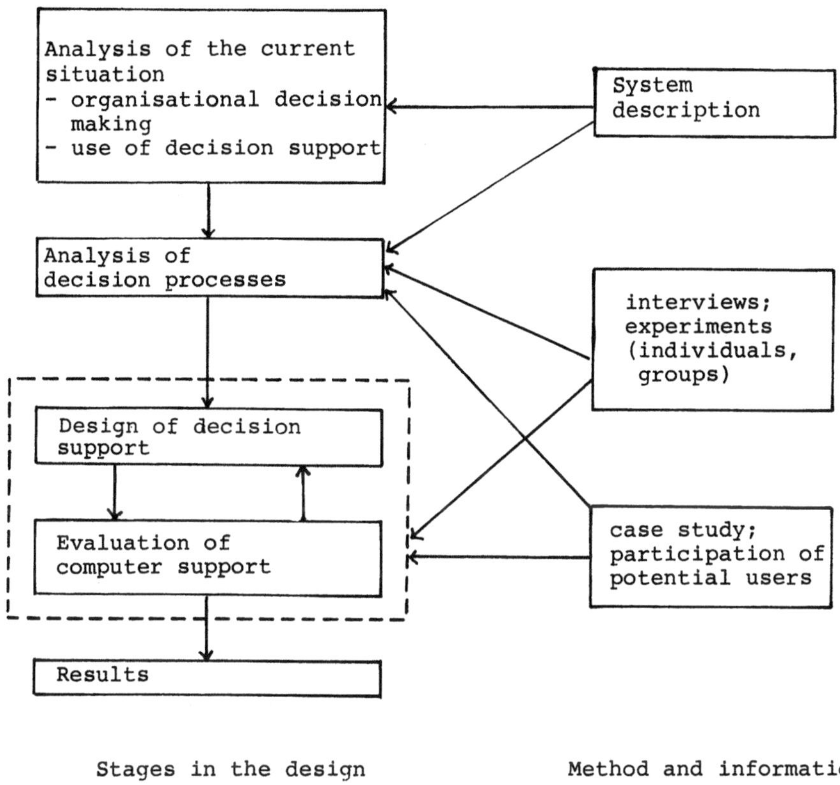

Figure 3. The design study

Figure 4 shows the stages in the design.

The design was originally thought of as a combination of separate processes of design an evaluation: pre-design and pre-evaluation by designers; evaluation by planning bodies and administrative bodies. In the pre-design stage, a simplified pilot model (interactive multi-objective capacity expansion of a water resources network) was designed as a base for discussion between designers and potential users. At the beginning of the participative design stage, general objectives were stated. Also, stages in the design process were identified: objectives formulation, model operationalisation, application of the model to the Twente region, presentation of results.

Soon it was discovered that ongoing communication between designers and potential users would be necessary to assure a more realistic character of models and the user-models interface (man-computer dialogues; choice and format of information presented to users) and to facilitate exchange of information (the physical system, the decision process, structure and results of models). During the design process, the problem definition has been developed and specified in formal models, and choice, design and structure of models have been related to preferences of users, data available, and existing problem solving strategies.

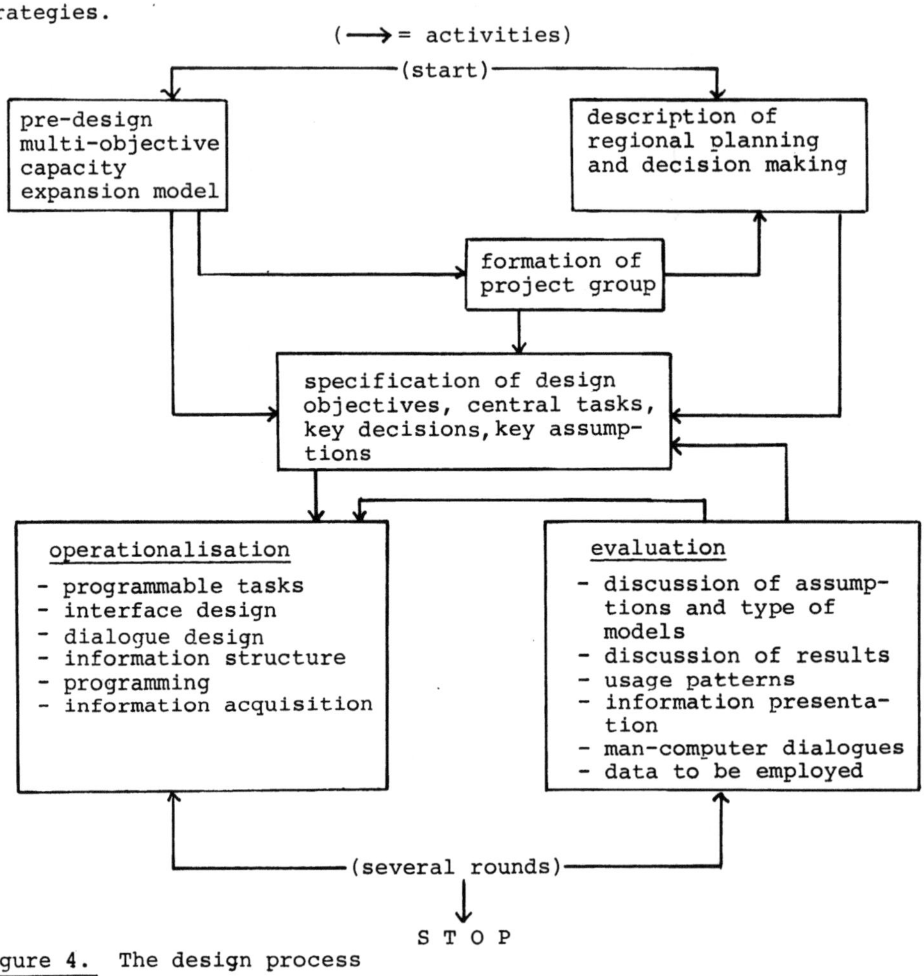

Figure 4. The design process

The process of modelling, especially with respect to formulation of objectives of the modelling process, the modelling methodology to be employed (optimisation versus simulation) and the assumptions involved in the specification of models, could be seen as a bargaining process between the designers and users, who had different priorities. Potential users stressed the need for a realistic approach, the use of realistic data, and the integration of existing decision rules in a general model, to be based on simulation methodology. Designers were concerned with development of normative methodology and proper evaluation of the design process. They aimed at integrating (multiobjective) optimisation methodology with traditional decision rules in an interactive system for alternatives generation and selection. Also, they wanted to investigate different dialogues and modes of presentation of computer-generated information and different usage patterns (interactive versus intermediary use of the computer) and its consequences for decision quality.

A compromise had to be made, involving a priority for 'realism' of models and data. As a conclusion, it can be stated that organisation of the design process as a 'laboratory' situation is not feasible when real-life decision makers participate; situational factors like time and status limitations of participants, the size and complexity of the problem and different priorities of the designers and users impose constraints on the organisation of the design.

Originally, computer-assisted group decision making was thought of as a feasible way of interaction between potential users and the models developed. Therefore, interactive Batch-mode computer programmes have been developed. However, interactive decision making has to be considered as one variable among many. Batch-mode computer-based generation of alternatives with emphasis on reports as a result of varying policy assumptions was preferred. The following reasons were important: a large interactive optimisation programme requires a very flexible structure to be tested carefully for unnecessary options that constitute decision points; the size of the optimisation problem results in computing times too high for man-computer interaction; time constraints of participants; group decision making using an interactive programme where many options (decision points) are open to the decision makers, results in a too time-consuming procedure; inputs needed in the programme (e.g. constraints on objective functions) were difficult to provide, due to the political nature of these decisions.

Users chose to formulate basic options for alternative plans in terms of attainment values for objectives; these alternatives then had to be developed in detail by an intermediary.

Three options with respect to man-computer interaction have been included: interactive execution; batch execution (input data by means of pre-processed data files), and mixed mode (input partly by means of files, partly user-supplied).

Choices in the decision process

The design process can be interpreted as a sequential choice (decision) process, constrained by situational factors such as: time available, objectives of designers and users, experience of participants with computer-assisted planning, existing planning procedures, information available, political aspects.

Major choices involve:
- physical and political system boundary
- objectives of the design process
- modelling methodology (simulation, multiobjective optimisation)
- participants
- design process: time available, frequency of communication between designers-users (user-involvement)
- models, decision rules, aspects in models
- interface characteristics (information presentation, man-computer dialogues)
- level of aggregation in data and models
- usage pattern (mode of interaction with computer)

For instance, the mode of interaction of users with the computer is constrained by their willingness to elicit tradeoffs on objectives. The sequential and iterative nature of the process, due to the ill-structuredness of the problem and political objectives of the participants (representing different organisations) gives rise to interrelatedness of choices. Often these choices are irreversible (e.g. choice of modelling methodology).

Key decisions in the design process can be clarified by means of different decision models (see also Allison 1971), e.g. the rational actor model, satisficing, organisational procedures, political process, individual differences. For instance, Janis and Mann (1977) would describe the design process as influenced by environmental stress (time available) and changing perceptions of risks of decisions. Political models (see Allison 1971, Kunreuther et al. 1982) would stress political objectives. Unfortunately, these models cannot serve as a useful normative (ex ante) guide. The best one can do is to trace effects of interrelating decisions; explicit specification of objectives of the design; proper choice of participants, specification of tasks for designers as well as participants.

User-involvement in the design

The opportunities for 'user-involvement', recommended in many studies concerned with design of decision support systems (e.g. Keen and Scott Morton 1978, Bennett(ed) 1983), are not always available. Time limits of potential users, but also organisational procedures and political processes limit the nature of the user-involvement. In our case study the design situation is part of a network. Actors belong to multiple decision situations with separate tasks, objectives and agendas. Inputs of actors in the design process reflect their position in the network, and do not necessarily mirror their knowledge and skills, but in group situations these skills (e.g. experience with computers) act as constraints. Several conclusions with respect to user-involvement can be drawn:

- when user-involvement is constrained, users will tend to control the design process as their objective. Then the decision process can no longer be defined as a learning situation.
- user-involvement is successful only if these users' role in the design is in accordance with their position in the organisation.
- user-involvement is successful only if these users are responsible for tasks in the design, and if bargaining between subgroups of users, reflecting 'real world' circumstances, can be brought into the design situation.

2.2 Computer support

As a result of the design process, a set of interrelated programmes have been developed (Figure 5). Solution strategies have been developed that involve man-computer interaction in order to reduce problem solving complexity. The central tasks in the programme are:

- analysis of the current water resources system; compared with future projections of demand
- design of a water resources system network ('layout')
- design of alternative plans, using the system network and multi-objective optimisation
- selection among alternatives.

Subtasks have been defined within the central tasks, directed to information production and information presentaton. A structure was developed for choice of and communication between subtasks and programmes. Models to support execution of (sub)tasks involve: multiobjective capacity expansion of a water resources network; allocation of supplies to users, costs, agricultural damages, protection of the environment, water quality.

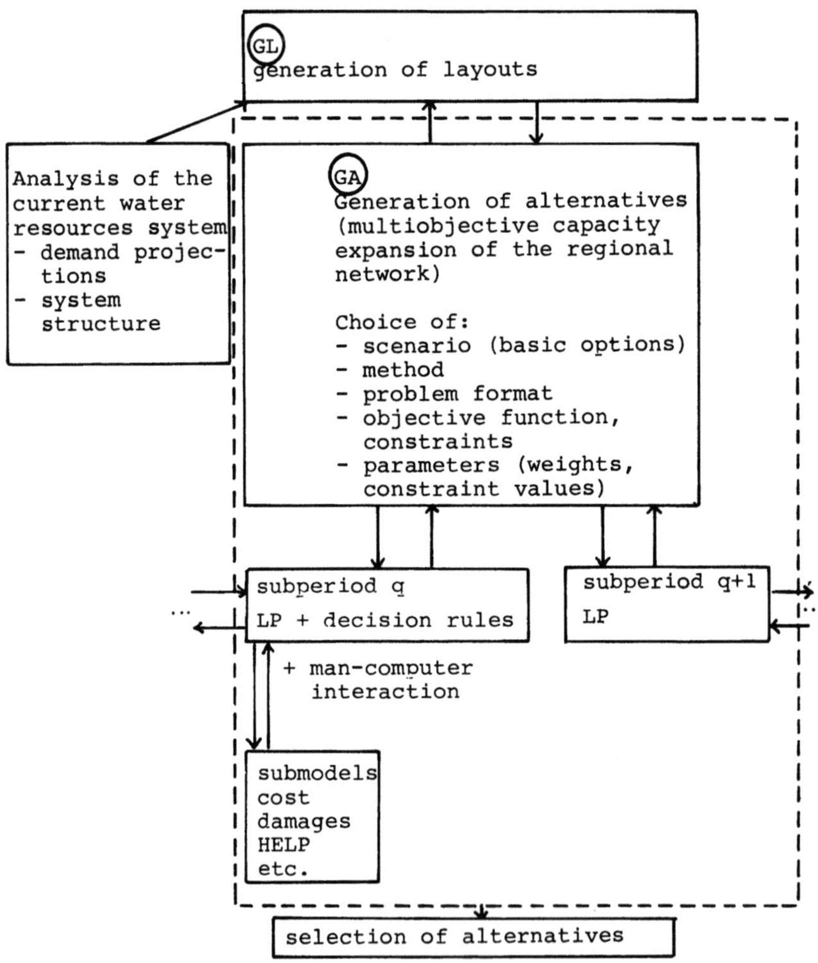

Figure 5. Structure of models

Generation of layout (GL)

The layout generation model supports the interactive design of a system network structure consisting of sources, demands, reservoirs and transport pipes. This structure provides a system of constraints and a matrix for the alternatives generation programme in that the set of permitted locations for projects, including pipelines, is chosen. Several possibilities are: design of alternative layouts; change of a specific layout, loaded from a library; test of a layout against alternative future demand schemes. Several interactive procedures have been designed varying from user-oriented to terminal (programme) oriented. Support involves choice and presentation of necessary information (e.g. damages, quality) and choice of design activities (selection of locations, selection of transports, test of a completed layout, change of a layout). The function of this programme involves a simplification of the alternatives generation problem, becuase of the connection of projects to locations.

Generation of alternatives (GA)

The central model for design of alternative plans consists of a combination of simulation and optimisation using decision rules to reduce complexity. A planning period is divided into subperiods, of which number and length can be chosen. A linear optimisation problem for each of the relevant subperiods can be generated using resulting decisions (locations, capacities, allocations) as inputs in subsequent optimisations. The layout structure acts as a set of constraints, besides those for damages, demand levels and supply capacities. Dynamic programming is used to rearrange project expansion schedules.

Alternative policy assumptions (level of future demands, allowable damages to agriculture and to protection of the environment, excess capacity levels of projects) can be investigated and compared.

The interactive structure allows the user to (re)formulate the optimisation problem (choice of method, choice of assumptions, choice of objectives and constraints, choice of subperiods). Also, dependent of the problem formulation, weights on objectives or constraint values on effects can be changed.

Different problem formulations result in series of projects appearing in the solution. A comparison of alternative series allows for projects to be singled out for further analysis. For instance, in Figure 6, results of cost minimisation are shown indicating expansion of projects 24, 25, 28 during the planning period for basic alternatives 0, 1, 2, 3, 4.

project	project 1	project 2	project 3	project 4
24	1,2,3	3	0,1,2,3,4	0,1,2,3,4
25	3	0,1,2,4		0,4
28	1,3	3	0,2,3,4	0,1,2,3,4

Figure 6. Some results

At the more aggregated subregional level, graphical representation of the development over time of inter-subregional supplies can be shown.

Basic alternatives involve as aspects:

1. agricultural damages,
2. protection of the environment,
3. quantity,
4. risk level.

The user specifies a matrix involving alternative (attainment) levels of aspects. These act as constraints in the alternatives generation programme. Although the programme is interactive, this method allows the policy maker to facilitate his interaction with the computer.

Results are written to a terminal or written to data files and collected in reports at different levels of aggregation; project level, subregional level and regional level.

2.3 Limits to integration of normative models in decision support systems

As a result of the design process, the man-machine interface consists of procedures for man-computer interaction translated into dialogues, that operate on formal models and data, and modes of presentation of information. Being a choice in the design process, the decision makers' usage pattern of the decision support involves two alternatives: 1) direct, interactive use; 2) direct use, involving an intermediary user of the decision support. The user is 1) the direct decision maker; 2) an intermediary (staff). The decision makers had a priority for indirect use of decision support. This is in line with their traditional work procedures.

Here, a conflict arises with respect to the nature of formal models and assumptions used in constructing the decision support. Several assumptions, for instance, linearity of causal relations; use of layout structure to simplify the decision; the multiobjective nature of the problem and the sequential optimisation procedure, involve the need for man-computer interaction as a means of controlling solution procedures. Our models do not pretend to produce implementable results; rather their function is to suggest directions for solutions and to provide insight into the causal system. This function, however, can be accomplished only if traditional interaction patterns of decision makers can be changed.

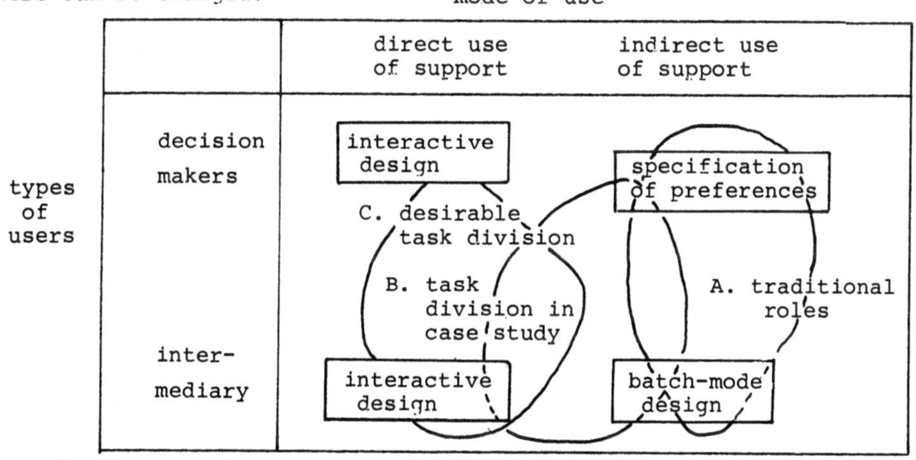

Figure 7. Usage patterns

In terms of Figure 7, where traditional task divisions (A) as well as the case study task division (B) is depicted, in terms of two dimensions (types of users, mode of use), more efficient task divisions should be investigated, e.g. (C).

A limit to integration of normative models in a decision support system is the political nature of the decision making process. Our case shows the existence of conflicting and strategic preferences (e.g. cost minimisation versus protection of the environment), but also conflicting perceptions with respect to the decision support process (adaption to existing organisational procedures versus integration of normative models). Thus, the importance of the process of problem structuring (von Winterfeldt 1980, Kunreuther et al. 1982, Humphreys et al. 1983a,b). Still, it has to be investigated whether several problem structuring methods just generate more potential for conflict, especially when diverging opinions exist.

3 INTEGRATION OF MULTIOBJECTIVE DECISION MODELS IN DECISION SUPPORT SYSTEMS

Development of multiobjective decision models (MODM) (see Hwang and Masud 1979, and Hwang and Yoon 1981, for a review) is primarily an answer to the problem of multiple criteria. The emphasis is on decision situations with one single decision maker. The nature of the problem (functional relations) and of the decision maker (preference structure) is presupposed. This static (rational actor) nature of the MODM framework limits application possibilities in an uncertain and dynamic environment with multiple users and ill-structured problems.

The field of decision support systems (DSS) has developed from thoughts about effective application of models in organisations. Models should be "simple, robust, easy to control, adaptive, complete and easy to communicate with" (Little 1970). At present, the methodology involves the applications of model management and data management capabilities, but the emphasis on the interface between the system and its users has remained a cornerstone. Here, the integration of multiobjective decision models in the broader DSS framework becomes promising. To the emphasis in MODM on man-model interaction, nature and logic of decision rules, utility of information presented to the decision maker and learning aspects, DSS offers realism in its organisational orientation, for instance, by focussing on adaptive and flexible tools to be developed in a design process where potential users do participate.

Decision support systems

The field of Decision Support Systems [1] (DSS), has been developed since the mid-seventies by Keen and Scott Morton (1978), Alter (1980), Sprague and Carlson (1980), Fick and Sprague (1980), Bonczek et al. (198) among others. It aims to integrate various disciplines (operations research, management science, decision analysis, organisation theory, data processing, cognitive psychology among others) in order to develop user-oriented tools to support and improve decision processes in semi-structured tasks. These tools involve interactive systems, and their scope varies from data-oriented to model-oriented (see

Alter 1980). Several most useful introductory or advanced articles and monographs on the subject of DSS design and methodology exist. Besides those already cited, Ginzberg and Stohr (1982) discuss various DSS definitions, underlying concepts, DSS technology building blocks (software, hardware), design process approaches, usage patterns. Ginzberg et al. (1982), Bennett (1983), Sol (1983), Humphreys et al. (1984) also present useful cases.

A useful framework is Sprague and Carlson (1982). 'Specific DSS' focusses on specific tasks in the organisation; they to be used by managers. 'DSS generators' are to be used by designers to produce specific DSS. 'DSS tools' involve basic technology components to be integrated to form a DSS generator. In the view of Sprague and Carlson, a DSS generator consists of several connected subsystems (dialogue subsystem, data subsystem, models subsystem). These subsystems use three basic elements of a DSS: a data base, a model base and a software system, providing the user with a means to interact with the data base and model base. In the terminology of the authors, the software system consists of data base management software, model base management software, and software for managing the interface between the user and the system. A different framework comes from Bonczek et al. (1981, 1983) related to artificial intelligence concepts. Three systems are proposed: a 'language system' where problems for the DSS to solve can be stated; a 'knowledge system', where application-specific knowledge can be handled, and a 'problem processing system' where problems are solved. Both frameworks can be integrated, as Minch and Burns (1983) have shown.

Here we limit the discussion to the model handling capabilities of a DSS. Several technological developments touch on integration possibilities for multiobjective decision models. Sprague and Carlson mention several capabilities for a models subsystem; e.g. the ability to create and extent new models quickly and easily, the ability to access and integrate model 'building blocks', the ability to catalogue and maintain a wide range of models supporting all levels of users. In financial planning, several simple modelling systems exist to be used on mainframe or microcomputers (Visicalc, IFPS, EPS, etc.). Spreadsheet systems for instance, offer a tool for devising and exexuting simple financial simulation or even optimisation models. More advanced model management systems, where models are generated by the DSS, include use of AI concepts (e.g. Bonczek et al. 1981, 1983).

A different technological development is interface design (man-computer dialogues, presentation of information). Carlson (1983b) shows the existence of tradeoffs between alternative types of interfaces. These involve choices in hardware, software for interface design, user support and are dependent on the type of decision making. Here, experimental research is clearly needed.

Carlson (1983a, b) has developed a methodology of 'contextual representations', where the user performs 'operations' (e.g. generate alternatives, change decisions, scale graphs) on 'representations' (e.g. tables, graphs, spreadsheet), using 'memory aids' (data base, library) and 'control aids' (menus, manuals).

Technological developments (for instance, the development of very high level programming languages with data base capabilities) show the possibility of more influence by end-users on development of applications. Martin (1982) even calls this 'application development without programmers'.

Although much DSS literature is technologically oriented, important studies relate to experimental or empirical research, e.g. characteristics of the design process in relation to the evaluation and use of the decision support (e.g. Henderson and Ingraham 1982, Keen and Gambino 1983, Alavi and Henderson 1981, King and Rodriguez 1981, Ginzberg 1981). This reflects a concern with the decision situation at hand (see also Stabbell 1983). In fact, two literatures exist: a technologically oriented literature, and a behavioural organisational oriented literature. Here, a problem is the integration of both in experimental and case studies. This integration should result in a (still not existing) 'theory of decision quality' [2].

In multiobjective decision problems, the following activities are important and can be integrated in a DSS:

- choice of causal relations and constraints,
- generation of causal relations using data base,
- assessment of the decision situation,
- choice of a MODM technique,
- specification of the MODM problem in an optimisation format,
- choice of fixed parameters,
- choice of alterable parameters (e.g. constraint values),
- value assessment in relation to choice of parameters.

In the traditional MODM framework, only 'choice of parameters' and 'value assessment' is supported in a man-computer dialogue. However, a DSS should involve support of all activities. DSS concepts, as model management, provide these opportunities. It has been shown (e.g. Dyer and Mulvey 1983), that optimisation models can be integrated into an information system. Integration of multiobjective models presents some new problems and opportunities. For instance, models could include structural models where qualitative relations between variables can be assessed (see Linstone et al. 1979). These models allow user-involvement. They could act as a generator of system models when integrated with a data base. A multiobjective model, chosen from a model base, could coordinate these systems models. Choice of a multiobjective model could be influenced by characteristics of the decision maker, to be reflected in his dialogue with the system. But, these technological potentials (see also Andriole 1982) in itself will not guarantee what remains as a puzzle: the definition of a 'good' decision.

4 CONCLUDING REMARKS

Development of decision support systems for complex decision problems (characterised by ill-definedness, multiple objectives and interests, interaction with related decision problems, and by the strategical nature of the decision situation) is of much interest. Many technological 'building blocks' (models, software systems for man-computer communication) are available; the design process, including the degree of user participation needed, has been studied extensively in the literature. It seems that, while technological developments have proceeded, organisational and political bottlenecks limit application of normative decision aids. Our case study shows the importance of factors as the position of participants in the organisational network, time available and existing decision procedures.

An important area of future research, therefore, will be the relation between systems for information generation and organisation structures (the problem of 'economics of organisation'). For instance, coordination and delegation involve transaction and manipulation of information between multiple participants in a strategic decision situation. Experimental research could be a first step in assessing design characteristics for decision support systems for these situations.

NOTES

[1] Ginzberg and Stohr (1982) adopt the following definition: "A DSS is a computer-based information system used to support decision making activities in situations where it is not possible or not desirable to have an automated system perform the entire decision process".

[2] See Edwards et al. 1984 for an interesting discussion of 'what constitutes a 'good' decision. Kleijnen (1980) offers a formal evaluation framework based on 'value of information'.

REFERENCES

Alavi, M. and Henderson, J.C., 'An evolutionary strategy for implementing a decision support system', Management Science, 27, 11, 1981, pp. 1309-1323.

Alexander, E.R., 'The design of alternatives in organisational contexts: a pilot study', Administrative Science Quarterly, 24, 1979, pp. 382-404.

Allison, G.T., Essence of Decision, Little, Brown, 1971.

Alter, S.L., Decision Support Systems, Current Practice and Continuing Challenges, Addison Wesley, Reading, Mass., 1980.

Andreoli, S.J., 'The design of microcomputer-based personal decision-aiding systems'. IEEE Transactions Systems, Man, Cybernetics, Vol., SMC-12, 4, 1982, pp. 463-469.

Axelrod, R., The Evolütion of Cooperation, Basic, New York, 1984.

Bennett, J.L. (ed), Building Decision Support Systems, Addison Wesley, Reading, Mass., 1983.

Bonczek, R.H., Holsapple, C.W. and Whinston, A.B., Foundations of Decision Support Systems, Academic Press, New York, 1981,

Bonczek, R.H., Holsapple, C,W, and Whinston, A.B., 'Specifation of modeling knowledge in decision support systems', in: Sol, H.G. (ed), Processes and Tools for Decision Support, North Holland Publ. Co., 1983.

Carlson, E.D., 'An approach for designing decision support systems', in: Bennett, J.L. (ed), Building Decision Support Systems, Addison Wesley, Reading, Mass., 1983a.

Carlson, E.D., 'Developing the user interface for decision support systems', in: Bennett, J.L. (ed), Building Decision Support Systems, Addison Wesley, Reading, Mass., 1983b.

Dyer, J.S., Mulvey, J.M., 'Integrating optimisation models with information systems for decision support', in: Bennett, J.L. (ed), Building Decision Support Systems, Addison Wesley, Reading, Mass., 1983.

Edwards, W. et al., 'What constitutes 'a good decision?'', Acta Psychologica, 56, 1984, pp. 5-27.

Fick, G. and Sprague, R.G. (eds), Decision Support Systems: Issues and Challenges, Pergamon Press, 1980.

Ginzberg, M.J., 'Early diagnosis of MIS implementation failure: promising results and unanswered questions', Management Science, 27, 4, 1981, pp. 459-478.

Ginzberg, M.J., Reitman, W. and Stohr, E.A. (eds), Decision Support Systems, North Holland Publ. Co., Amsterdam, 1982.

Ginzberg, M.J. and Stohr, E.A., 'Decision support systems: issues and perspectives', in: Ginzberg, M.J., Reitman, W. and Stohr, E.A. (eds), Decision Support Systems, North Holland Publ. Co., Amsterdam, 1982.

Humphreys, P., Svenson, O. and Vari, A. (eds), Analyzing and Aiding Decision Processes, North Holland Publ. Co., Amsterdam, 1983.

Humphreys, P. and Berkeley, D., 'Problem structuring calculi and levels of knowledge representation in decision making', in: Scholz, R.W. (ed), Decision Making Under Uncertainty, Elsevier, (North Holland), Amsterdam, 1983a.

Humphreys, P., Larichev, O.I., Vari, A. and Vecsenyi, J., 'Comparative analysis of use of decision support systems in R&D decisions', in: Sol, H.G. (ed), Processes and Tools for Decision Support, North Holland, Amsterdam, 1983b.

Hwang, C.L. and Masud, A.S.M., Multiple Objective Decision Making, Springer, Berlin, 1979.

Hwang, C.L. and Yoon, K., Multiple Attribute Decision Making, Springer, Berlin, 1981.

Henderson, J.C. and Ingraham, R.S., 'Prototyping for DSS: a critical appraisal', in: Ginzberg, M.J., Reitman, W. and Stohr, E.A. (eds), Decision Support Systems, North Holland, Amsterdam, 1982.

Janis, I.L. and Mann, L., Decision making. A Psychological Analysis of Conflict, Choice and Commitment, Free Press, New York, 1977.

Keen, P.G.W. and Scott Morton, M.,, Decision Support Systems. An Organisational Perspective, Addison Wesley, Reading, Mass., 1978.

Keen, P.G.W. and Gambino, T.J., 'Building a decision support system: the mythical man-month revisited', in: Bennett, J.L. (ed), Building Decision Support Systems, Addison Wesley, Reading, Mass., 1978.

King, W.R. and Rodriguez, J.I., 'Participative design of strategic decision support systems: an empirical assessment', Management Science, 27, 6, 1981, pp. 717-726.

Kleijnen, J.C.P., Computers and Profits. Quantifying Financial Benefits of Information, Addison Wesley, Reading, Mass., 1980.

Kunreuther, H., Lathrop, J. and Linnenooth, J., 'A descriptive model of choice for siting facilities', Behavioural Science, 27, 1982, pp. 281-297.

Mintzberg, H. and Raisinghani, D., 'A Theoret - The structure of unstructured decision processes', Administrative Science Quarterly, 21, 19 , pp. 246-274.

Schaffers, H., Computerondersteuning en Planning, PhD Dissertation, Twente University of Technology, Enschede, mimeographed, 1984.

Sol, H.G. (ed), Processes and Tools for Decision Support Systems, North Holland Publ. Co., Amsterdam, 1983.

Sprague, R.H. and Carlson, E.D., Building Effective Decision Support Systems, Prentice-Hall, Englewood Cliffs, 1982.

Stabell, C.B., 'A decision-oriented approach to building DSS', in: Bennett, J.L. (ed), Building Decision Support Systems, Addison Wesley, Reading, Mass., 1983.

Winterfeldt, D. von, 'Structuring decision problems for decision analysis', Acta Psychologica, 45, 1980, pp. 71-93.

Part B: Applications

13 Financial Planning with Conflicting Objectives

J. Spronk

1 INTRODUCTION

In this paper [1] we will demonstrate that financial planning in the private firm should be considered as a multiple criteria decision problem, the solution of which can be brought closer by employing multiple criteria decision methods.

Financial theory explicitly states that the firm is and should be maximising the wealth of its current stockholders. Since, for quoted companies, this wealth is being determined on the capital market through supply and demand for the firm's stock, much attention has been and is being devoted to the development of models describing the capital market. In summary, these models intend to describe the determination of stock prices or - in other words - the determination of prices of claims on future and uncertain income streams.

In our opinion, the determination of prices on the capital market does not (at least not directly) depend on the goal(s) of the firm. What matters to the capital market is the quality of the income stream that can be expected from the firm. As such, the empirical evidence on the fact that the firm takes account of multiple goals (see for a discussion Spronk 1981) should not be disturbing to financial theorists. Indeed, there seems to be a growing awareness among financial theorists that the classical assumption of stockholders' wealth maximisation as the firm's one and only goal should be rejected (see a.o. Amuhud and Lev 1981, and Jensen and Meckling 1976). Unfortunately, it is generally assumed that goals other than shareholders' wealth maximisation can either be tranlated into 'cost' factors which can be adopted in the stockholders' wealth formula, this re-establishing a single criterion decision problem or into hard constraints, subject to which the shareholders' wealth can be maximised again. Serious objections can be made to both approaches. These will be discussed in the next section.

2. MODELS FOR FINANCIAL PLANNING WITH CONFLICTING OBJECTIVES

In this section, we discuss a sample of capital budgetting and financial planning, which explicitly deals with multiple goals. These models will be characterised both by their technical and their (financial) economic properties.

One of the easiest ways to deal with multiple goals is to single out one of them to maximise, while requiring minimum values for the other goal variables. Such an approach was followed, e.g. by Robichek, Ogilvie and Roach 1969, who extended the capital budgetting problem by imposing constraints on each period's level of earning induced by the accepted projects. The objections against such a procedure are clear. It assumes that all goals formulated as constraints are equally important and, moreover, that they have absolute priority over the goal variable that is being maximised.

During the very early stages of the development of goal programming, it was suggested several times that this technique could be an important means of dealing with capital budgetting and financial planning involving multiple objectives. For instance, Ijiri, Levy and Lyon 1963, argued that their linear programming model for budgetting and financial planning could be combined with goal programming approaches to break-even budgetting. Indeed, a considerable number of authors have used goal programming in financial planning and goal progrmaming models. Its use in these fields corresponds with the decision maker's reality. In this respect, Ashton and Atkins 1981, state that "it is natural in financial planning to speak in terms of targets and goals; many of the indicators of company performance such a dividend cover, liquidity, or return on capital employed have target ratios adopted by customs and practice". Nevertheless, the employment of goal programming is not without difficulties. Notably, its need of a considerable amount of a priori information to be given by the decision maker should be mentioned. This shortcoming of goal programming clearly paved the way for other procedures.

Sealy 1978, describes a bank financial planning model that has been formulated as a vector-maximum problem. The relevant goal variables are assumed to be profit and solvency, where the latter is defined by two distinct (although related) goal variables: (1) the capital adequacy ratio (defined as the ratio of required to actual bank capital) and (2) the risk asset to capital ratio. The instruments are the amounts to be invested in each of the six available types of assets. Furthermore, the model is subject to a number of constraints, relating to capital adequacy, diversification, required reserves, and to the balance sheet. For this example, Sealy has found a set of seventeen solutions from which the decision maker has to choose a final solution.

This approach seems attractive. Nevertheless, a few important disadvantages should be mentioned. For instance, one may wonder whether for a given goal variable, more is always preferred to less (or vice versa). In many financial planning problems, goal variables like growth size, level of liquidity, amount of leverage, and several other ratios are considered to be important. For none of these goal variables is it obvious that they should be either maximised or minimised. Of course, one may maximise (or minimise) these kinds of goal variables subject to addition constraints, delimiting their values. As will be shown furtheron, there are more flexible solutions to this problem. A more serious problem consists of the fact that, in general, the number of efficient solutions is very large. The identification of them thus requires a considerable (and sometimes even prohibitive) amount of computer storage space and time.

Furthermore, the number of efficient solutions easily exceeds the information-processing capacity of the decision maker. The solution to this problem is offered by some of the interactive procedures.

Candler and Boehlje 1971, describe a two-period capital budgetting model in which the alternative activities consist of (1) two investment projects, to be undertaken either in period 1 or in period 2, (2) the 'opportunity to put cash in the bank', (3) net tax-free cash at the end of the planning horizon, (4) the value of the assets at the end of the planning horizon, (5) dividends paid to shareholders, and (6) pollution. At the same time, the latter four activities have been defined as goal variables, each of which has to be maximised or minimised. Furthermore, the dividends have been restricted to increase at a given (linear) rate. The outcomes of the existing operations have been assumed to be given and fixed and, consequently, to be independent of the investment projects. This problem has been formulated as a deterministic vector-maximum problem. The feasible region of the activity vectors x is described by linear (in)equalities in x. Some of the elements of x are integer. Because the goal variables

$g_j(x)$, j = 1, ..., 4, are at the same time activity variables, they can be expressed on a linear scale only. Candler and Boehlje aim at efficient (Pareto-optimal) solutions. The ultimate solution is to be found by an (unstructured) iterative and interactive approach.

Chateau 1975, gives a numerical example of a capital budgetting problem with multiple goals. The problem is to choose from a set of investment projects, some of which are indivisible. Internal capital rationing is assumed to have the highest priority. Furthermore, three other goals are assumed (an acceptable level of cash, a desired level of dividend disbursement, and a minimum target asset value). These goals are expressed entirely in present values.

This problem has been formulated as a deterministic, mixed-integer, goal programming model employing preemptive priority factors. Chateau shows the results for a variety of objective functions, including the one originally used by Weingartner. Although Chateau finds merit in the goal programming model's flexibility, he also mentions a number of its disadvantages. In his opinion, "The ordering and weightings on a priori ground and in absolute or relative terms may constitute a rigidity factor of the goal programming approach". Not surprisingly, he proposes an interactive procedure. However, for this he has chosen an approach that also requires very detailed information from the decision maker - i.e. marginal rates of substitution for multiple criteria.

With regard to multiple objective decision models, many interactive procedures have been shown to be very powerful tools in the process of searching for a final (compromise) solution. However, as mentioned above, financial planners usually express their preferences in terms of goals and targets. Therefore it seems useful to search for interactive procedures that correspond to this use. An attempt in this direction was made by Ashton and Atkins 1981. They describe an interactive procedure based on goal programming, in which both weights and targets are changed parametrically. Two important technical problems they have met are the choice of the metric distance in the goal programme and the considerable number of goals that is being used in their financial planning model. They developed a three-stage methodology that could deal with these problems in an ad hoc way. In their opinion (with which we wholeheartedly agree), a specific methodology is necessary for financial planning problems involving multiple objectives. Moreover, in view of the possible applications in this field, the efforts to find such a methodology seem to be justified.

Ashton and Atkins described an eight-period financial planning model incorporating a set of investment opportunities and financing alternatives available to the firm. Furthermore, the model contains a number of accounting variables that correspond with the UK tax law and accounting standards. For each of the planning periods, eight goal variables are defined (six of which are ratios). Thus the problem contains a total of sixty-four goal variables. Such a large number of goal variables constitutes a source of difficulties in using multiple objective programming methods.

3 GOALS AND CONSTRAINTS IN FINANCIAL PLANNING

In the remainder of this paper we assume a single decision maker who has to choose from among a set of implicitly described financial plans. Thus we have a series of instrumental variables and a number of constraints limiting the admissible values of the instruments. Together, the instruments and the constraints determine the set of admissible plans. Within the set of admissible plans, the most preferred solution should be chosen. Which alternative is most preferred depends on the goals strived for by the decision maker and on his perception of the goals of others. By using the term 'goal' we assume the existence of a 'goal variable' depending on the instruments, together with a specification of what is wanted with respect to this goal variable (e.g. maximisation, attainment of some minimum value, etc.).

Even when financial planning problems are formulated as single criterion optimisation problems, the corresponding planning models generally contain - apart from the already mentioned cost factors - a series of 'policy constraints' [2] which are intended to take account of policy considerations other than wealth maximisation . In our opinion, these policy constraints should be explicitly considered as goals rather than as constraints. To clarify this point, we will distinguish between three different kinds of policy constraints:

i. <u>constraints which are self-imposed</u>, i.e. the decision maker can determine the exact position of the constraint. For instance, the decision maker may have several goals, of which all but one are formulated as constraints subject to which the remaining goal variable is to be maximised. The main objection to such an approach is that the goals formulated as constraints have preemptive priority over the one which is to be maximised. A better approach is to deal with all goal variables simultaneously, because then the tradeoffs between all goal variables can be considered explicitly, while the positioning of the constraints becomes a result rather than an input of the planning process.

ii. constraints which are externally imposed, which means that the decision maker himself cannot choose the position of the constraint. Examples of the first case are existing governmental regulations, existing production capacity, etc. Of course, these are all examples of hard constraints. Alternatively, the position of the constraint may be uncertain to the decision maker, for instance, because this position has not yet been chosen. An example is a governmental regulation, of which the precise influence is yet unknown, but which is known to be announced in a future planning period: A fisherman who wants to buy a new ship, may have to take account future catch limits set by the government. A more or less traditional way of dealing with such constraints is to formulate them as chance constraints. Nevertheless, situations might arise in which it makes sense to replace such a constraint by a goal variable. In our example, the fisherman might formulate 'the catch limit to be set by the government' as a goal variable - thus being able to influence the risk that the plan chosen will be (in)feasible in the future.

iii. constraints which result from a game situation, where the positioning of the constraint is determined both by the actions of the decision maker and by the actions of other participants, and where neither the decision maker nor any of the other participants have complete control over the game. In his planning model, the decision maker may insert estimates of the ultimate position of constraint, although game theory learns that this estimation is a hazardous if not impossible task [3]. For example, the decision maker may set certain limits on the firm's market share or on the magnitude of the firm's labour force. However, competitors of the firm will anticipate and react upon the firm's actions, thus influencing the market share that will be realised. Similarly, trade unions may anticipate and react upon the firm's actions which influence its employment level. Instead of trying to predict the outcome of these games a priori, without considering the complete profile of the firm's plans, it is better to translate the variables, which are the subject of the game, as goal variables. In principle, every plan can then be described by means of a coherent vector (profile) of values attained for each of the goal variables respectively, after which it is the decision maker's task to judge whether a particular profile is desirable and whether it has a reasonable chance of realisation.

In summary, most of the above types of policy constraints should be viewed as goal variables rather than as rigid constraints. Of course, on the basis of the above classification of policy constraints, a corresponding classification of goal variables can be made. In a particular financial planning problem, any of these different types of goal variables can be present, separately or in combination with other types.

Similarly, it is generally very hard - if not impossible - to translate policy considerations by means of cost factors, which should be included in the formula of the firm's single goal variable. If calculated on an ex post basis, the difference between the stockholders' wealth in case that the goal has been adopted and in case 'it would not have been adopted', should be calculated. On an ex ante basis the problem becomes even more difficult, because then the 'cost factor' may depend on the decision to be taken. Unfortunately, it is in the very nature of (financial) planning to deal ex ante with these different goals'cost factors. In more technical terms, the latter complication arises when the functional form of one goal variable depends on the value of other goal variables. For instance, the goal variable 'wealth maximisation' may depend on such entities as the quality of the products of the firm, the job security of the management, the well-being of the workers, the firm's public relations, etc. Sometimes it is possible to specify more or less exactly how one goal variable depends on another. For instance, one might try to express the stockholders' wealth as a function of the quality of the firms' products. More often however, it is practically impossible to describe how one goal variable depends on the other. In our opinion, this is among others the case for the dependence of the stockholders' wealth on private goals of managers (and other workers) such as their own job security. Amihud and Lev 1981, provide empirical evidence that this almost silently assumes that these private goals can be translated ex ante into so-called agency costs [4], independent of the decisions to be made and thus also independent of the profile of the financial plans to be chosen.

In practical planning problems, one should of course be aware of the fact that the value of one goal variable may influence the functional form of other goal variables. However, it will seldomly be possible - and if so, probably too costly - to find out a priori how the functional form of each of the goal variables concerned precisely depends on the values of the other goal variables. Instead, one may proceed by selecting financial plans on the basis of profiles which do not completely reflect all possible interdependencies between the goal variables. Then, once a plan seems attractive enough to be adopted, a more detailed study of these interdependencies can be made. Within the interactive framework to be discussed in the following section, such an approach can be integrated in a straightforward manner.

4 FINANCIAL PLANNING AS A MULTIPLE CRITERIA DECISION PROBLEM

In the preceding section we showed not only that in financial planning there is generally a multiplicity of goal variables, but also that these goal variables may be of different kinds. The first point is an invitation to use multiple criteria decision methods in financial planning. The second point leads us to assume that it is practically impossible to find an overall preference function defined over the set of admissible combinations of goal variables. Among others to avoid the need for constructing such an overall preference function, it is better to choose one of the interactive multiple criteria decision methods. To select from among the set of interactive methods, several rather common characteristics of financial planning models may be helpful (cf. Spronk 1981):

- financial planning models generally include several policy constraints;
- in financial planning it is not unusual to use goal variables that are defined as ratios;
- sometimes, financial planning models include chance constraints;
- in many financial planning models, goal variables occur which are neither to be maximised nor minimised (e.g. 'growth of earnings over time' and 'amount of cash to be held'). Instead, the values of these goal variables will have to meet certain upper and lower

limits or will have to be as close as possible to a given target value;

- financial planning models very often include discrete (0,1) variables to represent the yes-no options inherent in the selection of capital investment projects.

Given these characteristics, it is not surprising that in literature, very often goal programming models have been proposed to deal with the financial planning problem. Because goal programming requires the specification of a detailed (dis)preference function by the decision maker, we have developed an interactive procedure which can handle the same class of problems as goal programming does, called IMGP (Interactive Multiple Goal Programming).

IMGP needs no more a priori information on the decision maker's preferences than other multiple objective programning methods. Nevertheless, if available, such a priori information can be used in a fruitful manner, while giving the opportunity to the decision maker to reconsider his a priori information. Since IMGP has been described in detail elsewhere (see Nijkamp and Spronk 1980, and Spronk 1981) we give only a brief sketch of the procedure.

In IMGP, the decision maker has to provide information about his preferences on the basis of a pessimistic solution and an ideal solution [5] presented to him. A pessimistic solution is a vector of lower limits (for the goal variables to be maximised) and upper limits (for the goal variables to be minimised) for the respective goal variables. These limits are either defined directly by the decision maker or, in cases in which this is possible and useful, derived mathematically from known properties of his preference structure and the set of alternatives. The ideal solution shows the optimal value, for each of the goal variables separately, given the goal values of the pessimistic solution concerned. The decision maker merely has to indicate whether or not a solution is satisfactory, and if not, which of the pessimistic goal values should be changed. Nor is there any need to specify weifhting factors (however, if available, these kinds of information can be used fruitfully within the procedure). On the basis of the above information, a new pessimistic solution together with the corresponding ideal solution is calculated and presented to the decision maker. Then, the decision maker has to indicate whether the shifts in the pessimistic solution are outweighed by the shifts in the ideal solution (and in possible other indicators). If not, the goal values in the current pessimistic solution are imposed as constraints on the set of admissible alternatives. Within the thus reduced set of admissible alternatives, the pessimistic solution can further be improved upon, and so on, until the decision maker is satisfied with the remaining set of alternatives. This remaining set may be an ε-region around an optimal or Pareto-optimal solution, but may also - depending on the decision maker's preferences - be a much larger set of alternatives, which for instance can be investigated further on the basis of policy considerations that could not be accounted for within the model.

5 A FINANCIAL PLANNING MODEL WITH MULTIPLE GOALS: AN EXAMPLE

In this section we give an example of a financial planning model with multiple goals, and we show how a financial planning model might be selected by using IMGP. The described model includes some features of financial planning, which are in practice rather unual. Nevertheless, every financial planning in reality has its own peculiarities. The purpose of the present section is merely to show how IMGP might help to cope with some of those peculiarities occurring frequently.

Assumptions

We assume that management has to choose a combination of capital investment projects. Furthermore, it has to consider a series of financial decisions, which - assuming no equity issues and no dividend payments during the planning period - consist of a series of debt issues. Next to these decisions, management has to decide upon the amount of cash to be held in each period.

One of the most important goal variables is assumed to be the firm's total market value, defined as the sum of the unlevered present values of the projects adopted plus the market value of the tax savings implied by debt financing plus a correction term for the opportunity costs of cash holdings (cf. also Myers 1974, and Myers and Pogue 1974). Among others, the costs of a possible bankruptcy have been ignored. The unlevered present values are assumed to be determined by the capital market which also takes account of the risks associated with the projects. Independently of possible other goal variables, however. Of course, the negligence of certain goal variables might have a negative effect on the firm's total market value. Instead of accounting for such goal variables either by translating them into correction terms of the market value formula or by imposing hard constraints on the goal values, we deal with these goal variables explicitly and separately. As such we have chosen goal variables relating to the stability of the earnings over time, the amount of debt outstanding, the minimum and the maximum cash levels, and the firm's employment level.

The model

The definition equations of the model are given by

$$E_t = \sum_{n=0}^{20} E_t^n . x^n \qquad \text{for } t=1, \ldots, 10 \; ; \tag{1}$$

$$C_t = \sum_{n=0}^{20} C_t^n . x^n \qquad \text{for } t=1, \ldots, 10 \; ; \tag{2}$$

$$W_t = \sum_{n=0}^{20} W_t^n . x^n \qquad \text{for } t=1, \ldots, 10 \; ; \text{ and} \tag{3}$$

$$C_t + D_{t+1} \; [r.T-(1+r)].D_t + L_t - L_{t+1} + + [(1+r)-r.T].Z_t - Z_{t+1} = 0 \tag{4}$$

x^n, n=0, ..., 20; are (0,1) decision variables representing the possibility of adopting or rejecting each of the twenty available projects (x^0=1) represents the existing firm).

E_t stands for the firm's total accounting earnings before interest and taxes in period t and E^n is the part of the period t earnings, contributed by project n. C_t represents the firm's total after tax cash flow in period t and C_t^n is the period t cash flow associated with project n. W_t is the firm's average number of employees in period t and W_n^t is the average number of employees demanded by project n in period t. The sources and uses of funds constraints are given by (4), where D_y represents a one-period loan (borrowed at the beginning and repaid at the end of period t), r is the interest rate, T is the tax rate, L_t is the amoung of cash held during period t and 2_t are the firm's lending during period t.

One of the firm's most important goal variables is its total market value, defined as

$$V = \sum_{n=0}^{20} A^n . x^n + \sum_{t=0}^{10} r.T.D_t/(1+t)^t - D_0 - \sum_{t=1}^{10} r.L_t/(1+r)^t + L_0 , \quad (5)$$

where A^n is the unlevered present value of project n. Clearly, this goal variable is to be maximised.

A second desire of the firm is to smooth the time path of its total accounting earnings before interests and taxes. To this end, the following time path has been defined:

$$E_t^* = E_0 . (1+g_E)^t \qquad \text{for } t=1, ..., 10; \qquad (6)$$

where E_t^* is the target for earnings in period t and g_E is the target growth rate. The second goal variable is defined as the maximum deviation from this growth path, which is to be minimised. Thus we have:

$$\text{Min! } e^-_{max} , \text{ s.t.}$$

$$e^-_{max} > e^-_t/(1+g_E)^t \qquad \text{for } t=1, ..., 10; \qquad (7)$$

$$E_t - e^+_t + e^-_t = E^*_t \qquad \text{for } t=1, ..., 10;$$

In order to limit the risk of being unable to pay interest on debt out of current earnings, the firm in our example employs a rátio which is often used in practice: the interest cover (or times interest earned), defined as the ratio of earnings before interest and taxes to the interest charges. This ratio can be defined for each period of the planning horizon. However, in order to avoid too large a number of goal variables, we assume that the firm wants to maximise the smallest value of the ratio during the planning horizon. Or, in other words:

$$\text{Max! } \mu , \text{ s.t.}$$

$$\mu < E_t/(r.D_t) \qquad \text{for } t=1, ..., 10. \qquad (8)$$

To solve this non-linear problem, we adopted an approach suggested by Charnes and Cooper 1977. Assuming $r.D_t > 0$ for t=1, ..., 10; the variable μ is fixed at a value $\mu = \bar{\mu}$. Then we solve

$$\text{Max! } \upsilon \text{ , s.t.}$$

$$\upsilon < E_t - \bar{\mu}.r.D_t \qquad \text{for } t=1, \ldots, 10; \qquad (9)$$

and υ unrestricted in sign.

If the maximum υ^* is negative, $\bar{\mu}$ is infeasible and should be lowered. A positive value of υ^* means that $\bar{\mu}$ is feasible and can be raised. A zero value of υ^* corresponds with the optimal value $\bar{\mu} = \mu^*$. Notwithstanding its heuristic nature, this procedure worked quite well in our computations. Besides (9), a set of lower limits

$$E_t / r.D_t > 1.0 \qquad \text{for } l=1, \ldots, 10; \qquad (10)$$

was defined. These lower limits have been changed systematically during the interactive process.

The fourth goal variable concerns the minimum cash level, which is desired to approximate 5 per cent of the per period cash flow plus 5 per cent of the per period interest charges. As with the preceding goal variable, this was formalised as

$$\text{Min! } \lambda \text{ , s.t.}$$
$$L_t / (C_t + r.D) + \lambda > 0.05 \qquad \text{for } t=1, \ldots, 10. \qquad (11)$$

Using the same heuristic as above, λ can be fixed at $\lambda = \bar{\lambda}$, after

$$\text{Min! } \xi \text{ , s.t.}$$
$$\underline{L}_t + (\bar{\lambda} - 0.05).(C_t + r.D_t) + \xi > 0 \qquad \text{for } t=1, \ldots, 10; \quad (12)$$

gives either a positive or a zero value for ξ. If $\xi > 0$, the 'tolerance' $\bar{\lambda}$ in meeting the target ratio value 0.05 is too tight and should be relaxed. If $\xi = 0$, $\bar{\lambda}$ can be tightened. The best value of $\bar{\lambda}$ that can be thought of is $\bar{\lambda} = 0$, which occurs in the case that $L_t > 0.05 \cdot (C_t + r.D_t)$ for all t. Together with (12), the set of limits

$$L_t > \lambda^{min} \cdot (C_t + r.D_t) \qquad \text{for } t=1, \ldots, 10; \qquad (13)$$

is formulated, where λ^{min} can be raised systematically.
The fifth goal value is defined as

$$\text{Max! } \sum_{t=1}^{10} \eta_t \text{ s.t.}$$

$$L - 0.15 \cdot (C_t + r.D_t) + \eta_t = 0 \qquad \text{for } t=1, \ldots, 10; \qquad (14)$$

in order to keep the amount of cash as low as posisble, while assuring that the amount of cash in each period is less than or equal to 15 per cent of the cash flow plus interest charges.

The last goal variable has been introduced to minimise the maximum number of dismissals of workers per period, in order to promote the conditions of employment and to avoid work disputes.

This desire can be formalised as:

$$\text{Min! } W^-_{max}\text{, s.t.}$$

$$W^-_{max} > W^-_t \qquad \text{for } t=1, \ldots, 10; \qquad (15)$$

$$W_t - W^+_t + W^-_t = W_{t-1} \qquad \text{for } t=1, \ldots, 10;$$

Results

We have done several experiments with the above model, which are described in detail in Spronk 1981. Here, it suffices to give a brief outline. We did two kinds of experiments. First, we assumed the variables x^n, n=0, ..., 20; to be continuous (0,1) variables. In the next stage, we assumed these variables to be discrete (0,1) variables. In both cases, we made the decisions necessary to reach a final solution by ourselves. In Table 1, it is shown how this final solution was reached in the continuous case. First, minimal values for the amount of cash hold, the interest cover and the market value are required, respectively. Then, the earnings goal is formulated as a constraint in iteration 5, after which the maximum number of dismissals is limited and the constraint on the interest cover is further tightened. In iterations 8 and 9, the minimally desired market value is raised. However, given the solutions in iteration 9, the minimally desired value is pushed back in iteration 10. Finally, in iteration 11, the interest cover is raised further.

In the discrete case, we started with the pessimistic solution values of the fifth iteration in the continuous case. Of course, the choice of this starting point is somewhat arbitrary. Therefore, in practical problems, this starting point should be selected with more care. Furthermore, in the discrete case, we dropped the goal to keep the amount of cash as low as possible, since the experiments in the continuous

Table 1.

Potential goal values during the interactive process

goal variable	potential goal values	iteration number										
		1	2	3	4	5	6	7	8	9	10	11
current market value	pess.	588.108	588.108	588.108*	700.0	700.0	700.0	700.0*	750.0*	775.0*	762.5	652.5
	ideal	849.097	843.743	838.817	838.817	838.817	790.97	775.19	775.19	775.19	775.19	765.08
underattainment min. earnings	pess.	14.87	14.87	5.79	1.90*	0.0	0.0	0.0	0.0	0.0	0.0	0.0
	ideal	0.0	0.0	0.0	0.0	0.0	0.0	0.0	0.0	0.0	0.0	0.0
interest cover	pess.	1.0	1.0*	2.0	2.0	2.0	2.0*	3.0	3.0	3.0	3.0*	3.25
	ideal	3.69	3.68	3.68	3.68	3.58	3.58	3.58	3.48	3.03	3.32	3.32
underattainment min. cash level	pess.	0.5*	0.0	0.0	0.0	0.0	0.0	0.0	0.0	0.0	0.0	0.0
	ideal	0.0	0.0	0.0	0.0	0.0	0.0	0.0	0.0	0.0	0.0	0.0
amount of cash below upper limit	pess.	0.0	0.0	0.0	0.0	0.0	0.0	0.0	0.0	0.0	0.0	0.0
	ideal	647.15	431.43	323.32	323.32	323.32	306.44	257.93	257.93	204.13	253.74	224.4
max. number of discharges	pess.	13.33	13.0	12.0	12.15	12.15*	5.0	5.0	5.0	5.0	5.0	5.0
	ideal	0.0	0.0	0.0	0.48	0.48	0.48	0.81	2.88	4.98	3.87	4.76

* Goal values chosen to be improved

case had shown that this goal variable was less relevant [6]. However, the constraint limiting the amount of cash to 15 per cent of the cash flow plus interest charges remained in the model. The results of the discrete experiments are not very different from those in the continuous case. Pessimistic goal values, differing only slightly from those in the final iteration of the continuous case, could be found. There are four different solutions satisfying these minimally required goal values. In Table 2, we show some outcomes for the case that market value if maximised.

We can be quite positive about the computational aspects of IMGP in this integer case. The standard package for mixed integer programming offered by IBM, MIP, was used. The branch and bound procedure used in MIP offers several options which appear to be quite useful. For instance, if bounds on the goal variable to be optimised are known (which is one of the features of IMGP), these bounds can be inserted - generally simplifying the branching process. Another possibility that was used to lighten the computational burden is to start each iteration of IMGP with an integer solution which is known to be feasible, subject to the newly added constraint. As such, the preceding optimal solution of the goal variable, of which the minimum value is raised in the new iteration, can be used. Using an IBM 370/158 computer, the CPU-time needed for each iteration was on average less than one minute, notwithstanding an incidentally limited amount of real storage. Finally, the similarity of the optimisation problems, both within and between each iteration, might offer additional opportunities for simplifying the computational process.

6 CONCLUDING REMARKS

The main purpose of this paper is to stress the idea of considering financial planning as a decision problem involving multiple goals. Furthermore, we want to show that IMGP can be a useful tool in dealing with these kind of problems, because (a) it can handle many of the peculiarities inherent in financial planning, (b) it is a simple method and (c) it does not require very sophisticated information on the decision maker's preferences. The fact that IMGP uses target goal values is, in our opinion, attractive from both a technical point of view and - since the use of targets is rather common practice - also from the user's point of view.

Table 2.

Some outcomes when the market value is maximised, final iteration, integer case

projects n	x^n	n	x^n	time	D_t	Z_t	L_t	C_t	E_t	W_t	λ_t
0	1			0	400.0		15.0	80	110.0	100	3.29
1		11	1	1	334.67		5.67	80	115.5	105	4.24
2	1	12		2	272.54		3.46	42	146.0	99	5.97
3	1	13	1	3	244.41		0.97	-5	174.0	96	6.25
4		14	1	4	278.29		15.19	276	184.5	98	106.46
5	1	15	1	5	17.33		13.54	269	201.5	96	
6	1	16		6		256.67	7.5	150	193.5	95	
7		17		7		418.52	11.05	221	205.5	95	
8		18		8		664.63	11.05	221	201.5	95	
9		19		9		931.0	5.55	111	191.5	95	
10	1	20	1	10		1093.36	10.05	201		95	
										95	

$V = 760.90$ $\quad L_t \geq 0.05\ (C_t + r.D_t)$

$\bar{e}_{max} = 0.0$ $\quad \bar{w}_{max} = 6$

$E_t \geq 3.29\ (r.D_t)$

For a successful implementation it is necessary to verify not only whether the proposed procedure is not in conflict with the organisational framework of the financial planning process, but also whether its implementation is really desired and at least not counteracted by the participants involved in the planning process. For instance, managers may be quite reluctant to even mention their goals, let alone specify them in such a way that these goals can be incorporated within the model. To overcome this type of resistance, it is necessary to:

- inform all participants concerned about the aim, the assumptions, and the operation of the method;
- build the financial planning model in close cooperation with the participants;
- pay very much attention to the formulation of the goals;
- give sufficient opportunity to change and rechange the model and the goal variables, and to revise earlier choices made during the interactive process.

Some practical consequences of these desirata are a.o. that the necessary computer software should be as user-friendly as possible, and that attention should be paid to the development of an adequate information system.

Once it is recognised that financial planning should be viewed as a multiple criteria decision problem, many areas for further research can be formulated. We mention the problem of how to deal with large numbers of goal variables, the problem of the (0,1) instrumental variables, the problem of uncertainty and fuzziness, and the problem of interdependencies between goal variables (cf. also Spronk 1981, Chapter 9). Another interesting area for further study concerns the phenomenon that in practice, not all potential capital investment projects are known at the beginning of the planning period, but are often proposed in the course of the period. Furthermore, if one is willing to accept the fact that the set of available investment projects is not completely given and fixed, a next step might be to include the design of new projects within the planning procedure (cf. Zeleny 1981). Finally, we would like to mention the problem of financial planning in decentralised organisations. The procedure proposed in this paper offers interesting opportunities to deal with the decentralisation problem, because it uses lower and upper limits on the goal variables, which can be used as guidelines or budgets for different decision levels. Although it may not be expected that all of these problems can be easily solved, we believe that the use of multiple criteria decision methods in general, and of the described interactive procedure in particular, can already be beneficial to financial planning in practice.

NOTES

[1] This paper has been based on material published earlier by the same author.

[2] Apart from policy constraints, a planning model may include definitional constraints and logical constraints. The present discussion is limited to policy constraints.

[3] See for a more detailed discussion Spronk 1981, p. 26.

[4] The costs the stockholders have to make to 'persuade' management to work in the best interests of the stockholders.

[5] Possibly accompanied by other information on the state of the current solution, that may be required by the decision maker.

[6] Because the maximum cash level is defined as a percentage of cash flow plus interest charges (see (14)), the underattainment of this maximum cash level can be enlarged by simply raising the 'antagonistic' variables D_t and Z_t simultaneously by equal amounts.

REFERENCES

Amihud, Y. and Lev, B., 'Risk reduction as a managerial motive for conglomerate mergers', Bell Journal of Economics, 1981, pp. 602-617.

Ashton, D.J. and Atkins, D.R., 'Multicriteria programming for financial planning, some second thoughts', in: Nijkamp, P. and Spronk, J. (eds), Multiple Criteria Analysis, Gower, Aldershot, 1981, pp. 11-24.

Candler, W. and Boehjle, M., 'Use of linear programming in capital budgeting with multiple goals', American Journal of Agricultural Economics, 53, 1971, pp. 324-330.

Charnes, A. and Cooper, W.W., 'Goal programming and multiple objective optimizations - Part I', European Journal of Operations Research, 1977, pp. 39-54.

Chateau, J.P.D., 'The capital budgeting problem under conflicting financial policies', Journal of Business Finance and Accounting 2, (Spring 1975), pp. 83-103.

Ijiri, Y., Levy, F.K. and Lyon, R.C., 'A linear programming model for budgeting and financial planning', Journal of Accounting Research, 1963, pp. 198-212.

Jensen, M.C., and Meckling, W.H., 'Theory of the firm: managerial behaviour, agency costs, and ownership structure', Journal of Financial Economics, 1976, pp. 305-260.

Myers, S.C., 'Interactions of corporate financing for capital budgeting', Journal of Finance, 1974, pp. 1-25.

Myers, S.C. and Pogue, G.A., 'A programming approach to corporate financial management', Journal of Finance, 1974, pp. 579-599.

Nijkamp, P. and Spronk, J., 'Interactice multiple goal programming: an evaluation and some results', in Fandel G. and Gal, T., Multiple Criteria Decision Making Theory and Applications, Springer, Berlin, 1980, pp. 278-293.

Robichek, A., Ogilvie, D. and Roach, J., 'Capital budgeting: a pragmatic approach', Financial Executive, 1969, pp. 26-38.

Sealey, C.W., 'Financial planning with multiple objectives', Financial Management, (Winter 1978), pp. 17-23.

Spronk, J., Interactive Multiple Goal Programming: Applications to Financial Planning, Martinus Nijhoff, Boston, 1981.

Zeleny, M., 'A case study in multiobjective design: de novo programming', in Nijkamp, P. and Spronk, J. (eds), Multiple Criteria Analysis: Operational Methods, Gower, Aldershot, 1981, pp. 37-52.

14 Interactive Multiple Goal Programming for Bank Portfolio Selection

J. Spronk and G. Zambruno

1 INTRODUCTION

In this paper, we describe and illustrate a new tool for the management of bank portfolios. This new tool, Interactive Multiple Goal Programming (IMGP), is certainly not intended to replace management by prescribing how 'the' optimal bank portfolio can be found. Instead, IMGP is a systematic procedure for gaining insight into the role of the various conflicts, uncertainties and other complexities inherent in bank portfolio management. On the basis of these new insights and assisted by the procedure, management is able to find new solutions and to get a better idea of the implications of these solutions for the bank's position.

In bank portfolio selection, conflicts of various kinds may arise. In general, there is the usual risk-return dilemma. More particularly, the bank has often to choose between short-term obligations and profitable opportunities in the long run. The setting of this decision problem is the complex and uncertain world of modern banking.

Various, but mainly linear, programming methods and models have been proposed, and used, to solve bank portfolio problems [1]. The apparent power of mathematical programming to visualise complex interrelationships is often counterbalanced by the rigidity of assumptions underlying these methods. This mainly explains the tendency to develop more 'realistic' models which, unfortunately, rather often become very large and Babylonic and - by implication - difficult to be understood by managers. Another way to make programming methods and models more useful in practice is to amend the most rigid assumptions behind these methods. Along the latter line of thought, Booth and Dash 1979, propose goal programming to deal with the choice conflicts in bank portfolio selection and two stage linear (goal) programming to deal with uncertainties. Apart from some dangers in the use of goal programming, which will be discussed in Section 2, we agree with Booth and Dash that goal programming is a powerful technique to take account of various, possibly conflicting, objectives and policy constraints. However, a difficulty in applying goal programming (and many other programming procedures) is its requirement of a detailed and formal representation of the decision-maker's preferences. In practice, and certainly in the complex and uncertain environment concerned, managers (and their advisors) are generally reluctant to define exactly what they want prior to knowing more or less reliably what the available actions and their consequences are. The problems becomes even more serious when the decision-maker is asked to define his preferences in terms of (exact) weights, priorities and aspitation levels. Since the latter is exactly what is done in goal programming, we have searched for a method that is less demanding on the decision-maker's abilities, while preserving the positive aspects of goal programming. This technique, IMGP, is described in Section 2 and illustrated in Sections 3 and 4.

The two stage linear goal programming models proposed by Booth and Dash to cope with uncertainty have the same drawback as goal programming. In Section 5 we present - within the IMGP framework - an alternative way to deal with uncertainty. That is, IMGP offers the possibility to systematically investigate the sensitivity of a programming model for external uncertainties. In this sense, IMGP is much more robust than what is generally meant by sensitivity analysis.

2 THE INTERACTIVE PROCEDURE

Recently, interactive methods have become rather popular in decision analyses. They are based on a mutual and successive interplay between a decision-maker and an analyst. These methods do neither require an explicit representation or specification of the decision-maker's preference function nor an explicit quantitative representation of tradeoffs among conflicting objectives. Obviously, the solution of a decision problem requires that the decision-maker provides information about his priorities regarding alternative feasible solutions, but in most interactive procedures only a limited amount of information about the decision-maker's preferences for the various objectives has to be specified in a stepwise manner. The task of the analyst is to provide all relevant information, especially concerning permissible values of the criteria and about reasonable compromise solutions.

Interactive Multiple Goal Programming (IMGP) was developed to combine the advantages of goal programming with the advantages of interactive procedures. Because of its use of aspiration levels and pre-emptive priorities, goal programming is in close agreement with decision making in practice. Although it is one of the stronger methods available, some important drawbacks should be mentioned. First, goal programming requires a considerable amount of a priori information on the decision maker's preferences. Moreover, this a priori information must be precise: the decision maker has to define exact aspiration levels and exact weighting coefficients. Second, goal programming does not always produce optimal or even Pareto-optimal solutions. The third drawback concerns the fact that, in financial management practice, objectives often concern ratios of variables. These ratios are non-linear by nature and cannot be dealt with by means of standard linear goal programming. Obviously, if there is a multiplicity of objectives in ratio form the problem is even more complicated. Unfortunately, this fact is generally ignored in applications of goal programming to financial management problems. Our experiences with the application of goal programming in financial planning stimulated us to develop an interactive variant of that technique (see Spronk 1981).

In IMGP the decision maker has to provide information about his preferences on the basis of a <u>potency matrix</u> presented to him. This matrix consists of two vectors, representing the <u>ideal</u> and the <u>pessimistic</u> solution, respectively. The ideal solution shows for each of the objectives separately the maximum value, given a series of constraints representing a minimally required value for each of the objectives. The vector of these minimum values is defined as the pessimistic solution [2]. The decision maker has to indicate only whether a pessimistic solution is satisfactory or not, and if not, which of the minimum values should be improved, and by what amount. Then a new ideal solution is calculated and presented to the decision maker. He then has to indicate whether the shifts in the ideal solution are outweighed by the shifts in the pessimistic solution. If not, the pessimistic solution must be redefined, a new ideal solution must be calculated and so on. IMGP may be characterised as a systematic procedure (guided by the decision maker) of imposing constraints on the set of feasible actions. A simplified flow chart of the procedure is given in Figure 1.

We conclude this section by mentioning some key properties and possibilities of IMGP. In IMGP the objectives are assumed to be known and concave in the instrumental variables. The preference function of the decision maker is <u>not</u> assumed to be known. However, it is assumed to be either concave, both in the objectives and in the instrumental variables, or lexicographic. Given these assumptions, both optimising and satisficing behaviour can be incorporated. Furthermore, IMGP deals with ratios in a straightforward manner.

The decision maker has to give information only on his local preferences. However, all available a priori information can be incorporated within the procedure. The decision maker has the opportunity to reconsider this a priori information during the interactive process. In order to benefit most from this learning opportunity, the decision maker may wish to repeat the procedure several times.

As shown in Spronk 1981, IMGP converges within a finite number of interactions to a final solution, which does exist and is feasible. Apart from an ε-neighbourhood, this solution is optimal. Whether this solution is unique or not, depends on the decision maker's preferences (for instance, if the decision maker is a satisficer having formulated targets which are all attainable within the feasible region, the final solution is, by definition not unique.

Given a new (proposal) solution, the ideal values of the objectives must be (re)calculated during each iteration of IMGP. This can be done with the help of any optimisation method which meets the fairly unrestrictive requirements imposed by IMGP. Instead of requiring the development of special computer programs, IMGP can make a straightforward use of one of the widely available mathematical programming routines. At this moment, we have several positive practical experiences with the application of IMGP in problems having up to approximately 1,000 constraints (see Spronk and Veeneklaas 1983).

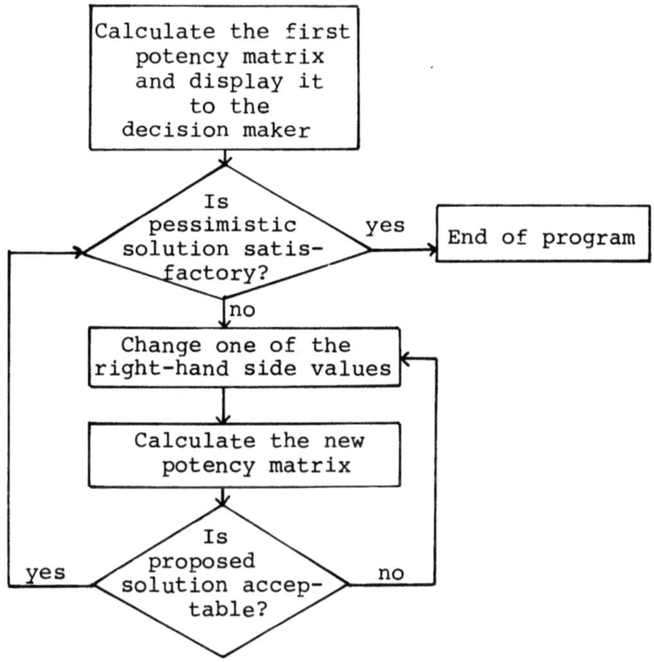

Figure 1. A simplified flow chart of interactive multiple goal programming

3 SOME DETERMINISTIC MODELS AND A REFORMULATION

The aim of this and the next section is to illustrate the relative merits for bank portfolio selection of interactive multiple goal programming as compared with traditional linear (goal) programming. In order to simplify the exposition, we will use a simple bank portfolio model. To save valuable space, we will refer to models and results described earlier in this journal by Booth and Dash 1979, in a discussion of several programming procedures.

For a discussion of programming procedures, these models can best be kept simple. According to Booth and Dash, in order to be operationally useful, the models should 'be expanded to fit the specific decision making requirements of the bank'. To be more precise, the discussed models cover one period only, employ a very simple balance structure and ignore taxes. The variables and parameters included are described in Table 1, together with their values assumed in this example. Variables with prime superscript refer to beginning period values. Booth and Dash formulate both a linear programming model and a linear goal

Table 1.

Variable and parameter definitions and their sample values

Balance sheet variables			Decision variables	
B_1	Cash	180	P_2	Securities purchased
B_2	Securities	300	P_3	Loans made (purchased) ·
B_3	Loans	520	S_2	Securities sold
B4	Deposits	900		
B_5	Equity	100		

Parameters and other variables

a	Portion of desposits associated with liquidity reserves		0.15
b	Portion of securities maturing within period		0.20
c	Portion of loans maturing within period		0.20
d	Maximum new loan demand within period		\$ 200
e	Maximum supply desposits within period		\$ 925
	in the two stage models	e_1	= \$ 950
		e_2	= \$ 900
f	Maximum desired loan/deposit ratio		0.6
r_2'	Current security interest rate		0.06
r_2	Security interest rate in the next period		0.0625
			= 0.065
			= 0.06
r_3'	Current loan interest rate		0.08
r_3	Loan interest in the next period		0.11
r_4	Deposit interest rate		0.05
P	State of nature probability (in two stage models)	p_1	= 0.5
		p_2	= 0.5
h^+	Overachievement variable (in goal programming models)		
h^-	Underachievement variable (in goal programming models)		

Table 2.

Deterministic model specification

(a) LP model specification

Max. B_5	(LP-1)
s.t. $B_1 \geq aB_4$	(LP-2)
$B_2 = (1+b)B_2' + P_2 - S_2$	(LP-3)
$S_2 \leq (1-b)B_2'$	(LP-4)
$B_3 = (1-c)B_3' + P_3$	(LP-5)
$P_3 \leq d$	(LP-6)
$B_4 \leq e$	(LP-7)
$B_3 \leq fB_4$	(LP-8)
$B_5 = r_2'(1-b)B_2' + r_2P_2 - [r_2' - (r_2'/r_2 + 1]S_2 + r_3'(1-c)B_3' + r_3P_3 - r_4B_4 + B_5'$	(LP-9)
$B_1 + B_2 + B_3 = B_4 + B_5$	(LP-10)

(b) LGP model specification

Min. $Z_1[h_1^+] + Z_2[h_3^- + h_5^- + h_6^-]$	(LGP-1)
s.t. $B_1 - h_1^+ = aB_4$	(LGP-2)
$B_2 = (1-b)B_2' + P_2 - S_2$	(LGP-3)
$S_2 + h_2^- = (1-b)B_2'$	(LGP-4)
$B_3 = (1-c)B_3' + P_3$	(LGP-5)
$P_3 + h_3^- = d$	(LGP-6)
$B_4 + h_4^- = e$	(LGP-7)
$B_3 - h_5^+ + h_5^- = fB_4$	(LGP-8)
$B_5 = r_2'(1-b)B_2' + r_2P_2 - [r_2' - (r_2'/r_2) + 1]S_2 + r_3'(1-c)B_3' + r_3P_3 - r_4B_4 + B_5'$	(LGP-9)
$B_1 + B_2 + B_3 = B_4 + B_5$	(LGP-10)
$B_5 + h_6^- = 10^6$	(LGP-11)

(c) IMGP model specification

Max. B_5	(IMGP-1)
Max. B_1/B_4	(IMGP-2)
Min. h_3^-	(IMGP-3)
Min. B_3/B_4	(IMGP-4)
s.t. $B_5 \geq B_5$	(IMGP-5)
$B_1/B_4 \geq \underline{a}$	(IMGP-6)
$h_3^- \leq \underline{h}$	(IMGP-7)
$B_3/B_4 \leq \underline{f}$	(IMGP-8)
$B_2 = (1-b)B_2' + P_2 - S_2$	(IMGP-9)
$S_2 \leq (1-b)B_2'$	(IMGP-10)
$B_3 = (1-c)B_3' + P_3$	(IMGP-11)
$P_3 + h_3^- = d$	(IMGP-12)
$B_4 \leq e$	(IMGP-13)
$B_5 = r_2'(1-b)B_2' + r_2P_2 - [r_2' - (r_2'/r_2) + 1]S_2 + r_3'(1-c)B_3' + r_3P_3 - r_4B_4 + B_5'$	(IMGP-14)
$B_1 + B_2 + B_3 = B_4 + B_5$	(IMGP-15)

programming model which are summarised [3] in Table 2, which also includes a reformulation of these models to make them suitable for interactive multiple goal programming. Since the three models differ only with respect to the way the bank's objectives are translated, we restrict ourselves to a discussion of the formulation of the objectives within the three models.

Objective 1 Maximise stockholder's equity

In the LP-formulation, the (only) objective is 'maximise stockholder's equity, B_5, at the end of the planning period'. This objective was also adopted in the LGP-model, be it in a unnecessarily complicated way [4]. In the IMGP-formulation, this objective was defined by IMGP-1, being identical to LP-1. Through IMGP-5, management is able to guarantee a minimum equity level, $\underline{B}_5$. This minimum level can be changed interactively. Stockholders' equity is defined by IMGP-14, which is identical to LP-9 and LGP-9.

Objective 2 Cash covering of bank deposits

By means of LP-2, the end of the period's cash and reserve holdings B_1 are required to equal or exceed a predetermined fraction of the bank's deposits, B_4. According to Booth and Dash, this fraction a represents legal requirements as well as managerially determined surplus to handle unexpected cash needs. In their goal programming model, Booth and Dash introduce the new objective that the amount of cash above the required level a. B_4 should be minimised. In our opinion, this objective does not make much sense because within the model there is no incentive to hold more cash than is strictly necessary. This is witnessed by the LP and LGP model solutions, where the ending cash values are exactly the same (see Table 3). A more interesting managerial decision concerns the determination of the fraction a, the portion of the bank's deposits that should be covered by cash holdings. Therefore, in the IMGP-model we investigate the ratio between cash and deposits [5]. This ratio is required to equal or exceed the value $\underline{a}$ (IMGP-6). Using IMGP, the value of $\underline{a}$ can be determined directly by the decision maker, within the interactive framework and in relation to the values of the other objectives. At each iteration, IMGP produces the maximum value of the cash/deposits ratio, given the constraints on the values of the objectives (see IMGP-2).

Objective 3 Maximise loans made

In LP-6, the amount of new loans made is constrained by an externally given parameter d, which reflects the fact that the bank concerned is able only to engage in local lending activities. In the goal programming model, Booth and Dash want to maximise the amount of loans, given the local lending constraint. This is accomplished by adopting the underachievement variable h_3^- in LGP-6, which variable is minimised through LGP-1. In the IMGP-model, we have IMGP-7, which is exactly the same as LGP-6, except that h_3^- is minimised through the separate objective function IMGP-3. Moreover, the maximum value $\underline{h}$ can again be changed interactively.

Objective 4 Target loan-deposit ratio

In the linear programming formulation, loans are not allowed to exceed an a priori determined fraction f of deposits (LP-8). This ratio is used to reflect the risk attitude of the bank. In the goal programming model, Booth and Dash introduce the possibility of deviating from this still predetermined, ratio value (LGP-8). However, only the over-attainment of the target ratio value is penalised in the objective function (LGP-1). Here, like in the second objective, the most important problem is the determination of the fraction f. Therefore, in the IMGP-model, we introduce constraints IMGP-8 by means of which $\underline{f}$ can be changed interactively by management. The ratio itself is minimised through IMGP-4.

4 RESULTS OF THE IMGP-MODEL, CERTAINTY

In Table 3, the solutions of the linear (goal) programming models and some of the solutions of the interactive model are given. At each iteration, the interactive procedure produces four solutions, i.e. one solution for each objective. To illustrate, we have selected the solutions in the first, third and fifth iteration resulting when stockholders' equity, B_5, is maximised. At each iteration, we have simulated the decisions of management.

In the first iteration, we chose a minimum value of 0.10 for the cash/deposits ratio and a maximum value of 0.80 for the loans/deposits ratio. Given these conditions, the equity value resulting from maxiisation of B_5 is better than the corresponding value in the LP and LGP solutions (cf. IMGP(1) in Table 3). Of course, this could only be accomplished at the expense of a less safe cash/deposits ratio. In the first iteration, the best and the worst values of each of the four objectives are as follows:

	B_5	B_1/B_4	h_3^-	B_3/B_4
Best	130.09	0.642	0	0.45
Worst	89.92	0.1	200	0.8

In the second iteration, before improving the cash/deposits ratio, we wanted to be sure that the original equity ratio (100) would not drop. In terms of the best and worst objective function values, the addition of this constraint resulted in:

	B_5	B_1/B_4	h_3^-	B_3/B_4
Best	130.09	0.505	0	0.45
Worst	100	0.1	200	0.678

In other words, the best attainable cash/deposits ratio drops and on the other hand the worst value of the loan/deposits ratio improves. In the third iteration, we wanted to guarantee a higher cash/deposits ratio. We chose a value of at least 0.15 for this ratio, resulting in the following best and worst objective function values:

	B_5	B_1/B_4	h_3^-	B_3/B_4
Best	127.01	0.505	0	0.45
Worst	100.00	0.15	200	0.678

Clearly, the best attainable equity value dropped, but that seems to be a reasonable price for the less risky cash position. IMGP(III) in Table 3 is the solution resulting from the maximisation of equity. It turns out that this IMGP solution exactly equals the LGP solution. Obviously, this is caused by the fact that in this iteration of IMGP, we have set the constraint on the cash/deposits ratio exactly equal to the corresponding target value in the goal programming model.

	B_5	B_1/B_4	h_3^-	B_3/B_4
Best	123.92	0.505	61	0.45
Worst	100	0.15	200	0.60

Apart from a drop in the best attainable equity value, the tightening of this constraint implied a minimum value of 61 for h_3^- which means that approximately 30% of new loan demand could not be met. Therefore, we judged this shift in the constraint value too restrictive. Instead, in iteration 5, we chose a constraint value for the loans/deposits ratio in the midle of its values in the two preceding iterations. This resulted in:

	B_5	B_1/B_4	h_3^-	B_3/B_4
Best	125.79	0.495	24	0.45
Worst	100	0.15	200	0.64

It turned out that one of the solutions of this iteration, the one resulting from equity maximisation, was quite satisfactory (see IMGP(V) in Table 3). Therefore, we stopped the interactive process. Of course, in practice, the decision to stop or to continue the interactions is made by the decision maker. In Figure 2, the interactive process is described graphically.

Comparing the results of the three models, we see that depending on the decision maker's preferences, IMGP is capable of yielding both the LP and LGP-solutions. If the LGP-solution is not Pareto-optimal (which is generally not excluded in goal programming), IMGP clearly shows there are better solutions. However, more important is that IMGP gives the opportunity of systematically investigating the tradeoffs between different objectives and policy constraints without requiring much a priori information and without asking the decision maker to define exact weighting or priority factors.

Table 3.

Deterministic model solutions*

		Beginning values	Ending values				
			LP	LGP	IMGP (I)	IMGP (III)	IMGP (V)
Balance sheet							
Cash	(B_1)	180.00	138.75	138.75	92.50	138.75	138.75
Securities	(B_2)	300.00	355.17	297.26	346.59	297.26	320.04
Loans	(B_3)	520.00	555.00	616.00	616.00	616.00	592.00
Deposits	(B_4)	900.00	925.00	925.00	925.00	925.00	925.00
Equity	(B_5)	100.00	123.92	127.01	130.09	127.01	125.79
Decisions							
Purchase Securities	(P_2)		115.17	57.26	106.59	57.26	80.04
Make Loans	(P_3)		139.00	200.00	200.00	200.00	176.00
Sell securities	(S_2)		-	-	-	-	-
Objective functions							
B_5		100.00	123.92	127.01	130.09	127.01	125.79
B_1/B_4		0.20	0.15	0.15	0.10	0.15	0.15
h_3^-		n.a.	1.00	0.00	0.00	0.00	24.00
B_3/B_4		0.58	0.60	0.67	0.67	0.67	0.64

*Of the IMGP-solutions, only those resulting from maximisation of B_5 have been given

5 DEALING WITH UNCERTAINTY

An obvious limitation of deterministic programming models is their poor ability to deal with uncertainty. Of course, most programming procedures offer the possibility of a post-optimality analysis. Although these analyses may provide valuable insights, they may also have their limitations. First, the post-optimality is only concerned with the analysis of the optimal solution and its neighbouring solutions. Second, the sensitivity analysis of some kinds of problem parameters (e.g. technical coefficients in linear programming) may become quite cumbersome. The analysis of simultaneous changes of more than one problem parameter is even far more complicated.

Another widely used procedure for dealing with uncertainty while using deterministic models is to define different scenarios (i.e. different sets of problem parameters) and to rerun the deterministic model for each scenario. Scenarios may be defined at the beginning of the analysis but just as well during the analysis, if the outcomes of one scenario give rise to questions which may be answered by means of a new scenario. Of course, such a procedure is ad hoc and unsystematic and, therefore, often too costly and too time-consuming. This in turn may lead the decision maker not to pose all questions he would like to have answered. Ultimately, these shortcomings of the analysis may lead to the rejection of the whole model.

The two abovementioned procedures for dealing with uncertainty can also be used in combination with the interactive multiple goal programming approach in this article. In addition, two other procedures can be used. The first is to use the interactive framework to reduce the set of decision alternatives to a new set satisfying a series of minimum requirements with respect to the objectives. From this reduced set, a number of decision alternatives can be selected (for instance by means of a random sampling procedure such as proposed by Törn 1980) which are then subjected to a more detailed sensitivity analysis.

A better approach for dealing with uncertainty while using deterministic models is very different from the usual procedures. It is closely related to the philosophy behind the interactive approach and will be described in detail below.

From time to time, stochastic programming models are proposed as tools for dealing with uncertainties. There is a large variety of stochastic programmimg procedures, but in principle they require the definition and the specification of a probability distribution over the outcomes of the uncertain events concerned. Furthermore, the objective function in stochastic models should reflect the risk attitude of management, thus requiring the definition and specification of management's utility function. It hardly needs to be said that these information requirements impose a heavy (generally too heavy) burden on the decision maker. For example, consider deposits in the example of the preceding section and assume that they are stochastic. Management may have a fairly good impression about future deposits, but to conjecture that it is able to translate such an impression into a well-defined probability distribution would - at least in our opinion - be an inadmissible oversimplification of reality. To a large extent, the same holds for the specification of the utility function (see e.g. Shoemaker 1980). These problems become even more complex when there are dependencies between the outcomes of the events and between the preferences for these outcomes. Together with the fact that the use of stochastic models easily becomes costly and time-consuming, the above-mentioned specification problems explain why stochastic models are so seldom implemented in practice.

In much of the literature on decision making, it is quite generally assumed (and/or advised) that decision makers facing uncertainty first specify a probability distribution (or something alike, but less well-defined) and then specify their preferences. However, as suggested by experimental economics, there are good reasons for assuming that managers, like other decision makers, instead of assuming two separate scales for utilities and probabilities, combine both into a single scale. Furthermore, the complexity of decision problems is often reduced by establishing a framework of aspiration levels (see Tietz 1983). An illustration of management not separating between its assessment of probabilities and the expression of its risk attitude, is the definition of lower cash limits such as for instance in the example of the preceding sections. Such a cash limit not only reflects management's estimate of the probability of running out of cash, but also reflects management's (dis)preference for such an event.

The IMGP-framework described and illustrated in the preceding sections offers the possibility to translate the above described assumption into operational terms. In short, variables which are considered to be random variables are treated in IMGP as if they were objectives. For instance, the uncertain deposits of the preceding section would be defined as an objective. Next, it is assumed that management is able to define a 'confidence interval' for this objective having a high probability of including the value of the random variable/objective that will ultimately result. In the example, management may state that it is more or less certain that deposits will be between 850 and 1000 dollars during the next period. Obviously, the definition of such an interval puts much less demand on the decision maker than does the specification of a complete probability distribution. To take proper account of management's preferences let us distinguish between the preferences for the deposits itself (clearly, management prefers more deposits to less) and the attitude towards the risk that the level of deposits, which is necessary for the realisation of the plan adopted by management, will not be attained. It is this risk attitude that we propose to be represented with the help of the objective 'deposits'. Obviously, in the example, the best value for deposits would be $B_4 \leq 850$ since then the risk of not attaining the required deposits level is practically zero. The most risky and thus worst objective value would be $B_4 \leq 1000$. So, in the first iteration, deposits would obtain the pessimistic (because of the risk) upper limit 1000. During the following iterations this upper limit can be lowered, thus reducing the risk that the chosen level of deposits will not be attained. Thus with an upper limit for deposits of say 925, no plan requiring a higher deposit level will be chosen. Of course, this does not mean that the real deposits level cannot become higher than 925. It just means that management does not want to base its plans on the risky assumption that deposits will be higher than 925. And if that deposits target is overattained nothing is lost. On the contrary, such a message would be received wholeheartedly. Thus, instead of defining a probability distribution and a preference function or some x-percent confidence limit, management can now directly determine what risk it is willing to accept with respect to the random variable concerned. More important, this choice can be made in relation to other risks and other objectives, implying that management gains insight into the pros and cons associated with varying risks. To some extent, this procedure also offers management the opportunity to take account of stochastic dependencies between different random variables. For instance, management may wish to set another lower cash limit in case there is a high risk that the target deposits level will not be attained as compared with the case that this risk is low.

6 CONCLUSIONS

In this article it is shown that mathematical programming models may be quite helpful in bank portfolio management. However, many of the existing approaches are not used or not used on the scale one might expect because of rigid assumptions with respect to the bank's objectives, poor ability to deal with uncertainty and heavy requirements with respect to the amount and precision of the information to be provided by management. In the article, an approach is proposed by means of which most of the above problems can be circumvented or at least relieved. The approach can deal with different objectives in a straightforward manner. It is also shown that risk factors can often be formulated as separate objectives, to be traded-off against each other and against the other objectives, without requiring the formulation of probability distributions or preference functions.

NOTES

[1] Quite a large number of scientific contributions on bank balance sheet management models have appeared. For recent reviews, we refer to Cohen and Gibson 1978, and to Cohen, Maier and Vanderweide 1981.

[2] In general, the pessimistic solution is not a single solution but rather a set of conditions describing a subset of the set of alternative solutions. During the interactive process, the conditions become stronger and - by implication - the subset of solutions satisfying these conditions becomes smaller.

[3] For a more detailed discussion of these models, we refer to the original article.

[4] Note that instead of introducing LGP-11 and the deviational variable h_6^-, which is to be minimised in the objective function LGP-1, the variable B_5 can be more easily included with a minus-sign in LGP-1, while dropping LGP-11.

[5] The presence of ratios poses serious problems in goal programming (see e.g. Awerbuch et al. 1976) but not in Interactive Multiple Goal Programming (see Spronk 1981).

REFERENCES

Awerbuch, S., Ecker, J.G. and Wallace, W.A., 'Hidden nonlinearities in the application of goal programming', Management Science, vol. 22, 1976, pp. 918-920.

Booth, G.G. and Dash, G.H., 'Alternative programming structures for bank portfolios', Journal of Banking and Finance, vol. 3, 1979, pp. 67-82.

Cohen, K.J. and Gibson, S.E., Management Science in Banking, Warren, Gorham & Lamont Inc., Boston, Mass., 1978.

Cohen, K.J., Maier, S.F. and Vanderweide, J.H., 'Recent developments in management science in banking', Management Science, October 1981, pp. 1097-1119.

Muhlemann, A.P., Lochette, A.G. and Gear, A.E., 'Portfolio modeling in multiple-criteria situations under uncertainty', Decision Sciences, vol. 9/4, 1978, pp. 612-626.

Schoemaker, P.J.H., Experiments on Decisions Under Risk: The Expected Utility Hypothesis, Martinus Nijhoff, Boston, 1980.

Spronk, J., Interactive Multiple Goal Programming: Applications to Financial Planning, Martinus Nijhoff, Boston, 1981.

Spronk, J. and Veeneklaas, F., 'A feasibility study of economic and environmental scenarios by means of interactive multiple goal programming', Regional Science and Urban Economics, vol. 13, 1983, pp. 141-160.

Tietz, R., 'Aspiration-oriented decision making', in Tietz, R. (ed), Aspiration Levels in Bargaining and Economic Decision-Making, Springer, Berlin, 1983.

Törn, A.A., 'A sampling-search-clustering approach for exploring the feasible/efficient solutions of MCDM problems', Computers & Operations Research, vol. 7, no. 1-2, 1980, pp. 67-80.

15 MCDM Problems in Rabobank Nederland

J. Telgen

1 INTRODUCTION

In The Netherlands there are nearly 1000 Rabo Banks each operating in its own geographical region completely independent of the others. All these Rabo Banks together have founded a cooperation that takes care of that part of banking business that can be handled more efficiently by a central (and larger) organisation, such as foreign affairs, high risk investments, money market transactions and automation. As a consequence of this organisational scheme, the central organisation, called Rabobank Nederland, should be considered as a daughter of 1000 mothers, which is essentially different from the rather common construction in which the central organisation is the mother of a number of daughters. Thus, Rabobank Nederland is limited in its possibilities to manage and direct the consolidated corporation.

The Rabo Bank organisation is among the 50 largest banks of the world with a balance sheet total of DFL. 116 billion (US $ 35 billion) and 27,000 employees (1983). Being such a large organisation in banking, Rabo Bank exhibits Operations Research problems common to large organisations and common to the banking sector. In this paper, two such problems (one from each class), both having an MCDM structure, are considered.

The next two sections outline these problems in more detail and describe the way we approach them. The final section contains some general remarks on MCDM in banking.

2 ESTABLISHING A BUDGET BALANCE SHEET

2.1 The problem

Top management of Rabobank Nederland controls the development of the organisation by comparing the 'budget balance sheet' for one year ahead and the current situation. In the past this budget balance sheet was composed of aggregated data from different departments (e.g. loans, savings, etc.) within Rabobank Nederland. These bottom-up data were partly forecasts, partly plans, partly budgets, but all based on the interests, knowledge and horizons of individual departments. Apart from simple checks on balance sheet totals etc. no systematic effort was put into transforming these individual data into an overall plan or budget.

Of course top management of Rabobank Nederland has its overall view and overall goals, but no formal mechanism was available to integrate these top-down data with the budgeted balance sheet.

The desires of top management are mainly related to the amounts of funds (as a percentage of funds available) that are available for investment in certain sectors of the economy. All these desires can be expressed in terms of balance sheet items.

A complication is the uncertainty in the amount of funds available to the total organisation one year ahead. Since this is of the order of DFL. 70 million, a 10 per cent change or a forecast that is 10 per cent off could have dramatic effects.

On the other hand, it is possible to be more or less active in attracting certain kinds of funds in order to achieve a limited increase or decrease in the amounts of funds available.

So, the problem is to determine the composition of the balance sheet for Rabobank Nederland one year ahead, taking into account the desires of top management, the 'budgets' of individual departments and the uncertainty concerning future funds available.

2.2 The model

The items to be determined are the amounts of money allotted to the different accounts in the balance sheet.

We denote them as:

a_i : amount of money allotted to asset i, $i = 1, 2, \ldots, n_a$

l_i : amount of money allotted to liability i, $i = 1, 2, \ldots, n_l$

Of course, the balance sheet totals should match:

$$\sum_{i=1}^{n_a} a_i = \sum_{i=1}^{n_l} l_i .$$

Furthermore, there are legal constraints on the liquidity of the total Rabo Bank organisation. Fixed percentages of the amounts involved in certain liabilities should be kept in short-term assets. Since Rabobank Nederland is required to fill any gaps, the individual Rabo Banks leave in this respect, the liquidity constraint can be formulated as:

$$\sum_{i=1}^{n_a} q_i a_i > \sum_{i=1}^{n_l} r_i l_i + g$$

in which q_i and r_i are legally required and fixed percentages and g is the 'liquidity gap' resulting from the individual banks. This gap is defined as:

$$g = \sum_{i=1}^{n_m} t_i m_i - c$$

in which:

m_i : means (liabilities) of the individual Rabo Banks of type $i : i = 1, 2, \ldots, n_m$

c : amount of cash money with the individual Rabo Banks

and t_i are legally determined and fixed percentages.

From this definition one can see that the individual Rabo Banks do not engage in short-term assets (money market, etc.), but use their account with Rabobank Nederland in that way.

Other constraints are formed by upper and lower bounds (some logical, some managerial) on all variables a_i, l_i and m_i. In addition, upper and lower bounds are specified for the balance sheet total

$$\sum_{i=1}^{n_a} a_i$$

and the total of all means with the individual banks

$$\sum_{i=1}^{n_m} m_i$$

Management desires can be expressed as functions of individual balance sheet items:

$$\sum_{i=1}^{n_a} f_{ij} a_i \qquad j = 1, 2, \ldots, n_f$$

which should equal fixed percentages of the total of all means with the individual banks:

$$F_h \cdot \sum_{i=1}^{n_m} m_i \qquad j = 1, 2, \ldots, n_f$$

Deviations from these desired are denoted as d_j^+ and d_j^- in

$$\sum_{i=1}^{n_a} f_{ij} a_i = F_j \cdot \sum_{i=1}^{n_m} m_i + d_j^+ - d_j^- \qquad j = 1, 2, \ldots, n_f$$

To incorporate these forecasts, plans and budgets contributed by the individual departments of Rabobank Nederland, we define

$$a_i = a_i^b + a_i^+ - a_i^- \qquad i = 1, 2, \ldots, n_a$$

and

$$l_i = l_i^b + l_i^+ - {}_i^- \qquad i = 1, 2, \ldots, n_l$$

With respect to the means available at the individual Rabo Banks, we define in a similar way:

$$m_i = m_i^b + m_i^+ - m_i^- \qquad i = 1, 2, \ldots, n_m$$

Now the goal is to minimise all deviations from the desires of top management, the budgets of the departments in Rabobank Nederland and the forecasts of the available means with the individual Rabo Banks. In terms of the variables, this implies minimising all of:

$$d_j^+ + d_j^- \qquad j = 1, 2, \ldots, n_f$$

$$a_i^+ + a_i^- \qquad i = 1, 2, \ldots, n_a$$

$$l_i^+ + l_i^- \qquad i = 1, 2, \ldots, n_l$$

$$m_i^+ + m_i^- \qquad i = 1, 2, \ldots, n_m.$$

2.3 Our solution

The model described above consists of 15 linear constraints in 200 variables. As such, it is a small LP problem that can be solved routinely. However, instead of one objective function, we have to deal with approximately 100 objectives formulated by different levels of management.

Even specific MCDM methods cannot cope with such a multitude of objective functions.

Therefore, we have to consider the specific problem setting for ways to cope with this problem.

As a starting point, we only paid attention to the desires of top mangement, since these were expected to determine the general direction the bank has to move towards. The balance sheet obtained in this way ignores the plans of the individual departments and the uncertainty about the forecasts of the means available.

Now the next step is to identify all goals that can be achieved without worsening the achievement of top management goals. These other achievable goals include the major part of all individual departments' plans. Consequently, these balance sheet items were fixed at their budget levels.
The remaining non-achieved goals of top management and the individual departments (about 10 items in total) were separated from the achieved goals and considered in a special discussion in which the achieved goals were not subject to discussion any more. Thus the discussion is concentrated on only 10 goals instead of the original 100.

We realise that this approach does not necessarily lead to the overall optimal solution, but this fact is considered less important than the practicality of the method.

In this (problem specific) approach, the decision maker does not have to be confronted with vast amounts of data at every iteration in the process. His attention is focussed upon those elements of the problem that cannot be easily solved. And for these he can evaluate a number of different solutions.

In this latter process the use of information contained in shadow prices (from the optimisation of individual objective functions) proved to be very helpful.

3 BALANCE SHEET MANAGEMENT

3.1 The scene

Rabobank Nederland performs all those banking activities for the entire organisation that can be done more efficiently by a central organisation: (international affairs, money and capital market transactions, automation, etc.). For one of these activities, providing mortgage loans, the Rabo Bank organisation has created a 100 per cent daughter called Rabohypotheekbank or RHB (hypotheek = mortgage). Although the member banks may provide mortgage loans to their clients themselves, frequently they choose to represent RHB and set up a mortgage loan with RHB for their clients. There are two reasons why member banks do this:

- they do not always have enough funds to offer mortgage loans themselves;
- they are restricted in providing mortgage loans with an interest rate that is fixed for some time (which is the most common form of mortgage loan).

RHB provides mortgage loans both to firms and individuals. The period during which the interest rate is fixed, varies (usually the repricing date is 3 or 5 years), as do the terms of payment of interest (monthly, halfyearly) and principal (linear, annuity, etc.).

3.2 The problem

Transforming maturity terms of deposits and loans is one of the basic functions of a bank. This transformation process inevitably leads to a mismatching of maturity dates in assets and liabilities. This mismatching is commonly referred to as interest rate exposure, since changing interest rates affect the return to the bank via this mismatching. A simple example may illustrate this point:

assets	loan I	loan II
liabilities	deposit	
time	0 5	10

In this figure, there is a certain interest rate exposure at time t=5. If both loans and the deposit amount to $ 1 million, we say that the interest rate exposure at t=5 is $ 1 million. The effect of this exposure on return depends on the interest rate at t=5:

interest rate at t=5	influence on return
- same as at t=0	no influence
- 1% higher than at t=0	$ 10,000 more return (per year)
- 1% higher than at t=0	$ 10,000 less return (per year)

Note that exposure may have a positive effect on return also.

In times when interest rates are changing quickly and drastically, the management of interest rate exposure is of great (and sometimes even vital) importance to the bank.

However, this management of interest rate exposure cannot be reduced to simply reducing the mismatching, since that may mean that the bank has to bypass certain profitable opportunities. Thus, the problem is to minimise the interest rate exposure, while at the same time, the return to the bank is maximised.

3.3 The model

The first step in managing interest rate exposure is to gain insight into the development of the gap between maturing assets and liabilities over time. This is uaually done by constructing a table with 3 rows (assets, liabilities and gap) and columns according to the various time periods that are of interest.

Table 1

Gap Management

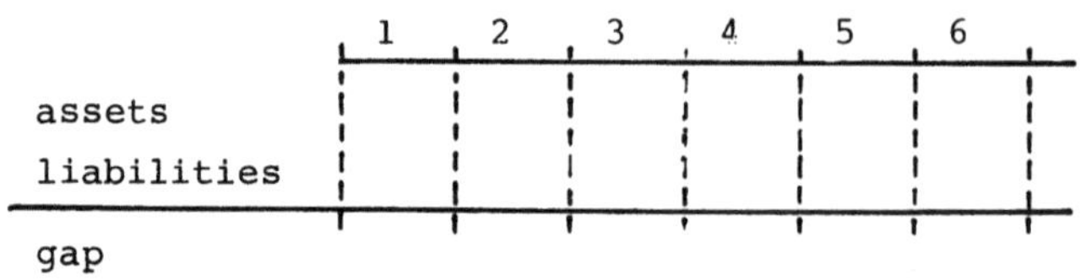

Now it is easy to see which maturity dates for new assets and liabilities are of interest to the bank: those that fill the gaps.

At the other extreme, we mention the classical balance sheet optimisation methods that are aimed at maximising the return for the bank without consideration of its interest rate exposure.

In this model we combine aspects of gap management and balance sheet optimisation methods in a multicriteria decision making framework. The two criteria considered are: (1) return, defined as interest received minus interest paid and (2) gap, as a measure for interest rate exposure. Both criteria cover more time periods and their values for these periods are weighted to produce one single compound value for each criterion.

Given an interest rate scenario and the future developments of assets (mortgages sold) it is possible to construct the bicriterion LP problem:

max! 'return'
min! 'gap'

subject to: logical constraints
legal constraints
bank policy constraints
etc.

In this problem the decision variables are to be found on the liability side of the balance sheet: the solution indicates how the funding for RHB should be.

In practice we transform the bicriterion problem to a simple LP problem as:

max! 'return'

subject to: 'gap' < c

all other constraints.

Then by starting out with c = infinity and gradually lowering c (parametric LP) we find the relation between 'return' and 'gap' as given in Figure 1.

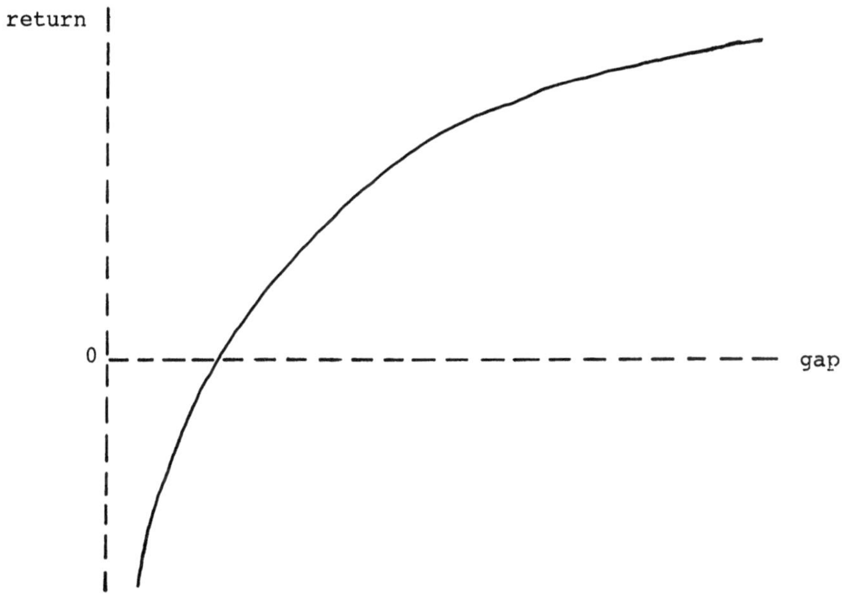

Figure 1. Return-gap relation

This relation is shown graphically to RHB management in order for them to choose a preferred gap-return combination. Only after this choice has been made, the funding combinations necessary to achieve these results are given.

This procedure is implemented in a DSS allowing bank management to change interactively:

- interest rate scenarios
- future developments in assets
- funding possibilities
- weights on different periods to produce the compound objective function.

As a DSS we believe this system has some extraordinary features:

- the underlying LP problem is rather large (800 x 2000) and dense (5 percent);
- the main interaction with the decision maker is a graphical representation of efficient gap-return combinations.

4 CONCLUDING REMARKS

The MCDM models described above are interesting only to the extent that they satisfy the needs of bank management. In this respect, the second model is more successful than the first. For the first model it was not the model (let alone the solution) that was most important, but the modelling process. The existence of conflicting goals and the degree to which they conflicted was only realised while modelling the system.

In developing the second model, it soon became apparent that only the implementation in a decision support system (DSS) would make it practical for bank management. Given this interface (DSS) there are virtually no restrictions to the complexity or the size of the underlying models used. Bank management accepts this hiding of the underlying model in a DSS.

In general, the application of MCDM in banking is a promising field for further development. This development may be hampered by a lack of software available to practitioners, since it is not general practice to build MCDM software in the course of an application.

ACKNOWLEDGEMENT

The development of the budget balance sheet model was carried out in cooperation with Cees van der Woude. The balance sheet management model was developed by Rien Huisman and Gerrit Hofstra.

REFERENCES

Huisman, M.C. and Telgen, J., 'Balance sheet management with multiple criteria', submitted to Journal of Bank Research, 1983.

Telgen, J., 'An MCDM problem in banking', in: Hansen, P. (ed Essays and Surveys on Multiple Criteria Decision Making, Lecture Notes in Economics and Mathematical Systems, vol. 209, Springer-Verlag, New York/Heidelberg, 1983, pp. 372-378.

16 On the Applicability of Game-Theoretic and Bargaining Methods to a Wage Bargaining Problem

G. Fandel

1 INTRODUCTION

Wage bargaining may formally be treated as decision problems among two parties with different utility functions. The decision consists of determining the increase of the wage rate for the time of the tariff contract commonly accepted by the both tariff parties representing the employers and the employees respectively. So far, on principle, the same solution methods of the game and the bargaining theory can be applied to such decision situations as they come into question for multi-person decision problems in organisations (Fandel 1979, Fandel 1981). However, because of the special problem structure in the case of wage bargaining one may restrict mainly to cooperative solution concepts without side payments.

In the following, analysis will be made in particular, of how far the methodical approaches of Nash (1953), Zeuthen (1930) and Contini and Zionts (1968) can be used in practice in order to explain and reconstruct the courses of and the agreements within wage bargaining processes. Thereby, the investigations refer to wage bargaining in the metal industry of the Federal Republic of Germany between 1961 and 1979.

2 WAGE BARGAINING IN THE METAL INDUSTRY

2.1 Preliminary remarks

The subject of the analysis will be the wage disputes between 'Gesamtmetall' as Organisation representing the employers and 'IG Metall' (Metalworkers Union) as the employees' representation in the Federal Republic of Germany in 1961-62 to 1979. The years 1964, 1967 and 1972-73, however, had later to be excluded from the study, since in these years agreements were either reached unusually quickly on account of political or economic events or were simply taken over from other areas; in these cases there were not any signs of bargaining processes.

The metal-processing industry seems to lend itself particularly well to investigations of this kind since first of all, within the DGB (German Trade Union Federation) IG Metall represents by far the majority of employees organised in this confederation and secondly, it shows a stronger tendency towards the strategy of cash wage than other trade unions (Zerche 1979, p. 25 and p. 117 ff.). The latter is often justified by the argument that the highest possible nominal wage increase strengthens the power position of the union leaders more efficiently than any other strategies. Therefore, additional claims will not be taken into account because of their secondary role and the difficulties to quantify them adequately within the wage movements. In this context the difference between the greatly centralised bargaining strategy of the employers and the unionists' will to negotiate regionally has to be allowed for in a suitable way; for this reason we have chosen as bargaining processes the wage negotiations in the pilot areas which in the year concerned were regarded as trend-setting for the total wage movement within the branch of industry under review, and whose agreement proposals have been approved by the members of the Gesamtmetall and the representatives of IG Metall.

2.2 The naive solution and the two-thirds hypothesis

Introducing the application-oriented considerations, let us first of all deal with two assumptions which are often expressed in connection with the wage disputes in the metal-processing industry with respect to the contract eventually signed by workers and employers:

1) The first assumption which is based on a general rule of the economic practice says that usually the later agreement with respect to the wage increase rate lies halfway between the union's initial claim and the employers' initial offer, that is to say, approximately corresponds to the arithmetic mean of these two quantities (naive solution). The initial claim, the initial offer and the agreement are to be expressed in percentages of the last basic wage.
2) The second assumption which can be found in the literature on the autonomy in negotiating wage rates starts from the discovery that the relations between the specific initial claim of the union and

the final result of the wage bargaining process have remained fairly constant in the course of time. Advocates of this assumption take the view that IG Metall, knowing what can reasonably be expected of the companies involved and to what extent the employers are ready to make concessions, increases its initial claim by a so-called bargaining amount in order to achieve a final result which amounts to about two-thirds of its initial claim and can thus still be regarded as a success (Weitbrecht 1969, p. 145 ff.). This two-thirds hypothesis seems to contradict in a way a statement according to which an acceptable contract has only then been achieved if 75% of the original claim could be realised (Müller-Jentsch 1972, p. 324 ff.); as a matter of fact, however, deals of this size have very rarely been made.

In order to be able to verify the validity of these two assumptions by means of regression analysis, Table 1 has been compiled; it specifies the initial claims of IG Metal $\bar{w}_t$, the initial offers made by Gesamtmetall $\underline{w}_t$, the actual contract w_t^*, the naive solution $\tilde{w}_t$ as well as the two-thirds values w_t' for the years t from 196 -62 to 1979.

Table 1.

Survey of the wage negotiations 1961-62 to 1979

Year t	Initial claim of IG Metall $\bar{w}_t$	Initial offer made by Gesamtmetall $\underline{w}_t$	Actual contract achieved w_t^*	Naive solution $\tilde{w}_t=\frac{\bar{w}_t+\underline{w}_t}{2}$	Two-thirds values $w_t'=0.67\bar{w}_t$
1961-62	10.0	1.5	6.0	5.75	6.67
1963	8.0	3.0	5.67	5.5	5.34
1965-66	9.0	2.4	6.63	5.7	6.00
1968	7.0	4.0	5.5	5.5	4.67
1969	12.0	5.0	8.7	8.5	8.00
1970	15.0	7.0	11.0	11.0	10.01
1971	11.0	4.5	7.0	7.75	7.34
1974	18.0	8.5	12.25	13.25	12.01
1975	11.0	6.0	6.8	8.5	7.34
1976	8.0	4.0	5.4	6.0	5.34
1977	9.5	4.75	6.9	7.125	6.34
1978	8.0	3.0	5.4	5.5	5.34
1979	6.0	3.0	4.3	4.5	4.00

Setting up the homogeneous linear regression equations

$$w_t^* = \beta_1 \tilde{w}_t + \varepsilon_t \qquad (1)$$

and

$$w_t^* = \beta_2 \bar{w}_t + \varepsilon_t \qquad (2)$$

respectively for the connection between the actual contract and the naive solution and between the actual contract and the union's initial claim with regard to the two-thirds hypothesis respectively, where the perturbation variables ε_t are to be normally distributed with the expected value zero, one obtains the regression lines

$$\hat{w}_t^* = 0.96\tilde{w}_t \tag{1'}$$

and

$$\hat{w}_t^* = 0.69\bar{w}_t \tag{2'}$$

respectively with the correlation coefficients $r_1 = 0.97$ and $r_2 = 0.98$ respectively. On account of these correlation coefficients, the statistically founded correlation, and the fact that the regression coefficients β_1 and β_2 are near one and two-thirds respectively, it may reasonably be said that the connection expressed by the two assumptions cannot simply be brushed aside. Comparing the data for w_t^* and w_t', however, one may well suspect that the two-thirds hypothesis tends to be somewhat undervalued. The true relation between the actual agreement reached and the initial claim of the union will probably be placed between the two-thirds hypothesis of the literature and the union's ideal aim of 75%. Determining the confidence intervals for β_1 and β_2 at a level of significance of $\alpha = 0.05$, one obtains the intervals

$$\beta_1 \in [0.91;\ 1.01] \tag{1''}$$

and

$$\beta_2 \in [0.65;\ 0.73]\ . \tag{2''}$$

Both confidence intervals make the above assumptions appear quite evident.

2.3 Application of the cooperative Nash solution

The close connection between the naive solution and the actual agreement which has been described in the last section calls for an enquiry of the question to what extent the agreement points of the wage negotiations are interpretable in the sense of the cooperative Nash solution, since in case of linearly transferable utility this game-theoretic concept divides the bargaining cake available between two parties into equal shapes. For an analytic reconstruction of this possibility of interpretation, let us assume in the following that the cake to be divided between IG Metall and Gesamtmetall is each time defined by the difference of the changes of the wage sums resulting from the initial claim of the union and the initial offer made by the employers, thus reads

$$K_t = (\bar{w}_t - \underline{w}_t).L_t \tag{3}$$

and is consequently fixed, L_t denoting the wage sum before the wage dispute in the year t, and workers and employers possessing linearly homogeneous utility functions with respect to the shares which they eventually obtain of this bargaining cake. If IG Metall and Gesamtmetall are assigned the indices n=1 and n=2 respectively, the utility functions remaining constant over the years with respect to the shares can be written as follows:

$$u_{1t} = a.\frac{w_t - \underline{w}_t}{\bar{w}_t - \underline{w}_t} \tag{4}$$

and

$$u_{2t} = b.\frac{\bar{w}_t - w_t}{\bar{w}_t - \underline{w}_t} \tag{5}$$

respectively, the quantities a and b indicating the constant marginal utility. It is easy to see that the utility of IG Metall (Gesamtmetall) grows (declines) linearly with the rising wage increase rate w_t which the two parties have to agree upon in year t and for which $\underline{w}_t \leq w_t \leq \bar{w}_t$ holds in general. For $w_t = \bar{w}_t$ IG Metall reaches the highest utility, that of Gesamtmetall becoming equal to zero; correspondingly the ratio is inverse for $w_t = \underline{w}_t$. Moreover, let $\bar{w}_t > \underline{w}_t$ be presupposed. The cooperative Nash solution (Nash 1953) is characterised by the fact that the two negotiating parties involved in the case considered here agree upon a wage increase rate w_t^* or, which is equivalent, upon shares of the bargaining cake by which the product of their utility increases with respect to a disagreement vector $\bar{u} = (\bar{u}_1, \bar{u}_2)$ is maximised. To simplify matters the disagreement vector can be fixed by the zero utility levels of the negotiation parties. The following assumption which is fairly plausible is to justify this understanding: the bargaining cake corresponds to that part of the return of production for which in future they will have to work in common and the distribution of which to the factors work and capital must be agreed upon within the framework of the wage disputes; if one of the parties claims the total share this will be met by strike and lockout measures respectively by the other party; in such a case, the burden for the fighting fund on the union's part on the one side is opposite to the capital expenditure for the plant facilities on the employers' part on the other.

Assuming a disagreement vector $\bar{u} = (\bar{u}_1, \bar{u}_2) = (0, 0)$ in this sense, and considering (4) and (5), the cooperative Nash solution can be determined as follows:

$$\max u_t = (u_{1t} - 0)(u_{2t} - 0) = u_{1t} \cdot u_{2t} = a.\frac{w_t-\underline{w}_t}{\bar{w}_t-\underline{w}_t}.b.\frac{\bar{w}_t-w_t}{\bar{w}_t-\underline{w}_t}$$
$$= \frac{a.b}{(\bar{w}_t-\underline{w}_t)^2}(w_t-\underline{w}_t)(\bar{w}_t-w_t) = c(w_t-\underline{w}_t)(\bar{w}_t-w_t) \; . \qquad (6)$$

This expression is exclusively dependent on the wage increase rate w_t as variable which has to be determined optimally by both parties in the form of an agreement. As a necessary condition for determining such an optimal w_t^o one obtains from (6)

$$\frac{du_t}{dw_t} = c[-(w_t-\underline{w}_t) + (\bar{w}_t-w_t)] = c(-2w_t+\bar{w}_t+\underline{w}_t) = 0 \qquad (7)$$

and from this, because of $c \neq 0$,

$$w_t^o = \frac{\bar{w}_t+\underline{w}_t}{2} \; . \qquad (8)$$

Consequently, assuming the utility functions in (4) and (5) to apply, and taking the assumptions concerning the bargaining of the two parties and their disagreement vector as a basis, the cooperative Nash solution w_t^o tallies with the naive solution $\tilde{w}_t$, and its explanatory value with respect to the actual agreements reached w_t^*, as may be seen from Table 1, can be estimated accordingly. In this connection, the cooperative Nash solution has been derived from the initial claim $\bar{w}_t$ of the union and the initial offer $\underline{w}_t$ made by the employers; no statement, however, has thus been made about how these two initial values were obtained. As far as this is concerned, it may be enough to say that both employers and employees probably take the data of the past or the future economic trend as a basis; due to its limited methodical performance the Nash concept does certainly not allow these data to be elucidated and verified. Similarly, the deviations of the actual contracts w_t^* from the analytically derived values w_t^o cannot be explained on the basis of the Nash approach. Since these deviations are not too important, as a rule, they could be ascribed to the differences which are usually to be found between the rationally postulated and the empirically observable decision behaviour. Assuming constant marginal utilities for both parties, however, seems to be unproblematic in view of the fact that wage movements are generally of special economic importance, and IG Metall as well as Gesamtmetall represent a very large number of persons interested.

For the wage negotiations of 1969, the abovementioned analytic solution according to Nash is graphically represented in Figure 1. Here the coordinate axes are denoted by the utility argument $(w_t - \underline{w}_t)$ and $(\bar{w}_t - w_t)$ or $[-(w_t - \bar{w}_t)]$ from the expression in (6), so that the utility values u_{1t} and u_{2t} of both parties increase positively with the direction of the coordinates. Between the points A and B line L marks all contracts w_t for which $\underline{w}_t = 5 \leq w_t \leq 12 = \bar{w}_t$ holds.

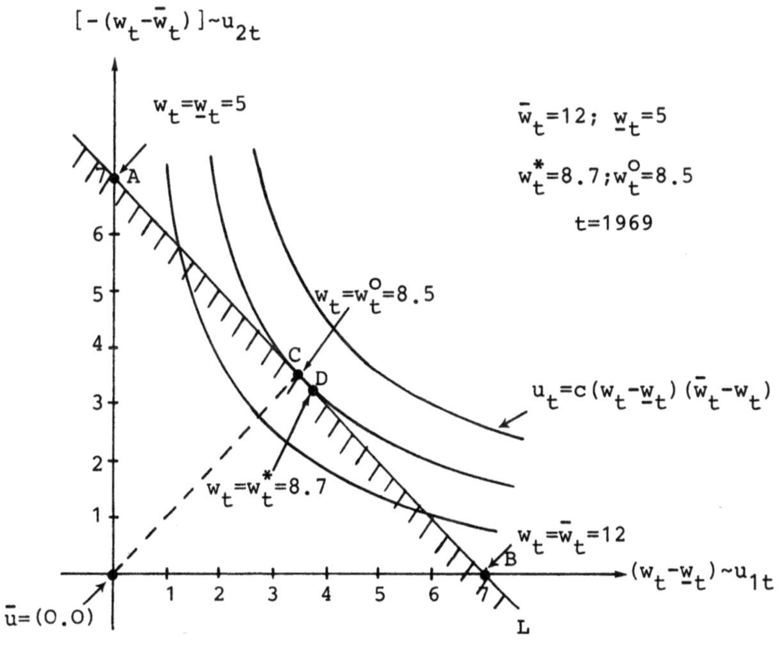

Figure 1. Nash solution w_t^o and actual agreement reached w_t^* for the wage negotiations in 1969

While any points above L are not feasible since for them the union's claims are always higher than the offers made by the employers, which means that no agreements can be reached there, the points below L represent a waste of the cake to be divided. From the condition of optimality $w_t^o - \underline{w}_t = \bar{w}_t - w_t^o$ according to (7) follows the Nash solution

w_t^o = 8.5, with 8.5 - 5 = 12 - 8,5 = 3.5, which in Figure 1 is near point C; the actual contract signed w_t^* = 8.7, however, corresponds to point D on L. As can be seen from (7) and (8) w_t^o is independent of parameter c in (6) due to the invariance of the cooperative Nash solution as to linear utility transformations; this parameter only represents a level constant with respect to the product of the utility increase which has to be maximised in common by both contrahents in comparison with the disagreement vector.

2.4 Verification of the wage bargaining processes with the aid of the theorem by Zeuthen

The bargaining theorem by Zeuthen (1930), which serves for rationalising the concession behaviour of decision makers in conflicting decision situations (Fandel 1981, p. 105 ff.), is identical to the axioms of the cooperative Nash solution, so that both concepts are equivalent with respect to determining an optimal agreement solution between the bargaining partners. But in comparison with the cooperative Nash solution, the bargaining theorem by Zeuthen represents a much more efficient instrument for verifying the behaviour-theoretic consistency of the decisions made by the bargaining partners. While according to Nash the optimal solution is determined statically, the bargaining theorem by Zeuthen, in order to reach this aim, requires a dynamic process consisting of proposals and counterproposals which consider the concessions made by the parties; in this way, the optimal solution is interactively approximated step by step and eventually reached.

In order to be able to properly check the rationality of the concessions made by IG Metall and Gesamtmetall during the pay talks of 1961-62 to 1979 according to Zeuthen while strictly maintaining the utility functions introduced in (4) to (6) the respective claims and offers which were submitted by the bargaining partners, until the agreement was reached, have been compiled in Table 2 for these different wage disputes in terms of bargaining rounds (Krelle 1976, p. 617 ff.). The claims and offers are given in wage increase rates and according to (6) can be immediately converted into the utility values that are necessary for applying the theorem of Zeuthen; to simplify matters, the constant c can be neglected here, i.e. set equal to one. Simultaneously, Table 2 shows that the wage negotiations are always to begin with an initial claim by the unions in the first

Table 2.

Survey of the claims and offers $w_t^n(r_t)$ (in terms of bargaining rounds) submitted by IG Metall (n=1) and Gesamtmetall (n=2) during the bargaining processes 1961/62 to 1979

r_t \ t	1961/62		1963		1965/66		1968		1969		1970		1971		1974		1975		1976		1977		1978		1979	
n	1	2	1	2	1	2	1	2	1	2	1	2	1	2	1	2	1	2	1	2	1	2	1	2	1	2
1	10		8		9		7		12		15		11		18		11		8		9.5		8		6	
2		1.5		3		2.4		4		5		7		4.5		8.5		6		4		4.75		3		3
3	10		7		9		6.5		11		15		7.9		14		7		8		9.5		8		6	
4		3		3.5		5.8		4.57		5		10		6		11.33		6.5		4.5		5.25		4.6		4
5	8.5		6		5.4		6.5		10		11		7.5		12.25		6.8		5.4		7		5.7		4.3	
6		4		4.5		5.8		4.67		7		11		6.5		12.25		6.8		5.4		6.5		5		4.3
7	6		5.5		5		5		8.7				7								6.9		5.4			
8		6		5.5		6.63		4.83		8.7				7								6.9		5.4		
9			5.67		6.63		5.5																			
10				5.67				5.5																		
			1)		1)																					

1) These values are not considered in the verification according to the theorem by Zeuthen

round, the following claims are always to be made in the respective odd rounds, and the offers by Gesamtmetall are to be made only in the respective even rounds. Moreover, as far as those cases are concerned in which between two different claims and/or offers made by the one side there was no reaction by the other side, it has been presupposed that the other side has maintained its last claim and/or its last offer in the intermediate round. In 1963, the last two rounds and in 1965-66, the last four rounds are not taken into account in the following considerations, since in these two years agreements could have been reached earlier, but the negotiations were continued for the time being due to the fact that additional claims were dropped and finally a higher wage increase rate was agreed upon. Accordingly, it should be noted that in 1968 the wage claim of the union increases again in round 9; consequently, no concession is made.

Let $R_t = \{r_t | r_t = 1, 2, \ldots, \bar{r}_t\}$ denote the set of round indices in year t, where $\bar{r}_t$ indicates the number of bargaining rounds in this year required for a (possible) agreement. Let $w_t^n(r_t)$ characterise the proposal made by partner n, $n \in \{1,2\}$ in the round $r_t \in R_t$ of year t; in this connection it should be pointed out that according to the arrangement described in the last paragraph index n=1 (IG Metall) can appear only in the case of odd and index n=2 (Gesamtmetall) only in the case of even round indices. Moreover, let $\hat{R}_t = \{\hat{r}_t | \hat{r}_t \in R_t\}$ be the set of round indices of year t in ascending order, for which one of the bargaining partners makes a concession, thus $w_t^1(\hat{r}_t) < w_t^1(\hat{r}_t - 2)$ holds for the union, and $w_t^2(\hat{r}_t) > w_t^2(\hat{r}_t - 2)$ holds for Gesamtmetall with $\hat{r}_t \in \hat{R}_t$ and $(\hat{r}_t - 2) \in R_t$. Then let the mapping $\rho : \hat{R}_t \to \{1,2\}$ be defined by the fact that it indicates for each concession round $\hat{r}_t \in \hat{R}_t$ that bargaining partner $\rho(\hat{r}_t) \in \{1,2\}$ who made the concession in this round. The new suggestion $w_t^n(\hat{r}_t)$, $n \in \{1,2\}$ of that bargaining partner which results from this concession leads - according to (6) - to the product of the utility increase

$$u_t^n(\hat{r}_t) = c[w_t^n(\hat{r}_t) - \underline{w}_t][\bar{w}_t - w_t^n(\hat{r}_t)] \; . \tag{9}$$

Moreover, in order that this concession may be rational according to the theorem by Zeuthen

$$u_t^n(\hat{r}_t - 2) \leq u_t^{n'}(\hat{r}_t - 1); \; n, n' \in \{1,2\}, \; n \neq n'; \; (\hat{r}_t - 2), \; (\hat{r}_t - 1) \in R_t \tag{10}$$

must hold (Fandel 1981, p. 106).

If the fact whether such a concession was rational or not is then mapped by the binary attribute function $\Psi(\hat{r}_t)$ with

$$\Psi(\hat{r}_t) = \begin{cases} 1, & \text{if } \rho(\hat{r}_t) = n \text{ and } u_t^n(\hat{r}_t - 2) \leq u_t^{n'}(\hat{r}_t - 1) \\ 0 & \text{otherwise} \end{cases} \tag{11}$$

then the result of the analysis can be illustrated in a simple form by Table 3. Here index i indicates the concession steps of the years 1961-62 to 1979. In order to be able to partly reconstruct the evaluation of the results of Table 3, by way of explanation the derivation of the results for the year t = 1969 is demonstrated in Table 4 using the symbols introduced. The common utility value $u_t^n(r_t)$ resulting from the proposals and counterproposals of the partners can be marked as points on line L in Figure 1; for the sake of clarity, however, this has not been done in this case.

Table 3.

Result of the verification with respect to Zeuthen rationality of the concessions made by IG Metall and Gesamtmetall during the wage negotiations 1961-62 to 1979

t	1961-62					1963						1965-66		1968					
$\hat{r}_t$	4	5	6	7	8	3	4	5	6	7	8	4	5	3	4	6	7	8	10
$\rho(\hat{r}_t)$	2	1	2	1	2	1	2	1	2	1	2	2	1	1	2	2	1	2	2
$\Psi(\hat{r}_t)$	1	1	1	1	1	1	1	0	1	0	1	1	1	1	1	0	1	1	1
i	1	2	3	4	5	6	7	8	9	10	11	12	13	14	15	16	17	18	19

t	1969					1970			1971						1974			
$\hat{r}_t$	3	5	6	7	8	4	5	6	3	4	5	6	7	8	3	4	5	6
$\rho(\hat{r}_t)$	1	1	2	1	2	2	1	2	1	2	1	2	1	2	1	2	1	2
$\Psi(\hat{r}_t)$	1	0	1	1	1	1	1	1	1	1	0	1	0	1	1	1	0	1
i	20	21	22	23	24	25	26	27	28	29	30	31	32	33	34	35	36	37

t	1975				1976			1977					1978					1979		
$\hat{r}_t$	3	4	5	6	4	5	6	4	5	6	7	8	4	5	6	7	8	4	5	6
$\rho(\hat{r}_t)$	1	2	1	2	2	1	2	2	1	2	1	2	2	1	2	1	2	2	1	2
$\Psi(\hat{r}_t)$	1	1	0	1	1	1	1	1	1	1	0	1	1	1	1	0	1	1	1	1
i	38	39	40	41	42	43	44	45	46	47	48	49	50	51	52	53	54	55	56	57

As can be seen from Table 3, 47 out of 57 considered concession steps by the bargaining partners in the years 1961-62 to 1979 to be rational according to Zeuthen; thus for the proportional value $\hat{f}$ of the Zeuthen steps

$$\hat{f}(\Psi=1) = \frac{47}{57} = 0.82 \tag{12}$$

holds.

Table 4.

Derivation of the results in Table 3 for the year t = 1969

r_t	$w_t^1(r_t)$	$w_t^2(r_t)$	$\hat{r}_t$	$\rho(\hat{r}_t)$	$u_t^n(r_t)$	$\Psi(\hat{r}_t)$	i
1	12		-	-	0	-	-
2		5	-	-	0	-	-
3	11		3	-1	6	1	20
4		5	-	-	0	-	-
5	10		5	1	10	0	21
6		7	6	2	10	1	22
7	8.7		7	1	12.21	1	23
8		8.7	8	2	12.21	1	24

If one starts from the assumption that Ψ is a random variable of quantitative binary quality and the concession steps of the years 1961-62 to 1979 represent a sample of the size m=57 from an infinite dichotomous parent entity consisting of the set of all concession steps made by the bargaining partners IG Metall and Gesamtmetall in the Federal Republic of Germany and for whose elements only the property $\Psi=1$ or $\Psi=0$ is interesting, then the number of Zeuthen steps in such a sample of the size m is binomially distributed with the parameters m and f, where f may designate the percentage of Zeuthen steps of the finite parent entirety. If on this basis the zero hypothesis is tested, that is to say the percentage of Zeuthen steps in the parent entirety is at the most 70%, i.e.

$$H_o: f \leq f_o = 0.70 \tag{13}$$

and if the sample proportion $\hat{f} = 0.82$ is chosen as suitable test variable which, due to $m \cdot f_o(1-f_o) = 57 \cdot 0.7 \cdot 0.3 = 11.97 > 9$ can be assumed to be approximately normally distributed, then the zero hypothesis is rejected with an error probability $\alpha = 0.05$ since the test variable $\hat{f}$ exceeds the upper limit c_o of the zero hypothesis (Wetzel 1973, p. 195 ff.), i.e.

$$\hat{f} = 0.82 > 0.81 = c_o \,. \tag{14}$$

Thus by inverse conclusion, it may be stated with 95% certainty that the percentage of Zeuthen steps in the parent entirety is higher than 70%. Moreover, if on account of the sample one determines the confidence interval for the parameter f on the level of significance of $\alpha = 0.1$, where because of $m \cdot \hat{f}(1-\hat{f}) = 57 \cdot 0.82 \cdot 0.18 = 8.41 < 9$ an approximation of the binomial distribution by the normal distribution is not possible but the F distribution must be used, then one obtains the interval

$$f \in [0.72; 0.90] , \tag{15}$$

that is to say, with 90% certainty the percentage of the Zeuthen steps in the parent entirety is between 72 and 90%. The latter two statements which have been derived statistically on the basis of the empirical analysis suggest that the theorem by Zeuthen, together with the utility functions (4) and (5) assumed when applying the cooperative Nash solution in the last section, is by all means acceptable as a methodical basis for substantiating the wage bargaining processes in the metal-processing industry under decision-theoretic aspects. Thus simultaneously, the explanatory value of the cooperative Nash solution and the naive solution is persistently backed.

2.5 Discussion of the concept of concession functions developed by Contini and Zionts

In this last section, eventually the question is to be examined to what extent the data available for the wage negotiation processes of 1961-62 to 1979 can be regarded as a basis for proving the existence of concession functions such as they have been assumed in the spontaneous bargaining model by Contini and Zionts (1968), and whether such concession functions actually follow decreasing convex courses, which is stated on account of empirical investigations. Convex decreasing concessions - counted in positive quantities - however, call for likewise convex decreasing utility values of that bargaining partner who makes the concessions. But on the other hand, according to (4) and (5) convex decreasing utility values are identical to the fact that the wage claims by IG Metall decrease convexly and/or the wage offers made by Gesamtmetall increase concavely. In order to simplify matters the discussion about concession functions can so far be reduced to the following two partial aspects:

1) Are there certain rules applying to the annual wage claim and/or wage offer curves of the bargaining partners which find expression

in uniform function parameters, and

2) do the wage claim curves of the union and/or the wage offer curves of the employers take decreasing convex and/or increasing concave courses?

In order to clarify these two partial aspects a series of methodical restrictions and simplifying additional conditions are required on account of the nature of the object to be investigated. For one thing, the data consisting of three to five wage claims and/or offers per year by the bargaining partners is rather meagre, so that, when deriving annual wage claim and/or wage offer functions for IG Metall and Gesamtmetall with the aid of the regression analysis, sometimes a statistical proof of the correlation for time dependent wage proposals cannot be established. As far as the time variable is concerned the wage bargaining processes can be considered in terms of days or bargaining rounds. While generally the scantiness of the data has to be put up with, thus not representing a specific objection, the preliminary investigations have revealed that with respect to the regressions for the description of time dependent wage proposals for both bargaining partners, the analysis in terms of rounds is to be preferred to the analysis in terms of days, since in the latter case no usable results are obtained. Under the first partial aspect of uniform function parameters, this is quite obvious, since the duration of the wage negotiations - between 10 days in 1969 and 86 days in 1978 - was subject to substantial variations, a consideration in terms of bargaining rounds, however, leads to something like a standardisation with respect to time. In view of these preliminary reflections, the regression analysis has eventually been based on the data prepared in terms of bargaining rounds in Table 2.

With respect to the clarification of the second partial aspect a further problem consists in choosing such regression approaches which due to their mathematical structure do not ex ante determine the individual course of the curve, but which rather leave it open for the time being, admitting as results, convex as well as concave structures. In view of the limited quantity of data available and the number of function parameters to be estimated, it seems reasonable here to confine oneself to such regression approaches of the logarithmic, exponential and potential forms which are linearisable, thus representing no computational difficulties. As things are, of these regression approaches, only the potential approach is eligible for deriving wage offer functions for

Gesamtmetall if for positively increasing wage offers, the question concerning concavity or convexity of the course of the curves is to remain freely answerable. Circumstances are less favourable with respect to IG Metall, since there, in all regression approaches mentioned positively decreasing wage claims would mean that simultaneously the course of the curve of the wage claim function is definitely fixed, this course being for example ex ante convex in the potential approach. In order to overcome this difficulty, a non-linearisable exponential approach has been used which showed that the estimated wage claim functions of IG Metall follow concave courses for the four years 1961-62, 1965-66, 1970 and 1979, but in fact take convex courses for the other nine years. On account of these additional considerations, eventually a potential approach has been chosen for the wage claim curves of IG Metall also. Moreover, with respect to both bargaining partners in an ex post analysis, the potential approach has proved quite successful in comparison with the other linearisable approaches without being dominant in each individual case.

Finally, another critical point to be dealt with in this connection is the fact that in the regression approach continuous courses of the annual wage claim and/of wage offer functions of the two bargaining partners are assumed which could contradict the discrete round-oriented expressions of wage proposals made by the two bargaining partners. This discrepancy might perhaps be modified by making the following helpful assumption: All rounds are considered to be of equal length, at the end of the individual rounds, the bargaining partners are asked in turn to submit their new wage proposals, the wage claims of IG Metall and the wage offers by Gesamtmetall are subject to a continuous change between these discrete points of information, and this behaviour is approximated by the regression approaches.

In view of these methodical preliminary remarks, now the round-oriented potential regression approaches for the annual wage claim curves of IG Metall and/or the annual wage offer curves of Gesamtmetall can be formulated as follows:

$$w_t^1(r_t) = a_t^1 \cdot r_t^{b_t^1} + \varepsilon_t \tag{16}$$

and/or

$$w_t^2(r_t) = a_t^2 \cdot r_t^{b_t^2} + \varepsilon_t \, , \tag{17}$$

where the exponents b_t^1 and b_t^2 can be interpreted as a measure of the two partners' readiness to make concessions. The regression results obtained on the basis of the data in Table 2 and by using (16) and (17) are specified in Table 5 where also the individual correlation coefficients r are given. For IG Metall the correlation coefficients r are naturally bad in those years in which the preliminary reflections on the basis of a non-linearlisable exponential approach called for concave wage claim functions. The wage claim curves according to (16) are decreasing and convex on account of $a_t^1 > 0$ and $b_t^1 < 0$. As far as Gesamtmetall is concerned, however, the potential approach according to (17) left ex ante open the possibilities of convex or concave courses of the curves of the wage offer functions. Strikingly enough, the regression has shown here that all wage offer functions of the years under review increase and follow concave courses on account of $a_t^2 > 0$ and $0 < b_t^2 < 1$, thus the wage offer behaviour of Gesamtmetall can be approximated fairly well by a function whose curves follow these courses. While consequently the empirically founded proposition concerning the existence of decreasing convex concession functions is supported by the regression results for Gesamtmetall, the same cannot be said with respect to the case of IG Metall, since expression (16) implies convex courses of the curves with wage claims decreasing, but the preliminary reflections mentioned did not lead to such unique results in this sense.

When comparing the regression coefficients of Table 5, the fact strikes us that for the estimated IG Metall wage claim curves of the 13 wage negotiations the parameter b_t^1 is confined to the relatively small range [-0.32; -0.13]. This impression could further be improved by excluding the year 1975 which is not typical to a certain extent, since the agreement then reached exceeded the initial offer by Gesamtmetall only by 0.8% which means that IG Metall lost comparatively many feathers. A correspondingly uniform picture for Gesamtmetall can be obtained only from 1969, however, if here too, the year 1975 is excluded on account of the reasons mentioned, the exponent b_t^2 of the estimated wage offer curves for Gesamtmetall is then in the interval [0.26; 0.42] over these eight years. Moreover, it is interesting that the regression coefficients a_t^1 and a_t^2 of Table 5 are quite well accounted for by the initial claims $\bar{w}_t$ and initial offers $\underline{w}_t$ of the bargaining partners (see Table 1). Setting, as in section 2.2, homogeneous linear regressions of the form

$$a_t^1 = \beta_3 \cdot \bar{w}_t + \varepsilon_t \qquad (18)$$

and/or

$$a_t^2 = \beta_4 \cdot \underline{w}_t + \varepsilon_t \qquad (19)$$

one obtains the results

$$\hat{a}_t^1 = 1.03\bar{w}_t \qquad (18')$$

and/or

$$\hat{a}_t^2 = 0.78\underline{w}_t \qquad (19')$$

Table 5.

Regression results for the annual wage claim and wage offer functions of IG Metall and Gesamtmetall

t	IG Metall a_t^1	IG Metall b_t^1	IG Metall r	Gesamtmetall a_t^2	Gesamtmetall b_t^2	Gesamtmetall r
1961-62	10.89	-0.22	-0.77	0.76	0.97	0.99
1963	8.18	-0.19	-0.97	2.12	0.43	0.96
1965-66	9.39	-0.24	-0.74	1.65	0.72	0.93
1968	7.23	-0.13	-0.93	3.54	0.17	0.95
1969	12.34	-0.15	-0.81	3.46	0.40	0.88
1970	15.66	-0.16	-0.74	5.31	0.42	0.98
1971	10.76	-0.23	-0.98	3.69	0.32	0.93
1974	18.04	-0.24	-0.99	6.80	0.34	0.98
1975	10.73	-0.32	-0.96	5.55	0.11	0.99
1976	8.45	-0.21	-0.74	3.28	0.26	0.96
1977	10.00	-0.18	-0.84	3.80	0.28	0.96
1978	8.52	-0.21	-0.85	2.34	0.42	0.97
1979	6.28	-0.17	-0.74	2.41	0.34	0.98

with the correlation coefficients $r_3 = 0.99$ and $r_4 = 0.98$ respectively. Consequently, while in the case of IG Metall the coefficient a_t^1 is approximately identical to the individual initial claim, in the case of Gesamtmetall a_t^2 amounts to about 78% of the individual initial claim. This difference is due to the functions assumed in (16) and (17) respectively, and to the representation in terms of rounds of the wage bargaining processes. a_t^1 and a_t^2 represent the estimated values for the wage proposals by the bargaining partners in the first round $r_t = 1$ of each year of wage bargaining. By representing the wage bargaining processes in terms of rounds it had, however, been laid down that in each first round $r_t = 1$ only the initial claim of IG Metall is known, whereas the initial offer by Gesamtmetall will be submitted only in each second round $r_t = 2$. As an example, for 1971 the wage proposal curves of the bargaining partners which have been estimated according to (16) and (17) are illustrated in Figure 2. Doubtless there is no definite answer to the question to what extent the concession behaviours of IG Metall and Gesamtmetall can actually be rationally accounted for in the sense of Contini and Zionts using such wage proposal curves. Yet, due to the results of the regression analysis, it can reasonably be assumed that certain rules do exist. This should encourage further investigations with a view to clarifying the rationality of wage bargaining processes. For even irrespective of the methodical reflections made here, the naive solution and the data compiled in Table 2 allow the assumption that the decision making of the two bargaining partners shows certain features of a heuristic procedure: on an average the partners expect about four double rounds of wage bargaining until an agreement is reached, and knowing the initial proposals they adapt their concessions accordingly, so that eventually the commonly defined bargaining cake is divided almost into halves.

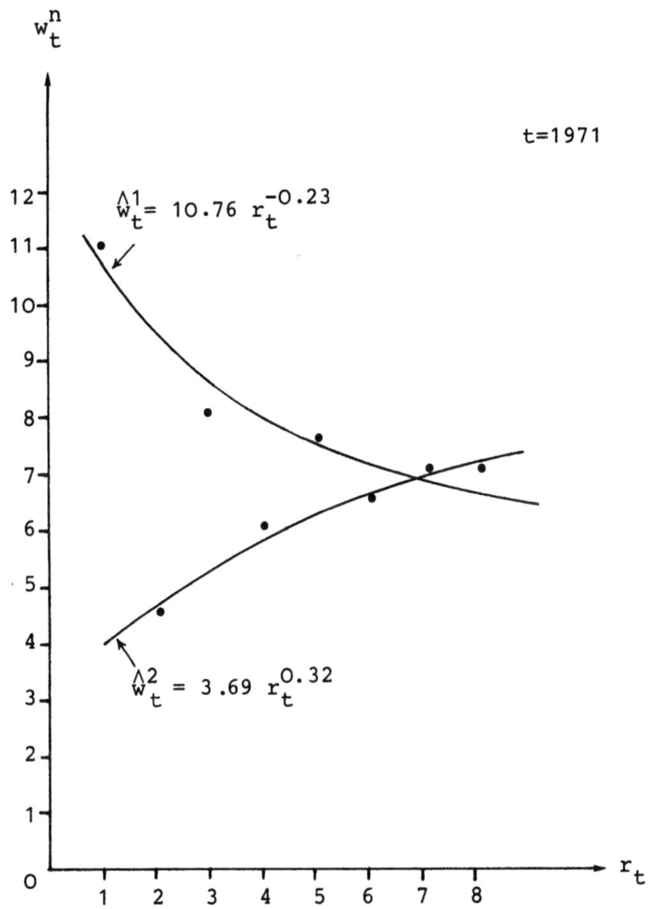

Figure 2. Wage claim and wage offer curves of IG Metall and Gesamtmetall in 1971

REFERENCES

Contini, B. and Zionts, S., 'Restricted bargaining for organizations with multiple objectives', Econometrica, 1968, pp. 397-414.

Fandel, G., Optimale Entscheidungen in Organisationen, Berlin-Heidelberg- New York, 1979.

Fandel, G., 'Decision concepts for organizations', in: Morse, J.N. (ed), Organizations: Multiple Agents with Multiple Criteria, Berlin-Heidelberg-New York, 1981, pp. 91-109.

Krelle, W., Preistheorie Teil II, 2nd edition, Tübingen, 1976.

Müller-Jentsch, W., 'Der Arbeitskampf in der Metallindustrie - Analyse der Tarifbewegung 1971', in Gewerkschaftliche Monatshefte, vol. 5, 1972, pp. 324-333.

Nash, J.F., 'Two-person cooperative games', Econometrica, 1953, pp. 128-140.

Weitbrecht, H., 'Effektivität und Legitimität der Tarifautonomie', Volkswirtschaftliche Schriften, no. 133, Berlin, 1969.

Wetzel, W., 'Statistische Grundausbildung für Wirtschaftwissenschaftler', vol. 2, Schliessende Statistik, Berlin, 1973, pp. 195-220.

Zerche, J., Arbeitsökonomie, Berlin-New York, 1979.

Zeuthen, F., Problems of Monopoly and Economic Warfare, London, 1930.

17 Computer Selection and Multicriteria Decision Aid

J. Fichefet

1 INTRODUCTION

We have shown elsewhere that computer selection involves many multicriteria problems and we have proposed a methodology taking this fact into account (Fichefet 1981). Hereafter, we shall confine to the final phase of such a methodology, when the decision maker is faced with a set A - named here the set of feasible actions - of narrowly defined computer configurations (e.g. a DEC 20/50 with three magnetic tape drives and two removable disk units) and has to select the most appropriate alternative in order to process a given (present and expected) workload as inexpensively as possible.

With the eventual help of an analyst (e.g. Ad Hoc Committee with regular staff members or a Consulting Firm), the decision maker has to go through two basic steps:

(i) determine the 'action - consequence' relation. To each action $a \in A$, this step associates n indices of value $X_1(a), \ldots, X_n(a)$ such as hardware efficiency, technical support, ease of conversion, etc. Each evaluator or attribute X_i evaluates any action on its own scale of measurement S_i so that the n evaluators $X_1, \ldots, X_n$ can be thought of as mapping each $a \in A$ into a point in an n-dimensional consequence space $\prod_{i=1}^{n} S_i$.

(ii) determine the 'consequence - value' or 'consequence - ranking' relation. This step can be viewed as assigning a value u(a) to each $a \in A$ or exhibiting a ranking of the feasible actions in terms of the n indices of value $X_1(a), \ldots, X_n(a)$.

The decision maker can make use of several measurement models in order to put the 'action - consequence' relation in concrete form, viz. global evaluations based on judgements collected in user groups and associations, professional reviews, technical documentations from manufacturers, professional support, congresses, etc., performance evaluations based on experimental techniques (instruction mixes, kernels, benchmarks, performance monitoring) or on modelling techniques (analytic models, simulation models).

The 'consequence - value' or 'consequence - ranking' relation implies identification of the decision maker's preference across attributes. This preference is generally expressed in terms of weights assigned to attributes. Scoring techniques are mostly used in order to exhibit the 'consequence - value or ranking' relation. The quickest scoring relies on an additive utility or value function of form:

$$u(a) = u(X_1(a), \ldots, X_n(a)) = \sum_{i=1}^{n} w_i X_i(a), \; 0 \leq w_i \leq 1, \; \sum_{i=1}^{n} w_i = 1 \qquad (1)$$

where w_i is a weight assigned to the i-th attribute and $X_i(a)$ is the score of action $a \in A$ on $S_i = [0,1]$ or $[0,10]$. Other possibilities are hierarchical scoring techniques with a decomposable set of attributes (Sarzotti 1977, Sharpe 1969, Timmreck 1973) and value function based on an extended continuous logic which aims at modelling conjunction of attributes (Dujmović 1975, 1977). Cost is seldom included as one of the attributes so that scoring methods are used with a cost - effectiveness view. Such methods are extremely criticisable on the theoretical side (Fichefet , Sharpe 1969, Timmreck 1973). The very simple forms conferred upon the value function are probably imputable to the computer selection complexity, and particularly to the fact that the decision maker's true value function is changing with time in the course of the selection process.

Our purpose is here to show the interest of another kind of method based on outranking relations rather than on value functions. It appears indeed that very few computer scientists are aware of the outranking relation concept introduced by B. Roy (1973, 1974). The following section is a brief description of a multicriteria method (ELECTRE II) relying on the outranking relation concept. The final section presents an illustrative example with data obtained in a real computer selection situation encountered at the Facultés Universitaire N-D de la Paix, Namur (Belgium).

2 ELECTRE II DECISION AND MODEL

ELECTRE II (ELECTRE = ELimination Et Choix Traduisant la REalité) has been focussed upon by B. Roy and P. Bertier at the SEMA, France, (Bertier and Bouroche 1975, Roy 1973), and is grounded on the concept of outranking relation introduced by B. Roy as a model of the decision maker's preference relation. Axiomatic properties of outranking relations are given in (Roy 1973, 1974, 1977).

ELECTRE II brings the set A of feasible actions in a relational structure which is a complete weak order. The actions are thus clustered in an ordered sequence of indifference classes ranging from 'best' to 'worst'. These notions of 'best' and 'worst' are put in concrete form by means of two outranking relations on A. It is assumed that each attribute X_i has been defined previously with a weight $w_i > 0$ which exhibits the global importance of attribute X_i in respect to the other attributes. Without loss of generality, it can be assumed that each S_i is included in the set of real numbers and, the greater $X_i(a)$, the greater is the decision maker's preference for a, with regard to the i-th attribute.

Let $I^+(a,b)$ be the set of attribute indices for which a is strictly preferred to b, $I^=(a,b)$ be the set of attribute indices for which a is indifferent to b and $I^-(a,b)$ be the set of attribute indices for which b is strictly preferred to a. Let us also define

$$W^+(a,b) = \sum_{i\in I^+(a,b)} w_i,\quad W^=(a,b) = \sum_{i\in I^=(a,b)} w_i,\quad W^-(a,b) = \sum_{i\in I^-(a,b)} w_i.$$

ELECTRE II makes use of a concord index

$$C(a,b) = \frac{W^+(a,b) + W^=(a,b)}{W^+(a,b) + W^=(a,b) + W^-(a,b)}$$

in such a way as the nearer C(a,b) is to 1, the more a is preferred to b. It also includes the possibility to specify that a and b are indifferent in respect to the i-th attribute if the absolute difference $X_i(a) - X_i(b)$ does not exceed some specified value on the scale S_i. It is necessary to choose the values of some parameters: (i) three concord values C_1, C_2, C_3 (standard values are $C_1 = 3/4$, $C_2 = 2/3$, $C_3 = 3/5$) such as $1 > C_1 > C_2 > C_3 > 0$; (ii) two discord values d_{1i} and d_{2i} for each attribute i so that $0 < d_{1i} < d_{2i}$. Then action b is said to be strongly outranked by action a if $W^+(a,b) \geq W^-(a,b)$ and

(a) either:

$$C(a,b) \geq C_1, \text{ and } X_i(b) - X_i(a) \leq d_{2i} \quad \text{for} \quad i \in I^-(a,b),$$

(b) or:

$$C(a,b) \geq C_2, \text{ and } X_i(b) - X_i(a) \leq d_{1i} \quad \text{for} \quad i \in I^-(a,b) .$$

There are thus two possibilities according to more demand on concord or more demand on discord. In the same way, action b is said to be weakly outranked by action a if $W^+(a,b) \geq W^-(a,b)$ and

$$C(a,b) \geq C_3, \text{ and } X_i(b) - X_i(a) \leq d_{2i} \quad \text{for each } i \in I^-(a,b).$$

Therefore, the outranking relation (strong and weak) concept has the following concrete meaning: (i) a outranks b means that it appears likely enough to admit the hypothesis that a is strictly preferred or indifferent to b when the available information is taken into account, viz. the decision maker's known preferences, the quality of the $X_i(a)$,s, the set A and the nature of the problem; (ii) a does not outrank b means that it appears unlikely enough to admit the hypothesis that a is strictly preferred or indifferent to b.

When working with the modified version of ELECTRE II which is proposed in Thiriez (1977), weak ordering of actions is established with the help of two rankings of actions:

(a) direct ranking : actions are ranked in such a way as action a precedes action b if and only if the number of actions which strongly outrank a is smaller than the number of actions which strongly outranks b;

(b) indirect ranking : actions are ranked in such a way as action a precedes action b if and only if the number of actions strongly outranked by a is greater than the number of actions strongly outranked by b.

In both rankings the weak outranking relation is used to disjoin actions of equal merit. When Condorcet paradox appears, indifferent actions are merged into a unique indifference class.

When both direct and indirect rankings are similar enough, the final ranking is a medium ranking: rank of action a is the mean of ranks assigned to a with direct and indirect rankings. Otherwise the decision maker and the analyst are asked to revise their 'action - consequence' relation.

The most notable facts in ELECTRE II rise out of the concept of (strong or weak) outranking relations. With such a model of the decision maker's preference structure:

(i) qualitative aspects of the decision problem are easily handled;

(ii) Two actions may be not comparable in the sense that neither strict preference nor indifference dominate. This situation is rather frequent in the course of the decision process when the available information is insufficiently discriminative. In case the decision maker is willing to remove incomparabilities, he is forced to look back upon his 'action - consequence' relation. Incomparabilities are usually not considered in classical decision theory;

(iii) as incomparabilities are taken into consideration, intransitivities are allowed, which is also current in practical situations;

(iv) the stability axiom is generally not satisfied. This axiom, which is classical in decision theory, should state here that, whenever R_A and $R_{A'}$ are outranking relations on A and A' respectively, with A included in A', then $a R_A b \Leftrightarrow a R_{A'} b$. But practice shows that the stability axiom is not necessarily realistic.

Let us also point out that:

(a) the choice of concord values C_1, C_2 and C_3 is not obvious: a sensitivity analysis of the rankings to these values is useful;

(b) sensitivity analysis with respect to weights is also useful;

(c) the form of concordance index shown above assumes some independence of attributes, but some solutions to this problem can be found in Roy (1974).

Two other ELECTRE decision aid models have been set up: ELECTRE I where the problem is to separate 'good' actions from 'bad' actions (Bertier and Bouroche 1975)), and ELECTRE III similar to ELECTRE II but using a concept of fuzzy outranking relation (Roy 1977, 1978).

3 ILLUSTRATIVE EXAMPLE AND COMMENTS

This section relies on a real computer selection problem encountered at the Facultés Universitaires N-D de la Paix, Namur, Belgium. Request for proposals concerned large scale computer systems and was stated by the Board of Administrators and an Ad Hoc Committee with five regular staff members: the Director of the EDP Department and four university professors who make intensive use of computers and are representative of the main computer users. Validation of proposed systems was accomplished by the Ad Hoc Committee and two full time computer scientists. The selection process took one year.

Table 1 lists the selected attributes together with rates assigned by the Ad Hoc Committee to the five computer systems (named here a to e) which had not been eliminated yet at the moment of the very final decision. Value system for each attribute was:

6 = excellent,	3 = acceptable,
5 = very good,	2 = poor,
4 = good,	1 = very poor.

It is impossible to describe here the exact meaning of each attribute but the reader can refer to André et al. (1978). Table 1 does not contain any political or cost considerations. The reason is that these considerations were the privilege of the sole Board of Administrators.

The additive value function (1) gives the following results, when applied to Table 1 with normalised weights:

$$u(a) = 4.675,\ u(b) = 4.695,\ u(c) = 4.678,\ u(d) = 4.555,\ u(e) = 4.766.$$

Figures 1 and 2 are two outranking graphs obtained with the hereabove modified ELECTRE II version. Because the five computer systems have the same rates in regard to attributes 5, 7, 11, 18 and 21, these attributes were not taken into account. In each figure, computer x and y are joined with an arc originating in x when x outranks y (dotted arc for weak outranking). The standard concord values were used. Figure 1 is related to discord values listed in Table 3. Tables 2 and 4 contain the rankings of computer systems produced with ELECTRE II for Figures 1 and 2 respectively. It is to be noted that computer system b is not comparable to other computer systems in the case of Figure 1. In such a case, the decision maker has to refine the available information when he wants to remove incomparabilities.

Let us point out that:

(i) Timmreck reports (1973) that attempts have been made to include costs of computer systems in the effectiveness calculation with

Table 1.

	Global Performances							Hardware Performances				Software Performances						Installation and Conversion Considerations				Management Considerations		Miscellaneous		
Attributes	1	2	3	4	5	6	7	8	9	10	11	12	13	14	15	16	17	18	19	20	21	22	23	24	25	26
Weights	3	3	3	3	3	3	2	3	3	2	3	3	3	3	3	3	2	1	2	2	2	2	2	2	2	1
Computer a	6	5	5	6	5	4	6	4.5	6	6	6	2	3	3.5	4	5	4	5	4	5	5	4	5	4	5.1	3
Computer b	4	5	6	2	5	5	6	6	6	4	6	6	3	5.5	3	6	2	5	4	4	5	5	3	4	6	4
Computer c	4	5	4	6	5	4	6	4.5	6	5	6	3	5	5	6	3	5	5	4	5	5	3	4	3	5	5
Computer d	3	6	2	6	5	4	6	4.5	5	5	6	4	6	6	3	2	5	5	6	5	5	2	4	5	5	3
Computer e	4	4	5	5	5	3	6	3	6	5	6	5	4	5.5	6	4	6	5	4	6	5	3	4	5	5.3	5

Global Performances

1. Capability to face batch workload
2. Response time in interactive mode
3. Capability to fulfil future plans
4. Extensibility
5. Reliability
6. Data communications scientific
7. Continuous operation without operator's intervention

Hardware Performance

8. Constraints related to storage
9. Disk units
10. Peripherals
11. Maintenance support provided by manufacturer

Software Performances

12. Ease of use
13. Programming languages available
14. Quality of essential programming languages
15. Packages available
16. Quality of available documentation
17. Staff support provided by manufacturer

Installation and Conversion Considerations

18. Delivery delay times
19. Conversion considerations
20. Facilities offered by vendor
21. Training courses offered

Management Considerations

22. Ease of operation
23. Accounting aids

Miscellaneous

24. Manufacturer's frame
25. User rating
26. What is possible for collaboration with

scoring techniques but that relative weights between cost and, say, hardware performance have been found to have little meaning. It is the reason why scoring methods are usually combined with a cost - effectiveness technique. With ELECTRE II, cost of computer systems can be considered as a supplementary attribute with a more or less heavy weight according to the importance imputed to cost.

(ii) When looking at Table 1 and considering the fuzziness of some data (see attribute n. 24 for example), one fain would introduce thresholds s_j and q_j so that, when

$$X_j(a) - X_j(b) = u \geq 0 ,$$

then :

. for $0 \leq u \leq q_j$: a is indifferent to b,
. for $q_j < u \geq s_j$: a is weakly preferred to b,
. for $s_j < u$: a is strongly preferred to b,

with respect to attribute X_j, these thresholds depending normally on the attribute X_j and eventually on an action chosen as frame of reference. ELECTRE III provides such an opportunity (Roy 1977, 1978) with the help of a concept of degree of credibility of outranking relation which fixes the more or less high credibility of the outranking.

(iii) As already mentioned, the rankings of actions produced with ELECTRE II model depend somewhat on the weights assigned to attributes. As computer selection involves several persons, we encountered (Fichefet and Leclercq 1979) four methods for collecting the judgements of experts concerning the relative value of sets of attributes: ranking, rating, partial paired comparisons and complete paired comparisons. The attributes were the DATAPRO attributes for computer systems. We questioned twelve computer scientists and computed the Kendall coefficient of concordance to determine the agreements among judges for each of the four methods: the values ranged from 0.28 to 0.31. Thus a consensual DELPHI-like method is probably more suitable to weighting. At this point, let us also mention another decision aid model, named ORESTE and recently proposed by M. Roubens (1982): this model can be considered as a member of the ELECTRE family but preferences across attributes are supposed to be expressed in terms of a preference relation of type (I,P,Q) (I = indifference, P = strict preference, Q = weak preference) rather than in terms of weights.

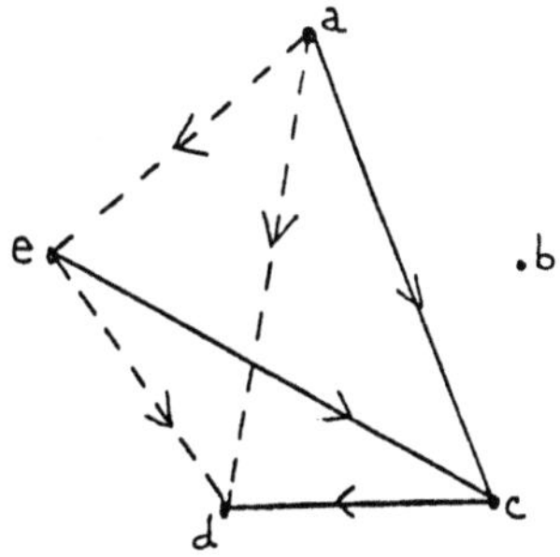

Figure 1.

Table 2.

Rankings \ Comp.	a	b	c	d	e
Direct	1	1	5	4	3
Indirect	1	4	3	4	2
Medium	1	2	4	4	2

Table 3.

Attributes	d_{1i}	d_{2i}	Attributes	d_{1i}	d_{2i}
1	2	3	14	2	2.5
2	1	2	15	2	3
3	3	4	16	3	4
4	3	4	17	3	4
5	2	3	18	3	4
6	1	2	19	2	3
7	2	3	20	2	3
8	2.5	3	21	2	3
9	2	3	22	2	3
10	1	2	23	1	2
11	3	4	24	1	2
12	3	4	25	0,9	1
13	2	3	26	1	2

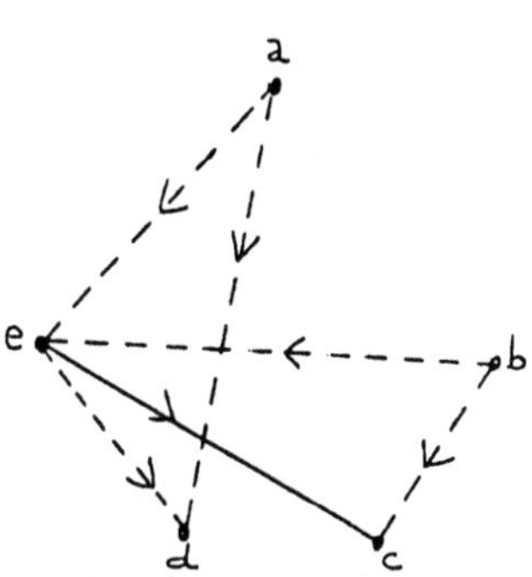

Figure 2.

Table 4.

Rankings \ Comp.	a	b	c	d	e
Direct	1	1	5	3	3
Indirect	2	2	4	4	1
Medium	1	1	5	4	3

ACKNOWLEDGEMENT

We express our thanks to the Ad Hoc Committee set up by the Facultés Universitaires N-D de la Paix, Namur. The Committee allowed us to have real-world data at our disposal.

REFERENCES

André, J.M., Feytmans, E., Guillaume, M., Ramaekers, J. and Bastelaer, Ph. van, Rapport sur une solution autonome destinée à satisfaire les besoins en moyens informatiques des Facultés durant la période 1979-1984, Note no. 75 de la Commission Plan-Calcul, Facultés Universitaires N-D de la Paix, Namur, 1978.

Bertier, P. and Bouroche, J.M., Analyse des Données Multidimensionnelles Presses Universitaires de France, Paris, 1975.

Dujmović, J.J., 'Extended continuous logic and the theory of complex criteria', Publikacije Elektrotehničkog Fakulteta Univerziteta U Beogradu, Serija: Matematika I Fizika, no. 461-497, 1975, pp. 197-216.

Dujmović, J.J., 'Professional evaluation and selection of computer systems', Proceedings of the 12th Yugoslav International Symposium on Information Processing, Paper 4-001, October 1977.

Fichefet, J., 'Some insights into the nature of computer selection', Revue Belge de Statistique, d'Informatique et de Recherche Opérationnelle, 21, 1981, pp. 49-89.

Fichefet, J. and Leclercq, J.P., Pondération de critères de comparaison de systèmes informatiques: résultats d'une enquête réalisée sur des critères DATAPRO, Internal Report, Facultés Universitaires N-D de la Paix, Namur, 1979.

Roubens, M., 'Preference relations on actions and criteria in multicriteria decision making', EJOR, 10, 1982, pp. 51-55.

Roy, B., 'How outranking relation helps multicriteria decision making', in: Cochrane, J.L. and Zeleny, M. (eds), Multiple Criteria Decision Making, University of South Carolina Press, Columbia, South Carolina, 1973, pp. 179-201.

Roy, B., 'Critères multiples et modélisation des préférences, l'apport des relations de surclassement', Revue d'Economie Politique, 1, 1974, pp. 1-44.

Roy, B., 'Partial preference analysis and decision-aid: the fuzzy outranking relation concept', in: Conflicting Objectives in Decision Making, John Wiley, Chichester, 1977, pp. 40-74.

Roy, B., 'ELECTRE III: un algorithme de classement fondé sur une représentation floue des préférences en présence de critères multiples', Cahiers du Centre d'Etudes de Recherche Opérationnelle, 20, 1978, pp. 3-24.

Sarzotti, A., Introduction aux techniques d'évaluation et de mesure des systèmes informatiques, Eyrolles, Paris, 1977.

Sharpe, W.F., The Economics of Computers, Columbia University Press, New York and London, 1969.

Thiriez, H., Initiation au calcul économique, Dunod, 1977.

Timmreck, E.M., 'Computer selection methodology', Computing Surveys, 5, 1973, pp. 199-222.

18 A Methodology for Multiple Criteria Environmental Plan Evaluation

R. Janssen, P. Nijkamp and H. Voogd

1 MULTICRITERIA ANALYSIS AND ENVIRONMENTAL IMPACT ASSESSMENT

In the past decade, multicriteria analysis has become an increasingly important analytical instrument in environmental evaluation problems. It offered many advantages over conventional tools, as it provided a framework for integrating non-monetary and even qualitative effects in plan and project evaluation. 'Soft' aspects of complex decision problems could be taken into account without reducing them to inferior criteria.

Unfortunately, the technical design of multicriteria methods has often taken place without due regard to the specific features of evaluation problems and of the specific conditions under which these methods may be applied. The usual approach was to select a (technical) evaluation method on the basis of its general features and, next, to adjust this method in an ad hoc fashion in order to comply with the specific nature of the evaluation problem at hand (see Figure 1).

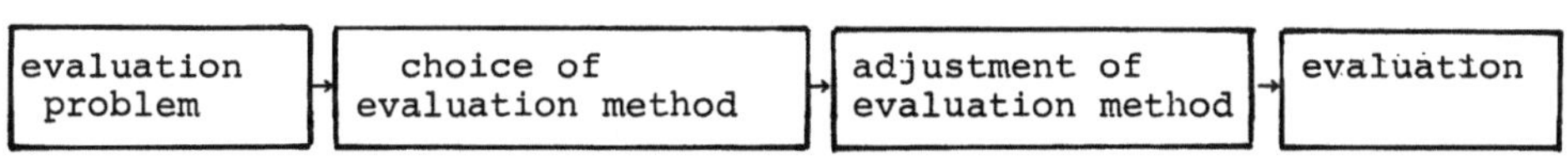

Figure 1. Conventional approach to environmental evaluation

In the present paper a reverse approach is adopted. After the definition of the evaluation problem, its general and specific characteristics are carefully described based on a systematic typology of environmental problems. Next, for each class of environmental (management) problems the specific requirements and criteria are specified in order to be able to provide a logical choice framework for the application of evaluation methods (see Figure 2).

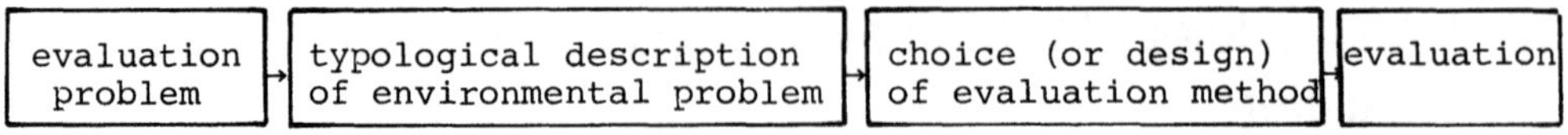

Figure 2. Schematic representation of the methodology adopted in the paper

The second approach also prevents an artificial adjustment of empirical data to the methodological requirements of a specific a priori selected evaluation technique. In a way, this problem can be regarded as a meta-multicriteria problem: how to select a specific evaluation method for a complex decision problem, while taking into account a multidimensional set of methodological criteria. A closer investigation into this question requires a systematic inventory and typology of environmental assessment problems, based on a set of relevant classification principles (see Nijkamp 1981, and Rietveld 1980). Altogether, the present paper will direct the attention to the following research question: is it possible to identify a set of discriminating criteria for environmental management problems in order to be able to choose an appropriate evaluation method for a specific environmental management problem?

The following research phases will be treated in the sequel to this paper:
- a systematic description of relevant activities in the framework of environmental management,
- a coherent representation of relevant impacts of the abovementioned activities,
- an adequate description of the institutional context of environmental management,
- a systematic identification of selection criteria for choosing a certain appropriate evaluation method.

These phases will be illustrated by means of an empirical case study in The Netherlands (for more details see Janssen 1984b).

2 RELEVANT ACTIVITIES FOR ENVIRONMENTAL EVALUATION

The first phase is made up of a typology of relevant activities which lead to environmental problems. Examples are traffic, resource extraction, industrialisation, noise annoyance, recreation, etc. Such activities are only regarded as relevant if they cause a significant environmental impact (see Section 3) and if the government through public policy can influence these impacts (see Section 4). Furthermore non-environmental consequences will only be taken into consideration if they play a role in the evaluation of environmental policies.

Types of activities to be distinguished are: (1) transport (including infrastructure), (2) land use, (3) urban building and construction, (4) water management, (5) resource extraction, (6) waste disposal, (7) industrial production and (8) environmental management.

These activities can be further classified according to their nature and their spatial scale.

The nature of activities is aligned to the degree of precision and the range of impacts and to the extent of policy intervention. Three major classes of activities may be distinguished, viz. projects (pr), plans (pl) and regulations (re).

The spatial scale of activities concerns the geographical dimensions of these activities, such as an international (in), national (na), regional (re) or local (lo) scale.

Activities can now be typified by means of an attribute profile (see Table 1). Table 1 can be used as a framework for classifying all activities relevant in an environmental context.

Table 1.
An Attribute Profile of Activities

types of activities	example of specific activities	nature of activities pr	pl	re	spatial scale in	na	re	lo
(1)	highway construction							
	:							
(2)	land reallocation plan							
	:							
(3)	urban renewal							
	:							
(4)	water extraction							
	:							
(5)	oil extraction							
	:							
(6)	nuclear waste processing							
	:							
(7)	steel industry							
	:							
(8)	air pollution							

3 RELEVANT ENVIRONMENTAL IMPACTS

Impact assessment tries to gauge the expected effects of the activities at hand. As mentioned before, impacts can be distinguished into environmental and non-environmental impacts.

Environmental impacts may concern inter alia effects upon: (i) soil and ground water, (ii) surface water, (iii) air, (iv) plants, (v) animals, (vi) landscape, (vii) noise annoyance, and (viii) climate.

Non-environmental impacts may concern: (ix) employment, (x) income, (xi) accessibility, (xii) housing, (xiii) energy use, (xiv) level of amenity, (xv) security, and (xvi) health.

In addition to the main division into environmental and non-environmental effects, one may also classify impacts according to their features in terms of time, space and otherwise.

Temporal. Impacts may be unique (un), repetitive (re), continuous short-term (cs) or continuous long-term (lo).

Spatial. Impacts may be stationary (st), mobile (mo), international (in), national (na), regional (re) or local (lo).

Otherwise. Finally, the impacts may be characterised by applicability of formal regulations (ar), non-applicability of formal regulations (nr), marginal contribution of effects (mc) or non-marginal contribution of effects (nc).

Given a typological approach, one may again design an impact table that contains in a systematic way all relevant activities and their impacts, distinguished according to the abovementioned features (see Table 2). This table may serve to provide a coherent picture of all expected types of impacts associated with the implementation of relevant activities.

Table 2.

A typological impact table

types of activities	specific activities	environmental types of effects	non-environmental types of effects	features		
				time	space	otherwise
(1)						
(2)						
(3)						
(4)						
(5)						
(6)						
(7)						
(8)						

4 INSTITUTIONAL CONTEXT OF ENVIRONMENTAL MANAGEMENT

Evaluation problems in environmental policy analysis can be characterised by the number and nature of alternative choice possibilities and by the information content of these problems.

The number and nature of alternatives may relate to discrete versus continuous alternatives, to point versus sequential alternatives, and mutually exclusive versus non-exclusive alternatives.

The information content of evaluation problems may relate to quantitative versus qualitative information, to certain versus uncertain information, to extensive versus limited information, and to complete versus incomplete information.

Next, the decision space of environmental management problems may be marked by the institutional structure and by the objectives of the evaluation. The institutional structure may again relate to the spatial dimensions (international, national, regional or local), to the number of objectives (single objective versus multiple objective decision making), to the policy structure (hierarchical policies, negotiation, participation, informal decision making), to the (policy) creativity needed (routine versus non-routine decision) and to the decision style of policy makers (analytical versus heuristic approaches).

Environmental evaluation may have several objectives: ex ante versus ex post evaluation, internal versus external communication between policy makers or interest groups, and selection of one alternative, a series of feasible alternatives or a ranking of alternatives

It is clear that for all activities again a matrix can be designed that integrates the abovementioned features (see Table 3).

Table 3.
A typology of activities on the basis of institutional and decision attributes

types of activities	specific activities	alternatives	information content	institutional structure	objectives of evaluation
(1)					
(2)					
(3)					
(4)					
(5)					
(6)					
(7)					
(8)					

5 IDENTIFICATION OF AN APPROPRIATE EVALUATION METHOD

In the past years, a wide range of evaluation methods have been designed (see also Janssen 1984a, Lichfield 1975, McAllister 1980, Rietveld 1980 and Voogd 1983). Dozens of techniques have been used in different policy situations and for different choice problems. In the present section, a methodology will be presented for identifying appropriate evaluation methods for specific classes of environmental decision problems, based on the typological approach discussed in Sections 2-4.

This identification process is a multiple criteria procedure. Following Duchstein et al. (1981), a two-step approach will be adopted by making a distinction between <u>first-order</u> selection criteria (necessary or mandatory conditions which have to be fulfilled) and <u>second-order</u> selection criteria (desirable conditions which should be fulfilled to a maximum extent).

It should also be noted that some selection criteria do not discriminate between specific evaluation methods, as they are more <u>general</u> methodological, e.g.) in nature. However, many selection criteria are aligned to specific features of the environmental management problem at hand, which means that the methods at hand can only be judged in the light of the practical problem to be solved.

Example of general selection criteria are: the evaluation method should make a consistent tradeoff between different policy goals, the results of a method should be conceivable to a decision maker, the method should be able to process information with different dimensions in a comparable way, and the main principles and assumptions of the evaluation method must be explicable to the decision maker at hand.

The following specific selection criteria for the choice of an evaluation method may be envisaged inter alia:
- discrete or continuous nature
- quantitative or qualitative information
- certain or uncertain information
- point or process evaluation
- stationary or mobile effects
- presence or absence of external constraints
- presence or absence of learning effects
- separation or combination of alternatives
- rish or non-risk averting behaviour
- hierarchical versus non-hierarchical decision structure
- balance or imbalance between computation complexity cq. costs and size of choice problem
- inclusion or exclusion of past information
- inclusion or exclusion of subjective elements
- presence or absence of space for (policy) creativity
- presenve or absence of optimising behaviour
- presence or absence of information on priorities
- absence or presence of computer support
- cheap or expensive application of evaluation method

Both the general and specific criteria may be subdivided into first and second order criteria. The abovementioned selection criteria can be confronted with both the specific nature of a certain environmental evaluation problem based on the abovementioned typological approach to activities, and the specific generic features of the long series of evaluation methods which are currently available. Then the following identification table may be constructed (see Table 4).

Table 4.

Identification table for the selection of evaluation methods for specific types of evaluation problems

Type of activities	specific activities	selection criteria
(1)		
(2)		
(3)		
(4)		
(5)		
(6)		
(7)		
(8)		
Evaluation methods		

For the sake of brevity, the various evaluation methods will not be listed here, but surveys of such methods can be found inter alia in Chankong and Haimes (1983), Hwang and Masud (1979), Rietveld (1980), Nijkamp (1980) and Voogd (1983).

For more specific details the reader is referred to Janssen (1984b). By comparing the upper part of Table 4 with its lower part, one may select a set of appropriate evaluation methods for the environmental management problem aligned to a given activity. Instead of presenting here a general large table, the identification procedure will be illustrated by means of a case study for The Netherlands.

6 ILLUSTRATION BY MEANS OF A CASE STUDY

The procedure developed in this paper for characterising environmental problems and selecting evaluation methods according to these characteristics will be illustrated by means of an evaluation study carried out on behalf of the Dutch Ministry of Culture and Recreation - by a consortium of Dutch research institutes (see Ministry of Culture and Recreation 1981). Given a certain expected demand for water in the Dutch province of North-Golland (in the so-called Kennemerland area), this evaluation study aimed at ranking 11 potential water extraction sites (see Janssen 1984b for more details).

In terms of this paper, this choice problem is an evaluation problem with a discrete set of distinct alternatives. This evaluation study is aimed at a complete ranking of all alternatives.

Some relevant features of this problem will be listed below. Each alternative gives rise to a wide range of effects which differ considerably in various aspects. These effects include inter alia impacts on ground and surface water, flora, fauna, landscape and health. Most of these effects are long-term effects, for example, the change of the flora due to a change in groundwater level. Some effects are stationary, but most of them will vary over time. For certain effects (e.g. the effects on health) formal standards can be specified.

The available information is extensive and is partly quantitative and partly qualitative. An important part of the information (e.g., information aligned to ecological effects) is uncertain with an unknown probability function. The decisions regarding this water management project will be made in a negotiation between different policy institutions at different levels (national, regional, local). This decision process is carefully and critically judged by environmental interest groups.

The features of this evaluation problem are summarised in Table 5. The selection criteria which are aligned to these features are listed in Table 6. Table 6 can be used for the selection of an appropriate evaluation method for this problem. This approach will be briefly outlined here.

The first-order criteria pertaining to this problem are presented in the shaded columns on the left hand side of Table 6. It can be seen that no method in its basic form complies with all these criteria. Most methods listed however, can be extended in a way which makes application of these methods to the problem possible.

Next from the right hand side of Table 6 one can conclude that no evaluation method meets all relevant second-order criteria. In this case, the following two second-order criteria seem to be of special relevance:
S2: The evaluation method must allow for the introduction of constraints. This criterion is of special importance because several constraints, such as the quantity of water to be supplied and environmental standards, are applicable to this problem.
S12: The evaluation method may not include implicit subjective choices and must be repeatable. This criterion is of special importance because a wide range of people and groups with many different views and interests are involved in the decision making process, both inside and outside the government.

The features of evaluation methods corresponding to criterion S2 and S12 are represented in the shaded columns on the right hand side of Table 6. One can see that according to these criteria especially the <u>scorecard</u> method and the <u>key issue</u> method can be applied to this problem. These methods also comply with the greatest number of other second-order criteria.

Scorecard methods aim at presenting available information in such a way that the alternatives can be judged without applying arithmetic computations to the scores.

The scores are listed in a scorecard and clarified by the use of graphic Scorecards can contain all types of information (cardinal, ordinal, nominal). By adding an additional commentary column, an indication of the level of uncertainty in predicting the effects can be provided.

The key issue method, which can be seen as a variant of the scorecard method, also aims at making a judgement without applying arithmetic exercises to the scores. Reduction of the amount of information presented takes place in three steps:
1. cross out inefficient alternatives,
2. cross out alternatives which cause effects that exceed set constraints such as environmental standards on the available budget,

Table 5.

A typological matrix for the water extraction plan, Kennermerland

features	projects: gov.dir.infl.	projects: gov.indir.infl.	plans: facet policy	plans: sectoral policy	legislation: facet policy	legislation: sectoral policy	international	national	regional	local
water extraction	x								x	x

EFFECTS – effect categories	environment: ground water	surface water	air	flora	fauna	landscape	noise	climate	non environm.: employment	income	accessibility	housing market	energy consumption	level of amenity	security	health
water extraction	x	x		x	x	x										x

EFFECTS – features	time: one point in time	more points in time	continuous short term	continuous long term	space: stationary	mobile	international	national	regional	local	otherwise: env. standards	no env. standards	marginal effect	non marginal effect
water extraction	x		x	x	x	x			x	x	x			x

DECISION STRUCTURE – solution space	alternatives: continu	discrete: one alt.	discrete: few alt.	discrete: many alt.	point alternatives	serial alternatives	mutually excl.alt.	non-mut. excl.alt.	information: quantitative	qualitative	certain	uncertain: known distr.	uncertain: unknown distr	extensive (much data)	limited	complete	incomplete
water extraction				x		x		x	x	x	x	x	x	x			x

DECISION STRUCTURE – decision space	institutional structure: international	national	provincial	local	one policy goal	more policy goals	hierarch.dec.struct.	dec.through negotat.	presence interest gr	routine situation	non-routine situat.	analytic	heuristic
water extraction		x	x			x	x		x		x		

DECISION STRUCTURE – decision space	objectives: pol.making (ex ante)	pol.evaluat. (ex post)	internal communicat.	external communicat.	gen.one optimal alt.	gen.set satisf.alt.	complete ordening alt.	much exp.and use comp	little exp.no compute	much time and money	little time and money
water extraction	x		x	x			x	x		x	

Table 6.

Identification table based on features of the evaluation process

FIRST-ORDER CRITERIA

Activity	S1 The EM must be based on a continuous decision function	S2 The EM must be based on a decision function for discrete choices	S3 The EM must be able to handle quantitative information in an efficient and methodologically sound way	S4 The EM should be able to handle qualitative information or a combination of qualitative and quantitative inform. in an efficient and methodologic.sound way	S5 The EM must be able to process uncertain information	S6 The EM must be able to process effects occuring on different points in time	S7 The EM must be able to process effects which occur continuously over time	S8 The EM must be able to include the spatial pattern of the effects
water extraction		x		x	x		x	x
1. concordance analysis		x		x	o	o	o	o
2. frequency method		x		x	o			
3. lexicographic ordening		x		x	o			
4. permutation method		x		x	o	o	o	o
5. eigen value method		x		x	x	o	o	o
6. regime method		x		x	o	o	o	o
7. multidimensional scaling		x		x	x	o	o	o
8. metagame method		x		x	x	o	o	o
9. mixed data method		x		x	x	o	o	o
10. trichotomic choise method		x		x	o	o	o	o
11. score card method		x		x	o	o	o	o
12. key issue matrix		x		x	o	o	o	o

SECOND-ORDER CRITERIA

Activity	S1 The EM should be able to include effects at different spatial scales	S2 The EM must allow for the introduction of constraints	S3 The EM must be able to relate the size of an effect to the importance of an effect	S4 The EM must be able to relate the importance of an effect to the importance of all other effects	S5 The EM must be able to include information on past decisions in the analysis	S6 The EM must be able to include alternatives both separately and in combination	S7 The EM must take account of the decision maker's attitude to risk	S8 The EM must not be based on an algorithm of which the amount of required calculations increases exponentially with the amount of data	S9 The EM must be able to integrate decisions at different decision levels	S10 The EM must be able to incorporate easily information from the past	S11 The EM must stimulate the imagination of the decision maker	S12 The EM may not include implicit subjective choices and must be repeatable	S13 The EM must be based on a decision rule related to optimizing behaviour	S14 The EM must be based on a decision rule related to satisficing behaviour	S15 The EM should not require a priori information on preferences and should not provide to detailed results	S16 The EM must be simple and applicable without the use of a computer	S17 The application of the EM must be cheap and not time consuming
water extraction	x	x	x	x	x			x				x		x			
1. concordance analysis					x							x	x			x	x
2. frequency method					x								x			x	x
3. lexicographic ordening					x			x				x	x			x	x
4. permutation method					x							x	x				x
5. eigen value method					x			x					x			x	x
6. regime method					x						x	x	x			x	x
7. multidimensional scaling					x						x	x	x				x
8. metagame method					x				x		x	x	x				x
9. mixed data method		x			x	x							x				x
10. trichotomic choise method		x			x	x							x	x	x		x
11. score card method	x	x			x	x			x			x	x	x	x	x	x
12. key issue matrix		x			x	x				x		x		x	x	x	x

3. cross out effects that do not differentiate between the alternatives or due to their relative size are of minor importance for the decision.

In the abovementioned evaluation study, as carried out for the government, a combination of a scorecard and an eigenvalue approach was used. First, a scorecard containing the different criterion scores was drawn, and secondly, the criterion scores in combination with different weight sets were transformed to a complete ranking of the alternatives. The eigenvalue method is based on a pairwise comparison of criterion scores using a semi-qualitative scale. This procedure implies a subjective judgement of the criterion scores and therefore does not comply with second-order criterion S12.

In this paper a systematic typological approach has been developed to link available evaluation methods with specific practical evaluation problems. The inability to integrate time, space and uncertainty features of environmental evaluation problems into the analysis turned out to be a major shortcoming of most of the available evaluation methods.

REFERENCES

Changkong, V., Haimes, Y.Y., Multi-Objective Decision Making, Theory and Methodology, North-Holland Publ. Co., Amsterdam, 1983.

Duckstein, L., Bogardi, I. and Gershon, M.E., Multi-Objective Decision Making: Model Choice, Working Paper, IIASA, Laxenburg, 1981.

Hwang, C.L. and Masud, A.S.M. (eds), Multiple Objective Decision Making, Springer, Berlin, 1979.

Janssen, R., Beoordeling van de Gevolgen van Ruilverkaveling met Behulp van Multicriteria Analyse, National Institute for Forestry and Landscape Research, De Dorschkamp, Wageningen, 1984a.

Janssen, R., Evaluatiemethoden ten behoeve van het Milieubeleid- en -Beheer, Economic and Social Institute, Free University, Amsterdam, 1984b.

Lichfield, N., Kettle, P. and Whitbread, M., Evaluation in the Planning Process, Pergamon Press, Oxford, 1975.

McAllister, D.M., Evaluation in Environmental Planning, MIT Press, Cambridge, Mass., 1980.

Ministry of Culture and Recreation, Milieu-Effect Rapport Waterwinning Zuid Kennermerland, Staatsuitgeverij, The Hague, 1981.

Nijkamp, P., Environmental Policy Analysis, Wiley, Chichester/New York, 1981.

Rand Corporation, Protecting an Estuary from Floods: A Policy Analysis of the Oosterschelde, Rand Corporation, Santa Monica, 1977.

Rietveld, P., Multiple Objective Decision Methods and Regional Planning, North-Holland Publ. Co., Amsterdam, 1980.

Voogd, H., Multicriteria Evaluation for Urban and Regional Planning, Pion, London, 1983.

19 An Example of Comparison of Two Decision-Aid Models*

B. Roy and D. Bouyssou

1 INTRODUCTION

i The two competing models

Let us consider a situation where a decision is necessary and where several criteria are involved. The analyst who has to help an actor in such a decision process by using as rigorous a method as possible, generally has the choice between several approaches, which involve several ways of viewing the real world and can lead to significantly different models. The objective of the present study is to compare two of these models that are frequently used, and thus to shed light on two different currents of thought that have been developing on either side of the Atlantic.

The first of the two models derives from multiattribute utility theory. This theory is based on a set of axioms referring to a highly coherent and complete preference system, considered as an objective reality, not influenced by the analyst. His task is therefore supposed to consist merely of delimiting such a preference system and making it explicit. To this end he has to consider that probability distributions can always be used to analyse the uncertainty affecting the evaluations of the various consequences of each solution, alternative, programme or possibility, what we will call actions, relevant to the decision problem. The analyst may then assess using this probabilistic description, partial utility functions u_i (the subscript i referring to an attribute or a 'point of view'), and aggregate them into a global utility function u. It is then a logical consequence of the set of axioms (cf. von Neumann and Morgenstern (1947), Fishburn (1970) and, for a critical discussion, Allais (1953)) that the expected value of the global utility is a criterion representing the preference system. More precisely, for any two actions a, a' :

*This is an abridged version of Roy and Bouyssou (1983)

$$E(u(a')) > E(u(a)) \iff a' \; P \; a$$
$$E(u(a')) = E(u(a)) \iff a' \; I \; a$$

(where P and I represent respectively strict preference and indifference relations). Accordingly, we will call this expected utility criterion a 'true criterion'.

The second model does not claim to deal with an objective reality to be 'described', but with the relationship with reality that the actors of the decision process have or wish to have. This model is thus a construction designed to illuminate possible decisions by means of pragmatic ideas and intentional actions. It is therefore difficult to connect this model with a set of axioms. In addition to probability distributions, it uses dispersion thresholds and discrimination thresholds as a way of defining what is uncertain but also what is imprecise and ill-defined in the evaluation of the consequences of the actions. This model no longer refers to a complete and coherent preference system. It considers instead that, given any two actions a and a', and given their evaluations in terms of different criteria, each of the following statements

"a' is to be considered as at least as good as a" (a' S a),
"a is to be considered as at least as good as a'" (a S a')

can be either accepted, or refused, or, in ambiguous cases, appraised on a scale of credibility. Moreover, the acceptance or refusal of one of the two statements does not imply any information as to the acceptance or refusal of the other; if both statements are refused, the two actions are said to be incomparable.

The definition of such a relation S - which is called an outranking relation- involves not only the thresholds mentioned above, but also diverse variables ('indices of importance' and veto thresholds), whose function is to reflect the respective part to be played by each criterion. The formulas defining S are constructed in such a way as to respect certain qualitative principles, and, in particular, they rule out the possibility that a major disadvantage on one criterion could be compensated for by a large number of minor advantages on other criteria. They do not imply that S should necessarily be transitive or complete. The only justification for such formulas is the application of common sense to these principles.

In contrast with expected utility, S does not in general provide a clear ranking of the actions in the form of a complete preorder. In this approach, the systematic search for such a preorder cannot be justified, and, accordingly, the model only leads to the establishment of a partial preorder. A detailed 'robustness' analysis then allows one to determine which of the comparisons of actions are convincingly justified by the model in spite of the element of arbitrariness in the allocating of values to certain of the parameters (thresholds, indices of importance, ...).

Further details of these models and their theoretical background can be found in Keeney and Raiffa (1976) and Roy (1977, 1978).

ii The methodology of the comparison

In order to compare the two models and, more generally, the two corresponding approaches, we examined a particular example, the siting of a nuclear power plant on the North-West Coast of the United States. The Washington Public Power Supply System (WPPSS) requested Woodward-Clyde Consultants to carry out a study on this subject a few years ago. In many ways, this study seems to be a very good example of the application of the first of the abovementioned approaches. It has been described in a number of papers, most notably by Keeney and Nair (1976) and Keeney and Robillard (1977).

After an initial stage of the study, the set of potential sites was reduced to 9. In order to judge and compare them, 6 points of view were chosen, leading to 6 partial utility functions (and consequently 6 criteria if one is arguing in terms of expected values). Our aim was to carry out the work that could have been done using the outranking model - henceforth model S - instead of the utility one - model U.

iii The objectives of the comparison

We had three objectives in comparing the two different models applied to the same decision situation:

a) to emphasise the different ways in which the two models explored reality and drew on what are officially (and mistakenly) called 'data' (data are more often 'built' than 'given');

b) to understand better the extent to which the two models are arbitrary, vulnerable, realistic or robust (all elements necessary for assessing their respective degrees of reliability);

c) to appreciate better how and when the two models produce similar or different recommendations.

It would certainly have been interesting to attempt to place the comparison on another level: that of their contribution to the decision process, in other words, their acceptability to the different actors and their impact on the course of the process. However, this would have required an experimental study of a different nature from the present one.

The final section of this paper will be devoted to an assessment of the study in terms of these three objectives.

2 THE CRITERIA

i Introduction

The designers of model U used 6 relevant points of view for comparing the sites, which we will accept for the purpose of the present study, assuming that the WPPSS was willing to impose them. The 6 points of view are:

a. the health and security of the population in the surrounding region;
b. the loss of salmonid in streams absorbing the heat from the power-station;
c. the biological effects on the surrounding region (excluding the salmonid loss);
d. the socio-economic impact of the installation;
e. the aesthetic impact of the power lines;
f. the investment costs and the operating costs of the power station.

(Further details may be found in Keeney and Nair (1976)).

The description of the consequences of an action s (the installation of a power station on site s connected with any one of the 6 points of view is clearly not simple. Here again, we based model S on the description carried out by Keeney and Nair in the perspective of model U. We will give details of this description in the next paragraphs. But first we must emphasise what such a description consists of, and how one deduces from it a representation of the preferences in model U vis à vis each point of view. We must also indicate how model S differs in these respects. We will thus see that, in each approach, a distinctive submodel of preference is constructed. This submodel constitutes what is usually called a criterion; it will be denoted g_i for the point of view i.

In model U, it is an a priori condition that the consequences of an action s be describable in terms of 6 random variables $X_i(s)$ $(i=1,...,6)$. Each variable is regarded as an attribute linked to the action in question. The carrying out of this action must be accompanied by a realisation of $X_i(s)$ by means of a random draw according to its probability distribution. The particular value $x_i(s)$ thus realised must encapsulate on its own all the information to be taken into account concerning the point of view considered. The first step must therefore be to determine this information in a concrete fashion, in order to be able to define the attribute and thus make the probability distribution explicit.

In the particular case we are considering, but also in general when dealing with real decision-aid problems, it is accepted in practice that:

- the random variables $X_i(s)$ are probabilistically independent;
- the preference system benefits from two simplifying hypotheses: preferential independence and utility independence (cf. Keeney and Raiffa (1976) and Keeney (1974)).

These two hypotheses [1] together with the classical axioms of utility theory render the following procedure legitimate:

- the analyst questions the person who seems to possess the preference system to be represented, in order to assess a partial utility function $u_i(x)$ related to the point of view i;
- he makes explicit the marginal probability distribution of the attribute $X_i(s)$;
- he calculates the expected value of this partial utility for each of the actions: $g_i(s) = E[u_i(X_i(s)]$;
- in the preference system to be represented, the bigger $g_i(s)$ is, the better s is, other things being equal.

This possibility of comparing any two actions - other things being equal - is a prerequisite for model S. The points of view i must indeed be designed in such a way that these ceteris paribus comparisons constitute an appropriate departure point for the relationships that the analyst must establish between the actors (possibly the decision makers) and their vision of reality. Since the preference system of these actors is no longer regarded as pre-existing in this reality, the existence and the definition of the criteria g_i can no longer be a direct consequence of its observable properties. These criteria should, in particular, be defined in relation to the nature of the information available on each point of view and by taking into account as much as possible the elements of imprecision, uncertainty and indetermination which affect this information. Obviously, there is nothing to prevent a given criterion from taking the form of an expected utility criterion. However, in many cases, probability distributions may appear insufficient for taking into account the whole significance of these elements. In addition, the framework of the true criterion may seem too narrow to describe the conclusions of such comparisons. Model S therefore, leads one to substitute pseudo criteria for the true criteria of model U.

The pseudo criterion induces on the set of actions a structure generalising the semi-order one (see Luce (1956)) by introducing two discrimination thresholds: q_i (the indifference theshold) and p_i (the preference threshold). For the point of view of criterion g_i, we have:

- s' indifferent to s if $|g_i(s') - g_i(s)| \leq q_i$;
- s' strictly preferred to s if $g_i(s') > g_i(s) + p_i$;
- s' weakly preferred to s if $q_i < g_i(s') - g_i(s) \leq p_i$.

In the general case, the thresholds q_i and p_i may be dependent on $g_i(s)$ (or on $g_i(s')$). Further details may be found in Roy and Vincke (1982).

Since the only information available to us was the probabilistic description of model U, such a thorough analysis was not possible here. Consequently, we based the definition of the criteria involved in model S on common sense, although we tried to stay as close as possible to what we believe this part of the study could have been in a real context, with experts and decision makers. The type of reasoning used in the next sections is therefore more important than the precise numerical values elicited.

ii. Case of two criteria n° 1 and 5) based on quantitative single point evaluation

Amongst the 6 attributes used to describe the consequences of the actions in model U, there were two, X_1 and X_5, which were not regarded as random numbers, but as numbers that were known with certainty. In other words, a given site s is characterised in terms of these two points of view by two figures, $x_1(s)$, $x_5(s)$; and this is why we speak in this case of single-point quantitative evaluations. The evaluation on point of view n° 5 being in many ways simpler, we will use it to illustrate the differences between the two models.

The figure $x_5(s)$ represents the length of the high-tension wires (needed to connect the power station to the grid) which will harm the environment if the power station is constructed. For the 9 potential sites, it varies from 0 to 12 miles [1]. Although the measure of this attribute was not regarded as a random variable, it proved necessary to define a utility function $u_5(x_5)$ in order to take this attribute into account in the global preference model. The assessment of this function was carried out using the classical 50-50 lottery technique (cf. Raiffa (1968) and Keeney and Nair (1976)). The results obtained implied a linear expression:

$$u_5(x_5) = 1 - \frac{x_5}{50} .$$

It follows that the true criterion g_5 of model U is simply:

$$g_5(s) = 1 - \frac{x_5(s)}{50} .$$

Within model S, a criterion associated with this point of view could have been defined by letting $g_5(s) = x_5(s)$. Nevertheless, this number does not seem to be precise enough for one to be able to say that, if two sites s and s' are characterised respectively by:

$$x_5(s) = 10,\ x_5(s') = 9 ,$$

then site s' can necessarily be regarded (other things being equal) as significantly better than site S. The difference of one mile may indeed not seem convincing, given the uncertainty in the situating of the power lines and especially the arbitrariness inherent in the choice of the sections of line to be taken into consideration. We did not have access to the information necessary for evaluating the influence of these factors, and we consequently assumed that $x_5(s)$ was not known within an interval whose size grew with the distance involved but remaining no less than 1 mile for short distances. It seemed reasonable to choose a very low rate of growth: 3% (a rate of 10% would not have changed the results). This amounts to saying that $g_5(s) = x_5(s)$ is ill-determined over an interval of the form:

$$[g_5(s) - \eta_5(g_5(s)) \; ; \; g_5(s) + \eta_5 g_5(s))]$$

with $\eta_5(s) = 1 + \frac{3}{100} g_5(s)$.

The function η_5 characterises what is called a dispersion threshold (cf. Roy (1979-1982), Chapter 8). General formulas (cf. Roy and Bouyssou (1983), Appendix 4) can be used to deduce the two discrimination thresholds which complete the definition of the pseudo criterion g_5 :

indifference threshold: $q_5(g_5(s)) = 1 + \frac{3}{100} g_5(s)$
preference threshold : $p_5(g_5(s)) \simeq 2.0618 + 0.0618\, g_5(s)$.

iii The case of two criteria (n° 3 and 4) based on non single-point qualitative evaluations

To define the attributes X_3 and X_4, Keeney and Nair introduced two qualitative scales having respectively 8 and 7 adjacent intervals. The nature of the biological or socio-economic impact, covered by each interval, was determined by means of relatively concrete and precise descriptions of the future situation. For each of the two attributes and for each site s, approximately 10 experts were asked to use such descriptions to characterise the outcome which, in their view, seemed most probable in the hypothesis of the power station being constructed on that site. The proportion of votes received by each interval was used to define the (subjective) probability distributions of $X_3(s)$ and $X_4(s)$.

Two utility functions, $u_3(x_3)$ and $u_4(x_4)$ were then assessed (using a particular technique adapted to the qualitative nature of these scales, cf Keeney and Nair (1976)), $g_3(x_3)$ and $g_4(x_4)$ corresponding respectively to the expected utility of $X_3(s)$ and $X_4(s)$.

Once again, it is important to point out that we would have used a similar method to evaluate the biological and socio-economic impacts on the potential sites. The evaluation obtained by Keeney and Nair (a distribution of the experts' opinions, involving in general more than one interval of the scale in question) is called a 'non single-point one'. In order to define $g_3(s)$ and $g_4(s)$, only one of the intervals considered by the experts must be chosen. We selected the interval nearest the centre, that is the one which divides the experts most equally into those who are at least as optimistic and those who are at least as pessimistic as this value. Given the nature of the scales in question, constant discrimination thresholds were adopted. After examining the distributions of the experts' opinions, we used:

$$q_3 = 1, \; p_3 = 2 \; ,$$

$$q_4 = 0, \; p_4 = 1 \; .$$

iv Case of a criterion (n° 6) based on non single-point quantitative evaluations

The authors of model U considered that the investment and operating costs of a power station located on a site could be appraised relative to the costs of the cheapest site s_2. The attribute $X_6(s)$ therefore reflects a differential cost. It was supposed that the insufficient knowledge affecting this cost could be modelled by treating $X_6(s)$ as a normal random variable with a standard deviation equal to a quarter of its expected value. This expected value was estimated by the values $\bar{x}_6(s)$ varying from 0 to 17.7 (in millions of dollars per year, cf. Roy and Bouyssou (1983), Appendix 3). Let us point out that it is sure that $X_6(s_2) = 0$.

The criterion $g_6(s)$ of the model U is the expected utility of this random differential cost. Again invoking the lottery technique, the utility function $u_6(x_6)$ was defined as:

$$u_6(x_6) = 1 + 2{,}3 \; (1 - e^{0.009 \; x_6}) \; .$$

Once again, we would probably have constructed model S in a different way. Since it is not the same actors who are responsible for the investment and running costs, we would perhaps have introduced a criterion for each of them. But because we cannot analyse these costs in detail in the present study, we will merely set:

$$g_6(s) = \bar{x}_6(s) \; .$$

Lacking a more objective foundation, we can use the following reasoning to determine dispersion thresholds. Firstly, the values of $\bar{x}_6(s)$ which were suggested contain the assumption that the investment and running costs that are not included in the differential cost will actually lead to the same expenses as on site s_2 as on any other site s. This is obviously a source of sufficient error to cast into doubt the whole idea that a site s' is more economical than a site s when $\bar{x}_6(s) - \bar{x}_6(s')$ is small. We decided, on the basis of this single hypothesis, that the 'real' differental cost had to be regarded as ill-determined on an asymmetrical interval: $[\bar{x}_6(s) - 1 ; \bar{x}_6(s) + 2]$.

Secondly, the calculation of $\bar{x}_6(s)$ follows on from the evaluation of multiple factors which all involve specific expenses for site s. But the study carried out on each site remains brief until the construction is actually decided. In other words, these costs are not necessarily the only ones: they are relatively imprecise and possibly too optimistic. The margin of error resulting is asymmetric and its size is proportional to $\bar{x}_6(s)$ itself. The factors involved here seem to have no connection with the ones taken into account previously. We shall therefore assume that the effects can be added together. We have the following dispersion threshold:

$$[\bar{x}_6(s) - 1 - 0.1\,\bar{x}_6(s),\ \bar{x}_6(s) + 2 + 0.5\,\bar{x}_6(s)]\ .$$

Thus:

$$q_6(g_6(s))=1.1 + 0.11\,g_6(s),\ p_6(g_6(s))= 3.33 + 0.67\,g_6(s).$$

We refer to Roy and Bouyssou (1983) for a study of criteria 2, which is far more complex than the preceding ones. Let us simply mention that model S uses two different alternative forms of g_2 (g'_2 and g''_2) because of the difficulties encountered in order to take this point of view into account.

3 AGGREGATION OF THE CRITERIA AND GLOBAL PREFERENCE

i Introduction

Having in this way defined the true criteria of model U and the pseudo criteria of model S, we will now present the part of the model dealing with their aggregation. In the present section, we will briefly describe the parameters involved in the aggregation phase of each model. The following two sections will be devoted to the evaluation of these parameters.

Assuming that the WPPSS's preference system is a pre-existing entity that it conforms to the axioms of utility theory, that the hypotheses of independence mentioned in Section 1.ii are acceptable, and that the responses to the questions posed in order to assess the partial utility functions were governed by this preference system implies (using a general theorem - cf. Keeney and Raiffa (1976)) that this preference system is representable by means of a true criterion g(s) defined in terms of the criteria $g_i(s)$ by one of the following two expressions:

$$g(s) = \sum_{i=1}^{i=6} k_i . g_i(s) \quad \text{with} \sum_{i=1}^{i=6} k_i = 1 \tag{1}$$

$$g(s) = \frac{1}{k} [\prod_{i=1}^{i=6} (1 + k.k_i.g_i(s)) - 1] \text{ with} \tag{2}$$

$$k \neq 0,\ k \geq -1,\ k = \prod_{i=1}^{i=6} (1 + k.k_i) - 1. \tag{3}$$

The last expression of g(s) was the one chosen by Keeney and Nair (we will see the reasons why in Section 3.ii). In order to complete the characterisation of model U, it is consequently sufficient to assess the coefficients k_i (whose values increase with the relative importance attached to criterion i, once the utility functions have been defined) and to deduce the value of k from then by solving equation (3), which normally has only one non-zero root greater than -1 (cf. Keeney and Nair (1976)).

In model S - which corresponds to ELECTRE III (cf. Roy (1978)) - the aim is no longer to use the pseudo criteria $g_i(s)$ to determine a true criterion, or even a pseudo criterion. The more modest aim is to compare each site s to site s' on the basis of their values on each g_i, taking into account the thresholds q_i and p_i, and hence to adopt a position on the acceptance, the refusal or, more generally, the credibility of the proposition:

" site s is at least as good as site s' ".

As we pointed out in Section I.ii, this credibility depends on pragmatic rules of simple common sense, rules which are mainly based on notions called concordance and discordance. These notions allow one:

- to characterise a group of criteria judged concordant with the proposition studied, and to assess the relative importance of this group of criteria within the set of the 6 criteria;
- to characterise amongst the criteria not compatible with the proposition being studied, those which are sufficiently in opposition to reduce the credibility resulting from the taking into considera-

ation of the concordance itself, and to calculate the possible reduction that would result from this.

In order to be able to carry out such calculations, we must express in explicitly numerical fashion:

- the relative importance k_i accorded by the decision maker to criterion i in calculating the concordance;

- the minimum level of discordance giving to criterion i the power of withdrawing all credibility from the proposition being studied, in the case where this criterion is the only one of the 6 which is not in concordance with the proposition: this minimum level is called the veto threshold of criterion i; it is not necessarily a constant, and therefore we will denote it $v_i[g_i(s)]$.

It is important to emphasise that model S is different from model U in that the indices of importance (and also the veto thresholds) are not values stemming from the observation of a pre-existing variable but values designed to convey deliberate positions adopted by the decision maker, positions which are mainly of a qualitative nature. It follows that the techniques to be applied in order to evaluate the parameters we have just discussed for both models reflect two different attitudes towards reality (cf. 5.i) even more than the criteria do.

ii Modulation of the importance of the criteria

Within model U, the assessment of the scaling constants k_i is carried out by means of lottery comparisons.

Let us denote $\tilde{x}_i$ and $\underset{\sim}{x}_i$ the respective values used to scale the partial utility function u_i between 0 and 1. We have $u_i(\underset{\sim}{x}_i) = 0$ and $u_i(\tilde{x}_i) = 1$. Let us consider the following two multidimensional lotteries. The first one L_1 is a degenerate lottery resulting for sure in an 'imaginary site' which receives the worst evaluations on all the criteria except j, where its evaluation is $\tilde{x}_j$. The second lottery L_2 give rise to another imaginary site whose evaluation is either the best possible on all the criteria with probability p, or the worst possible on all the criteria with probability (1 - p).

The expected utility of L_2 is p; and the utility of L_1 is k_j in the multiplicative representation (2) - and indeed also in the additive one (1). If the decision maker is able to determine that particular probability p which guarantees indifference between the two lotteries, we can state $k_j = p$.

By iterating this procedure, one can therefore - in principle - assess the 6 coefficients k_i, and hence k, the solution to equation (3). The designers of model U used, in the end:

$k_1 = 0.358$; $k_2 = 0.218$; $k_3 = 0.013$; $k_4 = 0.104$; $k_5 = 0.059$; $k_6 = 0.400$.

One can observe that $\sum_{i=1}^{6} k_i = 1.152 \neq 1$, which justifies the choice of the multiplicative structure (cf. Keeney (1974)).

Solving equation (3) then gives $k = -0.3316$.

In model S, the only influence of the indices of importance is the ranking they impose of the different criteria or groups of criteria. If we had carried out the study, we probably would have tried to assess such a ranking interactively with the decision makers of the WPPSS. We would then have tried to find various sets of indices of importance compatible with these merely ordinal considerations.

Without access to the decision makers, we had to try to 'translate' the information conveyed by the utility function concerning the relative importance of the criteria into indices of importance, to attempt to produce a comparable system of values and hence to ensure that the comparison of the results of the two methods was still meaningful. The technique used is detailed in Roy and Bouyssou (1983, Appendix 7).

iii The veto thresholds

As veto thresholds convey deliberate and 'intentional' positions, they cannot be 'assessed'. It seemed reasonable in all cases to take the thresholds $v_j(g_j(s))$ as multiples of the preference thresholds $p_j(g_j(s))$ (not that there is necessarily any fixed link between these two figures). We imagined that the less important the criterion the larger the value of the coefficient α_j such that $v_j(g_j(s)) = \alpha_j \, p_j(g_j(s))$.

4 CONTENTS AND PRESENTATION OF THE RECOMMENDATIONS

One can summarise the results of model U in the following way [2]:

Table 4.1

Rank	Site	g(s)
1	s_3	0.926
2	s_2	0.920
3	s_1	0.885
4	s_4	0.883
5	s_8	0.872
6	s_9	0.871
7	s_7	0.862
8	s_5	0.813
9	s_6	0.804

The ranking obtained is therefore a complete ordering.

The authors of model U carried out a sensitivity analysis on this ordering. Nevertheless, the fact that they disposed of an axiomatic basis and that they had obtained the various data (shapes of utility functions, values of the k_i) by questioning persons supposed to represent the decision maker, led them to affect an analysis only of 'marginal' modifications of the data. This resulted in a virtually complete stability of the ordering vis à vis these modifications (cf. Keeney and Nair (1976)).

The robustness analysis is a crucial part of model S. We present in Roy and Bouyssou (1983, Appendices 9 and 10) the overall robustness analysis (which involves more than 100 different sets of parameters) and the results obtained.

We will merely observe here, of all the possible sources of variation, the form of criterion 2 selected (g_2' or g_2'') has the greatest influence.

The totality of these results may be represented, in very brief and qualitative form, as two graphs, corresponding respectively to the g_2' form and the g_2'' form of criterion 2 (the influence of the other parameters being less important). Figure 4.1 shows representative outranking graphs.

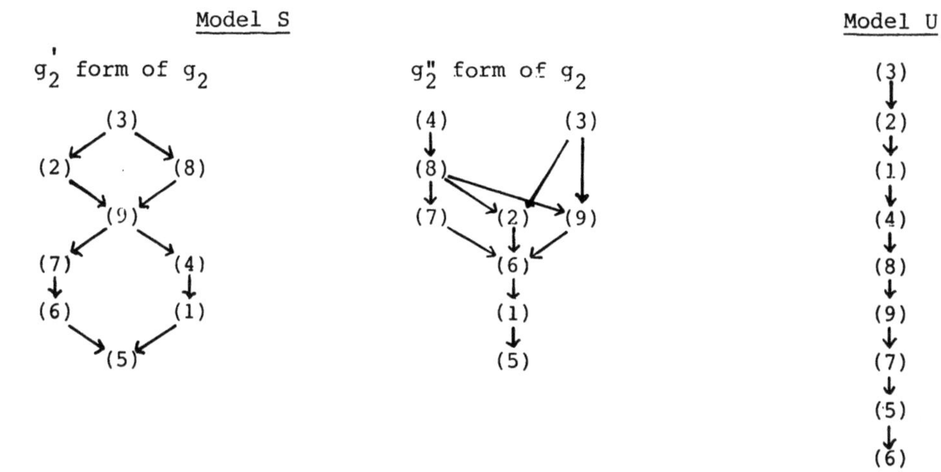

Figure 4.1.

The transitivity arcs have been omitted; two sites not connected by an arc (not considering the transitivity ones) are incomparable. The graph given for model U is a diagrammatic representation of Table 4.1.

iii The recommendations

The study of the ranking provided by model U shows that S_5 and S_6 can safely be eliminated from further stages of the study, and that S_3 and S_2 are in the leading positions with S_1 and S_4 just behind (cf. Table 4.1 and Figure 4.1).

The analysis of the results of model S (cf. Figure 4.2 and Roy and Bouyssou (1983, Appendix 10)) shows that there is a remarkable stability at the bottom of the ranking, with S_5, S_6 and S_1. Site S_3 is in the leading place, whatever form of criterion 2 is chosen. S_2, S_8 and S_4 are just behind, whereas S_7 and S_9 are to be found in a zone of instability in the middle.

Like the authors of model U, we would have recommended S_3, if the WPPSS had required that only one site be chosen. On the other hand, there is a major divergence between the two models concerning the position of S_1 and, to a certain extent, S_8 (we will come back to this point in Section 5.iii).

5 CONCLUSIONS

i The origin and the treatment of the data

In model U, the procedures used to assess the different parameters involved in the definition of the global utility function (partial utility functions $u_i(s)$, coefficients k_i) follow logically from the set of axioms underlying the analysis. These axioms imply that lottery comparisons can always be used to carry out this estimation.

This position is unassailable on the formal level, but the number of questions raised - and their complexity - imply that the decision maker (or his representative - cf. Section 4.ii) is obliged to collaborate closely with the analyst. The legitimacy of these techniques is inseparable from the hypothesis that a complete system of preference pre-exists in a form which is implicit but which is nevertheless in line with the axioms in the decision maker's mind [3]. It must also be assumed that the replies given by this decision maker or his representatives are in fact governed by such an implicit system, and that this system is not likely to be fundamentally altered during the dialogue with the analyst. The urgency of the decision problem to be solved and the analyst's experience then create the necessary conditions for the disclosure of these attitudes which are represented in terms of a utility function. When certain opinions brought up are in contradiction with the axioms defining the coherence, it is assumed that the normative character of the axioms (completeness, transitivity, independence) is sufficiently obvious for the decision maker to adapt his views of them (cf. Morgenstern (1979)). In such a perspective - unlike that prevailing in most of the other social sciences - the axioms of the formal model are also behavioural axioms - and, when necessary, normative axioms. This attitude underlies most of the studies based on model U. It explains why analysts place such great confidence in the data they gather and why they virtually never fundamentally question them when the sensitivity analysis is carried out.

The same is true when evaluating the consequences of the actions. The probability distributions provided by the experts are thus rarely questioned, even when they are clearly imprecise and/or arbitrary (cf. criteria 6 of the power station study). Once again, 'marginal' sensitivity analyses are carried out that imply generally a high level of stability in the ranking obtained.

Model S has no axiomatic basis, and consequently it is often difficult to interpret certain parameters used in it (veto thresholds, indices of importance). Only considerations based on common sense allow the decision maker and the analyst to give them a numerical value. This explains why the results produced by model S are significant only when the analyst has carried out a major robustness analysis, systematically exploring the numerical values of the parameters compatible with the qualitative 'data' he started with. This procedure should not be considered as merely a paliative for the lack of axiomatic foundations and the lack of sophisticated techniques for assessing the parameters, but constitutes instead one of the original features of the approach, which consists of trying to design a preference system and not of trying to represent an existing system in the most accurate way possible.

The difference observed between the two approaches in the way they obtain the data are in fact connected with a much deeper division: the one between a model drawing validity from a 'descriptive' aim of representing a pre-existing relation and a model whose validity is based on a 'constructive' aim of designing an acceptable preference relation in collaboration with the decision maker. Sophisticated assessment procedures only draw meaning with relation to a given reality, which must be adhered to as closely as possible.

ii Robustness and fragility of the approaches

The distinction between a 'constructive' attitude and a 'descriptive' one illustrates the relative advantages and disadvantages of models U and S. If the decision maker is clearly identified and possesses a sufficiently precise and stable preference structure, one can certainly adopt a purely descriptive attitude. Nevertheless, we consider that in most real decision-aid problems, an attitude of a constructive nature is inevitable.

Every decision forms part of the social structure of the organisation, which is often complex and conflicting, meaning that often the only single decision maker one can talk about is a fictional entity (see Walliser (1979) and Roy (1979-1982), Chapter 2)). It is then difficult to assume a collective group of decision processes for a pre-existing and coherent preference.

In fact, the designers of model U did not assess the various parameters included in the global utility function by questioning the decision maker(s) of the WPPSS (cf. Section 4.ii), but by using judgements provided by the study team itself. This practice is frequent in studies based on model U, and can cause reasonable doubt as to the reliability of the assessment procedures of the utility function: it implies that sensitivity analyses of the same scope as for model S may be necessary.

Once one has accepted the advantages - and even the necessity - of a constructive approach, one can understand better the implications of an axiomatic basis for decision-aid models. For many people, the attraction of an axiomatic basis is the legitimacy it apparently confers to their work. But this legitimacy is valid only for the 'theory' and not for the 'model' which is an 'interpretation' and a putting into practice of the 'theory'. Model U is based on a formal theory for representing an existing preference system. It is hard to imagine what a design theory of a preference system could be - a theory that would underly model S. If the axiomatic basis legitimises the theory, it does not follow that it does the same for the model. The legitimacy of the model must be sought in the effectiveness with which it enables the actors to arrive at convictions (possibly upsetting preconceptions) and to communicate with other people. A decision-aid model must not be merely a formal theory, but must form the basis for an interaction with reality and for an action on reality.

Finally, let us point out that model U can conceivably be used in a constructive perspective. This is in fact what is really done in most studies. However, model U should be considered in this case independently of its axiomatic basis: one should study the reliability of the assessment procedures of the partial utility functions and of the constants k_i as tools designed to construct and/or enrich the decision maker's preference relation between the actions.

Many of the misunderstandings in comparing models S and U seem to stem from the fact that model U designed in terms of a constructive attitude but only draws a particular legitimacy from its axiomatic basis if it derives from a descriptive attitude.

iii Agreement amongst recommendations

In Section 4.iii, we observed that, if there was a certain agreement in the recommendations on site S_3, there were also differences: the positioning of site S_1, in particular, was controversial. Model U ranked S_1 as amongst the best sites studied, while model S recommended that it be dropped from later stages of the study. In the same way, site S_8 is considered as a 'good' site in model S, but appears in the middle of the ranking in model U.

These disagreements in the two models reflect the contrasts in the qualitative principles underlying them, especially concerning the reliability of the differences between the evaluations on the different criteria and the more or less compensatory nature of their aggregation. Site S_1 (cf. Roy and Bouyssou (1983), Appendices 3 and 5) is evaluated very highly on most of the criteria (g_3, g_4, g_5, g_6), but receives the worst possible evaluation on health and security (g_1) and salmonid loss (g_2). Model S, being partially compensatory, ranks such a profile near the bottom whereas model U (perfectly compensatory) places the site among the best, because of its very good scores on many criteria.

Inversely, site S_8 may be interpreted as an average 'compromise' site (cf. Roy and Bouyssou (1983), Appendices 3 and 5), and is well-placed in model S; but in model U, it appears lower down, behind other sites where good performances on certain criteria compensate very bad ones on others.

In addition, conclusions of too great a generality should not be drawn from the good agreement of the recommendations on site S_3. An intuitive examination of the evaluations of this action shows that it seems to be a good site in terms of the information available. It is therefore 'normal' for S_3 to be in the first place in both methods. A good part of the agreement obtained is thus peculiar to the problem studied (in another problem, a site of type S_1 could have appeared at the top in model U).

Given such a fundamental opposition in the qualitative principles underlying the two models, it is not at all surprising that they culminate in dissimilar recommendations.

In our view, these inevitable disagreements do not imply that decision-aid is useless but simply that a single problem may have several valid responses. Given that two different decision-aid models cannot be implemented in the same decision process, the decision maker must be conscious of the qualitative choices implied by the different models

- often conveying the analyst's own ethical choices - before coming to personal conclusions on the choice to be made. In this domain, the many different approaches reflect in our view the complexity of the researcher's task much more than a scientific weakness.

NOTES

[1] All the numerical data used in models U and S can be found in Roy and Bouyssou (1983).

[2] The results in this paper are the ones we obtained by calculating from the data published in the articles quoted. They are slightly different from those given by Keeney and Nair (1976).

[3] In actual studies, the decision maker is supposed to be able to express a set of fundamental attitudes compatible with the axioms. Comparing complex actions is then equivalent to an extrapolation of those attitudes, whose validity is guaranteed by the set of axioms.

REFERENCES

Allais, M., 'Le comportement de l'homme rationnel devant le risque: Critique des postulats et axiomes de l'Ecole Américaine', Econometrica, vol. 21, no. 4, 1953, pp. 503-546.

Fishburn, P.C., Utility Theory for Decision Making, Wiley, New York, 1970.

Keeney, R.L., 'Multiplicative utility functions', Operations Research, 22, 1973, pp. 22-34.

Keeney, R.L. and Nair, K., 'Evaluating potential nuclear power plan sites in the Pacific Northwest using decision analysis', IIASA Professional Paper, no. 76-1; also in Bell, D.E., Keeney, R.L., Raiffa, H. (eds), Conflicting Objectives in Decisions, Chapter 14, Wiley, 1977 and in Keeney, R.L., Sitting Energy Facilities, Chapter 3, Academic Press, New York, 1980.

Keeney, R.L. and Raiffa, H., Decision with Multiple Objectives - Preference and Value Tradeoffs, Wiley, New York, 1976.

Keeney, R.L. and Robillard, G.A., 'Assessing and evaluating environmental impacts at proposed nuclear power plant sites', Journal of Environmental Economics and Management 4, 1977, pp. 153-166.

Luce, R.D., 'Semiorders and a theory of utility discrimination', Econometrica, vol. 24, 1956, pp. 178-191.

Morgenstern, O., 'Some reflections on utility', in: Allais, M. and Hagen, O. (eds), Expected Utility Hypotheses and the Allais Paradox, D. Reidel Publ. Co., Dordrecht, 1979.

Raiffa, H., Decision Analysis, Addison-Wesley, 1968.

Roy, B., 'Partial preference analysis and decision aid: The fuzzy outranking relation concept', in: Bell, D.E., Keeney, R.L., Raiffa, H. (eds), Conflicting Objectives in Decisions, Wiley, New York, 1977, pp. 40-75.

Roy, B., 'ELECTRE III: Un algorithme de classements fondé sur une représéntation floue des préférences en présence de critères multiples', Cahiers du CERO, vol. 20, no. 1, 1978, pp. 3-24.

Roy, B., L'aide à la Décision - Critères Multiples et Optimisation pour Choisir, Trier, Ranger, Book in preparation, Université de Paris-Dauphine, Documents du LAMSADE no. 4, 5, 9, 15, 19, 1979-1982.

Roy, B. and Bouyssou, D., Comparaison, sur un Cas Précis, de Deux Modèles Concurrents d'Aide à la Décision, Université de Paris-Dauphine, Document du LAMSADE no. 22, 1983, 102 p.

Roy, B., Vincke, Ph., Relational Systems of Preference with One or Several Pseudo-Criteria: New Concepts and New Results, Université de Paris-Dauphine, Cahier du LAMSADE no. 28, 1982, 29 p.

Von Neumann, J. and Morgenstern, O., Theory of Games and Economic Behavior, 2nd edition, Princeton University Press, New Jersey, 1947.

Walliser, B., Analyse Critique de l'Approche Rationelle des Processus de Décision, Ministère de l'Economie, Direction de la Prévision, 1979, 42 p. + 96 p.

Zeleny, M., Multiple Criteria Decision Making, McGraw-Hill, New York, 1981.

20 Multiple Criteria Analysis in Energy Planning and Policy Assessment

M. Grauer

1 INTRODUCTION

The explosive growth in the market price of energy (especially of oil) over the last decade or so has made the question of future energy supplies a major political issue in almost all countries of the world. Decisions concerning energy supply can have far-reaching consequences influencing, among other things, the quality of the environment, the state of the economy (balance of trade deficit, unemployment), the level of dependence on foreign energy sources, the standard of living of the population and the national distribution of costs and benefits. All of these factors should be considered in energy planning and policy assessment - the main objectives of this process are discussed in Section 2.

Analytic models may be used to help decision makers to cope with the wide range of issues related to the energy problem. Energy models have been developed for planning purposes at the regional, national and international levels; their scope ranges from engineering models of different energy conversion technologies, through sectoral models dealing with demand and/or supply of particular fuels and models encompassing the entire energy system, to models describing the energy system as an integral part of the economic system. A survey of these energy models is given in Section 3. Section 4 presents a multicriteria energy analysis based on a specific energy model (the energy-supply model MESSAGE developed at IIASA) and the reference-point optimisation method. The purpose of this case study is to demonstrate how multiple criteria analysis can be used to identify and quantify the tradeoffs, over time, between different, not directly comparable, objectives, and thus to assist policy makers to arrive at decisions which achieve the best possible compromise between conflicting strategic goals.

2 MAIN AIMS IN ENERGY PLANNING

When analysing the future development of an energy system it is necessary (i) to consider a number of quantifiable objectives, (ii) to take into account non-quantifiable objectives and (iii) to study the time dependence of these objectives and thus the interplay between them over time. A detailed discussion of which objectives can be included in an analytic model and which resist quantification is given in Cherniavsky (1981). The particular social impacts of decisions connected with energy research and development in The Netherland are discussed in Lootsma et al. 1984. The hierarchical structure of objectives in this case is presented in Figure 1: although this figure is based on the Dutch situation the objectives are quite general and include many currently crucial criteria such as impact on balance of payments effects on employment and environmental aspects.

Factors (i)-(iii) are taken into account in the case study using methodology derived from the paradigm of satisficing decision making, which makes it possible to combine the 'hard' information obtained from analytic energy models with 'soft' information on, for example, the social or political impacts of particular decisions. The 'soft' information is incorporated by involving the decision maker in an interactive dialogue with the computerised decision support system. This ensures that the decision process is an adaptive learning procedure driven by the decision maker. The achievement scalarising approach and its applications are discussed in more detail in Grauer et al. 1984.

3 A SURVEY OF ENERGY MODELS

It is now realised that the development of realistic energy models requires the use of theoretical and analytical methods from several disciplines: engineering, econometrics, operations research and computer sciences. The reasons for this lie in the history of energy modelling, which goes back some twenty years to the 1960s. Although efforts to develop energy models began well before the first oil crisis in 1973, it was growing awareness of the energy problem event that brought about an explosion in energy modelling.

The energy models developed in the sixties focussed mainly upon the

Energy R&D should help to achieve a well-balanced national energy economy and to consolidate the ability of Dutch industry to compete on both home and foreign markets					
Thus, the aims of energy R & D should be					
To diversify and secure energy supply by:	To increase energy efficiency by:	To increase the social acceptability of new energy systems by:	To create innovative industrial activity by:	To facilitate long-term energy management by:	To promote high-level scientific activity by:
• minimizing strategic risks	• improving extraction, conversion, distribution, and consumption technologies	• adapting modern energy systems to demands related to public health, safety & environmental protection	• urgent updating of technical know-how and implementation of modern technology	• achieving a sustainable society	• long-term industrial development
• studying short- & long-term availability of supplies	• development of high-yield technologies	• awareness of pressure groups pro & con	• exploiting advantages related to the Dutch energy position and industry	• funding basic R&D or research aimed at a breakthrough	• creating and maintaining scientific "cutting edges"
• studying technological & economic feasibility of supply options	• reduction of energy demand	• studying problems faced by public authorities	• studying commercial feasibility	• addressing problems connected with the depletion of finite high-quality energy sources	• exploiting specific features of Dutch R&D
• studying the flexibility & adaptability of existing & new facilities	• utilization of residues		• studying the impact on employment	• management of uncertainty in the long-term development of energy prices	• promoting international interest in results
• studying the impact on the balance of payments			• studying the impact on other developments in science and industry		

Figure 1. Hierarchy of main objectives of energy R&D in The Netherlands (based on (2))

supply and demand of a single form of energy or fuel such as electricity, oil and natural gas. Faced with the complex problem of optimal allocation and routing of crude oil and oil products between different sources, refineries and demand centres, the petroleum companies have developed (and used) particularly large allocation models, as well as models of the defining process Rath-Nagel and Voss (1981). Another example of a successful application of sectoral models is provided by the models used to analyse the operation of electricity plants. These models may be used to evaluate the optimal expansion strategy of a power plant system that has to satisfy an increased electricity demand. The models determine the technology mix and time of introduction of new power plants that satisfies the electricity demand over the planning horizon at minimum discounted overall cost (i.e., capital, fuel and operating costs). This multiple criteria problem is usually solved as a single-objective problem by assigning weights (discounted rates) to the different criteria.

Both of the energy models described above focus on the supply side, that is, on the best way to satisfy an assumed energy demand. Energy demand is an exogenous input to these models and is often provided by econometric demand models which estimate energy or fuel demand as a function of energy prices and other determinants such as population, economic growth, etc.

A major criticism made of sectoral, single-fuel or energy form models is that they treat the development of the sector or fuel in question in isolation from the rest of the energy and economic system, thereby ignoring the fact that there are many different ways to satisfy demand for, say, space heat, industrial process heat and transportation. A sectoral, single-fuel model cannot adequately describe the interfuel substitution brought about by changing energy prices, technological development or environmental considerations in the different sectors of energy use.

The need to take these factors into account was the main reason for the development of models which describe the energy flows from different primary energy sources through various conversion and utilisation processes to different end users. Work on these energy systems began in the early 1970s.

Figure 2 shows an energy reference system which can be viewed as a single static energy system model of the type described above.

Most energy system models are based on network representations and the energy balance approach. Using a network describing the flow of resources (coal, oil, gas, nuclear power, solar power) to various demand sectors (industrial, transportation, commercial, household) as a simple accounting framework, it is possible to stimulate and evaluate the consequences of different ways of satisfying an estimated increase in demand in each of the major end-user sectors in terms of primary energy consumption, required conversion capacity, etc. This type of model may also be extended to analyse the impact of alternative energy supply strategies on the environment (e.g., the effects of acid rain).

In addition to the development of network accounting models, work on a process of optimising models of energy systems was initiated at the beginning of the 1970s. These models were designed to determine the optimal allocation of energy sources and conversion technologies to end-users using a network representation of the energy system. The models are either static, with the optimisation process seeking to minimise costs for a single target year, or they are quasi-dynamic, attempting to minimise the present values of the total costs over the whole planning horizon, subject to the demand and to a set of constraints reflecting resource availabilities and/or environmental considerations.

Accounting and optimisation models of the types described above focus on the technical structure of the energy systems and usually take the energy demand as an exogenous input. With demand as a fixed input, these models do not allow for the variations in demand due to higher energy prices or to changed GNP growth caused by rising energy costs and limited energy supplies. To take this into account it is necessary to have models which link the energy system with the rest of the economy. Most of the more recent energy modelling work is concerned with the area of energy/economy/environment interaction. Linear programming techniques have been used far more than other mathematical programming methods in this type of work because of their capacity for solving large problems. Linear programming models formulated in terms of energy flows also provide useful economic information about the optimal solution via shadow prices.

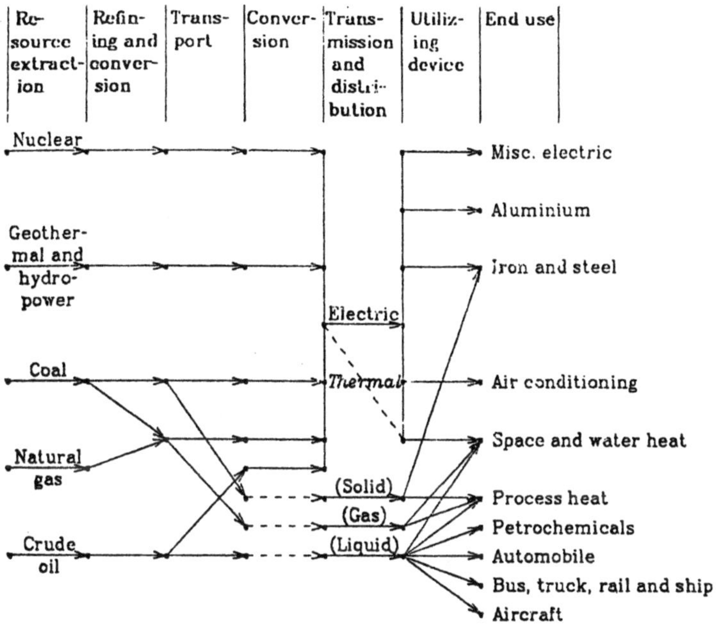

Figure 2. Energy reference system (Ormerod 1980)

A number of energy models based on input-output techniques, the system dynamic approach or the methods of game theory have also been developed.

Table 1 lists several well-known energy models, together with the methodology used and their principle applications.

4 A CASE STUDY IN MULTIPLE CRITERIA ENERGY STRATEGY EVALUATION

This section describes an experiment based on the achievement scalarising approach to multicriteria analysis, and the energy-supply model MESSAGE (Schrattenholzer 1981). In its original form, MESSAGE is a dynamic linear programming model (see Table 1) with the single objective of minimising the total discounted costs of meeting a set of energy demands over a given time horizon. The experiment described in Grauer et al. (1982) shows that it is possible to consider more than one objective and thus to study the interplay between costs and other

Table 1.

A survey of energy models (based on (4) and (7))

		MODEL	METHODOLOGY	APPLICATION
ENERGY SYSTEM MODELS		BESOM (Brookhaven)	Linear optimization	Evaluation of energy technologies for US R&D policy.
ENERGY SYSTEM MODELS		EFOM (Grenoble)	Linear optimization	Originally built to develop energy scenarios for France. Now used within the CEC set of models for policy assessment.
ENERGY SYSTEM MODELS		MARKAL (Brookhaven/ Jülich)	Linear optimization	Optimization of end-use and supply side. Applied to 15 countries of the IEA for evaluation of new and conservation technologies.
ENERGY SYSTEM MODELS		MESSAGE (IIASA)	Linear optimization	Applied to 7 world regions in the context of IIASA's set of models.
ENERGY-ECONOMY MODELS	INTEGRATED MODELS	ETA–MACRO (Stanford Univ.)	Non-linear optimization, informal econometric	Studies of nuclear and alternative energy systems in the US.
ENERGY-ECONOMY MODELS	INTEGRATED MODELS	PILOT (Stanford Univ.)	Dynamic linear optimization	Exploration of energy and economic growth in the US.
ENERGY-ECONOMY MODELS	INTEGRATED MODELS	Soviet Union	Dynamic linear optimization	Study of the interconnected balanced growth of energy and the economy in the Soviet Union.
ENERGY-ECONOMY MODELS	INTEGRATED MODELS	SRI (Stanford Res. Inst.)	Process representation, informal econometric	Analysis of US synfuels strategy.
ENERGY-ECONOMY MODELS	INTEGRATED MODELS	HUDSON–JORGENSON	Econometric	Long-term energy and economic growth analysis of the US. Taxing policy in the US.
ENERGY-ECONOMY MODELS	INTEGRATED MODELS	ESPM (Bechtel Co.)	Accounting	Framework for energy supply planning and accounting of industrial, capital, labor and material requirements. Applied to the US and developing countries (Peru, Egypt, Indonesia).
ENERGY-ECONOMY MODELS	INTEGRATED MODELS	PIES (Project Independence Evaluation System)	Process representation, linear optimization, econometric	Analysis of alternative strategies for the national energy plan of the US.
ENERGY-ECONOMY MODELS	MODEL SETS	DRI–BROOKHAVEN [combination of Hudson–Jorgenson and BESOM models]	Linear optimization, econometric	Studies of economic impact of alternative energy futures in the US.
ENERGY-ECONOMY MODELS	MODEL SETS	CEC (Brussels) [combination of macro-economic growth, energy demand, input–output and energy-supply models]	Linear optimization, econometric	Application to member countries of the European Communities for Energy System Studies.
ENERGY-ECONOMY MODELS	MODEL SETS	IIASA (Laxenburg) [combination of macro-economic, energy-demand, energy-supply and energy-impact models]	Linear optimization, econometric	Applied to studies of the energy/economy growth of 7 world regions. Investigations of energy strategy impacts.

factors such as import dependence, the need to develop infrastructure, and so on. The main purpose of the case study described below is to illustrate the methodology; the data used in the MESSAGE run serve only as examples and the policy implications of the results are therefor not discussed.

4.1 The energy-supply model MESSAGE: problem formulation

We used the energy-supply model MESSAGE in conjunction with the reference-point optimisation approach to study energy supply policies for the countries of the European Economic Community (Grauer et al, 1982) over the period 1980-2030. The main aim of this model is to meet the predicted demand for secondary energy by manipulating the vector of annual consumption of resources, the vector of energy production, and the vector of annual increases in energy-producing capacity. The feasible set is determined mainly by strategies for the supply of primary energy resources involving a variety of possible technologies (see Figure 3).

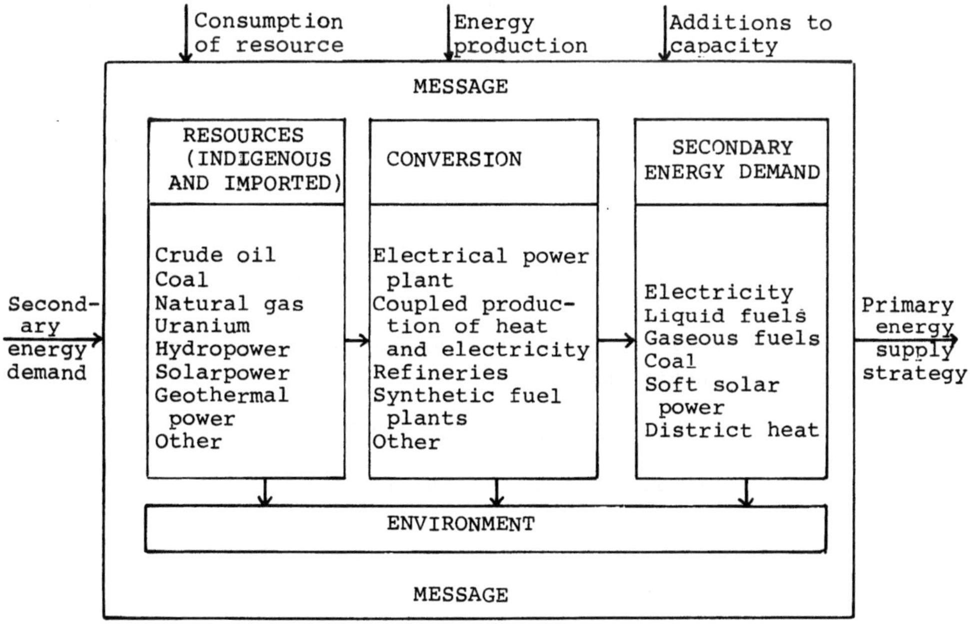

Figure 3. Structure of the energy-supply model MESSAGE

The resulting problem can be formulated as a standard dynamic linear program. The general form of the state equation is:

$$y(t+1) = \sum_{i=1}^{\nu} \bar{A}(t-n_i)y(t-n_i) + \sum_{j=1}^{\mu} \bar{B}(t-m_j)u(t-m_j), \quad t=0,1,\ldots,T-1 \qquad (1)$$

where

y is a vector of state variables

u is a vector of control variables

$\bar{A},\bar{B}$ are matrices of input data

$(n_1,\ldots,n_\nu),(m_1,\ldots,m_\mu)$ are sets of integers which characterise time lags in state and/or control variables

T is the length of the planning period (50 years in 5-year steps, i.e., T = 11).

Examples of equations of this type in the energy-supply model are:

Capacities of technologies

$$c(t) = c(t-1) + 5z(t) - 5z(t-6), \; t = 1, 2, \ldots, 11$$

where

c is a vector describing the capacities of the different technologies

z is a vector describing annual additions to capacity

t-6 reflects a 30-year service life.

Resource balances

$$s(t) = s(t-1) - 5r(t), \; t = 1, 2, \ldots, 11$$

where

s is a vector of reserves (stocks) of primary energy carriers or synthetic fuels

r is a vector describing the annual consumption of primary energy carriers or synthetic fuels.

The general form of the inequality constraints is:

$$\bar{G}(t)y(t) + \bar{D}(t)u(t) \leq f(t), \; t = 0, 1, \ldots, T \qquad (2)$$

where

$\bar{G},\bar{D}$ are matrices of input data

f is a vector of input data.

Examples of constraints of type (2) are given below.

Demand/supply balance

$$Dx(t) \geq d(t) + H(t), \; t = 1, 2, \ldots, 11$$

where

D is a matrix describing supply/demand paths

x is a vector of annual supply activities

d is a vector of annual secondary energy demands (exogenous inputs)

H is a matrix of coefficients reflecting secondary energy inputs to technologies.

<u>Capacity utilisation</u>

$$B_i x(t) \leq c(t), \; i = 1, 2, \ldots, n, \quad t = 1, 2, \ldots, 11$$

where

B_i are matrices defining load regions and the availability of technologies in each load region i=1,2, ..., n (input data).

<u>Build-up constraints</u>

$$\sum_{i \in I_1} z_i(t) \leq GUB(t), \; t = 1, 2, \ldots, 11$$

where

GUB is a vector of absolute upper limits (input data)

I_1 is a subset of the set of technologies.

<u>Resource consumption</u>

$$Gr(t) \geq Q_1 x(t) + Q_2 z(t) - Q_3 z(t-6), \; t = 1, 2, \ldots, 11$$

where

G is a binary matrix which aggregates resource categories

Q_1, Q_2, Q_3 are matrices of parameters describing the specific consumption of resources by conversion technologies (input data).

<u>Resource extraction</u>

$$G_1 r(t) \leq p(t), \; t = 1, 2, \ldots, 11$$

where

G_1 is a matrix which aggregates indigenous resource categories (input data)

p is a vector of annual production limits for each type of resource (exogenous inputs).

The general form of the <u>bounds</u> is:

$$L(t) \leq \begin{bmatrix} u(t) \\ y(t) \end{bmatrix} \leq U(t), \; t = 0, 1, \ldots, T \tag{3}$$

where

U is a vector of upper bounds

L is a vector of lower bounds.

The planning period (T) is fixed and the initial state of the energy system is also given:

$$y(0) = y^o \tag{4}$$

The performance function in the scalar case has the general form:

$$J(u) = (a(T),y(T)) + \sum_{t=0}^{T-1}\left\{(a(t),y(t)) + (b(t),u(t))\right\} \tag{5}$$

where a and b are input vectors.

MESSAGE was originally run with the following scalar objective function, which minimises the total discounted costs of energy supply:

$$J(u(t)) = \sum_{t=1}^{T}\left\{\beta_1(t)(\alpha_1(t),x(t))+\beta_2(t)(\alpha_2(t),z(t))+ \beta_3(t)(\alpha_3(t),r(t))\right\} \rightarrow \min \tag{6}$$

where

$T = 11$

$J(u(t)) = J(x(t),x(t),r(t))$

$x(t)$ is a vector of energy production

$z(t)$ is a vector describing the annual increase in energy-producing capacity

$r(t)$ is a vector describing the annual consumption of primary energy carriers or synthetic fuels

β_i are discount factors

α_i are vectors containing annual cost coefficients.

To demonstrate the qualitatively new character of the multiple criteria analysis we decided not to simply minimise a single aggregated function at the end of the planning period (as represented by (6)) but to 'minimise' the trajectory of certain criteria of interest. As a test we considered the problem of simultaneous minimisation of the undiscounted costs $J_{cost}(t)$, the amount of coal extracted $r_{coal}(t)$, and the volume of oil imported $r_{oil}(t)$ in each time period. This leads to the following vector of 33 criteria:

$$J_{cost}(t) \;;\; t=1,2,\ \ldots,\ 11$$
$$r_{coal}(t) \;;\; t=1,2,\ \ldots,\ 11 \qquad (7)$$
$$r_{oil}(t) \;;\; t=1,2,\ \ldots,\ 11$$

where

$$J_{cost}(t) = \left\{(\alpha_1(t),x(t))+(\alpha_2(t),z(t))+(\alpha_3(t),r(t))\right\} .$$

Here $r_{coal}(t)$ and $r_{oil}(t)$ are subvectors of the vector $r(t)$.

The minimisation of vector (7) under constraints (1)-(4) reflect a wish to minimise both current costs and the use of fossil fuels in the production of energy. Our approach to this multiple criteria problem is based on a methodology derived from the paradigm of satisficing decision making and linear programming techniques. The mathematical background to this approach (based on aspiration formation and the concept of scalarising functions) is outlined in the next section.

4.2 The achievement scalarising function approach

In satisficing decision making it is assumed (March and Simon 1958) that people set up aspiration levels for various outcomes of interest, modify them as they accumulate more information, and then make decisions that satisfy or come close to these aspiration levels. Many of the methods of multiobjective analysis, such as the displaced ideal point approach (Zeleny 1976) and goal programming (Charnes and Cooper 1977) have more or less consciously adopted this approach. A generalised method that combines the satisficing and aspiration level concepts with mathematical optimisation techniques was proposed by Wierzbicki (1980, 1980a). This approach concentrates on the construction of modified utility functions (called achievement functions) which express the utility or disutility of attaining or not attaining given aspiration levels. We will now describe the problem and explain the mathematical basis of the method.

Let $E_o \subset E$ be the set of admissible decisions or alternatives to be evaluated and G be a (linear topological) space of objectives, performance indices, or outcomes. Assume that a mapping $Q: E_o \to G$ which assigns a numerical value to the consequences of each alternative is given, and let $Q_o = Q(E_o)$ denote the set of attainable objectives. Assume that there is a natural inequality (a partial preordering) in G; to simplify the presentation, we shall suppose that the preordering is transitive and can be expressed by a <u>positive cone</u> (any closed, convex proper cone) $D \subsetneq G$:

$$q_1, q_2 \in G,\ q_1 \le q_2 \iff q_2 - q_1 \in G \ . \tag{8}$$

The corresponding <u>strong partial preordering</u> is given by

$$q_1, q_2 \in G,\ q_1 < q_2 \iff q_2 - q_1 \ \tilde{D} \stackrel{df}{=} D \setminus (D \cap -D) \tag{9}$$

If the cone D has a nonempty interior $\mathring{D}$, it is also possible to introduce <u>strict partial preordering</u>:

$$q_1, q_2 \in G,\ q_1 << q_2 \iff q_2 - q_1 \in \mathring{D} \tag{10}$$

Suppose that we wish to maximise all objectives (gains, etc.). A generalised Paretó (nondominated) objective $\hat{q}$ is then a D-<u>maximal element</u> of Q_o:

$$\hat{q} \in Q_o \text{ is D-maximal} \iff Q_o \cap (\hat{q} + \tilde{D}) = \emptyset \tag{11}$$

A slightly weaker definition, which includes a few points that are not nondominated, is that of <u>weak</u> D-maximal elements:

$$\hat{q} \in Q_o \text{ is weakly D-maximal} \iff Q_o \cap (\hat{q} + \mathring{D}) = \emptyset \ . \tag{12}$$

For a normal space G, we can also have a stronger definition (D_ε-<u>maximality</u>) which does not include all nondominated points:

$$\hat{q} \in Q_o \text{ is } D_\varepsilon\text{-maximal} \iff Q_o \cap (\hat{q} - \tilde{D}_\varepsilon) = \emptyset \ , \tag{13}$$

where

D_ε is an ε-conical neighbourhood of D:

$$D_\varepsilon \stackrel{df}{=} \left\{ q \in G : \operatorname{dist}(q,D) < \varepsilon \|q\| \right\};\ \tilde{D}_\varepsilon \stackrel{df}{=} D_\varepsilon \setminus (D_\varepsilon \cap -D_\varepsilon) \tag{14}$$

and

$$\operatorname{dist}(q,D) = \inf_{\tilde{q} \in D} \|q - \tilde{q}\|$$

is implied by the norm of the space G.

If the space G is normed, we can define an <u>achievement scalarising function</u> (often shortened to <u>achievement function</u>) $s: G \to R^1$, where s is assumed to satisfy either (15) or (17) below (the order representation case) or (16) and (18) below (the order approximation case).

Thus, an achievement function should be

(a) strictly order-preserving: for all $\bar{q} \in G$, all $q_1, q_2 \in Q_o$:

$$q_1 << q_1 \Rightarrow s(q_1 - \bar{q}) < s(q_2 - \bar{q}) , \qquad (15)$$

or, if possible, strongly order-preserving: for all $\bar{q} \in G$, all $q_1, q_2 \in Q_o$:

$$q_1 < q_2 \Rightarrow s(q_1 - \bar{q}) < s(q_2 - \bar{q}) , \qquad (16)$$

where strong order preservation implies strict order preservation.

(b) order-representing:

$$S_o \overset{df}{=} \left\{q \in G : s(q - \bar{q}) \geq 0\right\} = \bar{q} + D; \; s(0) = 0 , \qquad (17)$$

or, at least, order-approximating for some small $\varepsilon > 0$,

$$\bar{q} + D \subset S_o \overset{df}{=} \left\{q \in G : s(q - \bar{q}) \geq 0\right\} \subseteq \bar{q} + D \; ; s(0) = 0 , \qquad (18)$$

where, clearly, order representation implies order approximation.

We see that the achievement function s is taken to be a function of the difference $q - \bar{q}$, where $q = Q(x)$, $x \in E_o$ is an attainable objective but $\bar{q} \in G$ is an <u>arbitrary</u> aspiration level, which is <u>not constrained</u> to Q_o, nor otherwise constrained. Moreover, an achievement function is usually constructed such that, if $\bar{q} \notin Q_o - D$, then maximisation of $s(q - \bar{q})$ over $q \in Q_o$ represents minimisation of the distance between $\bar{q} + D$ and Q_o; if $\bar{q} \in Q_o - D$, then maximisation of $s(q - \bar{q})$ represents allocation of the surplus $q - \bar{q} \in D$.

Using the above definition of an achievement scalarising function we shall now show how this approach may be used to minimise the vector of criteria (7) subject to (1)-(4). To do this we have to construct an achievement functional with $G = L^2[0,T]$ and $D = \{q \in L^2[0;T]: q(t) \geq 0$ on $[0;T]\}$:

$$s(q - \bar{q}) = \int_0^T \left\{[q(t) - \bar{q}(t)]^2 - s[\bar{q}(t) - q(t)]_+^2\right\} dt \qquad (19)$$

where $q(t)$ is the criteria vector (7) and $\bar{q}(t)$ is the vector of reference trajectories for these criteria.

The implementation of this approach in the Dynamic Interactive Decision

Analysis and Support System (DIDASS) developed at IIASA is described in more detail in Grauer et al. (1982), Grauer et al. (1984), Grauer (1983).

Here we shall give only a short overview of the use of this approach for multiple criteria analysis in energy planning and policy assessment.

4.3 Implementation and computational aspects

The software for the energy-supply model MESSAGE has been combined with the DIDASS package for linear multiple criteria reference point optimisation to produce a system capable of solving the problem described above. The combined structure of the energy model and the multiple criteria software is given in Figure 4. This figure also illustrates how a model (e.g., the energy supply model) may be used in conjunction with an interactive multiple criteria analysis procedure. The left-hand side of Figure 4 gives the usual stages in a computer run of MESSAGE. In the combined case, however, the MPS format input file must be prepared according to the formulation of the multiple criteria problem: for large models such as MESSAGE, the original matrix generator (Matrix Gener. I) must be altered (Matrix Gener. II) to modify the MPS input file in this way.

The right-hand side of Figure 4 illustrates the multiple criteria optimisation procedure. This begins with an interactive 'editor' (lpmod) which is used to define the trajectories of the various criteria and to manipulate the reference trajectories and scaling factors. In the next step, the preprocessor (lpmulti in Figure 4) converts the prepared MPS format input file into its single criterion equivalent (19). This single criterion problem is solved using the MINOS system (Murtagh and Saunders 1980). A postprocessor (lpsol in Figure 4) extracts selected information from the LP system output file, and computes the values of the objectives and displays the information to the decision maker. Figure 5 shows the results obtained if the problem is to minimise the use of imported oil and indigenous coal in energy production (to save them as feedstocks for other industries), while at the same time minimising investment in the energy sector. The decision maker can then change the reference trajectories on the basis of this information, on the basis of his assessment of the nonquantifiable impacts, and possibly on the basis of experience gained in previous sessions, thus generating new efficient energy supply strategies which he can analyse in future iterations.

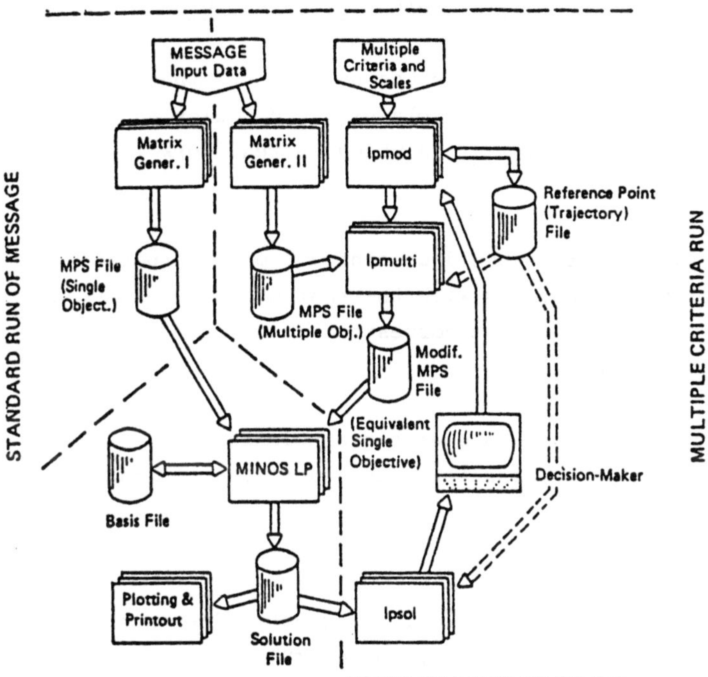

Figure 4. The combined structure of the energy-supply model MESSAGE and the DIDASS package

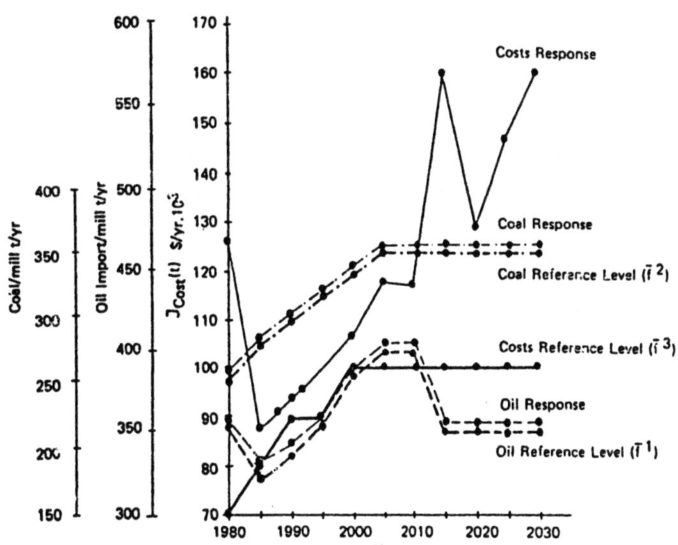

Figure 5. Reference trajectories (objectives) for imported oil supply, indigenous coal supply, and cost

5 SOME UNRESOLVED ISSUES AND POSSIBLE DIRECTIONS FOR FUTURE RESEARCH

The aim of this paper was to demonstrate the need to use the techniques of multiple criteria analysis in energy planning and policy assessment. We shall now consider a number of ways in which current work in this area could usefully develop.

Future energy modelling research should concentrate on incorporating into the models the interconnections with the rest of the economy, and especially with the environment. The corresponding decision analysis would then have a broader basis.

We have discussed here only situations with a single decision maker. However, the decision making process often involves several individuals or groups, so that the problem of multiple decision makers with different criteria should be studied.

The efficient use of decision support tools is greatly dependent on the user interface. The use of graphics, for example, can often improve the decision maker's appreciation of the problem. Further work on the user interface could also help to bridge the gap between the decision maker (planner) and his policy analysts.

The treatment of uncertainty and risk in decision making situations is another subject which deserves more attention. In view of the fact that there is considerable uncertainty in many of the key parameters which influence current decision making, e.g., economic growth, oil (fuel) prices, consumer behaviour, air pollution, etc., there is clearly a need to have some means of identifying efficient and 'robust' policies. This would require further research in the field of multiple criteria analysis under uncertainty.

REFERENCES

Arushanjam, J., Belensky, V. and Belostotsky, A., 'Energy and economic growth - modeling and results', Angewandte Systemanalyse 3, 1982, pp. 58-71.

Charnes, A., and Cooper, W.W., 'Goal programming and multiple objective optimization', European Journal of Operational Research, 1, 1977, pp. 39-59.

Cherniavsky, E.A., 'Multiobjective energy analysis', in Bayrastar, B.A. (ed), Energy Policy Planning, NATO Conference Series, Series II: Systems Science, Plenum Press, New York, 1981.

Grauer, M., A Dynamic Interactive Decision Analysis and Support System (DIDASS) - User's Guide, WP-83-60, International Institute for Applied Systems Analysis, Laxenburg, 1983.

Grauer, M., Lewandowski, A. and Schrattenholzer, L., 'Use of the reference level approach for the generation of efficient energy supply strategies', in Grauer, M., Lewandowski, A. and Wierzbicki, A.P. (eds), Multiobjective and Stochastic Optimization, CP-82-S12, International Institute for Applied Systems Analysis, Laxenburg, 1982.

Grauer, M., Lewandowski, A. and Wierzbicki, A.P., 'DIDASS - theory, implementation and experiences', in Grauer, M. and Wierzbicki, A. (eds), Interactive Decision Analysis, Springer-Verlag, Berlin, 1984.

Lootsma, F.A., Meisner, J. and Schellemans, F., Multi-criteria Decision Analysis as an Aid to Strategic Planning of Energy Research and Development, Report 84-02, Department of Mathematics and Informatics, Delft University of Technology, 1984.

March, J.G. and Simon, H.A., Organizations, John Wiley, New York, 1958.

Murtagh, B.A. and Saunders, M.A., MINOS/Augmented, Technical Report SOL-80-14, Systems Optimization Laboratory, Stanford University, 1980.

Ormerod, R., 'Energy models for decision making', European Journal of Operations Research, 5, 1980, pp. 366-377.

Rath-Nagel, H. and Voss, A., 'Energy models for planning and policy assessment', European Journal of Operations Research, 8, 1981, pp. 99-114.

Schrattenholzer, L., The Energy Supply Model MESSAGE, RR-81-31, International Institute for Applied Systems Analysis, Laxenburg, 1981.

Wierzbicki, A.P., A Mathematical Method for Satisficing Decision Making, WP-80-30, International Institute for Applied Systems Analysis, Laxenburg, 1980.

Wierzbicki, A.P., Multiobjective Trajectory Optimization and Model Semiregularization, WP-80-181, International Institute for Applied Systems Analysis, Laxenburg, 1980a.

Zeleny, M., 'The theory of displaced ideal', in Zeleny, M. (ed), Multiple Criteria Decision Making - Kyoto, Springer-Verlag, 1976.

List of Contributors

Denis Bouyssou
LAMSADE
University of Paris-Dauphine
Place du Maréchal De Lattre de Tassigny
F-75775 Paris Cedex 16
France

Alain Checroun
Centre d'Etudes et de Recherches
en Informatique Appliquée
University of Paris-Dauphine
Place du Maréchal De Lattre de Tassigny
F-75775 Paris Cedex 16
France

Gerard Colson
Faculté de Droit
Ecole d'Administration des Affaires
University of Liège
Boulevard du Rectorat, 7 (B at. 31)
B-4000 Liège (Sart-Tilman)
Belgium

Günter Fandel
Fern Universität
Postfach 940
5800 Hagen
West Germany

Jean Fichefet
Faculté Universitaire Notre Dame
de la Paix
Institut d'Informatique Rue Grandgagne 21
B-5000 Namur
Belgium

Manfred Grauer
IIASA
Schloss Laxenburg
A-2361 Laxenburg
Austria

Heinz Isermann
University of Bielefeld
Postfach 8640
4800 Bielefeld
West Germany

Eric Jacquet-Lagrèze
LAMSADE
University of Paris-Dauphine
Place du Maréchal De Lattre de Tassigny
F-75775 Paris Cedex 16
France

Ron Janssen
Free University
Faculty of Economics
P.O. Box 7161
1007 MC Amsterdam
The Netherlands

Matthias Jarke
Department of Computer Applications
and Information Systems
Graduate School of Business Administration
New York University
90 Trinity Place
New York, NY 10007
USA

Mohamed Tawfik Jelassi
Department of Computer Applications
and Information Systems
Graduate School of Business Administration
New York University
90 Trinity Place
New York, NY 10006
USA

Benedetto Matarazzo
Università di Economic e Commercio
Istituto di Matematica
Corso Italia 55
92125 Catania
Italy

Peter Nijkamp
Free University
Faculty of Economics
P.O. Box 7161
1007 MC Amsterdam
The Netherlands

Anna Ostanello
Politechnico di Torino
Dipartimento di Automatica e Informatica
Corso duca Abruzzi 24
10129 Torino
Italy

Bernard Roy
LAMSADE
University of Paris-Dauphine
Place du Maréchal de Lattre de Tassigny
F-75775 Paris Cedex 16
France

Hans Schaffers
Erasmus University
Faculty of Economics
P.O. Box 1738
3000 DR Rotterdam
The Netherlands

Jaap Spronk
Erasmus University
Faculty of Economics
P.O. Box 1738
3000 DR Rotterdam
The Netherlands

Jan Telgen
Rabobank Nederland
Laan van Eikenstein 8
2705 AR Zeist
The Netherlands

Philippe Vincke
Institut de Statistique
CO 210 Campus Plaine ULB
Boulevard du Triomphe
B-1050 Brussels
Belgium

Henk Voogd
Department of Civil Planning
Delft University of Technology
P.O. Box 6048
2600 GA Delft
The Netherlands

Giovanni Zambruno
Istituto Università di Bergamo
Via Salvecchio
24100 Bergamo
Italy

Stanley Zionts
State University of New York and Buffalo
Department of Operations Analysis
201 Crosby Hall
Buffalo, NY 14214
USA

MIX
Papier aus verantwortungsvollen Quellen
Paper from responsible sources
FSC® C105338

If you have any concerns about our products,
you can contact us on
ProductSafety@springernature.com

In case Publisher is established outside the EU,
the EU authorized representative is:
Springer Nature Customer Service Center GmbH
Europaplatz 3, 69115 Heidelberg, Germany

Printed by Libri Plureos GmbH
in Hamburg, Germany